JAW.67
The Unwanted Truth

Sebastian Ronnie Smith

SJW Books

First edition published 2008 by SJW Books

ISBN: 978-0-9556851-0-1

Copyright © Sebastian Ronnie Smith 2007

All rights reserved. No part of this publication may be reproduced, stored in or introduced into a retrieval system, or transmitted, in any form or by any means (electronic, mechanical, photocopying, recording or otherwise) without the prior written permission of the publisher or author.

E-mail: jaw.1967@hotmail.co.uk
Phone:07960-312-082

A CIP catalogue record for this book will be available from the British Library.

Printed and bound by Lulu Enterprises, Inc.

BIGS' BEDROOM

It was 2:45 am; the moon was full and shone its grey light into Bigs' unlit bedroom. Bigs stared at the long shadow that was cast over the room. 'It looks like a deformed man or creature... no, it looks like a man on a surfboard,' he thought. He shook his head... 'Why do I care?'

He looked at Michelle, who was fast asleep as usual; unlike Bigs, she didn't suffer from insomnia. It always took Bigs two to three hours to get to sleep, only to wake up three hours later and have to start the whole process all over again, just to get another three hours sleep. Bigs first lay on his back, then his side, then his stomach, but no matter how he lay on the bed, he could not get comfortable. His side of the bed was too hot and uncomfortable. He got up, fell to the floor and began to pray.

'Lord, how can YOU be so kind to me? All of the things I have done and YOU are still here for me. I know YOU have protected me all of these years. The governments of this world want me dead and yet I live. Please tell me what to do for YOU; I will do anything for YOU. I will give my life for YOU. I owe YOU everything and YOU owe me nothing. Please tell me how to serve YOU.

'I can never repay YOU for giving me life itself... I am always in YOUR debt. No matter what I do, I will always owe YOU everything and YOU will always owe me nothing. What would I do without YOU?'

Bigs knew he was alive because of unseen forces. He knew those forces were connected to THE MOST HIGH. What he didn't know was why; why he had been chosen, why he had been saved. He could remember the way it had been when he was a little boy, how he had felt his life was being protected and guided by unseen forces.

He was always able to get out of the most serious and dangerous situations, most times without help from the physical world. From a young age, Bigs had thoughts and ideas that he knew were not his own; he knew he was not that smart. Yet it was as if there was a voice inside his head, saying things that made him think in ways he could not have dreamed of on his own.

The voice would ask him questions to which he did not know the answers. The questions made Bigs think about things he would never have thought about otherwise. As he got older, he would sometimes call this his 'brain' or 'the voice.' He knew it wasn't his brain... but what he believed it was, he was too scared to call it. So by calling it 'the brain' or 'the voice,' he could comfortably
acknowledge it as a separate part of him that was inside of him.

The voice, or brain, had been directing him for all of his life. His awareness of this force was growing day by day. It was this force that had allowed Bigs to out-think his brothers and friends; it helped him to be better at whatever he tried to be. Whether he was good or bad, this force never left him. The voice would tell him when it was time to change direction in his life, how he was to see himself, when he should be unhappy with his actions and what he should give up or keep.

Most of the time Bigs would find it near-impossible at first to understand what was wrong with what he was doing, never mind commit to changing or doing what the brain had told him to.

For Example, smoking Marijuana made him calm and helped him to sleep, without it he could become extremely aggressive and violent; but the voice had told him to stop smoking. Bigs could not understand, he was extremely healthy and trained harder than people who did not smoke.

After a hard days training which covered Mixed Martial Arts Ju-jitsu, Mauy Thai boxing, Roman Greco wrestling and Jeet Kune do, followed by weight training and a five mile run; Bigs would like to sit down and chill out with a smoke, which to him seemed like no big thing. To Bigs Marijuana was his best friend, it helped to keep a side of him that he was afraid of under control.

The brain would tell him who he could trust and who he couldn't trust, and in his early years, Bigs didn't usually believe that the brain was right about people; so he'd continue to hang around them... until, as usual, the voice would be proven right. It was hard, because the voice held no one out of bounds. Bigs, on the other hand, couldn't bring himself to think such bad things where his family or so-called close friends were concerned; but as time went on, the brain always proved itself right.

Bigs went backwards and forwards in his mind about calling it the brain or the voice. He knew it was not a part of him, it was always right and he was always wrong. Most of the time he would fight with the voice, until he finally realised, that the problem was, the voice could see things he couldn't... not just physically, but spiritually. It was the brain that could somehow see into the future and informed Bigs of things that would be happening years from that point.

In the early years that made it hard for Bigs to believe in the voice, but as the years passed by, Bigs began to realise more and more that the problem was not with the voice, but with him. He was caught up too much in the physical and in the present. The voice taught him that there was more than one dimension and more than one time scale. Somehow, the brain was connected to all of them.

More and more, in the deepest and darkest parts of Bigs' secret mind, he believed the voice or brain was connected to THE MOST HIGH (GOD). But he was sure someone like him had no right to make such a claim, so he continued to swap between the names 'brain' and 'voice,' not daring to use the word 'GOD' for this mysterious force inside of him.

By the time he was in his early teens, he only had to say in his mind 'I am nothing without GOD, but with GOD nothing is impossible,' and no matter what situations he was in, he would come out the victor. It had been the secret to his fearlessness and power all of his life. He told no one of these thoughts; they were his most private of thoughts and beliefs.

Yet there were many times when Bigs would be with his crew (what outsiders called a Gang) and he would drift off into private thoughts. When he did, it was as if no one was with him but GOD (THE MOST HIGH). In these moments he imagined being a soldier in the army of GOD, fighting to the death and beyond. It was what Bigs wanted more than anything.

He always said to GOD, 'I am not worthy of such an honour, but if you, GOD, ever need someone, I will always be willing to serve you. I'm not a saint and my thoughts and actions are mostly wicked, lustful and rotten, as nobody knows better than YOU; but I can fight, and with YOU, GOD, I have no fear. How can such a person know YOU and be protected by YOU, GOD? I will keep myself fit and I will clean up my mind as best I can, and pray that one day, before I go to hell, I may be of use to YOU just once. Every good thing in my life is because of YOU, GOD, and every bad thing in my life is because of me.'

Then, one night, the voice asked Bigs if he thought the word GOD was an appropriate word. Once again Bigs was completely taken by surprise and began to think in a new direction. As usual, at first, he couldn't see what the problem was; every person who was considered holy used the word GOD. But by now Bigs was beginning to learn that instead of questioning or fighting with the voice, it was best to take it seriously; his impulse was to reject it because he could not understand what the voice was saying or telling him, but instead he would now begin to think about why the voice might think the word GOD was a problem.

For the first time Bigs, rather than fighting with the brain, spent several days trying to work out what was wrong with using the word GOD. 'What is the mythology of Satan?' came a question from within Bigs' mind; it was the voice. 'Satan is the opposite of GO...' Bigs didn't finish his conscious thought. 'Satan is the opposite of the FATHER,' he thought carefully.

Bigs began to think about Satan worshippers. To him they were really stupid people; anyone who worshipped Satan needed their heads tested. After all, to believe in the FATHER, one must believe in Satan; to reject the higher power (The FATHER) in favour of the lower power (Satan) was truly mad. Bigs laughed to himself, thinking 'It must be all that head banging they do to that heavy metal music; they must be banging their brains off the sides of their heads.'

Bigs remembered that one night on the 9 o'clock news, there had been a warning telling parents to be careful when buying heavy metal records for their children. The TV presenter said that there were Satanic cults associated with the whole heavy metal scene, and that heavy metal records, played backwards, contained satanic messages that had led to a number of suicides in young teenagers.

So if Satan is the reverse and uses truth with non-truth, and has made it clear that his world is the reverse of the FATHERS' world, what word would he want millions of people to say, so that in reverse it would be an insult to the FATHER? The word GOD, in reverse, spells DOG.

Bigs shook his head; it seemed so obvious, but he had never thought of it in that way. Once again the voice had made him think in a way he would never have thought of on his own.

The voice spoke softly, as usual, to Bigs. It would always catch his attention as the subject matter it would speak of, would not be what Bigs was thinking of at the time. 'The first war is the war of self. Find yourself... who are you? You will not know your full self until you are at war. It is time to leave the life you have been leading behind.'

For the next two years Bigs would be consumed with trying to understand how to find himself and learning what he was supposed to do for the FATHER. Bigs was no longer into a life of crime. He had survived the Government's and the police force's bloody and vicious crackdown on his crew. It had been a violent war, with deaths on both sides. Bigs' mind drifted back to when he was a little boy, and for him where his life of crime really began...

THE BEGINNING

Bigs was four years old when he saw his first dead body. Bigs was the youngest of seven boys and three sisters born to Mr & Mrs Nayo, nicknames Ma and Pops. Howard, nicknamed H, was the oldest, followed by Tony, nicknamed T. Next was Clifford, nicknamed Duice, then Shania the eldest girl who was followed by Thomas, nicknamed Tc. Next was Fernando, nicknamed Fuzzy, then Leona followed by Nick, nicknamed Nicks, then Joy and lastly Ronnie, nicknamed Bigs.

THE DEAD BODY

Tc, Fuzzy, Leona, Nicks, Joy and Bigs were sitting on the porch watching the cars go by, drinking cool aide; when H, T and Duice came running up looking very excited and very aggressive.

Tc asked what they had been up to? H said he was going to tell them all something and that they could not tell anybody outside of the family. Bigs felt nervous, his stomach was getting tight; he almost felt like he was going to be sick. T looked at Bigs and asked if he was all right. Bigs said he had drunk the cool aide too quickly and his stomach was upset.

'When you see what we're going to show you, you'll properly be sick.' said Duice as he laughed. Bigs remembered they had left that morning with his Pops and now they were by themselves. He was getting more and more nervous. Bigs asked where Pops was. H, T and Duice, looked at one another and there was a moment of silence. H was about to speak when his face looked as if he had seen a ghost.

It was the police; they drove up the Street, towards Bigs' house. H, T and Duice ran into the house. The police car pulled up outside their home, and two white police officers got out and walked towards their front gate.

As the two officers came through the gate, Bigs couldn't take his eyes off of their guns; he looked at their guns in their holsters and wanted to grab one of them. Bigs didn't know why he felt like this, he just did. Maybe it was because he wasn't supposed to, or maybe it was because he just liked guns. Whatever the reason, he had made up his mind that he was going to grab the policeman's gun, as soon as he was close enough.

Just as the officers' gun was in reach, the door opened and Ma told them all to get inside. They ran upstairs onto the landing to where H, T and Duice were standing; who had positioned themselves so that they could hear what the police officers were saying and they had left the bedroom door and window open, just in case they needed a quick escape. H, T and Duice looked very nervous and were sweating.

Bigs' Ma asked what the police officers wanted and they replied 'Mr Nayo.' She told them he was not at home and asked if she could help? The police were very rude to Ma and said the only way she or any of her people could help, would be to go back to Africa.

'Well I guess I can't help you' she said, as she ignored their remarks and went to shut the door.

As she did, one police officer put his foot in the way to stop her from being able to close the door, and asked would she mind if they took a quick look around just to make sure he was not at home. H, T and Duice nervously moved towards the bedroom door.

'What do you want him for?' Bigs' Ma asked. They said they wanted to talk to him about a bank robbery in Dallas. Bigs didn't know where that was so he asked Tc. Tc told Bigs to shut up and slapped him on his head.

'He's not here and if you don't have a search warrant you can't come in.' Bigs' Ma said.
The police looked at each other and said 'we'll be back.' Ma closed the door and as she did they called her a black bitch.

'I'm black and proud of it,' she shouted through the door.

'We'll take your kids from you nigger,' they shouted back.

'Over my dead body,' she replied.

'That can be arranged,' they said, then kicked the door and left. Bigs' Ma began to curse all racist folks. H, T and Duice came back onto the landing and all three of them blew a sigh of relief.

T said that when Pops gets home, all hell was going to break loose. H told everyone to go into the bedroom and Ma called H, T and Duice downstairs. Bigs remembered what they were saying before the police came and his stomach began to get tight again. After all that had just happened, he didn't know whether he wanted any more excitement for the day.

Bigs asked Fuzzy what he thought they were going to show them.

'I bet it's a dead body,' said Nicks, who then went on to say that he had heard Pops and Uncle Joey talking this morning, about going to find a guy who owed Pops a lot of money. Uncle Joey was saying that Pops should stop wasting time and kill the mother fucker, because he was never going to pay Pops the money.

'You're lying!' Joy said 'Dad would never do something like that.'

The girls lived in a state of denial all their young lives and that was how Pops wanted it. He would have killed the boys if he had ever heard them talking like that in front of the girls. They were brought up to protect their sisters at any cost and they were never ever to put a hand on them. This gave the girls great power and they used it every day of their lives; in the way of bribes and the like. The boys were always powerless to react, if the girls did anything they didn't like.

Bigs tried to imagine a dead body. 'Can you catch anything from a dead body?' he asked.

'Like what?' replied Nicks.

'I don't know. May be it will come alive and eat us.' said Bigs. The girls screamed and said the boys were sick, and then the door flew open and H, T and Duice came in. They said that Ma had grilled them on what they had got up to with Pops that morning, and if he had said where he was going; they told her nothing and in doing so they thought she was going to beat the crap out of them.

They all laughed, but then stopped when Tc asked what was it they were going to show them? H pushed Tc on the bed saying, 'Shut up you idiot. Do you want Ma to hear?' H closed the door and told the girls it was time they left, but as the girls were a law unto themselves they decided they wanted to hear what H had to say. So, reluctantly H ordered Tc, Fuzzy, Nicks and Bigs, to meet him, T and Duice at the railroad track in 20 minutes.

'Don't all leave at the same time. Ma already knows something is up.' said H.

They agreed and H, T and Duice left via the bedroom window. Bigs' Ma was still cursing when they went downstairs. Bigs' Aunts had arrived and were telling Ma all the gossip from the social club. They would always know exactly what Pops and his brothers were up to, and always brought the news straight home to Ma, as she never really went anywhere; always saying 'a mother's place is at home with her children and not out on the town with her friends.'

She was too busy chatting with Bigs' Aunts to notice them slipping out the front door. They didn't wait more than five minutes to leave and left altogether; rather than wait the 20 minutes, as instructed by H.

They walked down Compton Avenue, around the alley, across the wasteland, over the canal and onto the railroad track. Bigs' brothers were already there.

'I thought I told you 20 minutes?' snarled H, as he struck out at Tc.

Tc was always the next in line to get it from Bigs' older brothers, as he was responsible for all of them below Duice.

'Let's go,' said H.

'Where are we going?' Bigs asked.

'Wait and see,' said Duice.

'But if I were you girls, I'd go home and play with your dolls. This is man stuff.' said T to the girls.

'Yeah! Well why are you going?' said Leona, as her and Joy began to laugh. T sucked his teeth and Fuzzy began to laugh, but thought better of it when T looked his way.

'Come on. I don't want to see what you're up to anyway.' said Joy.

'Good. Now they've gone let's go,' said H.

As they walked along an old railroad track, Bigs' stomach began to get tight again. There were five or six rusting old train carriages on the track and as they got to the last carriages H turned round to them and said, 'All right, I'll tell you what this is all about. We were out with Pops and Uncle Joey, and they were looking for a man who owed Pops some money. Pops was really pissed off and Uncle Joey kept going on that this man had to die, so we drove around going from one drinking hole to another, but couldn't find him anywhere.'

Bigs took a deep breath as he looked at Nicks and Nicks looked nervously at Fuzzy; Fuzzy smiled and moved back and forth excitedly. They were all waiting to hear the words dead body.

H continued, 'We were just about to give up, when Pops spotted the man's car outside a liquor store. Pops jumped out of the car followed by Uncle Joey, and then Pops gun butted the man and bungled him into the boot of the man's own car...' 'and this is where we dumped his body.' interrupted T, who just had to be the one to say what the surprise was.

H and T began to argue over T's interruption and as they shouted and H pushed T, Bigs looked around where he was standing. They were at the end of an old train track with just one semi-derailed, rusting, old train carriage, that was standing between them and what Bigs was sure to be a dead body. Then, just as quickly as it had started, H and T stopped arguing and looked at Bigs, Fuzzy, Tc and Nicks.

'Okay!' said H extremely excited. 'Behind this train is a man lying on the ground with a bullet in his head, and five in his chest and stomach.'

'Now anybody who doesn't want to see, better run home to the girls,' said Duice.

They all looked at one another and said in one clear voice, 'Let's continue.'

'Well come on,' said T who was already behind the train.

Bigs began to get that feeling in his stomach again and he notice that Fuzzy, Tc and Nicks were all behind him. Bigs really wanted to see the dead man but he seemed to be walking in slow motion. The end of the train was about two feet away, yet it seemed to take forever to reach the end. When Bigs finally did, he froze; it was as if he was about to jump out of a plane, at 2000 feet, without a parachute. Fuzzy pushed Bigs and before Bigs knew it, he was staring at a dead man with a bullet in his head.

Bigs was somewhat disappointed, it was as if he expected the man to get up and dance. Bigs thought how unnatural the man looked with a bullet in his head. Even though Fuzzy had pushed Bigs, he and the others had not yet looked; when they finally did, they too seemed disappointed. Bigs wanted to put his finger in the bullet hole in the dead man's head. I mean Bigs was only four years old, the seriousness for him had only lasted for five minutes and now he just wanted to play with the dead man's body; so did the rest of them. But as usual H had far more serious play in mind. T lifted his T-shirt and pulled out a gun.

'What are you going to do with that?' asked Tc.

'Nothing. The question is, what are you going to do with it?' replied T.

'What do you mean?' asked Tc, who was beginning to look like he wished he had stayed at home with the girls.

H took the gun from T and told Tc to shoot the man. Tc took a long hard look at the gun, and then he took an even longer look at the man.

'Go on, shoot him,' said Duice.

'Go on,' snarled T.

'He's dead,' shouted Fuzzy, who was really excited by the whole thing. Bigs watched Tc who was really having a hard time trying to do what had been asked of him.

'Give me the gun,' said Nicks, who was even more excited than Bigs or Fuzzy.

'No. I told you to do it. If you don't then you'll have to lose rank.' snarled H.

Tc still seemed unwilling, even after such a threat as to lose rank. H snapped and punched Tc in the stomach.

'You pussy! If you don't do it you'll...' before H could finish what he was saying Tc, still winded from the punch to the stomach, shot once into the ground.

'Open your eyes dummy,' shouted T.

Tc shot again and still managed to miss.

'You ass hole,' shouted T, who then slapped Tc on his mouth. Tc looked pale and sick, he threw the gun down and ran off; Nicks ran after him.

'Pussy! Can't even shoot a dead man.' shouted H.

Bigs thought back to the police officers that came to his house looking for Pops with their holstered guns, 'Oh how he wanted to grab their guns,' he thought, now there was one just a few inches in front of him. Then without a second thought he picked up what seemed to be a very heavy gun, and with two hands and a very bad aim, he fired three times.

The first two bullets were so far off target that they nearly killed his brothers, while the third went into the dead man's head. Fuzzy then took the gun and shot twice into the dead man's chest. They stood for a while as they looked down at the dead man. Bigs' eyes were burning and he couldn't hear a thing, his ears just kept ringing and his nose was full of gun powder. Until Bigs was four, he had never seen a dead body and he had never shot anybody; he had also never seen his Pops kill anyone.

Bigs always remembered his Pops saying that the only time the police were interested, was when it was a white boy that gets killed. Bigs, Pops and his brothers would marvel at how they could kill a black man in the middle of the street, in mid-afternoon, and no police would come. But kill a white man in the pitch of the night, in some remote place, and the police would be there in two minutes.

After looking at the dead man for a while and the holes that they had put in him, they left and went over a manmade river to the warehouses; this was heaven to them. They would break into the warehouses through the air conditioning systems or simply through the roof vents, and then they would tie a rope to Bigs and lower him into the warehouse. He would then hook or grab a box of goodies and the rest of them would pull him back up.

They would steal anything from boxes of crisps, toasters, TVs and the like and would then hide them in the waste grounds which, for most of the time, was their play area. H and T would then sell any electrical equipment and give the rest of them a small percentage of the money.

There really was nothing else for them to do but to learn how to rob, fight and to bully; rather than be bullied. As a four year old, Bigs was loaded; he had more money than any other four year old. In fact, he never really went around with anyone of his own age group, there weren't that many kids who would like the things he got up to with his brothers and the few that were, as they grew older, they became a part of his family and were like his brothers.

It was ten o'clock at night by the time they got home and Bigs knew he was in for a beating; this was a usual event for Bigs and his brothers Tc, Fuzzy and Nicks. Bigs' Ma would say 'stay in the backyard' and they would say 'Okay' but then be over the fence into the big wide world. Or she would say 'be in by six o'clock' if Bigs was with his brothers and they would stroll into the house at eight o'clock. But today they did not even ask her if they could go out and to make it worse, it was now ten o'clock at night.

Pops was now at home with his brothers and friends and Ma was in the kitchen with her sisters and friends.

They tried to sneak in, but Fuzzy sneezed as they got to the hall. Ma turned round towards the door.

'Well the big men have returned.'

'I can explain,' said Tc, as he tried to look as sorry as sorry could be. Ma raised her hand and looked at them all with steely eyes.

'Shut your mouth boy, I don't want to hear your bullshit.' shouted Ma.

Bigs tried to play the don't look at me I'm only four routine, which had a 10% chance of working, but not tonight; they all got a damn good hiding and went straight to bed. This was normal to them because tomorrow they would do the same thing all over again.

Let me just say this, what was normal to them and everybody else who lived in the ghetto, would be insane to a middle-class black or white family. Once in awhile they would see a middle-class family make a wrong turn and end up in South Central, City of Compton; they would have their windows up, even in the summer, and they would drive as if they were lost in Africa on a Safari. They would look at Bigs and the rest of them as if they were some rare dangerous lion and they would act as if they were about to become the lions next prey; and often they would.

That day by the railroad track, was the beginning of what was to become part of a normal life for Bigs; in fact by the end of that week Bigs had forgotten all about the dead man at the railroad track.

The following night his brothers stole a car and at three o'clock in the morning they came home to pick up Tc to go joy riding. Bigs heard Tc trying to sneak out of the bedroom window, so he went along for the ride. But it was a shorter ride than Bigs had hoped for, because by the time they had got to the bottom of the road, they were being followed by the police; who after a short chase arrested them all.

When the police informed Ma that they had five of her children in a police cell and that a Welfare Officer had to be called in as one child was only four, Ma thought it was a joke and said that Bigs was in his bed, and they could check for themselves.

Well I guess you know what happened to them once Ma got them home; Bigs could not sit down for a week because his bum was so sore from the spanking he got! For that week, Ma checked on all of them to make sure they were in bed and not on the street.

Poor Ma was fighting a losing battle, they were the seed of their Pops and that meant trouble; but she never gave up on them, not even as grown men. They all loved their Ma and tried as hard as they could to keep her from knowing what they were up to.

NEW SCOTLAND YARD, LONDON, ENGLAND.

Cigarette smoke filled the room, making the dimly lit room seem even darker. It was hard to see the faces sitting around the long oval table. The name tags sitting on the table were sometimes all that could be seen, the only indication that someone was sitting there.

'We have enough evidence to arrest him, and you're telling me I can't? I've waited over ten years to catch this bastard. I've lost too many friends and colleagues to count, trying to get this dick. What do their lives mean to you people who sit in the fucking dark telling us what we can and can't do? Who the fuck are you people anyway? How can you tell us, the fucking police, what we can and can't do?' shouted Sergeant Brown.

'Sit down. It's out of our hands. This is the head of MI5, this is the head of MI6, this is the head of the NSA, this is the head of the CIA, this is Admiral Goldberg and General Steven of special operations, and last but by no means least, is our boss, Police Commissioner Carter and

Assistant Commissioner Brink. This shit is way bigger than what we know,' said Commander Inspector Gold.

'Fuck me!' said Sergeant Brown under his breath, slumping back in his chair.

'We are all here to help one another with this problem. Sergeant Brown, you will give us your full cooperation,' ordered Police Commissioner Carter, in a well-spoken English accent.

'You're here because you know this guy well, but not well enough. You can help us by telling us what you know and fill in any blank spaces we have, so that we will know as much as possible about him,' said Admiral Goldberg, in a deep southern American accent.

'It's because you were about to arrest him. This is why we have decided it's time to bring the police force up to speed on what you're dealing with,' said General Steven, his American accent clipped and professional.

'At the moment, what you need to know is that we do not want this guy arrested. It's important that we work together on this matter,' said the head of MI5.

The head of the NSA sat forward. 'We know you have worked hard to get this guy and the sacrifice you have made in trying to get him. But the reason why you cannot make another attempt is for the safety of your officers.'

Sergeant Brown snorted. 'I don't understand why you are all so interested in this piece of shit? He's a scumbag gangster and we've got him. When we took out most of his crew in a bloody six-month war, where the fuck were you guys?'

Commissioner Carter leaned forward out of the smoke filled darkness.

'No disrespect Commissioner, but it's a bit late to be talking about safety of officers. We lost dozens of good men in the war... and believe me, it was a war, because these shitheads don't give a fuck about law and order.' shouted Brown.

'Just take it easy Sergeant, I understand your frustration but don't say something you might regret,' interrupted the Commissioner.

'We've never been able to get him. I mean, this guy's had more than nine lives, and now you're about to give him another one. I don't understand, what do MI5 and 6, the NSA and CIA want with this guy? His family is well–organised, but they're not terrorists. These guys live in their own criminal world and rarely venture out of it.'

'The reasons why, are not your concern right now,' said the head of the NSA.

'Just let us take him down and he will not be a problem for the next twenty years. Oh, I get it, you people think you can turn him into an informer. Yeah, I get it, you think he'll grass up on the Colombian drug cartels for time off of his prison sentence. Well, I can tell you, this guy will never crack. Believe me, you're wasting your time.'

'All we can tell you right now is that it is to do with National Security and the safety of you and your fellow officers. We will be sending out a memo to all of the Metropolitan Police force shortly, explaining that this is a very dangerous person; he is being monitored and is under constant surveillance,' said the head of MI5.

Police Commissioner Carter began to speak, but was interrupted by Sergeant Brown.

'Look, I can tell you for nothing you're wasting your time. He's not going to lead you to anyone. He's no fool, and he knows he is under constant surveillance. Do not underestimate him. I may hate his guts, but I have learnt to respect his intuition. I don't know how he does it, but he has the ability to outfox a fox. After the war he's just been through, I can tell you he's not going to be getting up to anything dodgy for awhile. He's too disciplined.'

Commissioner Carter stood to his feet and banged his fist on the table, as he leant as far as he could across the table towards Sergeant Brown. 'If you value your job,

Sergeant Brown, don't ever interrupt me. I've heard all I need to hear from you. The only thing I want to hear from you now is the door closing behind you as you go to get your files on this man and bring them here immediately. Oh and I mean *all* files. Leave none on your hard drive concerning this matter. Is that understood Sgt. Brown?'

'Yes sir.'

STREETS OF ROME

'Stop!' The shout came from a police officer, trying to stop a man who was running straight into the road with no concern for his life. Cars screamed to a halt, stopping just short of hitting the man. His main concern seemed to be a briefcase he was holding.

Puff... puff... two shots from a gun with a silencer. The first shot hit the police officer in the arm; he fell backwards, staggering to the floor. Cradling his arm, he watched blood trickling slowly out of a small entry hole in his arm, soaking his uniform in dark red blood. He began to howl in pain.

'*Shots fired... and I'm hit!*' the police officer screamed into his police radio.

The second shot just missed the man with the briefcase, smashing the windscreen of a car instead. The driver just missed being hit; he turned the steering wheel violently in shock as the glass shattered. His car was heading straight into oncoming traffic on the other side of the road. The oncoming traffic tried to avoid the car; the sound of tyres skidding and cars smashing into one another could be heard. Smoke rose in suffocating clouds, and the smell of burning rubber filled the air. In all of this mayhem, a calm voice said into a two-way radio 'He's on the move, heading towards the main shopping area.' It was a man in black clothing, known as Agent 1. He was holding a gun with a silencer on its end.

Agent 1 walked passed the injured police officer. Calmly, he pointed his gun at the officer and fired one shot into his head; then he continued walking towards the main shopping area. The officer, who had been holding himself up by leaning on a parked car, slid slowly to the ground; his eyes stared endlessly up into the blue sun-filled sky.

Agent 1 walked passed the crumpled wreck of cars, passed the smell of rubber tyres and burning cars. As black smoke rose into the atmosphere, people screamed for help, while others tried their best to do what they could. Many people were running to the nearest public phone booths to call the emergency services.

There were six cars involved in the crash. Two had been in a head-on collision, and it didn't look like either driver was alive. The four cars behind hadn't been able to stop in time and had all piled up on top of one another.

Agent 1 walked by as if nothing was happening and headed towards a narrow street that led to the main old market place and shops; the road twisted left then right, looking as though it had been built in the 18th century.

The old town was busy with people, and the market stalls buzzed with the daily sounds of the stall owners bidding for customers. 'Buy your fresh fish here; come on ladies, only the finest here,' said one stall owner. 'Get your ripe bananas here,' called another. People moved from stall to stall, looking and picking at the goods on offer.

The man with the briefcase tried to mix into the crowd. Sweat poured down his face but people were too busy to see the stress, panic and fear on his face.

'Shit! Shit! Where are you?' said the man with the briefcase to himself. He looked left to right and then back again. '*Shit!!*' he said once more, seeing the man in black clothing heading his way.

Suddenly a woman screamed and a small crowd immediately gathered around an old man.

'*He's been shot!*' shouted an onlooker. The crowd screamed and ran in all directions.

Agent 1 aimed again at the man with the briefcase, but the man with the briefcase ducked in the panic and headed for a dress shop.

'Please help me... where's your back door?' said the man with the briefcase to a shop assistant.

'That way!' she screamed, pointing to a hallway.

'I've lost him. I repeat. I've lost him in the crowd. Is he heading your way? Over.'

'Negative,' came back the reply over the two-way radio.

The shop assistant tried several times to phone the police, trying to tell them about the man who was bleeding heavily and leaning on the wall in the shops hallway. But the line was busy and she could not get through.

'I'm calling the police, I don't want any trouble. Do you want me to call an ambulance for you as well, sir?'

The man with the briefcase felt himself growing dizzy. He slumped to the floor, but the fall snapped him out of his slumber; he slowly scrambled to his feet as best as he could, staggered towards the shop assistant, and grabbed the phone out of her hand. She screamed and ran towards the door.

'*Don't come out here, there's a man with a gun!*' a man shouted as he ran passed.

The shop assistant stopped in her tracks; she turned and looked at the man with the briefcase. He couldn't stop his hands from shaking; sweat fell from his face onto the phone. He tried to slow down his breathing. '*Please help me, LORD,*' the man said to himself. He tried several times to dial the one number before he succeeded.

'*Where are you?*' he screamed down the phone.

'The police have closed the street on both sides. People are running everywhere. Where are you?' shouted the voice on the other end of the phone.

'I'm not going to make it. I'm in a dress shop. I've been shot...... I don't know how long I can hang on for,' said the man with the briefcase. His voice sounding weak.

'Shit, hold on, I'll find a way through. Just hold on,' said the voice on the other end of the phone.

MOBILE ONE COMMAND CENTRE

An extra-large black van, all of its windows blacked out, sat motionless, as though there were no one inside it. In contrast, the park that it sat near was the complete opposite. There were children playing in the playground and swinging on swings; the roundabout twirled frantically, and the children screamed as they tried to stay on. Laughter could be heard everywhere in the park.

'I wish I was like those children, not a care in the world,' said a man inside the van, sitting on a fixed swivel chair. The man turned away from the one-way looking glass and put on his glasses; in front of him was an array of monitors, keyboards, dials, buttons and flashing lights. The man pulled down his face microphone and sighed.

'I don't! It's better to be in the know,' said a second man, who was sitting on the other side of the van.

'Shut up! Target's making a call.' The two men began to tap codes into their keyboards at a dizzying rate.

'Satellite one in position,' said the man with the glasses, known as Operator One.

'GPS in position,' said the second man, known as Operator Two. The two men listened intensively to the conversation.

'Target one located. It's a clothes shop,' said Operator One, as he looked at two screens intently.

'This is Mobile One. We've just intercepted a call from a clothes shop 400 meters to your left. It's the target. Over.'

'Received, en route. Over.' replied Agent 1.

'Be advised, target is not moving. I repeat, target is not moving. Over,' said Operator Two.

'Received and understood. Over.'

'This is Mobile One, requesting secure link. Over.' said Operator One, speaking into his microphone headset and mouthpiece.

'This is Pegasus, Ocean operator. What is your designator and call sign? Over.' replied a voice on the man's headset.

'Bravo, Echo, Delta, 1, 9, 6, 7. Over.'

'Request received Mobile One. Enter code. Over.'

Operator Two in Mobile One typed a code into a computer keyboard and pressed enter.

'Code received, awaiting verification. Verification complete, secure link enabled Mobile One. Over.'

SCOTLAND YARD

A man stepped out of the dark and whispered into the ears of General Steven and the head of the CIA. The General put his hand out and was given a satellite phone. 'Excuse me one moment,' said the General to the rest of the people at the table. 'Go ahead Mobile One.'

'We believe the target is down and still has the package. Agents are en route; awaiting confirmation from agents now sir. Hold on sir, patching you into agents now. Over.' said Operator One.

The General plugged the phone into a loud speaker on the oval table. Everyone in the room stopped talking and listened closely.

'This is Agent One. Bravo team approaching shop front now. Agents Two and Three are moving around to the rear. Agent Four is in sniper's position; Five and Six are taking up positions on either side of shop. We are operating on a tight window here sir; the locals have blocked off the road and will be making some form of advance shortly. We are ready to commence. Over.'

'Proceed with extreme prejudice. Leave no one alive and retrieve package. Over.' ordered General Steven.

'Understood. Commencing with extreme prejudice. Over.'

'Big Bird is en route, two minutes to arrival Agent One. Over.' said Operator Two.

STREETS OF ROME

The little cobbled road was dead; not a soul was in sight except for Bravo team. It was a narrow, twisting street, with hardly enough room for two cars to drive down side by side. Police had set up road blocks on either end of the street.

The contrast between the street outside of the dress shop and the police road was shocking. The dead quiet outside the shop switched to the flashing police lights and sirens, while the busying movements of the police attempted to keep the crowds back. News vans began to pull up and reporters jumped out, jostling and trying to get the best spot to report from.

Police officers crouched behind their cars, guns pointing up and down the narrow, twisting street. It was a hot day; sweat poured down the faces and bodies of the police officers. The tension was great. 'What's going on?' said one officer to another. 'I don't know. All I heard was that shots had been fired by some madman, and an old man was killed. People were running everywhere, and in the panic three other people were knocked down and killed. The ambulance crews have helped the injured and moved them to safety, and the dead have been taken to the hospital morgue,' answered the officer.

'Police Chief, we have a call from the Vatican, and an FBI agent is here who says he needs to go through the road block to get to a man that's in a shop and may need medical attention.'

'No, not *may* need, *does* need medical attention,' interrupted the FBI agent, pushing his way past several officers. The Police Chief put his hand in the air for quiet. 'I have a call from the Vatican; I need to take this call.'

'I can't wait, the man could be dead already!' shouted the FBI agent.

'Hello, Your Holiness, how can I be of help?'

'I can't believe this! There are people dying here and you're on the phone to a vicar. You know what…' said the FBI agent, then he took a running jump over the barrier.

'*Stop*!' shouted the police, but the FBI agent kept on running. 'Chief, should we go after him?'

'Excuse me, Your Holiness, just for one second. No, let him go. Get the American embassy and let them know a suicidal FBI agent of theirs is on the loose and heading into an unknown, possible hostage situation. If he makes it out, he can tell us what the hell is going on without me having to risk any of my officers. Sorry about that, Your Holiness, please continue.'

A helicopter flew overhead. 'What now? Is that helicopter one of ours?' asked the Police Chief.

'No, we are still awaiting its arrival.'

'I'm so sorry, Your Holiness, but there's nothing I can do until we have air support. We don't know how many people we are dealing with or if there are any hostages.'

A police officer put down a police car radio and ran towards the Police Chief 'John Smith has worked for the FBI for 22 years and according to the American Embassy he's on holiday, and he's not due back to work for two weeks.'

The Police Chief looked puzzled and put his hand over his mouth.

'Okay, we can't wait any longer for air support; whatever is going on here, we're going to have to find out right now.'

FBI Agent John Smith ran as fast as he could towards the shops, but eventually he had to stop to regain his breath. 'Shit! I'm getting too old for this shit; two years ago I could run a marathon. This phone weighs a ton. Mobile? It's almost as heavy as a phone booth,' he muttered to himself. He looked down at his beer belly, wiped the sweat off of his brow and licked his moustache.

He began to jog the few feet towards the dress shop, only to find that there was more than one dress shop. 'What am I doing? This is crazy! I don't have a gun,' he thought to himself.

He moved slowly towards the first shop, looking quickly in through the front window. 'Come on, I can do this. I've spent 22 years in the FBI and put numerous highly dangerous criminals behind bars. Let's not lose our nerve now; this guy is relying on me. Come on; let's look in the next shop. Oh, shit, this is it,' he thought to himself. On the floor there was a woman who had been shot once in the head. A telephone was still gripped loosely in her right hand.

'Okay, I can do this; it may not be too late. But if it's not, how am I going to save him? Whoever has done this is in no mood to play. No time to think about that... I have to at least try to save someone.'

Smith pushed the front door open slowly. 'Where are those fucking police? They should be here by now,' he thought as he moved into the shop. The blood from the shop assistant was slowly covering a small area of the shop floor around her head, and dresses were scattered everywhere. '*It's the police. Is anyone in here? Come out with your hands up!!*' shouted the FBI agent. He could see a body slumped in the hallway. 'Pete, is that you?'

Pete was known by most as Father O'Reilly and was a priest from Washington D.C. He was a man devoted to the LORD, a kind and caring man of GOD. He spent his whole life studying the Bible and helping the needy. There was no reply. 'Oh, no, I'm too late. Shit! What did you get yourself into? How am I going to tell Lisa her brother's dead?'

Agent Smith ran straight to Father O'Reilly. 'Pete, can you hear me? Wake up! Shit! No, you can't die!' Agent Smith tried to breathe life back into the dead body of Father O'Reilly. He pumped three times on Father O'Reilly's chest and blew air into his mouth again and again, but it was no use. Father O'Reilly is dead, and nothing short of divine intervention would change that.

Agent Smith slumped to the floor, realising it was too late. He had to do something, somehow, to make it up to the dead priest. He vowed to find the killer or killers, no matter what. He then searched the priest's body for clues.

He found a map of the New York subway with the word 'key' at the top, and a set of keys on a chain, which looked like they might be keys to his house. His wallet was also in his pocket, and inside the wallet was a picture of Agent Smith's two children and his wife Lisa, Pete's only living family. Also inside the wallet was a small key with the number 8 engraved on it, a small piece of paper with the word 'Shane' written on one side and '1967.JAW' on the other side, two credit cards, and a hundred dollars.

Agent Smith felt the back pockets; the only thing there was a packet of chewing gum. 'That's weird, Pete doesn't like chewing gum,' thought Agent Smith. He put the map, keys on a chain, the small key with the number 8 engraved in it, the piece of paper, and the chewing gum into his pocket. He then put the wallet, the two credit cards, and the money back into Pete's pocket.

'Don't move! Put your hands in the air where I can see them and move away from the man slowly!' shouted the Police Chief.

Police Chief Inspector Roberta looked around the shop as two police officers put Agent Smith in handcuffs. 'Take him to the station, I will interview him myself. Right, let's preserve the crime scene and get forensics in here immediately. Let's find out what the hell is going on here,' ordered Chief Inspector Roberta.

ROME POLICE STATION

Agent Smith looked around the small interview room; he couldn't read the graffiti scraped all over the walls, because it was in Italian. He put his hands on the back of his head and laid his head on the grey table before him. He counted the cigarette burns in the top of the table; 'twenty-two,' he said, and stopped in mid-count. 'He's dead... my brother-in-law... he's dead. It's my fault. I should have got there sooner,' he thought. He looked up at the one-way mirror and yelled, 'It's your fault he's dead. I told you to get in there, but you were too busy making phone calls and now he's dead!'

The door opened and Chief Inspector Roberta entered the interview room. He took out a small cigar and lit it, all the while looking at Agent John Smith. He pulled a chair out from under the table and sat down slowly.

'Do you smoke, Agent Smith?'

'No.'

'It seems you have got yourself into a very serious situation, Agent Smith. I'm sorry for the loss of your brother-in-law. However, I have to say the circumstance in which he was killed seems rather, how would you say it... shady! Especially considering that he was a priest, no less! Tell me what you know, but before you do, I will tell you what I know. This was not a robbery. Your brother-in-law was chased over several miles, and many people were killed, people who by no fault of their own got in the way. We have lost an officer and your superiors want to know what you are involved in! What I don't know is this: how does a priest end up being killed by a hit man or men?'

A FEW HOURS EARLIER: MOBILE ONE COMMAND CENTRE, BLACK VAN

'Do you have it? Over.' asked Operator One.
'I have the Package. Over.' replied Agent 1.
'Confirm package is real. Over.'
Agent 1 took two CDs out of the briefcase that had belonged to the now-dead priest Father O'Reilly, and put them into a laptop computer.
'Running program now. Over.' said Agent 1.
'Big Bird is overhead and ready to pick you up. The locals are getting restless so move it. Over.' remarked Operator Two.
'Package good. On our way. Over.' replied Agent 1.

SCOTLAND YARD

'Great, good work everyone! We'll see you back at Langley in 24 hours.' General Steven gave the satellite phone back to the man in the dark.
'Good news... we've retrieved the package, and it's on its way to Langley.'
'Right, Commander Inspector Gold. We need a surveillance team made up of your best officers. We need to know everything this guy is up to, and from now on he will be referred to as Target One. Understood?'
Commander Inspector Gold nodded his head.
'Your team is to report directly to Sergeant Brown; he is to report directly to you, and you to Assistant Commissioner Brink. If Brown is obsessed with Target

One, as you say he is, we can use his enthusiasm to good effect. Your team needs to be split into two groups. Team One will be located at the special CCTV centre. From there they can pretty much monitor Target One around the whole of England. Team Two will cover the very few areas we don't have covered with CCTV.'

Commander Inspector Gold laughed nervously.

'You make it sound like all these cameras that have been put up in the UK were put there especially for Target One, sir!'

There was a moment of uncomfortable silence. Commissioner Carter ignored the comments from Commander Inspector Gold with a cold, blank expression.

'This whole situation is above Top Secret Classification. I do not need to remind you of your obligations as an Officer of Queen and Country, do I, Commander Inspector Gold?'

'No sir. I'm sorry if I made an inappropriate comment. We will not let you down,' replied Commander Inspector Gold.

'Good, Commander Inspector Gold. Special Branch has never had a more serious task at hand…. That will be all for now, keep me informed daily. You may leave now,' said Deputy Assistant Commissioner Brink.

'You know we will have our own teams watching Target One constantly, but it is important that you know where Target One is at all times Commissioner; because our shrinks say when he blows, it's going to be in your direction first. We need to make sure that won't happen for as long as possible,' said the head of the NSA.

'Admiral Goldberg, what is the status with War Hawk?'

'We are on schedule and will be ready to test in two weeks.'

'What's happening with Mother One?'

'We are tracking Mother One from the space station, along with the Hubble telescope and Satellite Signature One,' replied the head advisor from NASA.

'Right, I have to meet with the President's advisors and my boss in Washington. Our next collective meeting is scheduled for two weeks from now at Area 51, for the first testing of War Hawk... agreed?' asked the head of the NSA.

In the hallway Sergeant Brown met Commander Inspector Gold. 'National Security Agency, Central Intelligent Agency, MI5 and 6, NASA, and if that's not enough, Admirals and Generals. I thought when I entered that room I was dealing with auditors or some civil group, not the heads of the most powerful organisations on earth. What is going on, Sir?' asked Sergeant Brown, in total disbelief.

'I have never seen anything like that in all my years service,' replied Commander Inspector Gold.

'If he finds out that we can't touch him...' Sergeant Brown paused and shook his head.

'That's why we must make sure that this whole thing remains within Special Branch. How many Police Officers do you think this guy... I mean, Target One, as he is to be called now... would kill if he ever found out about this? No one will be safe. This is beyond our
understanding, so let's concentrate on what we do best. Our task is to make sure this cocksucker never leaves our sight. Whatever's going on, we know what we have to do, so let's do it and do it well.' The two men, somewhat bewildered, walked down the long pale corridor to Commander Inspector Gold's office.

Two years later.

Two years had passed since Bigs had been told by the voice to find himself. He had started to live as normal a life as he could. He had started a young family with his long-time girlfriend Michelle; they had been together for six years. Bigs knew she was the one for him, because the voice had told him so.

Bigs knew the police were still watching him. He would often point them out to Michelle as they drove. 'Look in the left-hand mirror... can you see that black Vauxhall Omega three cars back? Every time I take the back streets we pick up a tail. Those police are so thick. Do they really think I can't spot them following me? They really can't believe I'm going straight. To them it's once a criminal, always a criminal. It must kill them to think I got away with all of the shit I did. I tell you, if it weren't for the Father I would be dead or in prison right now. They probably think I'm running things from a distance. I don't know how they can keep getting the permission to keep this shit up, it must cost the taxpayers a small fortune. Shit, I forgot I'm a tax payer now; I should sue them for harassment. I told you they've still got listening devices in the walls. How can a judge keep giving them warrants to do that? I never knew I was that dangerous to them.'

Once again Bigs' mind drifted back in time to his days as a child and his life of crime...

ENGLAND

AIRPORT - DAY.

The sound of burning rubber can be heard from inside.
Flight 7417.
Arriving at terminal three,
Heathrow, London, England.
Time: 08:30 am. 10:31:1970.

It was cold. Bigs had a cold, everybody had a cold. Bigs hated England, it was cold. Two of Bigs' Uncles, had been in England for a couple of years, setting up business.

They had a lot of family in England and it seemed that business was good. The man Pops had killed at the party was an off duty policeman. Not that Pops cared, but it meant they could no longer stay in the USA. Well, as Pops said, 'we are going on holiday for awhile.'

So here they were in this cold, constantly raining place. They moved into a four bedroom house, it was small; everything was small. The roads, the cars, the food, everything and it was always so cold.

18 months later.

Things were tight. Business that used to be good was no more. So Pops changed businesses. One day Bigs came in from the street to find his Pops and his brothers sitting around a table stacked high with money.

They were back in the big times. Everything Pops made went on him and his family. They never wanted for anything and in the times when things or money was tight, they would just simply do without; until things got better.

They never got too used to anything. Pops always said that in this world only a fool thinks things last forever and that every day is a new one and that it should be lived as if it was your last, because it might be. They moved to a six bedroom house in the Midlands, where they kept low for awhile. Once again, they got used to their surroundings.

It was as if they were working with their Pops, because everywhere they went, they made trouble, money and respect. By the time Bigs was eight, he had a fearsome reputation. They all did. England was not ready for seven boys from the hood of LA.

It was another two years before they moved on. They knew England like the back of their hands. For a ten year old, Bigs was like an old man. He had seen things and done things, that most grown men wouldn't or couldn't imagine.

Bigs remembered when he was about eight, his Ma had put them all into school. Now for some reason many white people didn't like blacks, but especially blacks like Bigs' family, who were not afraid of anybody. Bigs remembered a white boy who was about 11 years old, he was picking on a black boy who was about six years old; calling him a nigger and so on.

Now Pops had always told them, that as black people they had been put through a lot of shit by many white people who still wanted to keep them apart, even after all the bad they had done, and that if black people allowed them to do this, then they would never become what they were supposed to become.

Now Bigs didn't understand all of what Pops had said, but most of it he did. Bigs understood that any time they saw something being done to black people, they were to help their brothers and sisters, rather than walk away. It didn't take much for him to want to fight anyway. Bigs decided that this was a good way to let all those white boys, who wanted to try that slave master shit, know that he wasn't that type of nigger.

This was the first time Bigs got into trouble with the British police. When Bigs finished with the white boy, he was just a pool of blood. The police couldn't believe that an eight year old child had done this and when the doctors report came back, they were even more horrified. The boy had 12 broken bones, from head to toe.

They made Bigs see a shrink, and every Saturday he had to attend a Discipline Centre for six months. This was where Bigs was first introduced to physical training, as part of the punishment was an hours' worth of circuit training.

Bigs shook his head as he remembered the Discipline Centre.

Bigs began to believe that the voice was definitely to do with the Father. Only the Father could know the things that the voice was teaching him. It was obvious to

Bigs that the Father was keeping the police from arresting him... what other reason could there be for them not arresting him, when they still seemed to be so interested in him?

Bigs and Michelle were happy, even though times were hard and they did not have the money or life style once afforded to them. Bigs had spent all of his life being a gangster. Money had come so easily in his former life, but he spent it even more easily. In the underworld he was a king, and great respect and fear were given to him. The mere mention of his name would cause grown men to shake and bow like humble servants. Bigs never queued for anything; people tripped over themselves to please him.

In the normal world he was a nobody, just another guy trying to make a living. Money did not come easy in this world, but bills did, and for the first time Bigs had to try to count the pennies.

People in the normal world would notice his physique and gangster attitude, which got him some respect, but normally the response was negative-fear, nothing more. In the underworld fear was a great asset and opened all kinds of doors. In the normal world it closed doors; people took one look at him and were afraid to do business with him. So he would dress in suits and talk in his best English, with no slang, but people would still find him intimidating.

Trying to be normal was extremely hard for Bigs. He had no qualifications and couldn't explain to people why he had never worked or collected unemployment benefits. It was as if he had not existed in the real world before walking into the interview room.

People in the underworld could not understand how Bigs could walk away from being king of the underworld. When he walked away he was at the top of his game, and seemingly untouchable; crews would bend over backwards to be associated with him. His war with the police was legendary and known all over the criminal world. The fact that Bigs had survived made him a legend. So many crews were willing to give him money because they had made so much money with him over the years.

The Zulus saw him as the head of its organisation and wanted to continue paying him a percentage of all profits. But Bigs refused, telling them that he had to leave the whole lifestyle behind, that included money. No one could understand what was going on, many thought Bigs had lost his mind. Those who knew him well couldn't understand how he could turn down such an easy life; he could have walked away from the life of crime but kept on getting the money, and no one could understand why he'd turn that down.

When word got around that it had something to do with the FATHER OF CREATION, even more people believed he had gone mad. It got even worse when all of the money Bigs had made was gone and it was clear he was struggling to make ends meet. Most were sure he would now have to turn back to a life of crime. But Bigs refused, saying the FATHER would provide the way; he just had to be patient and believe in the FATHER.

Many tried to make Bigs see how wrong he was, and even more laughed behind his back, calling him a fool and a madman. The great Bigs was now a big joke in the underworld, a one-time king now turned religious fool, turned mad by too many years of taking too many drugs and alcohol. Too many people said it was a fitting end to a stone cold killer who had more than his fair share of luck.

But those few who believed in Bigs would ask him what he thought was going to happen that would get him out of his present situation. Bigs had a lot to tell them.

'My life has always been in the hands of the FATHER,' he would say. 'I am alive today, sitting here in front of you, because of the FATHER. The FATHER has been my strength all of my life. I don't know what's going to happen to get me out of this pit I'm in, but I know it will be the FATHER who gets me out of it. All I have to do is believe in the FATHER of Creation for all things big and small.

'The FATHER has told me to leave the life I have lived behind. I have done that, and when the FATHER is ready THEY will tell me what to do next. Until then I will survive, because the FATHER has never let me starve or go without shelter. I know to you men, your life is about money and cars, clothes, gold chains and so on. But those things mean nothing to me now. If the FATHER does not want me to have them, I will do without them. I have a beautiful girlfriend and two beautiful children; all the money, cars, gold, name brand clothes, fear and respect in the world could never give me that. Only the FATHER can give you life... the most valuable things are alive. What we have loved all of our lives are dead things, and that's because we have been living like devils.

'How many of you have big houses, cars, money, and respect, but have no home to go to? Your girls know you have other women you are sleeping with and because of that they don't trust you, and because of that you don't trust them. All that money has brought you is a false happiness.

'On the outside it looks like you're living large; nice houses, brand new cars and clothes. But behind closed doors you spend most of your time paranoid about whom you can or can't trust. Are the police watching you, has someone grassed you up? Do people know you've got fifty grand in a hole under your toilet and twenty grand in your dressing room drawer? Did you spend the ten grand that's missing from your stack or is your girl stealing from you?

'The drugs and alcohol don't help; they blow everything out of proportion. The more success you have in the underworld, the more problems you have. It's a rat race, and in the end, how many people like you for you? Get to where you guys are and where I've been and you don't even know if your girl likes you for you, or for the lifestyle you can give her.

'Then you start wondering, has she started cheating on you yet? Or else you're wondering if she knows that you're sleeping with a new girl. I come to your houses and you can cut the atmosphere with a knife. Your kids don't know if mommy and daddy are going to argue tonight or just not talk for another week. Or whether daddy's going to beat mommy tonight before heading out into the night, not to be seen for another week. Beautiful houses, ugly homes.

'I hope one day you'll understand what I mean. Right now you think I still want all that shit just because it will put money back in my pocket, and you know what the worst thing is? You think I'm mad to be happy and broke. The funny thing is that I think you're mad to be unhappy and rich. I love you guys, but our paths are heading in different directions. I want to fight wars for the FATHER, not for Satan and money. I have enough demons to fight without adding all that shit from the life back into it.'

Most of the time what Bigs would say to them would go right over their heads and out the front door. He knew the only reason they were sitting there pretending to be interested and listening to what he was saying was their respect for him.

The only person who really wanted to know what he was saying was Michelle.

At times there was no money for basic food, because Bigs had spent it on weed. Even though once a week he would take a half ounce of weed for free from the Zulus, it still wouldn't be enough to last him more than four days. Bigs refused to take any more than that amount from the Zulus, even though he could have taken enough to last him for a week at a time; he refused out of guilt. He had been told by the voice to leave it all behind but could not give up the weed. So he decided to buy the rest with money he didn't have, as a half hearted gesture to the FATHER. In reality, though, it was so he could think he wasn't taking his entire weed from his old crew, the Zulus, and in doing so he was at least trying to do what the voice had told him to do.

It was pathetic, he was hooked, only the FATHER could get him off. Until that time came, Bigs kept using money that should have been spent on his children. After a while he didn't know whether he was feeling guilty because he couldn't stop smoking or whether it was because he was spending money that belonged to his children. One thing was certain, he had for the first time begun to realise that he had a serious problem with weed. He would stop for a day, sometimes three days, but the weed would call to him and in the end he would have to give in to its cries.

He begged the FATHER to remove the addictions from him. But in his heart he knew he didn't want to give it up. After asking the FATHER to remove the addiction, he would ask why he had to give up the weed. It was the one joy he had; why did he have to give it up? The voice simply replied, 'The weed is the key.'

Once again Bigs was arguing with the voice. It just didn't make any sense to Bigs. What was wrong with smoking his weed? It kept him calm. He loved the weed. It was his best friend. Bigs would go nowhere without his beloved weed. If he had to go to Michelle's parents house for dinner, he could only stay there for an hour and a half before the weed would start calling him to come home and smoke it. Bigs pleaded with the FATHER... 'Not the weed, I can't do it. I need it. Without it I can't sleep and that side of me I'm afraid of wakes up. I'll do anything; just let me keep the weed. Please.'

Michelle was afraid of his weed addiction; she found it hard to understand how things would get better under these circumstances. Bigs would say 'believe not in me, I'm nothing without the FATHER. Believe in the FATHER because with them all things are possible.'

FBI AGENT JOHN SMITH

Over the past two years, FBI agent John Smith had been trying to work out who killed his brother-in-law. It had become an obsession with him. After several weeks of investigating on the part of Chief Inspector Roberta, the case was put on file as unsolved. His brother-in-laws' body was released and sent back to America. The FBI put Agent Smith on leave while they investigated his part, if indeed he had any, in the killing of his brother-in-law.

Agent Smith, after several weeks of being investigated, was found not to be involved in his brother-in-laws' death. It was a trying time for Agent Smith... not only did he have to console his grieving wife and children; he himself had to deal with his own grief. The fact that he was not allowed to work because he was being investigated just added to the strain.

Whilst on leave he began to investigate secretly, for himself, the death of his brother-in-law. He went to the church where his brother-in-law was the priest, in order to find out why he had been in Rome; but he was greeted with a cold shoulder. It seemed that the death of one of their colleagues had little effect on them. They had no desire to help Agent Smith find the killer or killers. It was as if the board of deacons had fallen out with Father O'Reilly and didn't want to discuss anything to do with him, his death, or why he had gone to Rome.

Just as Agent Smith left the church and was about to give up, vowing never to set foot in their GOD-forsaken church again, a man standing in the dark caught his eye. The man signalled with his hands to Agent Smith to follow him down a dark corridor. Agent Smith unclipped his gun holster and held onto his Colt.45, but did not draw it. He followed the man down the dimly lit corridor, losing sight of the man as the man turned right. As the corridor twisted right, then left, Agent Smith held his gun even tighter.

When Agent Smith turned round the bend he saw a staircase leading down into the darkness. Agent Smith stopped and called to the man, but there was no reply. Agent Smith looked behind himself to see if anyone was following him, there was no one. The walls were damp and there was a strong smell of mould that filled the air. It seemed the further he walked, the smaller the space became between the ceiling, walls and the floor. The wind blew all around his body as if it was a force engulfing his entire body, feeling like it was touching him rather than just blowing past him. It just didn't feel right; it was as if some invisible force was there.

He felt a cold shiver run down his spine. His heart began to beat faster and he knew the next move he made could be fatal. He reached inside his jacket and pulled out a pen torch light. Pointing the light into the dark, he walked down the steps slowly, trying to see into the blanket of darkness. The walls looked like they were part of a dungeon, green moss covered the walls and water trickled down to the floor; dripping water could be heard splashing to the floor from all around him. It was so dark that the pen light hardly broke the darkness.

As he walked very slowly down the damp stairway, a hand reached out of the dark and covered his mouth and another hand pulled him into the dark. His penlight fell out of his hand as he jumped with fright. He tried to pull his gun out of the holster, but a hand gripped his hand with great strength. A voice whispered through the dark, 'Do not be afraid. I have no desire to hurt you. This is to make sure you are not being followed; if you are, they will not be able to follow you anymore.'

Agent Smith relaxed and allowed the stranger to lead him through the dark. Stumbling once or twice on the uneven ground, Agent Smith asked 'how can you see in the dark with no flashlight?'

'Huh! Modern man relies too much on his technology and has forgotten how to use his senses. I see with my mind.'

'Where are we going?'

'To a place long forgotten, where we can talk without risk.'

'Risk of what?'

'Not long now. Watch your step, and get ready to go down eight steps.'

'You didn't answer me. Risk from what? I'm an FBI agent; if people are threatening your life I can protect you.'

'Ha ha! You think it is I who needs protecting! what you seek is not a killer, but the reasons why someone would kill.'

'What? You're not making any sense. I seek the killer or killers of my brother-in-law. Their reasons for killing him mean nothing to me.'

'Stop. Wait here.'

'Where are you going? Don't leave me.' Before Agent Smith could finish, he was blinded by a light being switched on. He strained to focus as his eyes became used to the light.

They were in some sort of cell. It had been crudely modified with a single bed, chair and table. The walls were covered top to bottom with some sort of paper from books. Agent Smith squinted his eyes as he tried to focus in on the paper, trying to see what it said and which books the pages had been taken from.

Looking closer, he could see it was from all types of religious books and newspaper articles. 'Don't tell me this is where you live?' Agent Smith asked as he looked around the room with disgust.

'Yes, it is, and I'm happy here. I'm surrounded by the Holy Word, and the devil's world can't poison me with its blasphemy and lies in here. Your world will soon be over and there is nothing anyone can do Agent Smith. For it is the will of the MOST HIGH, and there are none greater.'

'This is no way to live, stuck in the dark and afraid to live in the real world,'

'Firstly, I am not stuck anywhere. This is how I choose to live. Secondly, I hate the world you live in and would rather cut off my head than live in it. Thirdly and most importantly of all, it is not your world I'm afraid of. It is what has come to your world because of your world's great sin and blasphemy; that is what I fear more than anything. Your world, Agent Smith, is about to be destroyed completely. What has come to your world is the most frightening thing you could imagine, and it cannot be stopped. There is nothing more frightening to the leaders of this world, for they cannot bribe it with money or power, nor can they fool it like they have been able to fool foolish mankind.'

'What does this have to do with my brothers' death?'

'Don't you mean your brother-in-laws' death, Agent Smith?'

'How do you know he was my brother-in-law? Who are you?'

'Who I am does not matter; just as who killed your brother-in-law won't matter to you if you continue to try to find his killers.'

'Is this why you dragged me down here, to tell me this?'

'No, I brought you here to tell you that Father O'Reilly left this address with me for you. He knew you would not let him down. But I must warn you once again that what you are going to find out is going to test your very sanity. Do you believe in the MOST HIGH, Agent

Smith? Because if you don't, you may be able to find your brother-in-laws' killers. But if you do believe in the MOST HIGH, what you will find out in the search for his killers will distract you completely and your killers will become less relevant. Take my advice, go home and look at your wife and children, and ask if you are willing to give them up. The people you are looking for are not that far away.'

'Don't play games with me! If you know who killed my brother-in-law you'd better tell me now!' shouted Agent Smith as he grabbed the man and pushed him up against the wall. The man began to laugh as he pushed Agent Smith to the floor.

'You want to know who killed your brother-in-law? I'll tell you, but it won't make a difference. Your brother-in-law killed himself by trying to reveal the truth to the world. The church and your government killed him for trying to upset their status quo, just as they're going to kill you and your family if you continue down this path.'

'Bullshit! All this time in the dark must have sent you bananas. Do you know what the truth is? And if you do, why haven't they killed you?'

'Because, unlike your brother-in-law, I have no desire to tell the world what I know. I hate this world and will rejoice in its demise.'

'Give me the address!' shouted Agent Smith.

The man passed the paper with the address written on it. 'You did not answer me when I asked you, do you believe in the MOST HIGH Agent Smith?'

'I am a Christian and I believe in GOD. If you have nothing else to tell me, then please guide me out of this hellhole.'

'I only have one last thing to say to you, and it is this: your religion can't help you.'

Agent Smith took the address and asked the mysterious man to show him out.

'What is your name?' asked Agent Smith, as they walked through the dark corridor once again. The mysterious man looked over his brow at Agent Smith, and for a moment Agent Smith could have sworn the man's eyes were like fire.

'My name..' paused the man, 'my name is... Death.'

'You people are all fucking mad. How could my brother-in-law be involved with a man who lives in the dark and is called Death?'

'All is not what it seems Agent Smith. All is not what it seems,' said the man as they reached the street.

Agent Smith walked a few feet in front of the man, saying to him, 'It seems to me my brother-in-law had gotten himself involved in some sort of occult practices.'

He turned around to face the man, but he was gone. He looked left and right then up and down the street; there was no one to be seen. Agent Smith felt a cold shiver down his spine, making him shake slightly.

Where had the man gone? This whole shadows-in-the-night thing was giving him the creeps. 'A man can't just vanish into thin air,' he thought. He felt the paper in his hand and took another look at the address, now that there was better lighting from the street lights. The address was a coach station three miles from where he was standing. He looked at his watch; it was three am. 'Shit, where did all that time go to?' He looked at the address and decided to go home and get some rest. He would start afresh in the morning, he thought to himself.

Beep! Beep! Beep! The alarm sounded at nine-thirty in the morning. Agent Smith rose slowly, wiping the sleep from his eyes. He turned to find that he was alone in bed; his wife must have taken the kids to school.

He looked in the bedside drawer; there was the address and his car keys. He couldn't even remember getting into bed. His mind ran back to the night before, and how the man calling himself Death had just disappeared;

once again a cold shiver ran down his back. 'Damn it, I'm an FBI agent with over twenty years experience. I've seen it all... why do I keep getting the shakes?' he said out loud, then got out of bed.

'Shit, where are my slippers,' he thought. Bending down he found them under his bed. He walked to the bathroom and sat on the toilet; the seat was cold, as usual. 'I've got to get a seat warmer,' he thought.

He felt a breeze and looked up to see that the bathroom window was open. 'Strange, nobody normally opens the window in the morning,' he thought to himself. He thought no more of it and took a quick shower; it was ten-thirty by the time he was fully dressed. He took a sip of his coffee and looked at the clock on the wall. His wife was still not back from dropping the kids to school. 'She must be running late,' he thought and decided to give her a call before he left the house.

He knew that today was going to be a long day and he probably would not be home before midnight. He phoned her mobile and left a message telling her to call him as soon as she got his message. Closing the front door, he headed for the coach station. He tried to remember what the man had looked like from the night before, but he could not remember his face at all. How could he not remember the man's face? It was as if he had not seen it the whole time they were talking. He couldn't remember what was correct, whether he had not seen it at all or if he just could not remember. He thought so hard about it that he nearly ran across a red light...seeing it just in time; he slammed on the brakes, skidding right up to the stop line. He parked the car and walked into the coach station. Looking around, he saw a booking clerk behind her desk.

He walked up to the window. 'Do you know Father O'Reilly?'

'No.' replied the clerk, too busy reading her magazine to be bothered to look up.

'Who else works here?'

'About four other clerks... who are you, and what is this all about?' said the clerk as she put down her magazine.

'Do you know where the other clerks are?'

'Until you tell me who you are and exactly what you want, I'm not saying anything.' smiled the clerk as she blew an enormous bubble from the gum she was chewing.

Agent Smith pulled out his badge 'I'm an FBI agent; I'm investigating the death of Father O'Reilly. This address has come up and I need to know why.'

'Well, I can tell you I have never heard of the man or priest.' Still chewing her gum hard she turned, 'Paul! Can you come here please? I'm sorry but I can't help you, maybe Paul knows him. If not you'll have to come back at three-thirty, that's when we change shift.'

A short fat man emerged from the back office. 'Hi, I'm Paul, how may I help you?'

The woman answered for Agent Smith. 'This man is from the FBI; he's looking into the death of a priest.'

Paul looked bemused, 'Did he die here? I didn't hear about that.'

Agent Smith shook his head, 'No, he did not die... he was killed, and it was not here. What I need to know is this, do you know a Father O'Reilly?'

The fat man looked at the clerk puzzled, 'Father O'Reilly... no. I don't go to church that much, sorry. I can tell you for nothing that neither of the other two on the other shift will know him either... they're both Gothic's. You could come back at the weekend; I think one of the reliefs is a churchgoer, or maybe she attends the mosque. I'm not sure, sorry.'

'Thanks for your time.' Agent Smith looked around, trying to find the connection. He walked into the toilets; nothing unusual. 'What am I missing?' he thought. He reached into his pocket and took out a see-through plastic evidence bag, which had inside it the contents he had found on his brother-in-laws' dead body. For a moment Agent Smith was back at the crime scene, and he had to refocus his mind on the job at hand instead of all the trouble that was surrounding him right now. The only things missing from the bag were the keys on a chain... they were the door keys to his brother-in-laws' house. Agent Smith had given them to his wife to sort out her brothers' last will and estate.

He looked at the contents in the bag, a map of the New York subway with the word 'key' at the top, a small key with the number 8 engraved in it, a packet of chewing gum, and a small piece of paper with the word 'Shane' written on one side and '1967. JAW' written on the other side.

Agent Smith went back to the clerk. 'Do you know anyone called Shane?'

'No, nobody in here is called Shane.'

'Okay, thanks again... Damn, what am I missing? ...That's it!' thought Agent Smith, walking quickly over to the locker compartments. Taking the small key out of the bag, he saw the number 8 engraved in it. He looked at the lockers for number 8. 'Could this be it?' he thought as he tried to push the key into the lock. '*Yes!*' he shouted as the key fitted. He turned it and the locker door opened.

Agent Smith looked inside and was disappointed to find nothing more than another piece of paper bearing the legend '1967. JAW'. Agent Smith turned the paper over; on the other side was a phone number. Also inside the locker was another key... this one had the number twelve engraved in it. Agent Smith phoned the number and waited.

'Hello, this Father Thomas. How can I help you?' There was a moment of silence.

'Hello, this is John Smith, Father O'Reillys' brother-in-law,' Agent Smith finally stated.

'So you have been chosen to carry out the work he started?'

'No, I'm trying to find out who killed him; all this knights-of-the-round-table stuff is not for me. I work for the FBI Father Thomas.'

'And now you work for good or evil; the choice will be yours John... if I may call you that?'

Agent Smith paused 'Good or evil? Not another Mr Death,' he thought. 'Sure, you may call me John, but I don't know what you are talking about. I think the occult is alive and well. Do me a favour; leave all that stuff for your midnight gatherings. I've had enough of that with your friend Death in his luxury condo.'

'I'm sorry John, I don't know what you are talking about, but I think we should meet as soon as possible. When can you come to Chicago?'

'I can't, unless you can tell me who killed my brother-in-law?'

'I don't know who killed Pete.' There was another moment of silence.

'Hello?' said Agent Smith.

'Yes, I'm still here. I didn't want to talk over the phone, but if you can't come here then I have no choice. Pete and I go back many years; he was a very close colleague and friend, and I shall miss him dearly. My only joy in all of this is I know he is with the Lord right now. He said to me that one day you might call, and if you did it would mean he was dead... For the past few years Pete has been involved in a very dangerous project, at the best of times.'

'Don't tell me he was involved in devil worship?' Agent Smith interrupted.

'No, but Satan is to do with it. It's about the inconsistencies in the Bible, a very touchy subject to the church.'

'I thought the Bible was written by GOD?'

'No, that is a misconception that people like your good self have, John. The Bible was written by men who claimed to be messengers of GOD.'

'So you are saying they may not have been messengers of GOD?'

'It's not that simple. The Bible has been translated from one language to another and versions upon versions have been put together through the ages. Look, I'm not the best person to speak to concerning this matter. All I know is that Pete stumbled across something that was major, to say the least.

'They were told by the Vatican to stop working on the project immediately and were ordered to Rome with their findings; they were not permitted to discuss what they had found with anyone. That's when Pete got in touch with me and told me that you might call me one day, and that that would be a sign that you had been chosen to complete their work. He believed he was doing the Lord's work, and that no matter what happened to him someone would carry it on to completion.'

For the first time Agent Smith stopped thinking this was some sort of occult, and that the people involved were weirdo's. He realised that the Church could be spooky and somewhat occult like. It began to dawn on him that this could be one of those conspiracy things you see on the History channel. Agent Smith re-evaluated his whole thought process on the subject and the people involved in the case. He had to try to see things how they saw them, and not so black and white; but he knew that was going to be hard to do.

'There are two things I would like you to explain to me. The first is... who are 'they'? Do you mean he was not working alone? Secondly, why would he think someone like me would carry on his work and not someone from the church?'

'All I know is that there were four priests working on this project. One died of a heart attack several months ago, and the other two are in hiding and have not been seen since they found out whatever they found out. Pete, being Pete, was not afraid of death, nor of the church, and continued to do his work until the Vatican called him to Rome. You would know better than I what happened there.

'It was because of his faith that he believed that even if he died, you would be compelled to find his killers and in doing so finish what he had started. He told me to tell you to find Father O'Brian and Shane. I suppose that being in the FBI, you can find anyone. The keys to all of this are the numbers 1, 9, 6, 7 and the word JAW. That's all I know John. I wish you all the best, and may the Lord be with you.'

'Do you know what the numbers and word means?'

'All I know is what I've told you; I have no idea what it means. I'm sorry I could not be of more help to you John, but if Pete was right the answers will come to you if you have faith.'

'Faith. That's something I have not had in a long time. My job only requires the facts, nothing more, nothing less' thought Agent Smith as he sighed.

'Thanks for your time, Father Thomas.' Agent Smith stood silent for a moment, trying to make sense of what he was dealing with. '*How the hell am I going to find two priests who don't want to be found, and will they be able to help me find the killer? What is going on?*' he thought.

Once again Agent Smith felt like he was at a dead end. Looking at his watch, he saw that it was four-thirty in the afternoon. 'Shit, time is running away from me,' he thought. He looked at the evidence bag and took out the map of the New York subway; at the top the word 'key' was written. He looked at the key he had taken out of the locker and the number 12 engraved on it. He knew for certain it was another locker key.

He decided to go home, pack a small case, and explain the situation to his wife, telling her that he was going to New York in the morning. Then it hit him that he had not heard from his wife all day. Fear struck him as his mind imagined his wife being kidnapped by a sinister occult organisation. Rushing towards his car, he quickly pressed speed dial on his mobile phone.

'Hello?'

'Thank GOD,' said Agent Smith; that hello was the most relieving hello he had ever heard. 'You're okay!'

'Yes, we're fine. I've been trying to get you all day, where are you?' Lisa asked.

'I'm on my way home right now, and I'll explain everything when I get home. I love you; tell the kids I love them too.'

Agent Smith blew a big sigh of relief. As he drove home, he thought of everything he had been told and had experienced over the past two days.

He was getting closer to the killers, he was sure of that; even though he had heard nothing that suggested that, he could feel it in his bones. But first he had to tell Lisa everything that had happened and ask her if she felt comfortable with him carrying on with the pursuit of her brother's killer.

At nine-thirty am the alarm next to Agent Smiths' bed began to beep. Agent Smith got up and began to shower, he was booked on the two o'clock flight to New York. After telling Lisa, his wife, what was happening, they both agreed that since they knew that whatever was going on Pete had thought it was worth dying for, they should honour him by finding his killers. Lisa was going to stay with Agent Smiths' sister in Houston while Agent Smith went to New York.

Agent Smith arrived in New York and headed straight to the subway, but there was no locker for the key he had. 'It can't be. I don't get it. Okay, think... where? Why would he lead me here when he knows the key is not for a locker here? Please help me, GOD,' he thought. Then, as he looked around, he saw a sign for Grand Central Station. 'That's it! Thank GOD,' he said under his breath.

He entered Grand Central station and headed straight to the locker area. He found locker twelve and put the key in... 'yes!' he whispered, and then looked around to see if anyone was watching him. He did not know what he was going to find but he was certain it would bring him closer to the killer.

Suddenly he felt a cold breeze rush across his face. It was the same thing he had felt when he was in the dark tunnel, talking to the man calling himself Death. Once again a cold shiver ran down his spine and he began to shake slightly. What was it about this breeze? It was as if it had a purpose. It didn't just pass by or over him, it was as if it had direction and it felt thicker than a normal breeze.

Agent Smith looked around him as he began to open the locker door; for the first time he felt as if he was being watched. Sweat began to cover his body as his heart rate increased; his mouth became dry as he tried to lick his lips. He slowly opened the door as if it was the most precious and delicate object he had ever touched. Half of him didn't want to open the locker door, afraid that it would contain yet another key and piece of paper, but the FBI side of him overrode the weaker side of him, and he continued to open the door.

Disappointment flooded him as the door was fully open and the contents within were clear to see; the locker contained no more than a Dictaphone and a computer disk. '*Damn*!' shouted Agent Smith. He picked up the
Dictaphone and computer disk, then slammed the door closed; his precious and delicate object had just become a

worthless and unwanted gift, which he was sure, was going to create more problems rather than solve any.

Placing the earpiece in his ear, he walked over to a coffee shop. The FBI side of him knew the information on the disk and Dictaphone would be plentiful and useful, but the human side of him knew it would only be part of a riddle; and this side of him just wanted the answer to who killed his brother-in-law.

Once he sat down, his disappointment was replaced with curiosity. Maybe this was the precious and delicate object he was looking for after all. His thought was broken once again by a cold breeze wrapping itself around his body and face. 'A hot coffee is definitely what I need,' he thought to himself, and called out an order to a passing waiter: 'One black coffee, no sugar, please. Thank you.'

Agent Smith looked at the Dictaphone and computer disk. 'How could these be so important?' he thought, as he ran his fingers up and down the stop, start, forward and rewind buttons, thinking about what could be on the Dictaphone. His heart began to race; he stared endlessly at the Dictaphone and computer disk as if he was in a trance.

His stare was broken by the words 'excuse me sir,' their repetition slowly tapping its way into his mind. He looked up to see the hand of the shop assistant waiting somewhat impatiently for payment for the cup of coffee on the glass counter. 'It looks like you really need this coffee sir, I called you five times. That will be $1.30, please. Are you okay?'

'Yes, I'm fine, thank you.'

Agent Smith sat at a table and sipped his coffee slowly; all the time keeping his eyes firmly on the Dictaphone and computer disk. Half an hour passed before he finally pressed the play button. He did not want to admit it to himself but he was feeling extremely nervous about what was on the Dictaphone. Why? That was the question he had been trying to answer for the last half an hour. For some strange reason he knew he was about to step into a world he was never going to get out of.

'Hello, I hope this is John listening to this message... although that would mean I'm dead. Anyway let's not dwell on the negative. I have died living my dream, and that dream was to live by the word of the MOST HIGH, searching for the truth no matter what it might cost me in this world. John, I know you're a Christian, but what you are getting into is the truth about the MOST HIGH, his first-begotten son, and the rest of the begotten of the MOST HIGH and the chosen.

'This is not religion, so most of what you are about to learn is not part of what they teach you in church. Before I go any further, you must understand a few things. The first and most important thing is that you must ask yourself... do you really want to do this? Please take your time and think if you really want to continue....

'To help you come to that decision I must explain to you what you are dealing with, then if you wish to continue, I will try to explain the best I can; but first you must let go of all you have learnt and been taught, up to now. Once you hear everything there will be no going back.

'Going straight to the basics: what you are dealing with is the word of the MOST HIGH (GOD). You may be thinking that that's what you did every Sunday at church, but the word of the MOST HIGH cannot be found in a book. It is just as alive as you are right now, and will live forever after you have died. This world you live in that you call 'physical' is only one of an infinity of worlds otherwise known as dimensions; some can be seen, such as other solar systems and galaxies.

'Believe me when I say that we are not alone in this physical world and that there are more beings, both more intelligent and less intelligent than humans, than there are grains of sand on the earth. Also, there are just as many unseen dimensions, filled with forces not visible to the naked eye. Some of these are a part of our world, while others are not.

'It is important that you understand this before you decide to continue. Whether you believe it or not, is not important. Still, you must understand that if you make a decision to continue without taking these factors into account, you will not be able to make it. Please do not think that being in the FBI can protect you, or that anything you know or have experienced can help you deal with what you are about to get into.

'Walk away now if your faith is weak or based on the laws of physics or this world. If you think you are the only being listening to this recording, you are wrong; right now there are beings that you cannot see that are listening as well. That is why before I go any further you must understand this; once you know what I know, you will become a part of the real game of life.

'Up until now your ignorance has acted like a buffer that has stopped you from experiencing too much of anything outside of the physical realm.

'Take your time, John. I know that you have what it takes to do this, but you must understand that the rules are very different from anything you have known before, and your adversaries have powers beyond your wildest fantasies. I understand that this may sound unbelievable to you, but it would be better to think of it as existing outside of this world. If you do not wish to continue, I will not be disappointed. I chose this life, John, so you should not feel that you owe me anything; I'm a grown man and this is the way I chose to live, just as you decided to be an FBI agent. Revenge is not what I seek or want from you. The truth is what I have searched for and found.

'We are a lot alike John; while you search for truth and justice in this world, I look for it in the MOST HIGH, what you call GOD. Think of our family; your wife, my sister, and the children. If you decide to continue, take the disk and put it into a computer. You will have to enter a password, followed by a four-digit code to access the information on the disk. I hope I have not overestimated your skills as a detective... I'm sure I have not. Tell Lisa and the children I love them very much. Take care John. Please press stop now and think.'

Agent Smith felt the breeze once again; feeling that same cold shiver run down his spine and the hairs on the back of his neck rising, he turned around quickly. For a second he was sure that he could see a mass of air that was see-through but definitely denser than normal air; it had the shape of a comet with a trailing tail. It moved quickly... left then right... and went through the wall.

Agent Smith squinted his eyes and tried to refocus but it was too late, it was gone. 'Did I see something or were my eyes playing tricks on me?' he wondered. He looked at the shop assistant, but she was busy taking another order. He turned around and looked at a man sitting in the corner of the shop reading a paper. 'Excuse me, did you see that?'

'See what?' asked the man, a puzzled look on his face.

'Nothing,' replied Agent Smith.

Agent Smith wasted no more time. He was certain of one thing, and that was that he was not going to stop until he found out what all of this meant.

As he drove to his office, he thought about what the man calling himself Death had said to him. Agent Smith realised for the first time that what he had said was coming true. For the first time, instead of being concerned with the killers of his brother-in-law, he was more concerned with knowing what his brother-in-law had been involved in.

As he reached his offices he pulled out his security pass and showed it to the guard at the gates. 'How are you today John?' asked the security guard.

'I'm doing fine Bill, and yourself?'

'Can't complain, but my name is Fred. Bill's about fifty pounds heavier and he's white.'

'Sorry Fred, I'm not myself today. Got a lot on my mind.' The gate rose and Agent Smith entered the FBI car park. As he parked his car and walked along the third floor car park to the lifts, all he could think about was what was on the disk.

A silver car pulled up alongside him. The window slowly came down and a deep-voiced man shouted 'Where have you been? I expect that report to be on my desk by tomorrow at noon John.'

'Yes sir, it will be. I'm working on it right now sir. I have to go into the field to gather information sir.'

'Are you okay John? You haven't called me sir for over fifteen years, and in the last two sentences you have said it three or four times.'

'Err... yes, Mike, sorry. My mind is on the job right now; I can't stop, got to get this report finished. Speak to you tomorrow.' Without stopping or even turning around Agent Smith kept walking to the lift. He reached his desk and switched on his computer. He tapped repeatedly on his desk with his pen as he waited impatiently for the computer to load up.

He pushed in the disk and once again impatiently waited for it to load up. Once it had, he realised that in his haste to get the disks' information, he had paid no thought to what the password might be. 'Shit!' he shouted, as the screen showed an 'enter password' sign. He got up and ran out of his offices like a madman, pushing passed his colleagues as if they were unwanted objects in his way. It was as if he was not himself, he could not deal with this situation with his normal black and white FBI professionalism.

He wondered whether it was a delayed mourning reaction over the death of Pete, or some sort of nervous breakdown? He felt like he was on a rollercoaster ride going up and down and around. He had to admit to himself that he was feeling a little spooked out by what he was now getting involved in, and for the first time he had no control over his emotional state of mind. 'Calm down, haste makes waste,' he thought to himself.

He entered the lift and took it down to the car park, then screamed as he reached the third floor, realising he had forgotten his car keys in his office. He took a deep breath and said out loud, 'Haste makes waste... calm the hell down.' His heart was pounding and sweat poured down his face.

He pressed the tenth floor button and went back up to his office. By now his shirt was totally soaked in sweat, half the buttons were undone and his tie was way off centre. As he walked to his office, his fellow work mates looked at him with bewilderment. 'Is everything okay John?' asked a fellow FBI agent.

'Everything's fine, I'm just in a rush trying to get two things finished at once, that's all. Fred has set me a dead line for tomorrow at noon.'

'Who's Fred? Don't you mean Mike?'

'Yeah, I mean Mike. Look, I can't stop.'

Agent Smith walked at a fast pace and finally got back to his office. He picked up his keys and went back to the lift. Once on the third floor car park he went to his car, opened it and took out the Dictaphone and evidence bag. He then made his way back to his office, locked his door, closed the blinds, sat at his desk and then played back the message on the Dictaphone; only to get annoyed with himself once again because the password, after hearing the message on the Dictaphone, seemed so obvious. He entered in the words JAW 1,9,6,7 and pressed enter. *'What!'* he shouted, as the screen showed him the words 'password not accepted.' 'Shit, come on think!' He said out loud. He pressed the Dictaphone and let it play past the point where Pete had told him to press stop and think.

As he did, he felt the breeze again and a cold shiver ran down his spine as the hairs on the back of his neck rose; but instead of shaking, as he had done in the past, he tried to focus in on the breeze. He couldn't see anything this time, but he could feel its presence.

'Okay John, you've decided to continue; I thought you would. The first thing I need to do is to let you know more about your enemies. I told you earlier that there are unseen forces everywhere and that most people are never aware of their presences.

'Just take a second and try to use your senses; you may feel something if you do. Don't worry if you can't, in this world it's not an easy thing to do as we rely on sight and hearing way too much, using our sense of touch much less; but what we use even less than that is our sixth sense, as it's called. Just believe me, there are forces present right now as you listen to this.'

For the first time Agent Smith did not think his brother-in-law was some kind of satanic nut. In fact, he believed everything his brother-in-law was saying; then a moment of fear struck him, like a nail being driven into a piece of wood by a jack hammer. His heart rate climbed so high that he felt pains in his chest and thought he might be sick, or worse, have a heart attack.

He pulled himself together as best as he could and had to rewind the Dictaphone because he had not heard a word that was said over the last several minutes. Suddenly he felt even more frightened as, once again, he felt the breeze rub all over his face and body; but this time he knew and believed that it was something that was not from this dimension and that made the whole experience that much scarier. He needed to know if it could harm him and what he could do to protect himself. His mind had been thrown deep into the abyss of the unknown and it seemed that there was no way out; he had passed the point of no return and felt as helpless as a baby.

He rewound the Dictaphone and tried to listen without thinking of his fears; he had to regain control of his mind. He pressed play and listened. To his relief his brother-in-law continued by saying, 'These forces are not your enemy, nor are they your friend. For the time being your real enemy is man, but things are going to change very soon. Anyway let's not get too far ahead of ourselves.

'You are not more powerful than these forces, nor are you weaker than they. However, their knowledge and understanding is far superior to yours. These unseen forces are governed by laws and will abide by them, their very existence is built upon these laws. These forces go by the name of Baphomd.

'They are one of many unseen forces that have the right to interact with mankind. Man, on the other hand, has the choice and can use these forces for good or for great evil. As your mind becomes aware of the laws, so will your senses grow; many have gone mad trying to understand the laws. Let me explain in greater detail...'

Agent Smith shook his head and smiled. 'It's just like you Pete to talk so matter-of-fact about such amazing and frightening things.'

'The works of THE MOST HIGH are the laws between Heaven and Earth and all dimensions. Knowledge of the laws can give great power to the holder of the knowledge, for in the laws are ways to control supernatural powers and the ability to control some of the unseen forces as well.

'The teachings of THE MOST HIGH are the ways to the works of THE MOST HIGH.

'The Ten Commandments, as they are known, are actually the steps towards the teachings of THE MOST HIGH.

'Secret organisations have fought bloody and violent wars to have and to hold the full knowledge of these laws and to keep them from the knowledge of all men, but they have never been able to hold the full knowledge of the works. I hope you can keep up John?'

'Of course I can Pete! It's a part of my FBI training; right after how to fly and make yourself invisible!' shouted Agent Smith as he put his hands on his head and continued to listen.

'These organisations have existed in one form or another as long as men have been on the planet. In the time of Adam and Eve, the full knowledge of the works of THE MOST HIGH was known. But when Adam and Eve chose to learn the knowledge of Good and Evil, the laws began to break up and were spread all over the earth. This was the price Adam and Eve chose to pay. They were fully aware that to hold the knowledge of Good and Evil, meant that some of the works of THE MOST HIGH would be lost in the exchange.

'Think of it as if Adam and Eve had been glasses of water filled to the brim with the powers or works of THE MOST HIGH. In order to receive any more knowledge, they knew that they would have to spill some water over the sides of the glass, and that once the knowledge was outside of them it would be lost to them. The spilt water ran down the drain, or into the earth, and was lost to them forever.

'Now you and I would think, having the knowledge of good and evil as we do, that Adam and Eve would have had to have been tricked by Lucifer to make such a gigantic mistake as to give up eternal life for death, just to know Good and Evil. However, that is because we have lived our entire lives knowing good and evil, and hindsight is always easy. But try to imagine what it would be like if you had only known Good and eternal life.

'Can you imagine the temptation you'd feel to know something like evil, an experience that was the total opposite of everything you had ever known? You would not fear death because you would have spent your entire life around THE MOST HIGH; death would have no real meaning to you.

'I mean, where are you going to go when you die? Back to THE MOST HIGH, as though you had never left in the first place. It's mind-boggling for us to try to understand this when we have spent our entire life away from THE MOST HIGH, knowing good and evil and death.'

Agent Smith paused the Dictaphone and looked up at the ceiling, he paused for thought... 'Shit Pete how can you be so calm about all of this?' then he pressed play again.

'So make no mistake, it was a choice they made. You have to understand that THE MOST HIGH is not religion and has nothing to fear. Religion is a business, and as in any business, there is competition. It has to find the best ways to sell itself to the masses; that's why there have been so many versions of the Bible.

'The western world is full of paganism and the earlier church had to compete with them; the old laws of the Old Testament just couldn't compete with the more, let's say, forgiving laws and gods of paganism. Even today, the church has had to change its position on same-sex marriages and gay vicars; this is not to say that THE MOST HIGH is for or against such things, but religion was. I don't think for one minute that THE MOST HIGH did not know that such things as same-sex relationships would be on the earth; but THE MOST HIGH is not trying to sell itself to anyone. On the other hand, when it comes to elements of religion that the world may not understand or like, religion has removed these things or changed them to fit in with the opinion of the masses.

'THE MOST HIGH had no need to put the tree of Good and Evil in their sight or to let them be tricked by Lucifer. THE MOST HIGH put it there because of the laws that THE MOST HIGH had set upon the earth; in this instance, the law of choice came into effect. It had to be Adam and Eves' choice between eternal life and death, between knowing just good and knowing good and evil.

'If THE MOST HIGH had made them do either, THE MOST HIGH would have violated their own law, the law of choice. So, left with the choice, Adam and Eve chose to know all things at the cost of eternal life... a choice that meant nothing to them as they had no concept of death; because it did not exist at that time.

'And so we will return to the parable of the glass of water. They were full to the brim with the powers or works of THE MOST HIGH and decided to take on some more water, spilling some of the water inside the glass over the side of the glass and down the drain. However, water that runs down the plughole and is lost to you and I, nevertheless continues to exist. To find it again you would simply have to be able to understand the drainage system, and this was what these secret organisations tried to do.'

Agent Smith paused the recording again. This time he wanted to take down some notes for reference, because if he was honest, this was way over his head.

'As time passed and the knowledge of evil grew, mankind had to make a choice as to what they wanted the knowledge for. They made their choice and men became less involved with the works of THE MOST HIGH for the glory of THE MOST HIGH, as they attempted to use the works of THE MOST HIGH for their own glory and power.

'As time continued to pass, men lost sight of THE MOST HIGH in their newfound ignorance, becoming focused on self-glorification and power. The other dimensions became less and less important as mankind found themselves kings of their own world, and as more time passed the knowledge of eternal life was lost so far down the drain that it was lost to men.'

For the first time Petes' voice showed signs of emotion. It was clear from his voice that what he was talking about made him sad.

'Yet they did not care because the little knowledge they had was so great in the world of men, that it made them kings and rulers.

'However, as the years went on, men realised the First-begotten son and other members of THE MOST HIGHS' family were going to come into the world of men, to show mankind the true works of THE MOST HIGH and to show the world what it had lost. It was then that they began to try and find the full works once again.

'They soon realised that they had lost touch with the few organisations and ancient cultures who out of a desire to ensure that the works would be for the glory and honour of THE MOST HIGH, had kept the works as pure as possible. It was these organisations who made it known that they were waiting for the First-begotten son to come.

'The world of men had sacrificed the works for self-glory and power, so they went back to their original plan. Secret organisations grew and competed with one another for supremacy and total control of the world system. As they destroyed one another, the groups that survived became ever more powerful and secretive. They became the masters of industries, the heads of religion and the rulers of government.'

Agent Smith made some notes and sat back in his chair releasing a long sigh. 'Jesus Pete, if what you are saying is true...' Agent Smith stopped and thought about what he was about to say out loud and thought better of it; thinking it instead... 'The very Government I serve is who you were going up against.' Leaning forward he pressed play once again.

'These organisations became the masters of industries so they could print and be in control of money. This would allow them to control mankind's desires and achievements. They became the heads of religion so they could control mankind's spiritual development and destiny, and they became the rulers of government so they could be the rulers of mankind's armies.

'Once they controlled the governments, they wasted no time in beginning their search for the scripts that contained information on the works of THE MOST HIGH. They killed anyone who possessed this knowledge and enslaved generations of indigenous people all around the world, in order to make sure none were left who knew the works of THE MOST HIGH.

'They would use their armies to destroy entire nations and leave them in ruin. Once this was complete they would remove all of a country's natural wealth... diamonds, gold, silver, copper, timber and so on.

'As we entered into the last days of the World, the Roman Empire controlled not only the works of THE MOST HIGH but also the scripts that contained the teachings of the First-begotten son of THE MOST HIGH. But the teachings of the First-begotten son were much harder to keep secret. This was especially true when the First-begotten son was alive and his disciples were preaching in the ports where travellers came and went to many different countries. So they decided to do what had been done throughout the ages when the works of THE MOST HIGH became general knowledge; they killed all those who knew.'

Pete spoke with anger and disgust in his voice. As he paused, it seemed to Agent Smith that Pete needed a moment to recompose himself; but the pause wasn't long enough, because you could still hear the contempt clear in his voice.

'They left none alive, killing the First-begotten son in the most violent way possible to show the world they were the masters of the earth. With this conquest under their belts, they truly believed that they had mastered the works of THE MOST HIGH. They believed that it was proof that men could be the masters of the world and that THE MOST HIGH would not be able to do anything; because of THE MOST HIGH'S own laws and works.

'With their organisation in place they had full control of mankind, and with full control of mankind, they had full control of the world. With full control of the world, they had full control of the supernatural knowledge of the world. With full control of the supernatural knowledge of the world, they would make sure that mankind stayed powerless to overthrow them and their successors.

'It did not matter if the whole world knew these rulers of the world were corrupt. Simply having control of these things meant that a few men could rule the billions of people in the world and conquer any nations that tried to come against them.

'Their bloodline would always be in power. Yet even though they had this control, they could not gain power over death. This was because they were wicked and evil, and in being so they could never truly connect with the spirits that could lead them to the knowledge of eternal life.'

'Pete seemed to find the irony as some sort of justice' thought Agent Smith, as he listened to the tone variations in Petes' voice; from anger and contempt, to a little chuckle of satisfaction.

'For men desired the things of the flesh more than those of the spirit. As time passed, once again they became less and less interested in the powers of the spiritual worlds and concentrated on gaining power and control over the world. For although in the spiritual world there was only one ruler, in the physical world they believed men could be the only masters; only calling on the spiritual world to see and to know what was happening in the physical world that was important to them, that they could not see and know.

'The secret sects such as the Illuminati, the Builderburg and the Freemasons, are by far the most secretive and powerful organisations. They were formed from the blood and misery of countless wars and Crusades throughout the centuries.

'The Freemasons are without doubt the most powerful and oldest; they have fourteen former Presidents as members, and the current President is probably a member as well. They have been known under many names over the centuries; the most notorious, apart from Freemasons, is the Knights Templar.

'The Knights Templar were sent out to secret places all around the world, to find the scattered pieces of the works of the MOST HIGH; which had been held by different powerful secret organisations spread all around the Globe. The Knights Templar were able to find many pieces but not all. Through wars and Crusades, they regained control of the world for a time.

'Before that it was the Roman Empire that had limited control. That has been the problem for all of these secret organisations, they have never had full control of the works. If they did, the war between them would cease and only one of them would rule it all.

'I hope you have been able to understand what I have been saying John. Right now, men are your problem. They are very powerful on the earth and their people are in all walks of life. They will summon the unseen forces such as the Baphomd, they will know what you are doing and they will come after you and maybe our family as well. Look them up in your FBI files, but trust no one... they are everywhere. If you do continue from here, you will have to find Father Shane. He will know what to do with the information on the disk. May the MOST HIGH be with you.'

Agent Smith didn't know what to think... he was lost for words. It was not confusing... and yet it was. It made sense, but it didn't make sense. It seemed believable, but how could it be real? Agent Smith stared at the computer screen and then played the Dictaphone message over and over again.

After some time, Agent Smith refocused himself and tried to concentrate on working out the password for the disk. He tried his wife's name and the year she had been born; no success. He tried combinations of names and dates, but nothing worked. He took a break and had to dodge his boss on the way to the coffee machine.

Agent Smith was still in a daze. Colleagues spoke to him and he had half-hearted conversations with them while he filled his cup with coffee. He spent hours going through this routine, going back and forth getting coffee and trying to work out the password.

It was around midnight and Agent Smith was just about to give up. Suddenly he felt the breeze circle his body and face, and he turned cold. 'Control yourself John; you know what you are dealing with.' He turned and once again he saw the transparent, murky shape of the force; but as he focused in on it, he noticed that this time it looked more like water rather than air. Then, as quickly as it had come, it disappeared into thin air.

Once again, Agent Smith began to realise that all this time he had not once thought about the killers of his brother-in-law. A shiver went down his spine as he thought of the man called Death... surely he wasn't the real Death?

Agent Smiths' stomach turned over as he attempted to reassure himself... 'No, he wasn't the real angel of Death,' he thought once more. But the truth was he didn't know what was real any more. His whole world had been turned upside down, and he was starting to feel well out of his depth. He felt as if he was starting to believe and that made him question his sanity, something he had never done before.

The room seemed to be spinning; his heart rate began to speed up, and he found it hard to breath. Agent Smith realised he was having a panic attack. Hastily he undid his tie and shirt. He switched on the fan on his desk as he began to feel hot. Reaching into his desk for a paper bag, he pulled it out, and a half eaten burger fell out onto the floor. As he breathed through the bag he began to slow his heart rate down. His left hand was in pain from gripping the arm of the chair so hard... he had almost passed out, but he had managed to keep himself from blacking out.

Out of the corner of his eye he saw the computer screen. The screen saver was active; it was a picture of his wife and two children. The picture immediately gave him strength and he breathed slowly and began to cool down. 'Shit, I'm getting too old for this,' he thought. He looked at the picture and smiled. Picking up the phone he called his sisters' home, where his family were staying until he could be sure it was safe for them to return and be in their own home.

'Hello?'

'Hello sis, its John. How are you and Paul?'

'We're fine, how's work?'

'It's very interesting right now. I hope my kids are behaving themselves and not causing you too much trouble?'

'Don't be silly. They're all asleep right now... we all were.'

'Sorry sis, I totally forgot the time.'

'Hold on John, Lisa has just popped her head around the door to see if it's you on the phone.'

'Hello John, it's me. Are you okay? John, are you okay?'

'Yes, I'm fine. Sorry, I lost track of time. I love you very much. Are you sure you want me to continue what I'm doing? It's very dangerous… I don't know if I should carry on, Lisa.'

'Why, what's wrong?'

'I can't tell you anything. All I can say is this is as big as it gets. The people that I'm dealing with are some of the most powerful people in the world. I think I should quit while I can.'

'John, whatever you decide to do, I trust you and I love you very much.'

'I love you too. I'm going to go to bed and I'll talk to you in the morning after I sleep on it. Kiss the kids for me.'

MEETING OF THE GRAND SECRET SECT

The mansion floor was covered in words written in goat's blood. There was a goat tied on an altar, and its throat had been cut. The blood trickled down a groove in the altar to a golden bowl, and the blood in the bowl had been used to write the words on the floor.

Twenty-four men in black silk hooded robes stood in a circle with their heads bowed. They spoke in an ancient language, summoning the beings of another dimension to come forth and to let them see and know what they knew. The room was filled with burning candles and incense filled the air.

Suddenly there was a rush of air and all the candles went out. The room was filled with the sound of rushing wind and the room became completely pitch black. Still talking in the ancient language, the men tried to keep their footing as their black hooded robes flapped violently in the swirling wind.

Candlestick holders began to fly through the air, smashing into the walls. The golden bowl was hurled into a wall and the blood inside of it splashed violently all over the room; the men were covered in goat's blood, but kept talking as if nothing was happening.

The goat, with its throat cut, began to rise into the air; from the altar it moved into the middle of the circle of men and exploded into pieces. The men were covered in bits of blood and guts from the goat, and once again they acted as if nothing had happened and kept talking in the ancient language.

Then, as suddenly as it had started, the wind stopped and all of the candles that remained standing in their candelabra relit themselves. The room began to reappear from out of the darkness, and as it did, in the middle of the men a force became visible. It was see-through, like a mass of air, just like the one Agent Smith had thought he'd seen in the coffee shop.

For the first time, the twenty-four men stopped chanting in the ancient language, staring at the force from another dimension. The men then linked arms and one of the men spoke to the mass of air in the ancient language.

'Oh great force from the spiritual dimension, tell us what we need to know and let us see what we need to see; for it is written that your knowledge is for those who seek it and your wisdom is for those who know how to possess it. We know there is only one ruling force and that they are THE MOST HIGH. We know that all living things are under them and belong to them. We know all may call upon the forces of the universe by knowing the word. Enter us now and reveal to us that which we seek.'

The unseen force rose almost to the ceiling of the room, some twenty feet high, and began to glow brighter and brighter. Soon it was so bright the men had to cover their eyes and bow their heads. They began to sweat as the room got hotter and the candles melted and withered to nothing. Then the force exploded into twenty-four pieces, flying at great speed into each of the men. The men were thrown to the floor, sliding until they hit the walls with great force. The room then turned back into complete darkness, followed by the sound of rushing wind leaving the room until it was dead silent.

The Grandmaster slowly stood and took a moment to gather himself together. The rest of the men slowly got up and began to compose themselves too. The Grandmaster felt for the wall in the pitch black and took another moment to get his bearings. He then felt his way to the light switch and turned the lights on. Taking a deep breath, he asked, 'Is everyone okay?' They all answered yes, although they were clearly somewhat dazed.

They removed their robes and wiped the blood and guts from their faces. Then, four at a time, they went into a shower room at the side of the room and washed themselves, putting back on their shirts, suits, ties and shoes when they were done; glancing into the mirrors on the wall to make sure they were completely rid of any goat's blood or bits. Still nobody said a word the entire time. When they had all cleaned themselves, they walked down a long corridor full of ancient African and Middle Eastern artefacts and entered another room.

Inside the room was an old oak round table with twenty-four chairs. There were twenty-four medieval knights suits of armour, complete with swords and shields. The shields had words engraved in them in Latin, which translated as "Knights Templar" and "Knights of the Round Table" and on the walls were very old pictures of knights in armour.

They sat at the table, and servants brought in tea and coffee and light refreshments for them. They drank and ate without speaking. Some of the men were brought plasters and Band-Aids for minor cuts and bruises.

When all of the servants left the room, they began to write on notepads on the table. Some moments later they all finished and they passed the notepads to the

Grandmaster. After reading each notepad, the Grandmaster stood up.

'So, we have a new problem to deal with,' he announced, with an evil look on his face. He stared into space, then with a sinister chuckle and smile, he asked 'Who is this Agent John Smith?'

AREA 51

The head of the NSA, the head of the CIA, the head of NASA, Admiral Goldberg, and General Steven of Special Operations sat inside a concrete bunker, staring out through binoculars over the desert. A voice came over an intercom telling them to put on their protective goggles and ear plugs.

Then a countdown began... *ten, nine, eight, seven, six, five, four, three, two, one*. They braced themselves as a green laser beamed down from a satellite in space. The beam touched the ground some seven hundred meters in front of them, then the sound of a rocket could be heard coming from the south of their position.

The rocket passed overhead at a height of about two thousand five hundred feet and at great speed. The laser immediately locked on and tracked the rocket, whilst a second laser inside the satellite beamed down and hit the rocket, vaporising it. There was a great explosion and the sky turned bright red; yellow and then white smoke trailed the wreckage to the desert floor. The men clapped their hands and patted each other's backs.

'Project Star Wars is progressing nicely. Our laser technology is improving vastly,' said the head of NASA with great pride.

'When will we be able to do this in the sea? And how long till we can hit turning projectiles?' asked the head of the CIA.

'Hopefully, very shortly. War Hawk is the answer to that question, and that's why we are all here.' said the head of NASA.

A jeep pulled up outside of the bunker and a young tall slim man stepped out. He took one last pull on his cigarette before throwing it to the desert sand and stepping on it. Stepping into the bunker, he stood to attention.

'Major Stone reporting for duty sir.'

'This is the replacement for Major Bruce that I was telling you about,' said General Steven.

Admiral Goldberg sighed. 'Very unfortunate, what happened to Major Bruce; he was a damn good man. He'll be missed. Welcome to Project JAW Major Stone. It does not get any bigger than this. Play your cards right and you'll be a Brigadier General in no time. Take the jeep back to HQ, and Lieutenant Colonel Grey will take you on a tour of our base and bring you up to speed. Debrief will be tomorrow at 0800 hours.'

'Yes sir. Glad to be aboard,' saluted Major Stone, before turning and heading back to the jeep.

'Well, with that out of the way, can we now please get on with the first test of War Hawk? I have to be in Washington for a briefing with the President. The budget for this project is spiralling out of control,' said the head of the NSA.

'This project is too important to have a limit on the budget. I explained that to Congress last week,' said the head of the CIA.

Admiral Goldberg picked up a phone. 'Professor Wolfgang, start Project War Hawk.'

HQ AREA 51

'Welcome to Project JAW, Major Stone. I'm Lieutenant Colonel Grey. General Steven has asked me to show you around and then to take you into the briefing room and give you the full history on Project JAW. I'll start off by telling you that you'd better fasten your seat belt. You're in for a hell of a ride.'

'I've spent ten years in Special Forces; I've seen it all sir. I'm here because I'm the best man for the job. I'm prepared for anything.'

'Relax with the "sir" on Project JAW unless you're told otherwise. We keep it informal below Brigadier General. This is your card; doors cannot be opened without this. Since you have security clearance for floors one to three you will have to give a retinal and finger scan for floors two and below.'

'How many floors are there?'

'Thirty-two, but as I said you'll only be using one to three. Anything below and you'll be entering the twilight zone.'

'The twilight zone?'

'Like I said fasten your seat belt. This is where worlds collide Major Stone. Believe me when I say that nothing can prepare you for Project JAW, or for area 51. Let's just take it step by step. First I'll show you around the base. Then we'll take it floor by floor... that way your eyes will be opened slowly. Ground floor, as you know, is made up of offices, factories and hangars. We have our own research centres for different projects on every floor below. Most people on floors six and downwards never leave area 51; their work is their life, you could say. It's not as bad as it sounds though, because these types of people are like kids in a toy shop. The stuff they get to play with is all they have ever wanted, and beyond.

'There are projects here that date back hundreds of years and have been passed down to the relevant governments and organisations throughout the ages. The more floors a project is on, the more significant it is.'

Major Stone was impressed by the sheer size of the place. To his right were airstrips, a Control Tower and views stretching for miles into the desert; interrupted only by mountains that sat on the horizon.

To his left were massive hangers the length of several football fields and three stories high. In front of him was the main road leading to several heavily guarded security gates, factories and offices.

'Project JAW is the biggest of them all; it covers all thirty-two floors and is older than any of the others. Here, it's time for you to use your card for the first time... these are the lifts for personnel. Over to the right are the lifts for planes, equipment and UFOs.'

'The crashed UFO from Roswell?'

Lieutenant Colonel Grey laughed. 'Everybody talks about Roswell. In 1952, over ten UFOs practically landed on the White House lawn. They were seen by Democrats, Republicans, police officers, ordinary people, radar towers, the Air Force, the Army, and the Secret Service.

'The Air Force sent interceptors to chase them out of the sky and every time they got in range, the UFOs would pull a couple of out-of-this-world manoeuvres and disappear; then as soon as the interceptors landed, they'd reappear. The interceptors would take off again, and as soon as they got in range they would pull the same manoeuvres and vanish into thin air again. This happened over and over again for a couple of days. Yet everyone always talks about Roswell and one UFO that may or may not have crashed.'

'So if it wasn't Roswell, where did we get the UFOs from?'

'Like I said, let's take it one step at a time; you have a lot to catch up on. Let me take you to your quarters and show you the canteen.'

Six hours later, Major Stone had been given a quick tour of three floors of area 51. He looked bewildered at what he had seen and had been told. He sat on his bed and looked at the massive pile of files on his computer; he knew it was going to be a long night, 'Lieutenant Colonel Grey was right... nothing could prepare me for what I now know,' he thought to himself. He quickly ran to the toilet and was sick for a second time.

BIGS' OFFICE

Bigs fell to the floor. Looking around his office, he saw the sunlight shining through the wooden blinds. As it brushed across his oak table, the metal handles on the brown cabinet drawers reflected the sunlight right into his eyes. Blinded for a moment, he began to pray.

'Lord, how can YOU be so kind to me? All of the things I have done and YOU are still here for me. I know YOU have protected me all of these years. The governments of this world want me dead, and yet I live. I have spent the last years trying to find out who I am and build a new life.

'Thanks to YOU, FATHER OF CREATION, I have a building company that has grown to great heights. YOU have given me a wonderful family, and now a successful business as well.

'Please tell me what to do for YOU; I will do anything for YOU. I will give my life for YOU. Please tell me how to serve YOU. I can never repay YOU for giving me life itself; I am always in YOUR debt. No matter what I do I will always owe YOU everything, and YOU will always owe me nothing. What would I do without YOU? I'm nothing without YOU, yet with YOU nothing is impossible.'

Bigs climbed back onto his black leather chair. 'I now know why I have lived the life I have lived. I know I am a soldier for YOU. I will try to build an army and await YOUR command.' Tears ran down his face as he prayed.

Bigs had tried to convince the underworld that most of them were soldiers and didn't know it. He told them that was why they lived the way they did.

The western world had tried to turn them into criminals and killers, by making most of its military forces racist and unwelcoming to young blacks. This left them with no healthy outlet for their natural aggression, so they only had the ghettos to release it in.

Yet if they wanted to follow him and build an Army for the FATHER, they were welcome to do so. They would prepare themselves for the end times that would be coming soon, and when anarchy ruled the streets they would take control and await orders from the FATHER. In the meantime, they would go to war with the racist groups that attacked their people.

If it wasn't for Bigs' reputation, they would have laughed him out of town. Behind his back, the whispers were clear; almost everybody was certain that Bigs had lost his mind. Yet there were three men who wanted to know more about what Bigs was saying. They were low-ranked criminals and they did not command much respect in the underworld. Still, this didn't matter to Bigs; it never had.

They began to train with Bigs. He taught them how to respect their women and to love and protect them and their children. They had to stop taking class A drugs and stop drinking alcohol. They were required to stop cheating on their women, and they were never to lay their hands on them or beat them. Bigs had never needed to beat a woman with his fist in an argument. He used his mind to beat them in arguments, unless they were right... and if that was the case he would admit it, eventually.

He had no time for silly egos and could listen just as well as talk. He told his men to face their weaknesses and to begin war against those weaknesses in an attempt to remove them from their minds for good.

'Do not pretend you have no weaknesses, for that path leads to eternal weakness. You must be prepared to fight every day, forever, against your demons. Your demons will not leave you, for they have great discipline and they use their invisibility to great effect.

'Your power is in choice. Use this power well, and you will be unbeatable. Treat people how you want to be treated, and do not hesitate to strike down your enemies. To be a man is to know truth, honour, peace, equality, justice, love, harmony, responsibility, and respect for oneself and for mankind.

'Ask the FATHER to guide you and make you into what the FATHER needs on earth. Ask them to clean your mind and use you for whatever they want. For you, no task is too big or too small. You must care not what the position may be, as long as it serves the FATHER. You must see yourself as nothing and ask the FATHER to make you something in their eyes, not in the eyes of this world.

'Care for physical and material things no more. Open your minds to the spiritual world, for this is where the FATHER lives and where you can find everlasting life and eternal power. Make the FATHER your foundation and trust not in yourself but in them; for in all things big or small.

'Your demons will try to keep you in this world, for this world has limits and cannot live forever. If you make this world your foundation and believe in it alone, you will only be able to see as far as your physical eye can see. You will only know what this world chooses to tell you and the wicked of this world who hold the knowledge, will keep you as a slave to the dead things of this world.

'The unseen forces of this world are in league with the wicked of this world. The wicked have fought day and night to win possession of the knowledge of the FATHER, and over the centuries they have killed all those, possessing this knowledge, who wished to share it with the world. By doing so, they have kept it to themselves and kept it secret from the world. In this way they have ensured that they alone have power and dominion on the earth.

'They have distracted you with beautiful things such as cars, clothes, jewellery and houses. In the end you have become slaves to them, working for them so that they will let you have the money and material things that they control. All of these things that you have become slaves to are dead and have no life in them.

'While in their secret places and organisations, they spend billions trying to understand the knowledge their forefathers have stolen from the righteous; for they know these things can give eternal life, not money or clothes.'

Bigs knew that what the three men really wanted to learn was how to fight and be fearless like him. The voice told him that they would not understand the world of the FATHER and that all they wanted was to be taught mixed martial arts. The voice told him to use this like a carrot on a stick and get them to clean up all of their devil ways first, before teaching them the things they really wanted to know.

The voice spoke to Bigs, 'Knowing you are a soldier is not enough... you are more than that.'

Once again Bigs had no idea of what the voice was telling him, but he knew by now that he would understand one day; so once again he began to try to work out how he would achieve this latest task. He thought about his nature. He knew he had a side to him that he was afraid of; he had been afraid of it all of his life and tried to keep it down in the darkest parts of his mind. It was full of rage and had no care or respect for anything in the world. Bigs had used a very small part of it when he was in situations of life and death or when he was threatened by great danger.

Yet even though Bigs knew it was a part of him and it had helped him to do the really bad things in his life, he also knew that he may not have been able to do those bad things without it. He was so afraid of this part of him... it feared nothing but the FATHER OF CREATION. It was pure anger and Bigs knew that if he ever let it control him, he would have killed everybody outside of his family and close friends. At times he struggled to keep it under control and he would think about taking a sword and killing anyone that would not bow in fear of him.

The police and any other authorities made this side of him even angrier. How dare they not realise they should be afraid of him? He was invincible; he could destroy all of mankind. All of their guns and bombs could not save them from him! That's how this side of him thought.

This side of Bigs was a raging psychopath that awoke inside of him anytime someone was ignorant, vicious, violent, or disrespectful. It would awaken even faster when blasphemy or profanity were used. This was the side of Bigs that the underworld knew and feared. It was this side of Bigs, as well as his insomnia, that kept Bigs smoking weed; that was his excuse anyway. When he felt his anger rising, he would smoke, and it would put that side of him to sleep. Two or three joints before bed would put the rest of him to sleep as well.

This was why Bigs could still not understand why the voice wanted him to give up smoking.

'Surely it is a good thing,' was his argument to the voice. He had been trying to stop, but by now he was hopelessly hooked.

Then the voice said, 'Who do you think made the suggestion to you to start smoking in the first place?'

Bigs paused for a moment. 'Me, wasn't it?' he thought. He remembered the first time he had smoked. He had been really young and dumb; still, it was something he enjoyed. 'It was me that decided to smoke. My Pops, brothers and friends did it, and I decided I wanted to,' he thought.

The voice replied, 'Who do you think suggested it to you? Do you think it was yourself, your Pops, your brothers, or your friends?'

'No, I did. I saw them doing it and I wanted to do it too. Please just tell me who it was, if it wasn't me,' thought Bigs.

'It was Lucifer and the demons. They have been talking to you, as well as yourself and I.' Bigs was shocked by this revelation.

'Lucifer? How come it's only now you're telling me this?' thought Bigs.

'Because it's time to tell you. You have always had the choice; nobody can make you do anything you don't want to. You are still to blame for making the wrong choice, but it was Lucifer and the demons who suggested it to you.

'Why do you think something as hard as smoking was still worth doing? The pitfalls you had to get through in order to become a true smoker were enormous, and even though you knew it could have killed you as well, you still did it. What force do you think had the discipline to keep you going through such an ordeal? Not you; you were too stupid from the effects of the weed to have had even half the discipline it takes.'

Bigs was blown away by what he was hearing, he couldn't quite grasp it at this point but it was starting to make some sense to him. As he absorbed what had been said so far, he kept wondering why the voice had taken so long to reveal this information. 'What pitfalls?' thought Bigs.

'At first you would have coughing fits, you would almost be coughing up your intestines and you would start vomiting. Once you got passed that, you began to try to take deeper intakes of smoke without the coughing fits. Then you had to get over the bleary vision and the way every sound you heard would echo. Once you got passed that, all that was left was the ringing sound that you could hear every time you smoked, which gave you panic attacks because you thought you might be going mad.

'Six months of dealing with all that and you finally made it! All of those things became the past, and then you could really enjoy being stoned,' said the voice.

'I'm mad! How could I go through all of that and still keep smoking?' thought Bigs.

'Have faith and trust, and be yourself. Fear not that side of you, for it is part of who you are. Stop smoking and be free,' said the voice.

'I can't! Please help me,' pleaded Bigs.

'It's not me you should ask.'

From that day on Bigs added 'Please help me to stop smoking,' into his daily prayer. He tried many times to stop smoking, but he failed every time. As time passed, the weed that had been his best friend for so long, slowly became his biggest enemy. He began to hate it, thinking, 'No true friend would stay when they were not welcome.'

Yet the more he hated it the more it gripped him, like a python refusing to let him be free. Every day Bigs begged the FATHER OF CREATION to remove this curse over his life. Never before had he seen how weak the weed had made him, it was as if a blindfold had been lifted off of his eyes. In the past he had asked the FATHER OF CREATION to help him, and when they did he would end up going back and start smoking again, telling himself that it was his only real vice.

But not now. Now it was driving him mad, insane; every time he had to smoke he could see that he was a slave to the weed. There was nothing he could do but hope that one day the FATHER OF CREATION would give him one more chance and come to his rescue.

In the meantime….

CHRISTIAN CHURCH

In his search for what he should be doing for the FATHER, Bigs had begun to look for the word of the FATHER in all religions. Bigs did not believe in any religion, but he knew religion had taken parts of the word of the FATHER to authenticate their piratical brand of teaching. For this reason, he was a bit uncomfortable going into Churches or mosques. He believed that religion had a big part to play in the destruction of mankind. Bigs had never needed churches, mosques, or their Bibles or Qur'ans to be close to the FATHER.

When Jehovah's Witnesses would knock his door he would invite them in, sit them down and ask why they needed a book to teach them about the FATHER OF CREATION. Did they not believe the FATHER wrote their word in the spirits and hearts of men and women, and that it was men and women who wrote in books?

He would also ask how they could know for sure, that most of their spiritual experiences had not come about as a result of reading their books. How did they know that their minds were not merely replaying what they had read? How could they be sure that the people writing the books didn't have agendas of their own? How could they be sure that man hadn't corrupted the word of the FATHER? Bringing him back to his original question, if their books were the first place they received inspiration, how could they know that their inspiration was not corrupt; if they had not received any spiritual guidance first?

They would politely say that he was wrong and that their book had been written by men of JEHOVAH, who had been chosen to write the word of JEHOVAH, so that all of mankind could receive the word of JEHOVAH.

Bigs would reply just as politely, saying he had no need for a book because the FATHER spoke to him in person. The Jehovah's Witnesses would respond immediately by getting up and leaving, with a look of disbelief and scorn on their faces.

It must have got around the Jehovah's Witness crowd because they never knocked on Bigs' door again.

What Bigs had learnt as the years passed by, were that the books were like codes. The things that Bigs had learnt from the FATHER OF CREATION could be confirmed in the Bible and Qur'an; it had taken many years for Bigs to realise this fact. This is what had brought Bigs to a Christian church. He had been told by the FATHER to find himself, and as usual it had taken years to understand how he could do this. The FATHER would tell Bigs the things he had to do... for example, that he needed to stop being a gangster and look for the new direction he had to take.

Bigs would work out what he had to do but it would always take time. Many times Bigs would want to give up trying to get to the new direction or task; he would rather stick with what he already knew. Making changes was hard to do, but Bigs always had the FATHER OF CREATION there to push him. The truth was, that without the FATHER Bigs knew he was nothing more than a junkie and a killer.

So here Bigs was in a church, looking for himself. It did not feel right; there was something about churches and their crosses that Bigs definitely did not like. The preacher started to talk about the Lord Jesus Christ.

'He will take care of us and we should all give praise to our lord and saviour Jesus Christ. Stand up and give the Lord Jesus a big praise.' The people stood to their feet and shouted and screamed.

Bigs felt his anger begin to awake and rise; he just wanted to kill them all. He closed his eyes and imagined taking out his sword and cutting and chopping off their heads, spilling their blood all over the church. His hand reached inside his long black leather coat and grabbed the handle of his double-edged sword. He began to draw it out.

'Not now,' said the voice, so Bigs got control of himself. Releasing the sword, he removed his hand from inside his coat. He then stood with his eyes closed, taking no part in the praise to the Lord Jesus Christ.

'Why am I carrying this sword if I'm not going to use it?' thought Bigs.

'Why have you started carrying the sword?' said the voice.

'I thought you told me to... I mean I thought it was the right thing to do. You told me to find myself. I know I'm a soldier and the side of me that I fear wants me to carry the sword. You told me not to fear that side of myself, so I'm trying not to... This is all so confusing.'

AREA 51 HQ

Major Stone pressed the Enter key on his computer and brought up the file labelled "Top Secret Your-Eyes-Only 1, 9, 6, 7. JAW." It had taken him over six months to get used to his new environment and his new understanding of the world. The world as he had known it was gone forever. His first six months on the base had been a mind-blowing experience. At times he thought he might not recover his sanity, but he was an excellent soldier and dealing with the extreme was his speciality. Even so, he had to admit that he was way out of his depth at area 51.

Project JAW dealt with alien beings, alien craft and technology, supernatural forces, space and other dimensions. Project 1, 9, 6, 7. JAW was split into different divisions. These divisions were connected to different organisations outside of the government or the military, all of which were highly powerful groups in their own right in the world. Together they were the world's most powerful organisation, known to most of the world as the New World Order.

The government was a part of all operations, but it was not the sole controller. It kept its share because it was the government and it had been the first to know of the full existence of UFOs in the skies around the world. The government had essentially also been in bed with the telecommunications companies from their inception and it even knew the dirty little secrets of the most powerful and secretive organisations. This meant the government had leverage and could claim a stake that could not be ignored. They could also provide a great deal of public money for funding, and they funded around thirty percent of all projects. However, there was a constant battle for control as governments came and went.

Somewhere along the way, the governments lost more and more control over the project, due to the ever-changing face of politics. This meant that more control went from the government to the Department of Defence, because these were the people who were always in the know. Then, unlike the governments, they too could pass the knowledge onto their successors and they gained more selective control from the fact that they did not have to worry about Joe Public's voting at the next election.

The secret organisations began to realise that Generals and Admirals were far more stable than Presidents and politicians. Not only that but they were the people who understood better than anybody, what the project dealt with. Thus, as time passed, the politicians lost their power as the representatives of government and the Generals and Admirals took the politicians places as the representatives of government.

This brought the same kind of stability to the government side of the operation as the secret organisations had, because they could now pass information down to people who had been groomed for the positions from a young age. Major Stone was one such official – not even thirty years old, with a promising career in the military, climbing the ladder quickly and willing to risk all for his beloved country. He was now a part of project 1, 9, 6, 7. JAW and he knew he would only be able to leave by death. Still, he also knew that his loyalty would push him further up the ranks, and to Stone that was all that mattered. He was a career soldier, the corps was his life. For Stone, like all people of his type, loyalty was the first priority; such people join the military in order to be a part of something that, provided that they work hard, will lead them to a position where they will know so much that they could never leave. To the average Joe such a commitment is mad, but to a soldier like Major Stone, it means that they are worth something in an organisation that has taught them all they know. Stone would rather die than betray the corps.

PROJECT 1, 9, 6, 7. JAW

Major Stone looked on the screen at the first page of the document. It was not the first time he had looked at these files; in fact, he almost knew them word for word. Yet every time he read them, it gave him the very same feeling that he had the first time he had read them. Aliens had been visiting the earth from the beginning of mankind. Major Stone stared at photos of ancient cave drawings depicting UFOs. As he did so, Lieutenant Colonel Grey entered the room.

'They get you every time don't they? I think it wasn't until I made Lieutenant that those files stopped giving me the goose bumps.'

'I can't believe it. I've been here almost a year and I still have to come in here every chance I get and put on my computer and read and look at this stuff. It's unbelievable.'

'Like I said, it took me years... and if I'm being truthful, I'm still amazed at how involved they have been in the creation and development of man.'

'How can such beings be kept a secret for all this time when, like you say, they have been involved in so much to do with man? I can't believe they are what they are. And I can't believe how close some of them really are.'

'Believe me, if they wanted man to know they were here, they would let it be known. But they take their orders as seriously as you and I do.'

'The database lists over a hundred different species, and that's just the ones we know of. I mean that's like saying there are a hundred different races of man. We have what? White, black, yellow, brown and red races... that's five, and really we're all just one species.'

'Now you can understand why I laughed when you spoke about Roswell.'

'But how do we prepare for the inevitable?'

'We can't, that's why the world can never know the truth. We would lose all control; the whole world would nosedive into anarchy.'

'Yeah... we're lucky they don't just say "to hell with them, let's have some fun"... they could let the whole world know that they're here and that we can't do anything about it. Or, worse, they could let the whole world know who they are and who they work for.'

'Luck has nothing to do with it. They have orders, just like you and I. They're here to do their job... that's it.'

'But they are going to introduce themselves slowly, according to Article 7.'

'Yeah, and that's why we have these sightings taking place. Most people think they exist, but they usually aren't a hundred percent certain. That's how you subliminally make people aware, without making a big splash.'

'That's what I'm saying; there is no part of what's happening that doesn't amaze me. People think that they are discovering aliens, when in fact it is the aliens who are slowly introducing themselves. By the way, are we meant to keep calling them aliens on base and in private, or can we call them by their real names amongst ourselves?'

'Never use any other name but aliens or E.B.Es... never. Is that understood?'

'Yes, absolutely.'

'I know all this is hard to contain, but we must. That's why we have been chosen. It's because we are the best of the best.'

'Can I ask you a personal question sir?'

'What have I told you? Don't call me sir. My first name is Kevin.'

'Sorry Kevin. I find that amazing... we've been working together for a year and it's only now that I'm learning what your first name is.'

'Do you remember when we first met and I told you to fasten your seat belt? Well, I think you can now loosen it a bit. What is the question you want to ask?'

'To be honest, I can't remember now.'

Lieutenant Colonel Grey and Major Stone began to laugh, shaking their heads in disbelief. Twelve months of working closely together, and it's only now that they had learnt each other's first names.

NATIONAL SECURITY AGENCY
OFFICE OF THE DIRECTOR OF OPERATIONS

Director Forbes put down the phone and immediately called for his office Assistant Director Sam Collins and Head of Field Operations Special Agent Ricardo Rodrigo.

'I've just got off the phone with the boss. He wants us to set up a special covert operation in sync with a team from the CIA... they're en route. Sam, I want you to coordinate this op. Set up a link with N.R.O. All intercepts are to be set at top secret. Ricardo, two tech teams are needed with full electronic capabilities. The military will provide the muscle heads, but we'll run the show.'

'Who's the target sir?'

'Right this is where it may get a bit tricky. He's an FBI agent by the name of John Smith.'

'I'll have his files pulled up immediately.'

'What are we looking for?'

'Right now we are to know all there is to know about this guy and await further instructions.'

'Do we inform the FBI of the ongoing investigation?'

'Not at this time, but I get the feeling this guy is not going to be around long.'

'Don't tell me the muscle heads are ex-military cut-outs?'

'Correct.'

'If this goes belly up who's going to take the fall sir?'

'Not me, you can be sure of that.'

'So should we run the usual get-out-of-jail program?'

'Most definitely. Anything to do with the CIA calls for it.'

'Do we know what this guy's done?'

'The chief was really clear about two things and two things only. We ask no questions, and we don't fuck this one up... that's all. Is that clear?'

'Yes sir.'

'Yes sir.'

'Good, then let's make it happen, gentlemen.'

AGENT SMITH'S HOME

It was 07.20 am when Agent Smith got out of bed for the fourth time that night; he had slept very little throughout the night. He had been tossing and turning, trying to make up his mind on what to do. He knew that if he continued, he could be putting his family at great risk. He also knew that things had changed, his motives were no longer the same. He was now no longer doing this to find his brother-in-laws' killers; he was doing this to find out what had gotten him killed in the first place.

If he was to continue, he would want to tell Lisa why he was continuing the investigation. He knew that to do so would make it more dangerous for her, but he didn't want to lie to her either. Feeling like his head was going to explode, he held his head in his hands over the bathroom sink. He looked up at the mirror and took a deep breath. 'Come on old timer, time to make a decision. What's it going to be?' he thought.

He brushed his teeth, washed his face with cold water and then he punched the mirror. The mirror cracked and split into four pieces and blood dropped into the sink from his clenched fist. Agent Smith had never lost his control like that before; but never before had he had to make a choice between doing his job and the safety of his family. The FBI side could not let this go, but the dad and husband side of him did not wish to risk the loves of his life. Frustration was starting to get the better of him.

'Shit, now look what I've done. Lisa is going to kill me.'

Agent Smith looked at the four pieces of mirror still hanging on the cabinet door.

'What am I doing? This thing has got me acting like a madman.'

He wrapped a small towel around his fist, went back into the bedroom and picked up the phone.

'Hello?'

'Hi sis, how are you? Sorry for waking you last night.'

'We're okay and don't be silly. You're my brother and that means that... unfortunately... you can call me at any time.' she laughed. 'I'm joking.'

'I hope so! I feel bad enough as it is waking you in the middle of the night.'

'John will you stop being silly? Honestly, I don't know what's got into you lately. Are you okay?'

'Yeah I'm fine, just a little overworked. You know how it is.'

'Don't get me started about the government and how unfair I think they are to you guys in law enforcement and the emergency services! Look at the criminally low slave wages and the lack of holiday leave... '

'It's okay. Most of us do it because we love it.'

'That doesn't mean you should be treated the way you are.'

'Sorry sis, I'll have to get into this with you another time, can I speak to Lisa.'

'Sure thing. Hold on I'll get her. And don't forget... you can phone any time. I mean it, okay.'

'Yeah thanks. Say hi to the family.'

'Hello John... are you okay honey?'

'Yeah I'm fine... well, as fine as I can be. I need to talk to you.'

'Sure honey, go ahead.'

'Not on the phone... in person.'

'Do you want me to come back home?'

'No I'll come to you. I don't want my sister or the kids to know though.'

'Okay tell me where.'

'No I don't think that's a good idea. On second thoughts forget the whole thing... forget about meeting me.'

'John are you sure you're okay? You sound like you don't know what to do. Is everything really okay? Is there anything I can do?'

'No... Look, I think I should stop with this stuff concerning your brother. I don't think I can help him anymore. I just want to get things back to normal.'

'Whatever you think is best John... you know I trust you and back you. I know Pete is in a better place now. You probably wouldn't be able to find his killer now anyway.'

'That's just it Lis... it's like I've lost track of what I was doing and now I could endanger you and the kids; without even finding his killer. It's just that I want to know more about what I've started to uncover and the truth is it has little to do with finding the killer or killers. Pete knows I won't find the killer Lis, but he wants me to help finish what he has started.'

'Can you tell me what is going on John?'

'No I can't. If I did that, I would really be putting you in danger. But if I continue, I will still be putting you in danger... you just wouldn't know why. I know it sounds crazy but believe me, I'm telling you in the saneness way I can. If I tell you everything, you will definitely think I'm mad.'

'Like I've said, whatever you want to do is all right by me. I know you will do the right thing. I love you John. I wish I could come home and hold you right now.'

'Me too. That's why I'm going to walk away Lis. I miss you and the kids, and my work is getting screwed up. I had to lie to Mike about what I'm doing... he expects a report on his desk today and I haven't finished it yet.'

'Well if that's how you really feel, then just go into work today. Get on with your work and put this whole thing in the past. Give me a call when you finish work and let me know when the kids and I can come home. They miss you too.'

'You're right. I'm going to go into work and get this report finished. I love you and I'll call you tonight around nine o'clock.'

'I love you too John. Bye.'

Agent Smith went back into the bathroom, took a quick shower and got ready to go to work. He was determined to put it all behind him, just like Lisa had said, and get back to normal life.

The door bell rang, he went to the front door and opened it. Two police officers showed their badges.

'Hello officers... what's the problem?'

'It seems someone has broken into your car.'

'What... no! Let me see... Oh shit, there's glass everywhere. Thanks, but how did you know, I didn't report it? I didn't even know until you just told me.'

'We were just in the area and saw the glass as we drove passed.'

'Well thanks for telling me. I'll have to get a repairman out.'

'Actually I know a good repair company. Do you want the number? These guys are really good, they come highly recommended and come out immediately... Can we come inside for a moment and get a quick statement from you? I'll give you that number.'

'Yeah... I mean, come in. I'd like that number as I'm in a bit of a hurry. I can't give a statement though, because like I said, I never knew my car had been broken into until you told me. Anyway come in... let's do this quickly. You know I work for the FBI so I probably could deal with this myself. It was probably just some kids looking for a quick buck.'

'Sorry to be a pain, but is there any chance I can use your bathroom? I need to take a leak.'

'Sure, I know how it goes. Upstairs, third door on your right.'

'Thanks, won't be a minute.'

'No problem. It should be me thanking you guys for spotting my car and giving me the number for a quick-response repair man.'

'Well as you are a fellow law enforcement officer, you know the pencil pushers want to keep us up to our necks in paperwork.'

'Yeah I hear you. Okay, my name is John Smith. I live here at number 1234 10th Street... here's my driver's licence. Do you have that number?'

'Sure, here... it's 555-2067. Give them a call; they'll come out within the hour.'

'Hey thanks for letting me use your bathroom. Are we done here?'

'Well here's your licence. Sorry about your car... we probably won't find the perps., so get a better alarm fitted. Anyway, have a nice day.'

'Yeah you're right... thanks for the heads up. Keep up the good work officers. Bye.'

John picked up the phone and dialled the number.

'Hello I got your number from a police officer, he said you come out within the hour, is that right?'

'Yes... what is the address, which window is broken and what type of car do you have?'

'10th Street, number 1234. It's the driver's side and it's a '74 Cadillac.'

'Okay, your name is?'

'John Smith.'

'Okay Mr Smith, we'll be there in one hour. Thank you for choosing us. Bye.'

'Bye.'

INSIDE MOBILE ONE

'Get into your glass repair uniforms. I want GPS trackers and microphones in this car.'

'What's the address?'

'The same one as these two just came from, idiot. 10th Street, number 1234. You muscle heads really are all muscle and no brains. Good job you two, he really believed you were the police. We got good surveillance of the inside of his home and of the type of mobile phone, clothes, shoes and belts he uses. Okay you two, get changed and go fix his car window and place the bugs. Let's go.'

FBI HEADQUARTERS

Two hours later; as Agent Smith sat at his desk, he took the evidence bag out of the drawer and looked at its contents. 'How did Pete think I was going to crack the password? I've tried every possible number and word. Shit, stop it! I need to put it away and get on with some work before I get into real trouble with Mike,' he thought. He placed the bag back in the drawer and closed it slowly; watching the bag disappear into the darkness of the drawer.

OUTSIDE AGENT SMITH'S HOME

A van pulled up outside of Agent Smith's house. Lettering on the side of the van read "Blocked Drain Busters", along with a telephone number for any blocked pipe or drain emergencies. Two men stepped out of the van dressed in plumbers' outfits; if anyone had been paying attention, they would have seen these were the two police officers from earlier on, but no one did notice. They made their way quickly to the front door of Agent Smith's home. One man stood with his back to the door and looked around at the houses across the street to see who might be watching, whilst the second man picked the front door lock with an electric lock pick device; he had the door opened in under twenty seconds. The two men entered the house; one went upstairs and the second went into the front room. Once inside they put earpieces into their ears.

'We're in the birds nest. Over.'

'Okay gentlemen, let's light up the birds nest. Over.'

'Yes sir. Over.'

The two men placed listening devices in all of the phones. They replaced the original smoke alarms with identical looking ones, but the ones they put in place had spy cameras inside them. They also changed plug sockets, with identical ones that had both listening devices and spy cameras in them. By the time they finished there was a total of twenty-five cameras and thirty-five listening devices in the house.

The man upstairs went into the wardrobes and drawers. He took out clothes and replaced buttons on shirts, trousers and coats, with buttons that were also listening devices. They placed tracking devices that looked like extremely small pieces of sticky plastic, under the collars of overcoats and also changed shoes and belts with identical ones that they had brought with them; which also had tracking devices in them. The two men worked in complete silence and moved through the house quickly. As they moved around the house they were careful not to move anything out of its place; and anything they did picked up, they made sure they put it back in its exact position.

INSIDE MOBILE ONE

The two men sat as usual at their monitors, talking into their headsets.

'Okay, let's make sure we have full optical capabilities. On my mark. Over.'

The second man in Mobile One held his fingers at the ready, preparing to flick the switches that would bring up on their monitors the different spy cameras and listening devices in Agent Smith's house.

'1, 2, 3, 4, 5, 6, 7, 8, 9, 10, 11... Agent 1, speak now please. Over... Okay, loud and clear... 12, 13, 14, 15, 16... Okay, Agent 2 speak now please. Over... Okay, Loud and clear... 17, 18, 19, 20, 21, 22, 23, 24, 25. All systems check.

Okay time to leave. Make sure nothing is out of place. Over.'

'Exiting now. Status quo green. Over.'

'Good work gentlemen. Birds nest is hot. Over.'

OUTSIDE FBI HEADQUARTERS

It was lunch time. Agent Smith went for some fresh air and walked four hundred meters to a small, grassy area with a few benches dotted around it. As he made his way there he decided to phone his wife at his sister's house. As he pressed speed dial he bumped quite heavily into a man and woman coming in the opposite direction. His phone fell out of his hand to the floor, and the woman's bag fell from her arm and spilled its contents onto the floor.

'What's wrong with you man, are you blind?' shouted the man, as the woman bent down to pick up her belongings.

'I'm sorry it's my fault... I was about to make a phone call. Here, let me help you with that,' apologised Agent Smith, bending down to help the woman pick up her things.

'Hey, look at me man! You should look where you're going! You could have hurt my lady, and if you did I would have knocked you out,' snarled the man. As he spoke he held Agent Smith's arm firmly, pulling him back up and looking straight into his eyes.

'Just calm down, it was an accident. I've said I'm sorry and if you hadn't just stopped me I was about to help your lady pick up her stuff.'

'It's okay I've done it now, here's your phone. I'm not hurt, there's no harm done,' smiled the lady.

'Okay. You're lucky this time man, but if I was you I'd watch where I was walking in future,' said the man, staring aggressively at Agent Smith.

'Come on, let's go. It was just an accident,' said the woman as she pulled at the man's arm. Reluctantly he walked away, giving Agent Smith the bird as he went.

Agent Smith shook his head and redialled his sister's number.

The man and woman walked around the corner and stepped into a black Range Rover with blacked-out windows. The Range Rover immediately pulled off at high speed. In the back of the Rover, the woman placed an earpiece in her ear.

'We have the package. Over.' She looked down at a mobile phone in her hand.

'Did the target suspect anything? Over.' said a voice in her earpiece.

'No, not a thing... it went as smooth as clockwork. You should be intercepting a call as we speak. Over.'

'Checking tracking device in phone. GPS tracker online, all signals clear. Green light, we have a painted eyeball on screen. Eyeball is in some sort of small park. Over.' said Operator Two.

'This is Mobile One, requesting real time imagery. Big Bird give us air support, sweep over target area. Over.'

'This is Big Bird providing air support, two kilometres south of eyeball. Sweeping now, maximum resolution in progress. Over.'

Inside Mobile One, Operators One and Two looked at their monitors.

'Received Big Bird, confirm eyeball in small park. Longitude 34 Latitude 73, recording imagery now. Over.'

'Okay report back to base, you two. Good job. He still thinks that's his original phone. Over. This is Mobile One, requesting secure link. Over.'

'This is Pegasus ocean operator. What is your designator and call sign? Over.'

'Bravo, Echo, Delta, 1, 9, 6, 7. Over.'

'Request received Mobile One, enter code. Over.'

Operator Two typed a code into a computer keyboard and pressed enter.

'Code received, awaiting verification. Verification complete. Secure link enabled Mobile One. Over'

'This is Mobile One requesting interception on 555 765 234. All calls on this number to be patched here. Over.'

'This is intercepting station operator. Request received and understood, signal located Mobile One. Patching through now. Over.'

'This is Mobile One, signal received. Over.'

'Starting recording now of 001 interception.'

Operators One and Two began to listen in to the phone call conversation between Agent Smith and his wife.

'Hi sis, it's me again... just on a lunch break. I need to speak to Lisa.'

'Hello again! What's with you and Lisa? She just said she was going to give you a call. I wish Paul phoned me as much when he's away for a few days. You're making me jealous. Hold on, I'll call her for you.'

'Hi honey, I was about to call you. Look, I know you John, you're not going to be happy until you know what's going on. It's that FBI side of you.'

'You know me so well. I just can't stop thinking of certain things I need to do. I think once I do this stuff, it will be a lot easier to leave this thing behind. I just have one puzzle to solve, and then I can truly leave it alone.'

'Are you sure you don't want to tell me? There's really nothing I can do to help?'

'No, I don't want you involved at all. I know it must be hard because it's your brother, but you must not ask me to tell you anything, okay?'

'Okay... so I guess we won't be coming home tomorrow?'

'I need a couple of days, if that's okay with you?'

'Since when have you needed my permission

John?'

'This time I do. I love you. I'll speak to you in a couple of days.'

'Bye honey.'

'I think I'm going to throw up,' Operator One remarked sarcastically, as the two men laughed.

'We'd better tell the boss what's happening.'

NATIONAL SECURITY AGENCY
OFFICE OF THE DIRECTOR OF OPERATIONS

'Well, what's happening?'

'Not good sir. The eyeball has indicated that they intend to carry on.'

'Is the FBI aware or involved?'

'No sir, that's the good thing. This guy is working alone. His wife and family are not fully aware of what he is doing either.'

'How aware are they?'

'His wife knows he is looking into the death of her brother, but that's about it. He is fully aware that it's not a good idea to involve her.'

'Are you sure there is no one else involved?'

'It's early days yet, so we will be more sure as the days pass and the Intel grows.'

'Okay. Keep me informed.'

The Head of Field Operations Special Agent Ricardo Rodrigo, walked down the hall to Assistant Director Sam Collins' office.

'I just got word that John Smith is still engaged in the investigation of his brother-in-law's death. It appears that he's working alone, without the Bureau's involvement or knowledge. None of his family members know what he's doing either. But it's early days yet.'

'Okay, keep me informed.'

Assistant Director Sam Collins walked down the hall to Director Forbes' office, knocked on the door, and waited.

'Come in.'

'Smith's still looking.'

'Without the FBIs knowledge?'

'Yes sir, that's correct. His family doesn't know anything either; other than that he's looking into the death of his brother-in-law.'

'But if this guy decides to involve the FBI, we need to have his credibility in our pockets.'

'What do you suggest sir?'

'I think it's time the CIA earn their keep in this op. They know better than anyone how to make someone look like an angel or like Satan.'

'Understood sir. I will inform my team.'

'No, this remains here. The fewer people who know the better, you understand?'

'Yes sir. I'll tell my counterpart in the CIA to begin the utter destruction of this man's credibility.'

FBI HEADQUARTERS

Weeks passed and Agent Smith was no closer to finding the password to gain access to the disk. He was now beginning to think that it might be better if he took the disk to the decoding specialists in his department; they would be able to crack it in hours. The question was though... how would he explain this to his boss? Especially given the embarrassment he had caused the department over his brother-in-law's death in Rome? He knew it was still fresh in his boss' mind. If he were to go behind his boss's back and take the disk to the decoding department, and if they told his boss, it could cost Agent Smith both his job and an old friend. It was too late now to try to explain that he had been lying and taking the piss out of his boss over the past months.

'No I can do this. I've just got to focus. What am I missing?' thought Agent Smith. He reached into his desk and pulled out the evidence bag once again, but nothing stood out. Agent Smith took the disk out, put it in his pocket, signed out of the FBI building and went home.

AGENT SMITH'S HOME

Lisa was setting the table for dinner and her two girls were in their rooms, listening to music and talking on the phone.

'It's almost dinner time and your father will be home soon. Get ready... I want you down here in ten minutes! Do you girls hear me?'

'Yes mom.'

'Sharon, do you hear me?'

'Yes mom I'm coming. Hang on.'

The front door opened and Agent Smith entered.

'Hi honey, you're right on time. I've just set the table.'

'Great, let me give you a hand bringing in the food. I'm so hungry I could eat a horse.'

'Come on girls, get down here and give your dad a welcome-home hug and kiss. John, go wash your hands before you sit down.'

'Sorry, I forgot! I'm so hungry and your food smells so good.'

'Hi daddy, how was your day chasing and capturing bad guys?'

'I would answer that if I thought for one minute that you were serious and interested. Give me a hug.'

'Sharon come on, get downstairs now! I'm not joking. John, will you tell her to get down here please.'

'Sharon, hurry up and get down here! I'm starving and you're keeping me from eating.'

'Sorry dad. Coming.'

'Okay, let's eat this delicious feast. It looks great dear.'

'I wasn't going to ask, but it has been a few weeks now, and you haven't mentioned whether or not you have finished yet with my brother's business.'

'Yes and no. I still haven't finished working out the puzzle, but as time passes I get more and more disheartened.'

'I know you don't want to tell me, but what can it matter now? Just tell me what it is you're trying to work out. You know I'm good at crosswords and puzzles.'

'Honestly, I think it's for the best if we don't discuss it. If only I could get this damn password to open this disk!'

'Password... does the disk belong to Pete?'

'Hey, that's enough Detective Lisa Smith! Like I keep saying, I don't want you involved.'

'I think it's too late for that John. You're my husband and Pete was my brother. I don't think you could get more involved than that.'

'I know how much Pete meant to you, but I just don't think you can understand how serious the stuff he was into is. Look, I promise, if I don't crack it by the end of the month I will throw this disk away and never talk about it again. But you must trust me when I say you cannot know exactly what is going on, okay?'

'Only if you promise to leave it alone at the end of the month. If you continue after that, I want to know everything... deal?'

'Deal.'

INSIDE MOBILE ONE

'Houston, we have a problem. 'The shit just hit the fan.'
'This is Mobile One, requesting secure link. Over.'
'This is Pegasus ocean operator. What is your designator and call sign? Over.'
'Bravo, Echo, Delta, 1,9,6,7. Over.'
'Request received Mobile One. Enter code. Over.'
'Code received, awaiting verification. Verification complete. Secure link enabled Mobile One. Over.'

NATIONAL SECURITY AGENCY
OFFICE OF THE DIRECTOR OF OPERATIONS

'Go ahead Mobile One, this is Assistant Director Collins.'
'Assistant Director Collins? I thought we dealt with the Head of Field Operations Special Agent Ricardo Rodrigo?'
'You do. He's out of the office, so his secure calls have been diverted to my office. What's the Intel on the eyeball?'
'Not good news, depending on how you look at it sir.'
'Well, spit it out.'
'Yes sir. It seems that the eyeball has a package from Rome.'
'What? Are you sure?'
'Yes sir, we have the entire bird's nest covered.'
'Have you seen the package?'
'No sir.'
'So how do you know for sure?'
'We know for sure, sir.'
'Has the eyeball seen what's on the package?'

'That's the good news. It seems there's a password that has to be entered in order to gain access, and the eyeball has not been able to work it out.'

'What... with all the technical know-how available?'

'That's why I say it's good news really, because it means the employers don't know what the eyeball is doing.'

'Get a team in there tonight and extract the package.'

'Yes sir, but what about the rest of the birds in the nest?'

'This is a matter of National Security. Use extreme prejudice if necessary.'

'Copy that, extreme prejudice if necessary. But because of protocol, should we still await orders by Special Agent Rodrigo sir?'

'He will be running the ops as usual.'

Operator One switched channels and removed his headpiece.

'Shit, I hate it when that happens. I don't like talking to the heads... it always seems so formal.'

'Yeah and especially when you have to tell them bad news.'

'Did you hear how he reacted to the news? I thought he was going to have a heart attack.'

'Those suits, they always want everything to run like clockwork up in their ivory towers.'

'We better get the team ready while we wait for Rodrigo to take charge.'

'I wonder where the hell he is anyway man?'

DIRECTOR FORBES' OFFICE

Assistant Director Collins walked down the hall to Director Forbes' office, knocked on the door, and waited.

'Come in.'

'Bad news sir... well it depends on how you look at it.'

'Bad news is bad news, no matter how you look at it. Close the door.'

'Yes sir. What I mean is...'

'Don't waste my time with what you mean. Get on with it.'

'John Smith seems to be in possession of a copy of the information from Rome.'

'What?'

'But it seems the FBI has no idea what he is doing.'

'How do you know that?'

'The information is on a disk and he doesn't know the password. If his boss had full knowledge of what he was working on, he would have passed it to the code-breaking team by now, sir.'

'Hold on a minute. I'd better make a call. Get me the Director of the CIA and call me when you have him.'

'I have ordered a team in tonight to get the disk. They will use extreme prejudice, and they will not fail.'

'They'd better not, but if they do, the CIA have been setting up one of their infamous propaganda ops; in the event that he gets to tell his story. I think it's time we let the CIA do their thing.'

The secretary buzzed the Director on the intercom.

'Yes?'

'I have the Director of the CIA on line one sir.'

'Okay, put him through and hold all my other calls.'

'Hello... are you ready for a game of golf?'

'Yes, I certainly am.'

'Okay, I will tell the club we will be playing.'

'Good. Speak to you soon.'

'Bye for now.'

CIA HEADQUARTERS
OFFICE OF THE DIRECTOR OF THE CIA

Director Johnson, the head of the CIA, put down the phone.

'Okay Rodrigo, it's time we played dirty with this guy. Are you ready to do what is needed for National Security?'

'Yes sir.'

'Okay, everything is set. John Smith's life is about to go down the toilet. After we finish tearing his life apart, no one will care what he has to say about anything. No one will even care if he dies. Just get me that disk and find out if he has any more.'

'So should we make it look like a robbery gone bad and kill him?'

'No, don't kill him yet; I want to keep the ops on him for now, just in case he has friends we don't know about who may be involved. Keep him under surveillance and bring me that disk without him knowing you were there.'

'And if there's a problem?'

'Then use extreme force.'

'On everyone in there?'

'Only those that get in the way.'

'But his wife could be a problem. Left alive, she could end up on Larry King live telling the whole story....'

Director Johnson thought for a moment.

'Okay, if it goes belly up kill them all. Make it look like a drug deal gone wrong.'

'Yes sir. But where will we get the drugs from?'

'Don't worry, my team will take care of all of the finer details. Just make sure you have surveillance covered.'

NSA COMMAND AND OPERATIONS CENTRE

Director Forbes, Assistant Director Collins and Head of Field Operations Special Agent Rodrigo, stood looking at several very large screens in front of them. Operating staff seated at desks, brought up on the screens certain information and images via National Security Agency Satellites, that had the power to see car number plates and read the small print on newspapers on the ground. They would also provide secure air waves for radio communications.

Director Johnson viewed the same information via satellite link. Johnson sat at his desk in his offices, looking at a very large wide screen TV that was split into several segments; information and imagery were being fed to it via the satellite link.

'This is Rodrigo. Operation Agenda is to commence. Extraction of package is primary objective. Stealth over extreme force required. If things go south, extreme prejudice authorised. Big Bird to provide air support. Satellite One will provide real time imagery to me at the command centre and Mobile One. Over.'

'All teams now in position, time zero. Zero on my mark. Mark. Over.'

'This is command centre, Mobile One has the ball. Command centre out, good luck. Over.'

INSIDE MOBILE ONE

'Mobile One real time imagery received. Over.'
'This is satellite operator, call sign Sat 1. Over.'
'Received Sat 1. Run visual test. Over.'
'Team One, switch to night vision now. Over.'
'Sat 1 loading and patching through images from Team One now. Over.'

'Received and crystal clear. All six cams online. Over.'

'Sat 1 received. Beginning visual test, night vision. Maximum resolution, Longitude 25 Latitude 77. Over.'

'Received and crystal clear. I can count the number of tiles on the roof. Over.'

'Sat 1 received. Beginning visual test, thermal imagery. Maximum resolution, Longitude 25 Latitude 77. Over.'

'Received and crystal clear. I can count four target heat sources and heat source of Team One. Over.'

'Sat 1 received. Beginning visual test, wire frame imagery of buildings, in conjunction with any tracking device in use in the building. Over.'

'Received and crystal clear. I have wire frame of house basement, ground, first and attic floors, plus twelve tracking indicators. Over.'

'Sat 1 received. Beginning visual test, keyhole visual imagery. Over.'

'Received and crystal clear, all systems good. Over.'

'Sat 1 received. Visual testing complete and confirmed good. Over.'

'Team One, move in and enter birds nest. Over.'

'This is Team One leader, we're moving into position now. In position now and entering birds nest. Over.'

AGENT SMITH'S HOME, 00:20 AM

Agent Smith and his wife Lisa were fast asleep in bed. Their two girls were in Sharons' room, lying on her bed and listening to music through their headphones.

Team One moved through the house silently. The six-man team split into three teams of two at the command of the team leader and began to search as quietly as possible.

As the men moved from room to room and floor to floor; Forbes, Collins and Rodrigo watched their every move on the big screens in front of them.

'This is Team One, proceeding upstairs. What is the status of targets? Over.'

'Hold your position Team One, we have movement in room two. Over.'

'Roger that. Team One holding position. Over.'

'This is Team Two. We have found nothing in the basement. Moving to ground floor and awaiting orders. Over.'

'Team Two, hold your position on ground floor and help with the search on that floor. Over.'

'Roger that. Team Two moving to ground floor now. Over.'

'Team One, there is still movement in room two. Proceed there and give us keyhole visual. Over.'

'Roger that. Team One moving into position now. Over.'

'Team Two, there is a door to your right; it leads to a small room. Sweep and clear. Over.'

'Roger that. Team Two proceeding to door now. Door is locked, picking lock now. Door unlocked, entering now. Over.'

'This is Team One, in position. Looking in room now. Over.'

The two men stopped outside of the room and quietly put a small cable camera through the keyhole.

Forbes, Collins and Rodrigo looked at the screens intently.

'Receiving imagery now Team One... Okay, two females; unlikely package is there. Team One, check the door and see if it is fitted with a lock. If it is, lock them in and jam the lock if possible. Over.'

'Roger that. Team One attempting to lock the door. Okay, door locked. Attempting to jam lock. Lock jammed. Placing sticky cam under the door for continuing visual of room two. Continuing search, entering room one now. Over.'

Forbes, Collins and Rodrigo looked at another big screen to the right.

'Receiving imagery from sticky camera. Females on bed and seem unaware of presence. Over.'

'This is Team Two. Room clear, no package found. Continuing search of first floor. Over.'

'This is Team One. Room clear, no package found. Moving to room three. Over.'

'Team Two, move to attic floor and sweep. Over.'

'Roger that. Team Two moving to attic floor now. Over.'

'This is Team One, entering room. Looks like other females' room. Over.'

'Receiving imagery, unlikely package is there. Move to primary target room and prepare tranquillisers. Over.'

'Roger that. Team One moving into position now. Over.'

'This is Team Three. Ground floor clear, no package on this floor. Over.'

'Team Three, hold your position on ground floor and await orders. Over.'

'Roger that. Team Three holding position on ground floor. Over.'

AGENT SMITH'S BEDROOM

Agent Smith was sleeping in his bed, totally unaware that outside of his bedroom Team One was preparing to shoot him and his wife Lisa with tranquilliser darts and search their room for the package. They were supposed to tranquillise the two girls as well, but the girls were still awake and Rodrigo had decided to lock the girls in their room rather than risking tranquillising them; as the next morning they would be able to remember what had happened. Rodrigo wanted to keep it a stealth mission for as long as possible.

Suddenly Agent Smith jumped up out of his sleep, feeling a cold breeze running all over his body. The feeling was unmistakable; it made him shake slightly, and a shiver ran down his spine. Looking up, he saw that the force floated in the air two feet above him. Agent Smith stared in disbelief; for the first time he could see it clearly.

It looked like a mass of water, but it was not as dense as water. The force moved to the door and began to change. First it reflected the door, but as Agent Smith watched in shock it changed again and showed him what was on the other side of the door. Agent Smith jumped with fright when he saw two masked armed men, outside of his bedroom door. He took a second to compose himself, wondering for a second if what he was looking at was an illusion. But the more he looked at the two men, who seemed to be preparing some sort of dart gun, the more he realised that what the force was showing him was real.

He quickly grabbed two guns and an ammunition belt full of bullet-filled clips, out of his bedside drawer. Putting his hand over his wife's mouth, he then woke her quickly.

'Don't say a word, and don't look at the door until you know you're not going to scream. I want you to get up slowly and move to the safe room; remember what we've practiced concerning a revenge attack. Okay, are you ready?'

Lisa nodded her head, and Agent Smith removed his hand from over her mouth. As she got up out of the bed, she looked at the door and froze. Her eyes widened and her jaw dropped as she saw the force for the first time.

'I will explain it all later. For now, I need you to move to the safe room. Now go, now!' Agent Smith whispered.

But Lisa did not move. Agent Smith had to pick her up by her arms and push her towards the safe room, but as soon as he had let go of her she stopped; her eyes fixed on the force. Agent Smith had no choice but to slap her across the face. As he did, the door handle began to turn slowly, and the force vanished into thin air.

Forbes, Collins and Rodrigo watched in horror as the thermal imagery from Satellite One showed two heat sources moving in the target room.

'This is Mobile One. Targets are on their feet and primary target may be armed; he is aware of your presence. Cover blown, I repeat, cover blown. Move to extreme prejudice status immediately. Over.'

Team One threw down their tranquillising guns and pulled out their hand guns.

'Roger that. Team One operating status now extreme prejudice. Over.'

'Teams Two and Three, move to extreme prejudice position now. Over.'

'Roger that. Team Two moving to extreme prejudice position now. Over.'

'Roger that. Team Three moving to extreme prejudice position now. Over.'

'Big Bird, move into extreme prejudice position now. Over.'

'Roger that. Big Bird moving to extreme prejudice position now. Over.'

Team Two made their way to the girls' room. Team Three split, as one member went to the backyard and took up a clear shot position, while the other member went to the front of the house and took up a clear shot position there; both waited. The helicopter known as Big Bird hovered over the house at a three o'clock position.

Team One stopped opening the door and took up firing positions. Agent Smith threw his wife into the safe room and closed the door, which automatically locked.

'*What about the girls*?' shouted Lisa.

'I will save them, I promise,' shouted Agent Smith as he took up aim at the bedroom door.

'Be advised, primary target moving into firing position. Move in with caution. Over.'

There was no reply from Team One. Agent Smith had fired repeatedly through the plasterboard walls and through the door; like a demon trying to break out of hell, he screamed as he shot. The veins in his head pumped out as his eyes became bloodshot and spit hung from his mouth. Moving towards the door, the only time Agent Smith stopped was to reload. By the time he moved to the door and opened it, the door looked like Swiss cheese. It fell off its hinges as Agent Smith opened it.

On the floor were the two lifeless bodies of the members of Team One; their bulletproof vests riddled with armour-piercing bullets. Blood dripped out of their bodies, down their black uniforms and onto the carpet. Agent Smith only stopped briefly to fire one shot, into each of the two men's heads, making sure they were truly dead.

Agent Smith raced to his beloved girls' room. His heart was in his mouth and his mind was filled with the most horrifying thoughts. Images flashed through his mind of his two girls dead, hanging over the edge of their beds, eyes staring coldly into space, blood dripping from the one hole in each of their heads.

Agent Smith felt like he was about to throw up. His stomach felt so tight that it seemed as if it wanted to push itself out of the back of his spine; but there was no time to be sick. His little girls, the loves of his life, were in mortal danger, and they needed daddy to come and rescue them... just like when they were little girls, falling off their bikes or getting stuck in trees. Sharon was the worst that way; she always was a tomboy. 'Please let me save them, GOD, I will do anything you want, just let me save them,' pleaded Agent Smith.

Team Two reached Sharon's room and tried to open the door, but it was jammed. One member of the team aimed at the door and shot the door lock off. Kicking the door open, he found that there was no one on the bed.

'Team Two, turn left. Go through the shower room and there's a door to the right. They seem to be hiding in there. Over.'

'Roger that. Team Two moving there now. Over.'

They moved towards the shower room and looked right at the door.

'Shit. This is Team Two, we have a problem. The door looks like a safe room door. If I try to shoot it open the bullet is going to come right back at me. Over.'

'Received Team Two, that's why you have C4 and shape charges. Over.'

'Copy that. Team Two placing explosives now. Over.'

'Received Team Two. Whilst one of you places the charge I want the other one to ask the girls to come out before you kill their dad... who, by the way, is en route to you right now. Over.'

As Agent Smith reached the outside of the girls' room he was greeted by a barrage of flying bullets.

'Do you hear that girls? If you don't open the door now we're going to kill your old man. This is your last chance, I'm running out of patience.'

'*No, don't open the door! If you do we're all dead! Remember what we have practiced for this type of situation. Girls can you hear me?*' shouted Agent Smith at the top of his voice, almost sounding like a man possessed.

'Yes we hear you Daddy. Be careful Dad, please! We're okay.'

'They're safe for now. I'm about to blow this door wide open old man... then what are you going to do, Daddy? Throw your guns in here now, put your hands behind your back and step into the doorway backwards. Do it now!'

'Okay, I'm going to do what you say. Don't shoot okay. I'm going to throw my gun through the door now, okay?'

'Okay old man, do it nice and slowly.'

'This is Mobile One Team Two, be careful. It looks like he has taken something out of his pocket. Over.'

There was no response from Team Two; they were too busy trying to clear their vision and stop the ringing sound in their ears. Instead of throwing his guns in, Agent Smith had thrown in a stun grenade. As soon as the grenade hit the floor, it flashed a brilliant white light that blinded Team Two, and there was an extremely loud bang.

Agent Smith stood in the doorway and pumped bullets relentlessly into the heads, bodies and legs of Team Two. Their bodies danced around, shaking and twisting in response to each bullet that hit them; until they fell backwards onto the wall. Leaving a trail of blood against the wallpaper, they slid to the floor in a lifeless heap.

Agent Smith also fell to the floor as his heart suddenly began to beat in triple-time. A sharp pain shot down his left arm, his eyes lost focus and he couldn't breathe. Sweat poured out his body and his head began to bang, as if someone was hitting him with a hammer. Then everything went black.

'Wake up, wake up, can you hear me?'

'Let me try.'

'Stop! Don't slap his face so hard.'

'Wake up! Go and get a glass of cold water.'

'Please don't die Dad.'

'Please don't die? Who's going to die?' thought Agent Smith, as the words pierced his unconscious mind.

Slowly Agent Smith opened his eyes and regained consciousness. As his vision cleared, the blur in front of him slowly became the recognisable faces of his two daughters.

'Here, drink some water. You gave us a big scare Dad. We thought you were going to die.'

'I thought I was going to use this glass of water to try and bring you around by throwing it on your face.'

'What is going on Dad? I'm scared... who are these two men?'

'Why were they trying to kill us?'

'Are they dead?'

'Where's mom? Is she okay?'

'What are we going to do?'

'Should I call the police? Is mom okay?'

'Hold on a minute, let me get my bearings. Your mom is okay and these men won't be bothering us again. We don't have time to phone the police right now. Let's get your mom and get out of here, just in case there are more of them. I'll call the police on our way.'

'But shouldn't we phone the police right now so they can come and protect us?'

'Yeah Dad, I agree with Sharon. Let's call the police now.'

'How long do you think it will take them to get here?'

'Not long.'

'Look, I'm not arguing with you. Let's go, now, move it. Stay right behind me and don't say anything.'

'You won't be needing these,' hissed Agent Smith as he picked up the two submachine guns that belonged to the two members of Team Two. He walked down the corridor and turned the corner. Moving towards his bedroom, he pointed the submachine guns straight ahead keeping his fingers firmly on the triggers; ready to shoot at the first sign of trouble. The two operators in Mobile One looked at one another with surprise.

'Who the fuck is this guy? He must be Super Agent John Smith.' shouted Operator One as he put his hands to his head in disbelief.

'This is Mobile One. We've lost Teams One and Two. Command centre please advise. Over.'

NATIONAL SECURITY AGENCY COMMAND CENTRE

'Shit! This was not supposed to happen. How long for support teams to arrive?' asked Rodrigo.

'E.T.A. nine minutes. Over.'

'Okay. Team Three, hold your positions and don't let anything get passed you. Over.'

'Roger that. Holding positions. Over.'

'This is Director Forbes. Patch me through to the Director of the CIA on secure link now.'

'Patching you through now sir.'

'This is Director Johnson. Things are not going according to plan, but don't worry, I have a plan for this situation. Let the primary target go. We will use the local police to hunt him down and pick him up.'

'Are you sure? What if he talks?'

'That's exactly what we want him to do. When the local police track him down, do you think a man in his state of mind is going to trust anyone? He's going to fight them thinking they're after him for us and that they are involved in this too. If they catch him without killing him, what's he going to tell them? That he has uncovered a plot involving his dead priest brother-in-law? Who is going to understand him, never mind believe him? He himself doesn't even know exactly what it is. This will help us to look more credible when we say he's a rogue agent who has become a traitor and has lost his mind. What evidence is recovered will be under the jurisdiction of National Security.'

'Hold on a moment. Rodrigo, tell Team Three to stand down immediately.'

'*What!* But they will escape, sir!'

'*Don't question me! Do it.*'

'Yes sir. Team Three, stand down. I repeat, stand down immediately. Over.'

'Roger that. Team Three returning to Mobile One. Over.'

'It's done sir.'

'Hello Johnson, it's done. What about the dead bodies of your ex-military cut-outs?'

'The teams on their way know what to do. Trust me, everything is in place.'

'What about the disk?'

'It's a copy... without the original it's nothing more than a bedtime story that he could have made up himself. Even if he cracks the code without help, he won't be able to explain it.'

'So what was the point of this mission in the first place?'

'To get him to run. Once he runs he looks guilty of something; all the time he has spent on this case means time missing from work. We'll fill in the blanks for the FBI and inform them that they have a spy inside their ranks. Like I said, you do your part and let me do mine. The CIA will take it from here. All you have to do is what you do best, and keep your eyes and ears open.'

'Okay. I will advise Rodrigo that you have the ball, and we'll sit back and watch the show.'

Director Forbes put down the phone and walked back over to where Assistant Director Collins and Special Agent Rodrigo were standing. With a face that could kill, he grabbed Rodrigo by the arm firmly and pulled him around to face him. He was foaming at the mouth as he shouted at Rodrigo; spit went flying into Rodrigo's face.

'If you ever question me again you will be giving out parking tickets in the North Pole! Do you understand?'

'Yes sir.' Rodrigo bowed his head in submission. 'I'm sorry sir, it won't happen again.'

Director Forbes clenched his teeth and looked hard at Rodrigo for a moment. 'It's been a disappointing night for all of us. Let's all stay focused and remain professional.'

Assistant Director Collins looked at Rodrigo and blew a sigh of relief.

'You know he doesn't like failure. You are one lucky son of a gun.'

Rodrigo shook his head. Looking up towards the ceiling, he blew an even bigger sigh of relief.

Director Forbes made his way back to his office and slammed the door behind him. He took a bottle of whiskey out of a cabinet and poured himself a cup as he sat back in his chair. Even though he knew Johnson had spent a lifetime spinning webs of deceit and lies, something in his gut was telling him Agent Smith was going to be trouble. It was time he called a meeting to decide what should be done next. He picked up the phone, dialled a number, and waited for an answer.

'Hello.'

'It's me. Get everything ready.'

'Very good sir. When will you be arriving?'

'At the weekend.'

'Everything will be ready and just how you like it sir.'

The man put down the phone and called to the other members of staff, who came immediately and lined up in a straight line.

'The master has called and will be coming this weekend. Make up the twenty-four beds and hang the robes in their rooms. Scrub the floors and prepare the shower room. Prepare the dining room and make sure the first aid kits are fully prepared. Separate five of the best goats and prepare them. I will take care of the sacred room and altar, as usual. As they are coming this weekend, the Secret Service will be here tomorrow doing their security checks; so have the extra staff house made up and ready first thing tomorrow.'

They were all dressed in maids' and butlers' uniforms, including the man who had just spoken to Director Forbes. In fact, he was the head butler and was the overseer at the Skull and Bone retreat mansion... the very same mansion that the twenty-four men had been at, when they'd found out that Agent Smith was a problem.

AGENT SMITH'S HOUSE

'Lisa, open the door it's me! Everything is okay! I have the girls with me.'

The door opened and Lisa hugged Agent Smith and the girls, relieved that they were okay.

'I tried to phone the police on the safe room phone but it was disconnected, and so were the surveillance cameras. It was so horrible! I thought you were all dead! I'm so glad to see you all.'

'So am I, but we don't have time to talk. We must get down to the car and try to get out of here.'

'Who are these people John? Why do they want us dead?'

'We don't have time to talk. Let's get moving. I don't want to sound like a killjoy, but we aren't out of this yet.'

They moved as quickly as they could down the stairs to the garage. Agent Smith would go a few meters or so first and make sure the coast was clear, and then the ladies followed. A trip that would have normally taken two minutes in a hurry, was now taking ten minutes in a hurry. Agent Smith truly believed he was going to run into masked gunmen all of the way to the garage. His heart was still pounding and his head was still thumping so much, that he could hardly keep his eyes focused.

By the time they made it to the car, he thought he was going to have a stroke. *'Come on John, we've done this a million times. Get a grip. Just because it's my family doesn't mean that the same rules don't apply; stay focused, look at them like any other victims who need my support and protection. Come on, get control. Deep breaths. We're going to make it... we're the good guys,'* he thought to himself as he entered the car.

'Are you okay honey?'

'Yes I'm fine. Don't worry Lisa, we're going to make it. I've done this a million times.'

'That's it, tell them they're going to be alright... you've got things under control. This is what I do,' he thought. As he did, he began to calm down; his heart began to slow and his breathing deepened.

'We're going to be alright aren't we dad?'

'Trust me, we're going to be fine. Don't worry. Now fasten your seatbelts, put your heads between your legs and hold on.'

'I don't know what's out there but I'll be damned if it's going to stop me from getting my family out of here,' he thought as he pressed the remote to open the garage door.

As the door slowly lifted, Agent Smith's heart began to beat faster again.

'Come on, hurry up and open,' he said, as he revved the engine as high as it would go. The garage door was hardly high enough for the car to get under, but that didn't stop Agent Smith; he was out of the garage like a bat out of hell, scraping the top of the car roof as he floored the throttle. Skidding onto the street like a hot rod racer, he drove the car at top speed, slamming on the brakes, using all of the evasion skills that he had learnt at the bureau, and not stopping once at any of the red lights that came across his path.

'Is everyone okay?'

'Yes... are we out of danger now?'

'I think so.'

Agent Smith pulled over and looked at his family. The two girls were deep in shock and his wife wasn't far from a nervous breakdown.

'I think I'd better get you lot to a hospital. I'm going to drive to the next state... I have to think for a moment while I drive.'

Agent Smith stopped at a petrol station and got a few sandwiches and drinks while the petrol tank filled up.

AREA 51, HANGAR 18

'General, we are working around the clock. We can't put this information together for you in an instant, just because you want it right now.'

'For the fifth time, I'm Major Stone, not General. It's my boss who is the General and he's the one who wants this information now.'

'Do you have any idea of the advancements in physics and technology that we are dealing with here?'

'No, but I do know I better have a very good excuse for my boss, when I turn up empty-handed.'

'That's the thing about you soldiers... you always want the best technology, but you never want to know how it comes about. I've been at this place since I was twenty-three years old, some thirty years ago, and I think in all that time I've only shown two Generals or Majors around; even though all of the advancements in the military in the past fifty years, have come out of this hangar and the floors below. Why do you think that is, Major Stone?'

'I guess it's like you say; we're soldiers not professors.'

'Maybe it's because of all my years stuck in here. We don't get out much, you know?'

'Sorry, you've lost me,' said Major Stone, a puzzled look on his face.

'I'll have the paperwork you need... on one condition. You pretend that you and the General are not just using me and my staff. You act as if you are interested and as if you appreciate what we do here day and night, and let me show you the hard work that goes into the information you now require from me.'

'Are you serious? I don't have the time for this Dr. Goodenberg.'

'Well I'm impressed that you know my name. But if you want me to tell my staff that we will be working late into the night because of you, you can at least show some appreciation, Major Stone. It's been a long time since I've shown anyone around the thirty-two floors below us.'

'I'm afraid that won't be possible. I'm only cleared for the first three floors.'

'Major Stone, when it comes to who can enter the floors of this facility, I have security clearance to show whomever I see fit.'

'Okay you're right. Without you guys we would still be chucking spears at our enemies,' said Major Stone. The truth was that he had hoped to see the twilight zone ever since he had first arrived at Area 51.

'Good, I'm so glad you want to know more about the tireless work we do for you guys. Shall we start here? This as you know is hangar 18, and we are standing on two massive moving floors that can swivel around three hundred and sixty degrees. They can ascend or descend to all thirty-two floors below and can carry a payload of up to one hundred and fifty thousand tonnes and any three hundred square meters.'

'That's quite impressive. In all the times I've stood here, I never knew that.'

'Oh that's nothing. The door over there is the staff elevator to the twilight zone. Shall we?' asked Dr. Goodenberg, as he gestured with his hands to move towards the door. Major Stone could hardly contain his excitement as he moved at a quick pace towards the door.

'You really do want to know what goes on in the twilight zone, don't you?'

'Yes. I have clearance for the first three floors but I have document clearance for a lot more. It took me almost two years to believe some of the stuff I have read and I'm still amazed at what I've read.'

'Well, I'm glad that today I can let you see the amazing things we have been able to reverse-engineer from the spacecraft.'

'Do you know where it comes from? I mean, did it crash in the desert like the rumours say?'

'Crash... first off, these things can't crash. It's impossible. The fail-safe systems are unbelievable.'

'So if it didn't crash, how did we get it? Did we shoot it out of the sky?'

'Shoot it out of the sky? You're going to make me crack my ribs if you keep making jokes like that.'

'So how did we get it then?' Major Stone was starting to get frustrated; he was so close to getting the answers to questions he had thought, up until now, he would never know the answers to. Mainly because he would never have dared to ask. Yet for the first time, instead of just collecting data and escorting sensitive material around the base, Dr. Goodenberg had opened the door and invited him in... and he'd almost missed the opportunity.

'Understand one thing Major Stone. We are in the Stone Age compared to the technology we are looking at. It will take ten or more generations of professors after me, to even come close to understanding anything above the basics of what we are dealing with.'

'I don't mean to be rude, but you're not answering the question. How did we get hold of the spacecraft?'

'We have more than one; we have five Major Stone. Please, after you,' said Dr. Goodenberg, as the elevator doors opened. Dr Goodenberg swiped his card and the elevator doors closed. There were three red lights above the lift door; one turned green after Dr. Goodenberg swiped his card, while the other two lights continued to blink red. A computer voice invited Dr. Goodenberg to give a thumb and eye scan. After Dr. Goodenberg had done this, the two remaining lights turned green and the computer voice spoke to him.

'What floor is required Dr. Goodenberg?'

'Fourth floor please Arthur,' replied Dr. Goodenberg, as if the computer was an actual person.

'Why do you call it Arthur?' asked Major Stone, with a smile on his face.

'Why not? I know to you it's just a computer voice but to me it's much more than that. Arthur is a supercomputer that controls a lot more than security and elevators. Let me demonstrate. Arthur, how many persons are in the elevator?'

'There are two of you Dr Goodenberg.'

'Wow, that's quite impressive.'

'I'm glad you think so Major Stone,' replied Arthur.

'How did it know that was me?'

'Like I said; Arthur is a supercomputer that is capable of much greater things than knowing how many people are in an elevator, or who they are. But to answer your question, he can read your cards magnetic strip without you having to swipe it. There is also a microchip inside the card.'

'Speaking of answering questions, are you trying to avoid answering the question I asked about the spacecrafts?'

The doors opened.

'After you,' said Dr. Goodenberg.

They walked towards a steel door; standing on either side of it were two armed guards. As they approached the doors, Arthur asked Dr. Goodenberg to give another thumb and eye scan. The steel door slid open and they walked along a white-lit corridor. As they approached a second steel door with two more armed guards on either side, a laser scanned both men.

'Don't I need to sign in anywhere?' asked Major Stone.

'Arthur has already done that. While we've being walking along this corridor he has weighed you, measured the distance between each step you've taken, measured your heart and breathing rates, and collected data on many more things concerning your every move. Whatever you do from this point on, Arthur will know about it and log it.'

As they reached the second set of steel doors, the doors opened and Arthur said "Welcome to the twilight zone, Dr. Goodenberg and Major Stone." There was a long corridor with two long glass walls on either side. On the other side of the glass walls, engineers and scientists were busy at work; some on computers, others working on prototype-looking machinery, robots, lasers and many other scientific projects. Major Stone didn't have any idea of what he was looking at.

Seeing that Major Stone looked lost, Dr. Goodenberg said 'This is the Reverse Engineering Department, eight floors below this are the spacecrafts. The seven floors directly below this one all take information about the spacecraft, break it down and then try to rebuild it using supercomputers.'

'I am very interested in what you are saying, but you're not answering the question I have repeatedly asked.'

'All in good time, Major Stone.'

They entered into the first room on the fourth floor.

'On this floor, computers make calculations on information sent up from the remote scanners inside the spacecraft and these machines recreate mock models. This model here we believe to be an Inertia Canceller.'

'You mean you don't actually go inside the craft?'

'No.'

'Why not?'

'For two reasons. One is that we cannot get the craft to open any doors large enough for a human being to fit through, and the second is that because when we sent a monkey in, it died after being in there for two minutes. So we put protective clothing on a second monkey, and it died after three and a half minutes.'

'What did they die from?'

'Their lungs collapsed, their hearts exploded, and they developed full-blown cancer across sixty percent of their bodies.'

'So you're using remote-control robots?'

'Yes. It has covered all of the craft, sending back air samples and video feed.'

'Is the craft still switched on?'

'Yes, they all are.'

'How long have you had them?'

'For over fifty years.'

'Do you have alien bodies?'

'No, and we refer to them as E.B.Es... Extraterrestrial Biological Entities.'

'So are you sure we won't get into serious trouble for me being here?'

'Major Stone, I know more about you than you think. You spent ten years overseas on several black ops, you think you're a replacement for some other Major who died on this base, and you think I do not know that from the time you arrived here, getting into the twilight zone has been one of your obsessions. You really believe I just happened to open a door and let you in to the world's most secretive ops ever?'

'I guess not.'

'I hand-picked you, like I hand-pick ninety-nine-point-nine percent of the personnel on this base. That is part of my job description.'

'I should have known. To be honest with you, I thought you were a bit of a crackpot.'

'Looks can be very misleading here at Groom Lake.'

'So if this is not an accident, what exactly is going on... or shouldn't I ask?'

'All will be revealed in time. First let's get some of the technical stuff out of the way. This is the Inertia Canceller department.'

They were now standing in a basketball court-sized hall. There were railroad tracks running down the length of the hall, with some sort of four-wheeled rocket propelled seat attached to it that was labelled "Sonic Wind 100". There were computers and monitors at the side of the track and cables ran from the rocket seat and the track, to computers that lined one wall of the hall.

'An Inertia Canceller... what does that mean?' asked Major Stone, as he looked around the hall and tried to make sense of what he was looking at.

'It has to do with the universal law of matter.'

'Come again?'

'Okay, let me try to explain it in layman's terms. You see that seat? It's called a rocket sledge and it's nicknamed the Sonic Wind. This one is number one hundred; we have been through quite a few over the years. It can go from zero to two hundred miles per hour in two seconds. The effect on the body is massive; the G-force that's created with that type of increase in speed, increases the weight of the body, making it feel extremely heavy. In turn, slowing down from two hundred to zero creates a negative G-force, which makes the body feel extremely light. In the next room is a positive G-force centrifuge rotary arm. Basically, you are strapped into a seat in a compartment and the rotary arm swings you around until you reach nine positive G-forces; which is the point at which G-lock is reached.'

'Sorry, what is G-lock?'

'G-lock is the technical term for a gravity-induced loss of consciousness.'

'Why does that happen?'

'The G-force becomes so great that it stops blood from being able to be pumped around the body, including the brain. The blood is pushed to the bottom part of your legs and you pass out.'

'That doesn't sound like a lot of fun.'

'That's nothing Major Stone. We have a train track outside in the desert with a rocket sledge like this one, only it moves at speeds of up to six hundred miles per hour and slows down to zero in under three seconds.'

'The G-force must be extreme.'

'The negative G-force is forty G's.'

'I bet no man can stand such G-forces.'

'You would lose the bet. Major Bruce, whom you have replaced, did.'

'And was he okay, or was it that what killed him?'

'No he didn't die, but he wasn't okay. He suffered a complete red-out.'

'A complete red-out... what is that?'

'Basically, he burst the capillaries in his eyes and many blood vessels all around his body.'

'And this has what to do with an inertia canceller?'

'Let me try to explain it this way. When you stand still, the whole of your body stays still; when you drive a car and slam on the brakes the car stops, but your body still wants to move forward and if you didn't wear a seat belt you could fly through the window.

'The inertia canceller is a high-tech seat belt that the E.B.Es use to fly their spacecraft. The force that Major Bruce's body had to deal with, because he was wearing a seat belt, was forty G's... going from six hundred to zero in two seconds. Not only can the E.B.Es spacecraft go from nine thousand miles per hour to zero in a second, they can turn left, right, up or down at the same time; which would create G-forces of around three hundred G's.

'With or without a seat belt, you and the seat and anything behind the seat, meaning the rest of the spacecraft, are going to be slammed and squashed into the front of the spacecraft without an inertia canceller.' They walked through a steel door and entered a room called Propulsion Systems. Major Stone was finding it hard to keep up with what he was being told and what he was seeing, but he knew it was important to understand as best as he could. He didn't know why it was important yet, but he was sure he was going to find out when the time was right. One thing he now knew was why it was called the twilight zone.

He looked around the hall they had now entered, inside he could see more computers and monitors. Cables ran to a funny-looking machine from which a light humming sound emanated; it was as if the humming had a physical presence, almost as if it were very lightly pushing him backwards.

'This is a force-field generator and it's very powerful. The Japanese use a less powerful version to run their high-speed railways, which they call maglev trains.'

'Yes, I've been on one... it works by using some sort of magnet.'

'Yes... not quite as simple as that, but you're on the right track. Magnets have a force field around them called North and South poles. North and South poles pull towards one another, while North to North or South to South poles push away from one another. We have learnt to use electro-magnetism as a propulsion system; basically, the force field around a magnet is super conducted to create a powerful levitation force. This force-field generator can be used to move over one hundred tonnes of machinery. Its full name is the electromagnet repulsive force-field generator. Some of the spacecrafts we have use water to create levitation force fields.'

'Water, how does that work?'

'Well I think I'll explain that to you later, as it is a bit more complicated.'

'That hasn't stopped you up until now.'

'Sorry, sometimes I get carried away. I just love my job. Is that sad?'

'If it is then you're in the right company, because I love my job too. Is any of this connected to Project Silver Bug?'

'No, not really. At the Air Technical Intelligence Centre the Project Silver Bug concentrated on vertical takeoff, supersonic speed and so on. We of course gave them the technical knowledge to do this, but it was to be used with a conventional aircraft. Although I wouldn't call the pancake aircraft conventional-looking, most of the stuff under the bonnet was normal.'

'Yes, I've seen pictures of the pancake. I do have to say it looks ugly.'

'We are also working on this,' said Dr. Goodenberg, pointing to a futuristic-looking piece of machinery.

'What is it?'

'It's called an anti-gravity drive. It manipulates the earth's gravity, reversing it against itself and creating a gravity wave.'

'I think my brain is about to explode. How does it work?'

They spent the rest of the day walking around the twilight zone. By the end of the day, Major Stone felt like his head was spinning because of all of the information he was trying to take in. He had seen amazing machinery with capabilities that were truly mind-blowing; yet he still hadn't found out how the spacecrafts had come to be in the hands of the military, or what his part was in the bigger scheme of things.

As they sat down in the staff canteen, Major Stone sipped his coffee slowly. Looking straight into Dr. Goodenberg's eyes he said 'This has been an interesting and eye-opening day, but I have to say what I found more intriguing than any of the equipment... if that's even possible... is the question, why you are showing all of this to me?'

'You soldiers, you always want to get right to the point. There are four known forces of gravity that we know of... electromagnetism, strong nuclear, weak nuclear and gravity. We know very little about gravity, but the E.B.Es know it well enough to manipulate it in many different ways. They can also use strong and weak nuclear power to travel at speeds we have yet to witness, never mind understand. The little that we have been able to use has advanced mankind greatly. Militarily, we've been able to create some pretty amazing equipment. We have two prototype crafts boasting great technical abilities... the X47 NASA aircraft, which is capable of flying in and out of the atmosphere and the War Hawk, which is able to fly like a plane in the sky at supersonic speeds and submerge under the sea like a submarine, to depths no submarine could match.'

'But what does that have to do with me?'

'Follow me through here,' said Dr. Goodenberg as he looked around the canteen. Major Stone followed Dr. Goodenberg to his office. As they walked Major Stone asked, 'Does any of this technology ever reach the general population?'

'In the last seventy years, mankind has shown greater, faster advances in technology than were seen in all of the technology developed over the last five thousand years. Why do you think that is?'

'I have no idea.'

'It's because they have wanted us to.'

'They?'

'The E.B.Es.'

They entered into Dr. Goodenberg's office; there was paperwork all over the place.

'Find the chair... it's under that pile of papers over there; it's the maid's day off as they say.'

Major Stone looked at the pile of papers and folders and tried to pick them up in one go, but there were too many. He laughed as he spilled half of them on the floor.

'I'm sorry, but don't you find it funny how we as humans can be so weird? I mean, you're a top professor. You've spent the day blowing my mind talking about stuff I cannot begin to comprehend, and yet we enter into your office and it's a complete mess. I just wouldn't imagine such a great mind would be surrounded by this.'

'That's what makes us what we are; the mind of the human being is made of many compartments. Some parts make us Nobel Prize winners, but the flip side of that can mean that we can become so obsessive and so absorbed in our particular field, that we turn out to be complete disasters when it comes to managing the simple things in life.'

'What about the aliens... sorry E.B.Es. Are they like us?'

'E.B.Es are a lot like you Major Stone. They are soldiers and most are extremely disciplined.' Dr.
Goodenberg sat back in his old leather reclining chair and looked up into space.

Major Stone finally removed all of the papers and folders on the chair. He sneezed as dust spiralled up into the air as he sat down.

'You haven't had any guests in a long time.' Major Stone coughed as the dust hit the back of his throat.

'Would you like some water?'

'Yes, thank you, I've got a bit of a dry throat.'

Dr. Goodenberg swivelled around in his chair to a water dispenser behind him and took out a plastic throwaway cup and poured cold water into it. Major Stone drank it all in one go.

'Thanks, I was really thirsty. How many times have you interacted with the aliens... sorry, the E.B.Es?'

'Interacted... you make it sound like some sort of inter-space docking. The E.B.Es communicate using telepathic means. However, apart from that the conversations are no different from those you and I have been having all day. They know every language on the earth; they were here before mankind was created.'

'If they were here before mankind, where are they now?' Major Stone looked anxious and began to fidget uncomfortably in his chair, as his mind contemplated the oncoming answer.

'They are here on earth, where they have always been. They have an entire country, way down in the deep blue sea.'

Major Stone took a deep breath of air and gulped down the last of the saliva left in his rapidly drying mouth.

'Wait a minute... Are you saying they don't come from out of space?' Major Stone looked more confused and nervous.

'That's the irony of it. All through the years we were looking in outer space for E.B.Es and all the time they have been in the one place we cannot explore, the sea. We know more about the moon and the nearest star... Alpha Centauri, which is some four light years away... than we know about the sea that surrounds us.'

'So they aren't coming from outer space?'

'They come from outer space, inner space, the sea and many more places about which we know nothing. Now do you understand why the government are unwilling to reveal the truth about UFOs? Look at how you are acting, and you are trained to deal with almost anything and have been exposed to classified information. The world at large would break down if it knew, and we would be thrown into chaos.'

'So how come we don't see them flying around all of the time?'

'Time, is why we don't see them all of the time. It's not time for us to see them all of the time. They are slowly making mankind aware of their existence.'

'Why be bothered about slowly letting mankind know they exist? Why not just pull up on the White House lawn and say, 'we're here to take over your planet?''

'Because they are soldiers, and they cannot act without the say-so of their General.'

'So why doesn't he give the order?'

'Because he doesn't know who he is.'

Major Stone shook his head and nervously laughed. 'What? How can he not know who he is?'

'I don't know why or how. I just know what I'm told. There are many things I don't know; this whole Project JAW is split into divisions, and only those right at the top have all of the information. All I can say is that they have been here since mankind was created and their technology is amazing.'

'Created... Don't you mean evolved?'

'Mankind was not an accident, nor is it chance that we look as we do.'

'But I thought most of the top scientists believed in evolution?'

'Do the words "conspiracy" mean anything to you?'

'You mean the theory of evolution is some sort of cover-up?'

'Now you really sound naïve. I would have thought that with all those covert operations under your belt, you better than anyone would understand that this world is ruled by lies and deceit.'

'Yes, but I thought you guys were searching for the truth to better mankind.'

'What we search for is how to survive the oncoming storm.'

'So E.B.Es are a threat to mankind?'

'No, mankind is the threat. Have you ever asked yourself why the most richest and powerful people in this world have done so little to stop global warming or the cutting down of the rainforests? I mean, hasn't it ever crossed your mind that the people whose children and grandchildren will stand to lose the most, don't seem to care?'

'Yes... I mean... no... aren't they trying to do something about it?'

'The truth is they know that no matter how much money or power they have, the world is on loan and the owner will one day return.'

'And is the owner the E.B.Es?'

'Like I said, E.B.Es are soldiers. You asked me how we got hold of the craft. The E.B.Es gave them to us so we would be able to advance mankind.' Major Stone sat back in the chair and rubbed his forehead.

'Why?'

'They have been influencing mankind from the time of our creation. It's their job.'

'If this is true, why does the government continue to cover it up? Why not just tell the people?'

'How much would the people want to know if they knew E.B.Es really existed? It's not their existence that is the problem; it's who and what they represent.'

'Who and what do they represent?' Major Stone sat forward again, this time rubbing his hands together repeatedly.

'The Creator of the universe, and they represent the opposite of this world. What are we in this world? The truth is that we are slaves to a system. No matter who you are or where you live, this world of ours affects the way you live. We are controlled by paper called money. And why is that a problem to the Creator? Because no man can serve two masters. Evolution says man came about by accident and not by design. The reason for this is that if man was designed, then it is clear that something more powerful than man exists, and that the earth does not belong to mankind. The ruling people of the world want to be the most powerful and want mankind to bow to them, not to some powerful force in the universe.'

'But they say that they can prove evolution?'

'Ha! It takes more faith to believe in evolution than it does to believe in a Creator of the universe.'

'Why?'

'Because what exactly is evolution? How does a fish in the sea know that there is dry land and that on that land it would be better to have legs instead of fins or gills? Why did a chimpanzee decide that to become a hairless man, would be better than being a chimpanzee? Why would evolution think it was better for a man to have just two legs and two arms and only have eyes in the front of the head? Why wouldn't an evolved man also have eyes in the back of the head? Why not continue and evolve mankind so that mankind had night vision like lions, or sonic radar like a bat, or thermal imaging like a snake, or the strength of a bear and gills as well as lungs? The point is that evolution seems to be able to see and know what the creature itself cannot. If evolution was independent, it would not have stopped with the present man. That means that something has a certain design in mind. Otherwise we should be seeing some and many more of the examples I have just mentioned. How did dirt decide to develop single cell organisms?'

'So evolution must be the Creator of the universe?'

'Look Major Stone, we are getting a bit sidetracked from what is important right now. Right now we are preparing for what can be best described as the war of the worlds, and it is my job to find the people that can put us in the best position to survive this war.'

'Don't you mean win this war?'

'No, I mean survive.'

'But I don't understand. If we are going to war with the E.B.Es, why would they give us technology that could help us to win the war?'

'It's a bit like if I was to give you a Rubik's Cube for Christmas; I may be giving it to you because I think you can complete it, or I might be giving it to you because I don't think you're smart enough to work it out. If that's so, by giving it to you I'm letting you know how stupid you really are.'

'So why haven't you asked them?'

'I understand your questions, but for now I need you to concentrate on why you are here.'

'Why am I here?'

'Good, now you're asking the right questions. You are here to take over the role of the recently killed Major; he was the gunner in War Hawk.'

'A gunner... shouldn't that be the job of a normal soldier?'

'There is nothing normal about War Hawk. Its weapons are state-of-the-art and need to be controlled by the best men we have. Tomorrow we will begin your training; it will become clearer to you once you sit inside the machine.'

'I hope we will be able to finish our discussion on mankind and the coming storm, sooner rather than later Dr. Goodenberg.'

'Yes, so do I Major Stone, so do I. But for now, go get some rest. Tomorrow is going to be a great day for you, if not the greatest of your life.'

'Just one more question... well actually two. Do you still have contact with the E.B.Es and when will you see them next?'

'Major Stone, all the things you want to know about the E.B.Es, you will soon have the answers for. Once you're up to speed in War Hawk, you will be meeting them.'

'What!'

'You will be the new representative for the USA.'

'But... '

'Don't worry; you will be well prepared when the time comes along. Now go and try to get some rest; we have a big day ahead of us.'

BIGS AND THE EVANGELIST

It was a sunny Sunday afternoon, and the music of birds could be heard all around the church grounds. Bigs sat on a bench and listened to the birds singing to one another. He watched people coming and going from the church.

It was almost three o'clock, and the great angelic preacher was about to start his session for the selected and special guests, who were known as "Angel Partners". They were also going to be recording the show, to be shown on a Christian cable channel. Bigs laughed as he read the leaflet promoting the show.

> *Be blessed by the HOLY SPIRIT, let the LORD into your life and have sweat-less victories in all parts of your life.*
> *Be healed from illness and financial problems.*
> *Learn how to get what you deserve: a new house, a new car, get married. All things are possible when*

you learn to be born again and confess Christ to be your Lord and saviour.

Don't miss this once-in-a-lifetime opportunity to get close to GOD with special speaker Dave Jones. In order to receive the great blessing the Lord has put aside for you, you must first sow a seed. Don't let your blessing pass you by because you were not willing to sow a little seed money to receive your blessing.

Become an Angel Partner and watch your life change forever.

Remember, the HOLY SPIRIT is waiting to bless your life.

Tickets are on sale for your love gift of fifty pounds or more.

Bigs screwed up the paper in his hand as he felt his anger begin to rise. What he had first found funny, had now triggered off his angry side; it was enraged at the profanity on the leaflet. He looked towards the entrance of the church; two doormen stood at the door and checked the tickets of people who wished to enter into the church. Bigs walked up to the door and was stopped by the doormen because he didn't have a ticket; however, the doormen soon realised who he was.

'Sorry Bigs, didn't recognise you for a moment... especially as this is, well, you know... I didn't know you were a Christian?'

'I'm not.'

'Oh, okay. Well, enjoy the show and sorry for stopping you.'

'I will, and it's okay.'

Bigs entered the church, it was packed with people; there were only a few seats left to sit on, and they were right at the back of the church. The church smelt old and musty; there were the usual stained glass windows with pictures of saints and angels, and the walls and arches featured statuettes of angels and fire-breathing dragons, while men with shields and swords drawn, fought the dragons.

'I wonder if it's just a coincidence or if it's symbolic that all the angels and saints are white or European looking?' said Bigs to a middle-aged, overweight ginger-haired white man; who was sweating as if he had just run a marathon... his suit and shirt were now two-tone in colour, a dark brown from the sweat and its normal light brown in the very few dry spots that were left.

'Try not to concentrate on the negative; just be glad to be in the presence of Jesus Christ our saviour. You must not let those devils inside you get the better of you. It doesn't matter what colour they are.'

'That's what you say, but it mattered to whoever built this church. I wonder if it matters to the Angels?'

As Bigs sat down, the doormen began to close the front doors and apologised to people who had not yet got in. As the doors closed, the sunlight that was filling the church through the open doors began to fade to a pin point. Bigs had to refocus his eyes as the church darkened and he watched people try to squeeze through the door as the doormen closed them.

'Sorry, the church is full... we can't let any more people in.'

'But I've got a ticket.'

'So have I.'

'We all have,' shouted people standing outside.

'Sorry, there's nothing we can do. You'll have to get a refund from the vendor who sold the tickets to you.'

The doors closed and the stage lights dimmed as a voice spoke over a microphone.

'Welcome to the New World Christian Church. Today you are going to feel the HOLY SPIRIT and supernatural blessings. Ladies and gentlemen, the body of Christ is blessed to have the great man of GOD here today, to share with you the wisdom of Christ our Lord and Saviour. Please stand and give a warm welcome for the man of GOD, Dave Jones.'

'I thought it wasn't a good idea to blaspheme against the HOLY SPIRIT?' said Bigs. The man next to him just looked at him with a frown. The church was filled with the sound of hands clapping and people shouting 'hallelujah.' Bigs looked around the room; the man sitting next to Bigs got up out of his seat and looked at Bigs who was still sitting in his chair.

'Come on brother, stand and show your appreciation for the man of GOD. Don't let your fear hold you back. Open your heart; you are in the presence of GOD.'

'How do you work that out?'

'Because you're in a church; the HOLY SPIRIT dwells here. This is the place of GOD, and we worship the Lord Jesus Christ here. That's why you have to stand and give praise to the man of GOD.'

'If he is a man of GOD, as you say, he will not want any praise from you or me; for all praise must be to the FATHER and not the messenger.'

'I know, but this is a man of GOD, so by praising him you are also praising the LORD. Come on, praise the LORD with me.'

Bigs ignored the man and remained seated. A spotlight lit and moved towards the side of the stage and out came Dave Jones; a forty-five-year-old white American. He had been a coach driver ten years ago, but he had a spiritual experience with an angel who told him he was to preach the gospel to the world. After one year of Bible study, he began his rise to become one of the great evangelists of the day.

'Thank you, please, you're too kind. Please be seated and I thank you once again for your warm welcome.

I can feel a supernatural blessing happening here tonight in the body of Christ.'

Bigs looked around and counted five bodyguards around the front of the stage and three more sitting on the front row of seats.

'What will Jesus do for a body when he returns?' said Bigs to the man who had told him to stand up.

'We will be taken up in the Rapture and become his bride in heaven. We will become one; he will be the head and we will be the body.'

Bigs began to laugh. 'I'm sorry, I don't mean to be rude, but you're saying that Jesus is going to marry you... a man... and thousands of other men and women too? And when that's done you will become his body? I know all things are possible to the FATHER OF CREATION, but what you are saying does not make sense.'

'That's why you have to open your heart and listen to the man of GOD,' replied the man with a sincere smile.

'Your man of GOD doesn't seem to have much faith.'

'What do you mean?'

'He has eight bodyguards. I would have thought a man of GOD, as you say, wouldn't need bodyguards because the supernatural forces would protect him.'

'Are you one of those Muslims who come to our churches to cause trouble?'

'Why, because I question his faith?'

'Yeah, we don't come to your mosques and cause trouble. Why don't you radical Islamic groups leave us alone?'

'I have no idea of what you are talking about. I'm not a Muslim, nor am I a Christian.'

'So why have you come here? What religion are you?'

'I have no religion. I'm a believer in the FATHER OF CREATION and I go anywhere I may find the word of the FATHER.'

'So if you don't believe in Christianity, why come here to find the word, as you call it?'

'Because all religions have taken the parts of the word of the FATHER that suit their beliefs and made them their own. I have to search in all religions to find the words of the FATHER.'

'Well, let me correct you. Christianity is directly from the son of GOD, who is GOD. We don't have part of the word of GOD, we have the full and glorious word of GOD; spoken directly to us by the followers of Christ, who is the only begotten son of GOD.'

'Really? From what I can tell, you follow a guy named Paul who wrote the New Testament in Rome.'

'Paul was a disciple of our Lord Jesus Christ.'

'Who is Christ?'

'Now I know you're mad. What kind of question is that?'

'I think it's a good one. If the Jesus you are talking about was here right now and you called to him... if you called out "Christ!"... would he turn around to see who was calling him?'

'Look, I'm not wasting any more of my time talking to you. I came here to hear my Christian word from our man of GOD, Dave Jones, not you.'

Bigs smiled and began to listen to Dave Jones, who was in the middle of singing, 'Christ is glory and Lord of the body of Christ, he is love, and we worship you, our Lord.'

'He's not a very good singer, is he?' said Bigs to the man next to him. The man ignored him and kept singing along with Dave Jones; they were both out of key, but everyone sang along with no care, waving their hands in the air. People at the front began to fall on the floor.

'The HOLY SPIRIT has entered into them, can you feel it? Come on, sing with me! Christ is glory and Lord of the body of Christ!'

After one hour the man of GOD, Dave Jones, began to wind down his appearance.

'All of you in the audience, who have not yet been saved, please come forward. We will pray for you and lay hands on you, that you may begin your rebirth as Christians. It is the only way to be saved; no other religion can save you... only our Lord Jesus Christ can. Hurry, come to the altar and receive your blessing from the Lord.'

Many people walked and many ran to the front of the stage to receive their blessing. Bigs followed and stood in one of the aisles. He watched as people fell on their knees. Some were crying, others lay on the floor, and still others held their hands up in the air asking Jesus Christ to save and forgive them. All the while, Dave Jones and his band sang 'Christ is our Lord and Saviour.' Bigs made his way to the side of the stage and began to walk up the stairs onto the stage. A body guard immediately stopped him, saying no one was allowed on stage.

'Do you have any idea who I am?'

'No sir, I don't, but it's my job to stop anyone from going on stage and as I take my job seriously, I can't let you pass.'

'Do you have a two-way radio?'

'Yes.'

'Then I suggest you call for backup, because if you don't let me pass you're going to need it.'

Two other bodyguards had made their way over, while Bigs and the bodyguard who had stopped him had been talking.

'Oh shit! Listen Bigs, we can't let anyone on stage. Please, if we do we'll lose our jobs.'

'Do you know this guy? He's just threatened me. I think we should take him outside and fuck him up.'

'Shut your mouth Tom, this is Bigs. If he wants us dead, we're dead! Do you understand? Just shut up and let me deal with this.'

'AAARRR,' Tom shouted as Bigs grabbed Tom by his testicles and squeezed. Bigs looked Tom straight in his tearful eyes. 'Take me outside and fuck me up... that's not very Christian-like, is it Tom?'

'No,' Tom cried out in pain.

'You're very lucky that I understand this is not personal and you're just trying to do your job. But I'm going up on that stage, with your balls in my pocket or not. Which one is it going to be, Tom?'

'Without, please.' Bigs released his grip, and Tom fell to the floor. Bigs walked up onto the stage and took a microphone out of its stand.

'Please brother, no followers on stage,' said Dave Jones, who looked to see where his bodyguards were.

'What's wrong Dave? You look a bit scared. Don't worry I don't want to kill you; I just want to ask you a few questions.'

'I'm not afraid, my faith in Christ is strong. It's just that there is a time and a place for questions and this isn't it my brother. Come and see me after the meeting and I'll gladly guide you to the Lord.'

'Thanks Dave, but I'm not going where you're going. I've tried several times now to talk to so-called men of GOD and none will talk to me in person.'

Bigs began to feel hot on stage; there were stage lights everywhere, pointing straight at him. The beams of light were hot, even though they were at least ten feet away.

Dave Jones motioned to his bodyguards to come up on stage, but they didn't.

'Look my brother, right now I'm bringing the lost sheep to Christ our Lord and Saviour. The Lord's work must come first. Please take a seat and I promise you, I will see you when the Lord's work is done.'

Bigs looked towards the audience, who seemed to be watching his every move. For a split second he thought about putting down the microphone and running out the back door, assuming there was one.

'Okay, but first can I ask you people here today a question? Are you looking to be saved, or are you looking for Christianity? Because if you're looking to be saved, I think you may want to hear the questions that I want answers to, before you get saved.'

'Get off the stage,' some people in the crowd shouted.

'Let him speak! This is the house of the Lord and he's looking for answers,' others shouted back.

Dave Jones looked lost for a moment. He scratched his head as he looked around at the crowd, trying to judge their reactions to this unexpected situation. *'It's important to remain in charge,'* he thought to himself, putting the microphone towards his mouth.

'Okay. Let me just say that this has never been done before; only at a Dave Jones revival could such things happen. Speak to the Lord Christ Jesus, my brother, go ahead,' said Dave Jones, in somewhat of a nervous voice.

'Who is Jesus Christ?'

'Phew! This guy hasn't got a clue. What kind of question is this? This is going to be easy,' thought Dave Jones as his confidence grew; he cleared his throat and forgot his nervous anticipation.

'That's simple. He is the only begotten son of GOD, sent as a lamb to the slaughter for our sins.'

'Who named him Christ?'

'Christ comes from the Greek word Christofis, which means chosen one.'

'So Jesus was a Greek?'

'No, he was a Jew.' *'This guy really doesn't know anything,'* Dave Jones laughed to himself.

'So why do you use a Greek spinoff as his last name?'

'I'm sorry, I don't know what you mean,' smiled Dave. He looked at the crowd, somewhat bemused.

'Well, the word Christ isn't Jewish. It's not exactly Greek and it's not exactly English... it's kind of a made-up word between Greek and English, right?'

'What's his point? I'm not a scholar... don't admit that out loud. Okay, get control and get this guy off the stage,' thought Dave. 'Look my brother, I don't let such things prey on my mind, for the glory of the Lord is my concern.'

'But don't you want to get his name right?'

'Jesus is love and cares not if you know his full name or not,' replied Dave, turning to the audience every time he answered a question.

'But what if his true last name is not Christ? Would that mean you were asking someone else to save you? What if someone made that name up for a reason, and what if that reason was a bad one?'

'Such as?'

'What if it was really a name that's related to Satan? I mean, you speak English, so why don't you say "Jesus the Chosen One?" Why do you have to use this word, "Christ?"'

'Like I said, Jesus is love and cares not if you know his full name or not. Now, if you don't mind, the people here today have paid good money to hear the word of GOD, so if...'

Bigs interrupted. 'I agree with you to a point but I would go one step further and say he cares not that you know his name at all; as long as you love the FATHER OF CREATION. But for someone like you, who claims to be a follower of the son of the FATHER OF CREATION, you should at least know his true name... otherwise how do you know you are following the real son?'

'No, that's where you're wrong my brother; for it is written that no man will reach GOD but through his son Jesus Christ.'

'Well, if you were to know the real Jesus instead of your Christ, you would know that no man who truly knows the FATHER, not even Jesus, would want to take any glory and praise away from the FATHER. Only Satan and his son want that. For it is the job of Satan and his son, whose name is Christ, to try and lead the praise away from the FATHER OF CREATION.'

'Are you calling Christ Satan? We praise him here and we won't be tricked by any Antichrist into disbelieving in him! Be careful young man, you are treading on very dangerous ground,' shouted Dave Jones, pointing his finger and shaking his fist at Bigs.

'Get off the stage, you devil worshipper, you blasphemer,' shouted people in the crowd.

'You call me the devil worshipper and Antichrist? I agree, I am anti your Christ... what is an Antichrist anyway? As I said already, this word "Christ" is made up. I know Jesus, the son of the FATHER, but you keep talking about Christ. It's not me that puts your Christ above the FATHER OF CREATION. Why do you raise the name of Jesus Christ above the FATHER?'

'Jesus is GOD,' shouted someone in the crowd.

'If you believe that, then why do you follow the teachings of Paul? He has almost the same status, if not a higher status than your Christ; for it is his books you quote the most.'

'You truly are a lost soul, full of hate and bitterness for our Lord Jesus Christ and his apostle Paul; who is one of the great men of GOD. If you're not careful Hell will be your home for all eternity!'

'Why can't you see the books have been tampered with? Jesus Christ is the name of the enemy of the true Jesus, who is the son of the FATHER OF CREATION, and is in the image of Satan, Lucifer and the Devil. The words you follow are from the Romans, like Paul, Mark, Matthew and Luke.'

'Why if I wasn't a Christian I would strike you down for your blasphemy! How dare you! I think it's time you left the stage,' shouted Dave Jones, frantically waving his fist at Bigs. He looked like he was about to explode.

'Do you have any idea of what Jesus meant when he said that he was the way and that you can only reach the FATHER through him?'

'Yes, he meant that he is Our Lord and Saviour. Look, you may hate him, but we love him and he loves us.'

'Really? How do you work that out?'

'You really don't know anything about Jesus Christ, do you? Let me make it simple so that you can understand. We know he loves us because he died on the cross for us. He is love, and that is why he was even willing to die for you.'

'Right I see. And that's why you love him?'

'It's one of the reasons, yes. Why?'

'So what if I told you the true Jesus didn't die for you at all, and that it was made to look that way by powers and principalities and wicked men? Basically, by the same people who gave you the Bible?'

'I would say you are truly a devil, sent here to try and affect the supernatural blessing upon this church tonight.'

'I know what the problem is; you keep thinking I'm talking about Christ. If you really knew Jesus, the son of the FATHER OF CREATION, you would know that he died for the FATHER OF CREATION and not for you. He lived for the FATHER OF CREATION and not for you.'

'Boo! Get off the stage!' some people in the crowd shouted.

'Shut up! Let him speak!' shouted another. Dave Jones looked left then right. He tried to judge which way the crowd was swaying. Many seemed to want to hear more of what Bigs was saying, but the majority did not like the fact that he had come on the stage and was trying to embarrass Dave Jones and Christianity. The boos got louder, but Bigs kept on talking.

'You would understand that when he said he is the way, he was referring to the way he lived. If you were like Jesus, the son of the FATHER OF CREATION, you would know that Jesus would never teach that he should be praised above the FATHER. He would tell you that all praises must go to the FATHER OF CREATION who sent him.

'Jesus didn't want to die for you; that's why, in the garden he asked the FATHER to remove the cup that he had to taste, from him. But then he understood that the emotion called fear had gripped him, and so he battled it and made it clear that he would do it because it was the will of the FATHER, whom he loved. It was not his will to die for you; it was his will to die for the FATHER, and it was the FATHER OF CREATION's will that he die for you. That right there should have told you that it is the FATHER you owe all praise and thanks to, not Jesus.' Dave Jones smiled as the hostile crowd became more antagonistic.

'It was the FATHER OF CREATION who loved man so much, that he sent his son to take the burden of your sins. I swear to you, if you knew the Jesus I know and not your Christ, you would know that Jesus hates the way you keep referring to him more than the FATHER. It was the FATHERS' works that Jesus did, not his own.

'His death was meant to show you that death is not to be feared and that he lived and died for the FATHER, because it was the FATHER who sent him, not himself.

Everything that he did was meant to show you that the FATHER OF CREATION is the most important being, that he is real and is not a figment of your imagination. If you really are a follower of Jesus, then you must stop putting your Christ above the FATHER. If you are a follower of Satan, then keep putting your Christ above the FATHER and keep saying that Christ is your Saviour and Lord; rather than saying that the FATHER OF CREATION is your Saviour and Lord.'

'Jesus Christ is GOD and GOD is Jesus. It is not we that must change our ways, it is you who must change your ways; your heart is filled with jealousy and hate.'

'Why? Because I tell you what you can't or don't want to see? Then how about this: the Jews of today are not the Jews of the times of Jesus. They came with the Roman armies from Europe and settled and learnt the ways of the original Jews, before all of the original Jews were all killed off by the Roman armies. The Jews of today are European in origin. We see the same thing happening today all around the world; immigrants settling in foreign lands and having children who grow up to call the foreign lands their own.'

'How dare you? Do you know what will happen to those who come against the Jews? Not only are you a blasphemer, but you are anti Jewish; a racist just like Hitler. You show all the signs of a true devil and Antichrist.'

'So how did European people end up in that part of the world two thousand years ago? If you did a genetic test on a Jewish person who lives in Israel today, in order to discover their origins or to trace their history or family tree; it would place their ancestors somewhere in Europe.'

'I will take no further part in your blasphemy. Christianity is the true religion of the Lord.'

'Where is it written that Jesus said he was a Christian or that Christianity is his church?'

There was no answer from Dave Jones, who stood with arms folded and his back towards Bigs. Nor did any of the crowd respond.

'Where is it written that Christianity is the true religion of the FATHER OF CREATION?'

No one on the stage or in the audience spoke.

'Why are the books written by people with European names?'

'I know, they were written thirty-five to eighty years after the death of Christ in Rome... I mean, Jesus,' shouted someone in the crowd.

'At least someone has an idea of what they are worshipping. Mark, Luke, Matthew and so on didn't ever meet Jesus in the flesh; they were not direct followers of Jesus. They were investigators who went to Nazareth and the surrounding areas and asked the people who knew and listened to Jesus, to talk about the man and his sayings. They went at different times, thirty-five to eighty years after the facts. That's why their accounts of Jesus have slight variations and their stories telling of the events of Jesus, are different.'

'So what? Who cares?' shouted someone in the crowd.

'Why are there no books that are written with the name Jesus above them?'

'Who cares? We're not here to listen to an Antichrist, get off the stage,' shouted another person in the crowd.

'Why are there books called Romans?'

'Because the word was spread around the world,' shouted another person.

'Do you know how crazy that sounds? Of course you don't, because you never lived in those times. But let me try to give you an example of how crazy the book of Romans in the Bible is. It's the same as calling it the books of the Nazis, because the Romans and the Nazis had the same attitude towards the Jews: kill as many of them as you can.'

'How do you know? You weren't there either,' shouted someone else in the crowd.

'It was not the FATHER OF CREATION who decided to make a Bible and select which books would be in it; it was a Roman emperor and then some men who claimed they were the righteous. Does that not bother anyone? Let me put it this way, there are sixty-six books in the Bible; what was the reason or motive to only have that amount and why was it decided that the rest did not matter? Do you know that there were hundreds of scripts that were left out of the Bible. Even in modern times, scriptures such as the Dead Sea Scrolls have been found and are kept from the general public.'

'So I suppose your religion is Islam?' said Dave Jones scornfully.

'I have no religion, religion is not important to me. I search for the FATHER wherever I may find them. Why can't you answer any of my questions, Dave?'

'Ha! I thought so, you admit it! You're an atheist, an Antichrist devil worshipper!'

'Why do I have to be religious in order to know or believe in the FATHER OF CREATION?'

'Because religion is GOD. See, now I have answered you,' replied Dave Jones. He smirked at Bigs, then turned to the crowd with a smile and shook his head.

'Religion is the work of Satan, Lucifer the Devil. The Bible you read contains the word of the FATHER, which is the truth; but it is mixed with the words of Satan, which are lies and deceit.'

'How can you continue with this blasphemy in the Lord's house? Are you deliberately trying to go to Hell? Who in their right mind could get up here and call Christianity the works of the devil? Are you crazy?'

'Because you constantly overlook the

inconsistencies in your teachings, you say that the word of the FATHER is pure, true and exact; that it does not conflict against itself and it is written in the hearts of men and women.'

'What you mean is, that you don't understand some things so you assume that the Bible is wrong and not you.'

'No. For example, you say Judas betrayed Jesus, but then you say that Jesus died on the cross for you. So either he knew he was going to die, or he didn't and was betrayed and tricked into dying for you. There is a script that was not put in the Bible that is called the Judas script. In it, it is claimed that Judas did not betray Jesus, but was doing what Jesus had told him to do. But because all you so-called men of GOD have taught that Judas was a betrayer of Jesus, you call this script blasphemy. Yet you will quote the Bible and say that the time had come for Jesus to taste the cup that he didn't want to taste; so he could never have been betrayed because he knew it had to happen.

'The Bible says he had a last supper with the disciples. He told them it would be the last one, because he was about to go somewhere they couldn't go and then he sent Judas on his way to do what he had to do.

'Why would he have had the last supper if he had not known and organized the time and place where the soldiers would arrest him. It is Satan Lucifer Devil, powers and principalities, and wicked men who want people to believe that this was all done by betrayal and not by the grand design of the FATHER.'

Dave Jones raised his hands in the air and then put them on his shaking head as he looked at the crowd, as if to say... *what is he talking about?*

'So what's your point? All I can hear is someone who wants to put down Christianity.'

'No. My point is that you have to be careful when reading a book, no matter what it claims, because all books are written by men or women; human beings who are not perfect. The whole Judas issue shows how Satan Lucifer Devil, powers and principalities, and wicked men have tried to deceive the world by putting their lies into a book that is supposed to be pure and true and from the FATHER. Satan Lucifer Devil, powers and principalities, and wicked men have been able in this instance, to take the point of true sacrifice and make it look like it happened because of betrayal and greed... all things that are dirty and are under the power of Satan.'

The crowd seemed to be in two minds, they did not like what Bigs was saying because it seemed to be purely against their religion, yet on the other hand, they were half interested in what he had to say. But their loyalty to Christianity meant they could not listen to the constant criticism of their beloved religion and Bible. Bigs continued.

'So Jesus, who is about to sacrifice his life for the FATHER, is doing it because of the Devil's intentions; rather than the divine works of the FATHER. Jesus was saying he would not die on the cross but would gain everlasting life. Satan Lucifer Devil has made man believe that it was about betrayal by Judas and that Judas' betrayal led to the death of Jesus. The message from Jesus was not about dying for mankind's sins; if that were true, there would be no Judgment Day for anybody, as all sins were paid for... even the sins of not making, as you say, Jesus Christ your Lord and Saviour. Jesus was showing mankind that true and real faith in the FATHER would conquer death; that was the message.'

'Oh come on, how long you are going to rant and rave,' Dave Jones put his hands on his hips and scorned Bigs. The crowd followed his lead and jeered at Bigs. Dave Jones seized the moment.

'But we Christians know that Jesus died for us, not because of Judas' betrayal. We know this because we have the Bible to tell us.' before he could continue, Bigs interrupted.

'If the Bible was written by the FATHER, why is it so hard to understand? Why do so many so-called men of GOD constantly add their own meanings to the written text; which always seems to be open to one's own interpretations? If religion is the work of the FATHER, why does it divide people rather than bring them together? Religion has killed more people than World Wars One and Two put together; it keeps man from coming together. Is that a lie?'

'Without Christianity, hundreds of thousands of people would be lost. We bring the words of GOD into their lives by introducing them to the Bible.' ranted Dave Jones, as spit flew out of his mouth and his smartly combed hair fell across his face.

'How many people of the FATHER in the Bible... or should I say, how many men of the FATHER in the Bible... do you find reading the Bible for guidance? Did Moses read it? Did Abraham or Noah? Did Jesus walk around carrying a Bible?'

'Christianity has saved millions of people, but I suppose to an atheist that doesn't matter.'

'You teach them lies and false promises. You tell them that if they become Christians and believe in Christ as their Lord and Saviour, they will enter into heaven... just like Paul who is your true messiah, not Jesus, has taught you. Because once again, what Paul says and what Jesus says are two different things.'

Dave Jones clinched his fist as his face got red with anger.

'How can you keep up this blasphemy in the Lord's house? Jesus came to save all mankind. He came to show mankind to love, not to hate like you do.'

'Yeah' shouted the crowd, almost in unison.

'Blasphemer! Satan worshipper!' others shouted at Bigs.

'No, you are the liar. Jesus came for the lost sheep and no one else. He did not come for the entire world. He made it clear that he would not talk to the Gentiles, and when a woman asked him for help he called her a dog, saying 'It is not for me to take the crumbs that fall on the table and feed them to dogs.' Like I said already, it was Paul who said that the message of Jesus was for everybody and that everybody could enter into heaven, not Jesus. Jesus said it would be easier to fit a camel through the eye of a needle than to enter into the Kingdom of GOD. Does anyone here claim they can fit a camel through the eye of a needle?'

'Oh please. Do you really think we are going to listen to you? Who are you anyway? Let me tell you who you are. You are the lost, trying to make us lost. We are the children of GOD and Christ is our Lord and Saviour. When the end comes... and believe me, it is coming soon... we will go to heaven, of that I'm sure, and you will be going to hell.' screamed Dave, as he completely lost his composure. The crowd had also lost their patience and just wanted this mad man off of the stage.

'Do you really believe that if Jesus came to tell everybody they could enter heaven, they would have all been against him; Jew and non-Jew? Only his people were for him... why? I listen to you making all these promises about going to heaven. Is that all the FATHER OF CREATION and Jesus are to you, a ticket to a better life in heaven? If you were here on the earth just to give praise to the FATHER everyday of your life and then die, would that not be a worthy life to you? Don't answer, because I already know the answer. No, it wouldn't be enough for all of you, because you have made yourselves more important than that.

'Paul and the Romans created the New Testament to lift themselves up above the angels. That's why, in the New Testament, man becomes the sons of the FATHER; but in the Old Testament, the sons of the FATHER were angels, not mankind. Your religions are full of vanity and pride. You have made yourselves gods and put yourself above the angels. You have said that because Jesus sits at the right-hand side of the FATHER, then so do you; but truth will always last over lies. You tell the people that you can offer them a place in paradise and that if they follow you they will become joint heirs; but I will strike you down with my sword before I will ever let that happen because for you to be heirs means my FATHER would have to die, so you may inherit that which is theirs. When did the angels die in order for you to become the new sons of the FATHER OF CREATION? Or what crime did they commit that would make the FATHER abandon his own for you?

'You have forgotten the most important thing about your life and that is that life is the most precious gift given to mankind. Thank the FATHER everyday for it because it was given to you for no price and when someone gives you an expensive gift for free you should be eternally grateful. That's why Jesus told mankind to live in love and not hate, because time is precious and you don't know when your time will be up. Use it wisely and enjoy it.'

Dave Jones was getting frustrated, he came to preach, not to get into an argument with this man; whose irrelevant questions were making him look like he didn't know what he was talking about. 'The people here don't want to hear all this crap,' he thought. 'We bring millions to the cross every year, all around the world.'

Bigs felt his anger rising, but the voice inside him told him to remain calm. 'The cross! I spit on your cross. I hate your cross with all my heart.'

'Oh, why am I not surprised by that! Just keep talking, because it is quite clear to us that you are nothing more than a true Devil, sent here to test us. I have to say that you almost got me, but I will not be tempted to turn my back on Christ and the cross.'

'The cross is a symbol of Rome's absolute power and authority. It was used to send the message that Rome would not tolerate any other authority above its own. It had nothing to do with Jesus, other than that the Romans used it to kill him. It was their way of totally humiliating their enemies and inflicting on them the greatest possible pain. You wear your cross as if it symbolises the meaning of Jesus and what he stood for. Jesus didn't say "I would like to die on the cross because I want the world to remember me that way; so don't hang me or stone me to death!" The truth is, it stands for the power and absolute authority of Rome, and it was the Romans who decided to kill him that way.

'This is another way that Satan Lucifer Devil, powers and principalities, and wicked men have been able to trick the world into worshipping them by mixing lies with the truth. What would you be wearing now if they had hung him or cut his head off with a sword? These are the things that tell me you are being misled by those who killed him, by the powers and principalities of darkness and wicked men hungry for power and control of mankind. Ask yourself this: if your father or mother were whipped, beaten, had a crown of thorns pressed into their head until it made their head bleed, were made to carry the cross they were to be crucified on all the way to the spot where they would be crucified, and then were stripped naked and left on the cross to die for all the world to see... would you still wear that cross around your neck in remembrance of the life of your mother and father? Knowing that the cross was brought into their lives to kill them?'

No one spoke at first. Then one man shouted, 'He speaks lies, just like his father Satan.'

Bigs closed his eyes for a second and composed himself before continuing. 'Romans were not against religion; they had many religions. What Rome was against was any teaching that said that Rome was not the absolute authority. That's why they killed Jesus and all of his disciples in the way that they did. Then they replaced the true Jesus with Jesus Christ, selected and kept only the teaching which spoke of love, so that they could keep the masses passive, and they replaced the disciples with their own. They selected what scriptures would be left in and what would be left out, and they made the Bible and called their new religion Christianity. They said it was the new religion of GOD and that the New Testament was to replace the Old Testament, or that it was to replace any parts of the Old Testament that did not correspond with their New Testament.' Bigs paused again.

'Do you really believe they went to all that trouble to kill Jesus, his teachings and his disciples, only to bring the same true teaching back to Rome and the rest of the world; so that the very teaching that they had found so threatening could now be taught to the world? The fact that you call yourself Christians, or any other religious name, proves you are lost. For what greater name is there than to call yourself a believer in the FATHER OF CREATION or GOD, ALLAH or whatever name you have for the SUPREME BEING? Isn't a 'believer' what you are supposed to be? To call yourself a Christian or a Muslim is nothing more than calling yourself a pagan. Paul said he was a follower of Jesus, but it is Paul who has made all of the changes to the teachings of Jesus. Jesus told us not to eat the swine named pig, whilst Paul told us to eat the swine named pig. Jesus told us not to go into the land of the Gentiles, and Paul told us to go to the land of the Gentiles. Jesus never named himself Christ, but Paul is always using the name Christ. Jesus never called himself a Christian, yet Paul always calls himself a Christian. He lies and says that Christianity is the religion of Jesus. These contradictions go on and on.

'You say the son of GOD is the colour of a European man and his name is Jesus Christ. What would you think if he was the colour of an African man and his last name was not Christ? Would you still worship him? Could you still love him?'

Bigs threw the microphone into the crowd, walked down the stage steps, and made his way out. People shook their heads; others shouted 'get out, devil!' Dave Jones shook his head saying, 'Well, I guess some people are beyond saving. I told you tonight was going to be filled with the HOLY SPIRIT, and anywhere people are about to be saved you must expect Satan to send his devils to try to deceive you. I think we can say Satan loss the battle tonight! Give me an amen if you still believe the Lord Jesus Christ is your Lord and Saviour.'

'Amen,' shouted the congregation.

Bigs walked out of the church and wondered what the point was. *'I don't know what I was trying to achieve,'* he thought.

'You were trying to deliver a message and find answers in the wrong place,' said the voice.

'So where should I have delivered the message? Where should I have looked for answers?'

'Where you have always known the message would be heard, and where you have always found the answers; in your heart.'

A tall, slim, tan-skinned, bearded man walked up to Bigs and grabbed him by his arm.

'Excuse me, but I think I know what you are looking for. I watched you in the church and I have to say you handled yourself quite well in there. The answers you are looking for can be found in Islam. We are not afraid of questions; we believe ALLAH will give answers to all questions if one is patient.'

'And what about you? Do you know the answers to my questions?'

'Come, let us sit on this bench for a moment and talk.'

Bigs was of two minds. He was not into religion, and he had made up his mind to listen to his voice and wait for the voice to show him the way he needed to go within himself. On the other hand, it could take months for the answers to be revealed to him; so he decided that while he was waiting he might as well waste time talking to some of the other religions out there and see what they had to say for themselves.

'Okay, let's sit down and talk.'

'So tell me... do you hate Christians and the way they live, or are you trying to be convinced that their religion is for you?'

'Neither. I have no time for religions. I simply want to see what comes out of my mouth when I talk to people like you.'

'Really? What is it that wants to come out of your mouth now?'

'Why do Muslims think that by going to Mecca they will be closer to Allah? And why don't you see it as idol worship?'

'It is not going to Mecca that makes them closer to ALLAH; it's the entire experience that brings them closer to ALLAH. Many people will have to save for years just to make it there once. Others will have to leave their families behind, and others must abandon their creature comforts. For others the experience is about being surrounded by millions of people who believe in and love ALLAH like they do. These things and many more, are what bring them closer to ALLAH. And it is not idol worship, because it is through sacrifice that one shows love for ALLAH.'

'So what if you can never go to Mecca? Does that make you less of a Muslim, or does it mean you have not gotten as close to ALLAH as those who have been there?'

'All Muslims should try their utmost to go to Mecca, but if they can't then ALLAH will come to them if they are worthy.'

'So it's not important to go to Mecca to be close to ALLAH? Is it not more important to live with ALLAH in one's heart, seek the way that will please ALLAH as best as possible, and hope that they may enter into your life? At the end of the day, the truth is that none of us are worthy of ALLAH.'

'Yes and no. It is important to try and go to Mecca for a Muslim, but like I said, if you cannot go because of financial reasons, then that's okay.'

'But that's not what I am saying. How could any Muslim be in financial difficulty? With so many other Muslims in the world, surely it would be the responsibility of all Muslims to make it possible for their fellow Muslim brothers and sisters to be able to go, if it is so important. I'm saying to you that ALLAH is everywhere and has no need to wait until a Muslim goes to Mecca to meet them. They should be as close to ALLAH as possible at all times, not at one time in their life when they get to Mecca. I strive to be as close as possible to the FATHER OF CREATION every day of my life.'

'So you think you are righteous every day?'

'What do you mean, righteous?'

'You pray five times a day and live your life without sin?'

'My life is full of sin. I don't pray every day; I speak with the FATHER every day and ask them to show me what it is I'm supposed to do for them. I ask them to forgive me and give me strength to defeat my sinful mind.'

'Then I can tell you that you are not close to ALLAH. Only by becoming a Muslim and studying Islam, will you become closer to ALLAH. You need to read the Qur'an and to come to the mosque five times a day to pray and to study.'

'Tell me something; if I were to spit on your Qur'an, what would you want to do to me?'

'Why would you want to do this in the first place?'

'To see how you would react; to see if the book is held in the same regard as ALLAH. Because some Muslims think the Qur'an is as holy as ALLAH. To me, a book is a book, whether it has the words of ALLAH in it or not. The true words of ALLAH are written in a man's heart.'

'In that case I would pray for you, because you would surely be on your way to Hell.'

'Why, if it's only a book?'

'No, it's more than a book. It's the word of ALLAH.'

'But isn't the true word of ALLAH in your heart, not in ink in a book?'

'No, because the words from the heart are written in ink in a book.'

'Does ALLAH write in ink or in the hearts of men and women?'

'ALLAH writes in the hearts of men, and then men write what is in the heart into a book.'

'So these are the words of ALLAH, written in ink by men?'

'Yes.'

'So it is a book. What makes you so sure that what is written has not been corrupted by the hearts of wicked men?'

'My belief in Islam.'

'My point is that men have stopped listening to their hearts and have replaced it with written text, which always seems to be open to interpretation. I believe this to be the work of wicked men, for the true word of ALLAH cannot be misunderstood. Most people I listen to who have religious beliefs, defend their religion more than ALLAH or the FATHER; they honestly believe that saying Islam or Christianity is the correct thing to say, rather than the name for their supreme being.

'Why not say I'm a follower of ALLAH or GOD? When I say things that you don't like, they are not against

ALLAH... they are against your religion. Yet you don't see that, because you believe your religion is ALLAH. The Qur'an is mans interpretation of the revealed word of ALLAH and any man who claims he is perfect should not be trusted. And if we agree no man is perfect then we must always remember that and understand that there may be mistakes made unintentionally or intentionally; it's the nature of man.'

'And that's why I can tell you the Qur'an is more than a book, for it is the clearest of holy books.'

'If that is true, then why are there so many different forms of Muslims, who hate one another so much that they will willingly kill one another? Who is correct and how did they decide that the one message from ALLAH to Mohammed, could be split into different messages for different groups? It is just like the Christians and their different groups who just like you, claim that they are the only way to the FATHER.'

'Like you say, some interpret the Qur'an with wicked hearts, but that does not mean it is the book that is wrong. It means that it is their hearts that are wrong.'

'Did you know that the Qur'an was not written by Mohammed?'

'No, that's wrong, and you shouldn't speak like that.'

'But it's the truth as I know it.'

'It's not the truth. Mohammed is the prophet of Islam and the revealer of the word of ALLAH to all Muslims. You must be careful how you talk.'

'I fear no man and I will talk how I please. What I have been told is that in the time and place where Mohammed lived they did not write things down, and Mohammed couldn't read or write. He spoke what was revealed to him to his followers, and they remembered what he told them.

'That is how the word revealed to Mohammed from ALLAH was kept, in their heads until he died. At that point they began to write them down so they would not be lost forever, because at those times the tribe of Mecca wanted Mohammed and his followers dead; as they were saying that the Kaaba housed idols and that Mecca was the centre for idol worshippers.

'The tribes of Mecca saw this as a threat, because many people travelled to Mecca to worship these idols inside of the Kaaba, just as Muslims do today. Mohammed was saying that it was wrong to do so and that there was no need to do this when worshipping ALLAH.

'The tribes of Mecca would lose a lot of money and status, if too many people listened to Mohammed and became Muslims and stopped travelling to Mecca to worship the idols in the Kaaba.

'Mohammed kept on talking and revealing the word of ALLAH. He told the people that they did not need idols to worship ALLAH, and if they didn't need idols, then they didn't need to go to Mecca. This made the tribe of Mecca so angry that they started a nine-year war against Muslims; torturing and killing all they could get their hands on in Mecca. Mohammed had to flee Mecca, fearful for his life.'

Bigs looked at his watch; one hour had passed and Bigs was losing interest in the conversation. In his mind he knew that religion was all about one's own point of view.

'It's been nice talking to you, but the truth is we all have our own opinions. It won't be until Judgement Day that we will all find out our fates and discover who was right and who was wrong.'

Bigs offered his hand, and the man shook it and smiled.

'If you ever want to really get close to ALLAH, come and see me at the mosque. I hold studies there on Friday afternoons and evenings after prayer. My name is Muqtar.'

'My name is Bigs.'

Both men paused for a moment. They looked at each other in the eyes and smiled, then turned and went their separate ways. Once again, as he walked to where his car was parked on the other side of the road, Bigs wondered what the point was.

He was so caught up in the moment that he failed to look left or right as he stepped into the road. If he had looked, he would have seen a speeding car coming towards him. It was too late; Bigs was about to take his second step into the road, and that would put him straight in the path of the car, which was now all but on top of him.

The car was travelling at high speeds and was about to hit him... but suddenly Bigs heard the voice say *'look out!'* and at the same time Bigs felt an unseen force hit him gently but with such power, that in a split second it pushed him back onto the pavement; which was the same time the car passed by the very spot he had just been standing in. All Bigs saw was a flash of red as the car passed; it all happened so fast that the driver didn't have time to blow his horn.

Bigs thanked the FATHER in his mind, because he knew that what had just happened had been supernatural. If it hadn't been for the FATHER he would have been dead, or at best a crumpled lump on the floor right now. He thought about the force that had hit him so gently but so powerfully at the same time. It didn't make sense, how could such a force push him back several feet in under a second and yet be so soft on contact with his body? His thought was broken for a moment, as he looked at a black van that was parked on the other side of the road with blacked-out windows. *'Fucking police, like flies around shit. Can't leave me alone for a minute,'* he thought as he got into his car.

As Bigs turned on the engine and turned down the volume on his stereo, he began to think about the force he had just felt. His mind slid back further, to what he had done on the stage in the church, and he wondered again what the point was.

Then again he began to think about the force he had just felt and then he thought of the Muslim brother he had just been speaking to. He decided to go to a barber shop that was owned by a friend of his who was a member of the Nation of Islam; he now wanted to see what would come out of his mouth. As Bigs pulled up outside of the barber shop, he noticed the black van pull up some four hundred meters further down the road.

Bigs smiled and entered the shop. He made his way to the back, greeting the many people in the shop as he went; many of the people in there hung around the shop all day, never getting their hair cut. It was a meeting place for many different types of characters... businessmen, thieves, members of the working, middle and rich classes, Christians, Muslims, and members of the religion that Bigs was interested in today... the Nation of Islam. He opened a door marked "Private" and walked into a room. It was full of men who were in the middle of what seemed to be an important debate.

'Listen blood, the white man is never going to let me and you make it in their world unless we are prepared to act like some kind of Uncle Tom. You know what I'm saying... Yes Bigs my brother, what's happening blood?' said the man who was standing in the centre of the room. There were ten to twelve men standing around him who had not even noticed that Bigs had entered the room; they all greeted Bigs, and then the tall, athletic, dark-skinned black man standing in the middle, who was known as H, said to Bigs, 'Tell the men about life as a gangster and how even in the underworld, the white man is still above the black man. They've got all the bent coppers in their pockets, grassing on the black man and getting them nicked; while the white criminals walk around untouched by the Babylon.'

Bigs took off his coat and began to smoke a spliff. As he pulled on it, smoke blew out of his nostrils like it would never end. 'Tell me something, you are all members of the Nation of Islam.'

'Yes, you know that Bigs,' replied H with a smile.

'Do you fear the FATHER OF CREATION more than Elijah?'

'Of course. ALLAH is the Supreme Being.'

'Then why do you refer to Elijah more than you do to the FATHER or ALLAH?'

'We bring up Elijah because he is the founder of the Nation, and without him we wouldn't know the truth.'

'But he is not the founder. ALLAH is the founder. Elijah is a messenger and should not be glorified as much as the FATHER, or even close.' Bigs paused and took another deep intake of smoke before slowly breathing it out of his nose.

H sat down and a man in his mid-thirties with light brown skin, slightly balding curly hair and two gold teeth at the front of his mouth; was sitting in a chair at the back corner of the room, he looked at Bigs and smiled. He seemed a little nervous and could not look Bigs straight in the eye, but he began to speak quietly. Finally Bigs told him to speak up, because he couldn't hear what he was saying. 'I said I respect you Bigs, but Elijah is more than a messenger. I believe he is ALLAH in the flesh.' There was a rumble of agreement in the room, but it was very low compared to when Bigs had first entered the room.

'Look, I know you man think if you disagree with me I'm gonna do something bad to you, but I want nothing more than to have a conversation with you,' said Bigs, as sincerely as he could. Still, he knew they wouldn't believe him.

Most of them knew Bigs from the days when he was the head of a murdering crew known as the Zulus, or, as most people called them behind their backs, the stone cold killers.

'Look, put aside what you think of me and tell me honestly, how could you kill Malcolm X for expressing his views about the fact that Elijah had been having sex with his sixteen-year-old secretaries? If it was the truth, why did it need to be kept a secret?'

'Boy, to be honest with you Bigs, I agree. Killing Malcolm X was a bad thing to do. The only thing I know is that he wasn't interested in telling the truth about Elijah; he was just using it to get back at Elijah because Elijah had banned him from speaking publicly about the death of the president,' replied H.

'But why would the Nation be afraid to say what they thought about the President?'

'Boy, you would have to speak to Minister Farrakhan about that. All that stuff is before my time and way above my head.'

'Fair enough, but do yourselves a favour. Stop putting Elijah and Minister Farrakhan above the FATHER, and know that black people are just as much Devils as white people. The problem I have with your teachings is that they are based upon hate for the white man. You blame him for everything. Now in times gone by, such statements were correct: slavery, segregation and lynching; those types of things were pure evil and the whites that did such things were devils. But look at Africa today, some of the wickedest things ever done are being done right now by the great-grandchildren of slaves. The days have gone when you could blame things on one colour or race.

'Look I got nuff love for you man, and unless you come against me you don't ever need to fear me. I know the word on the street is I've gone mad, but the truth is I was mad before the gone, in gone mad, if you can feel me.' Bigs put a fist in the air and said goodbye.

He realised he would not be able to have a true conversation with what he saw as his own people... not because they were the Nation of Islam, but because they were from the street and whether the street thought he was mad or not, it still feared him greatly. Once again he thought, *'what was the point?'* and once again he noticed the black van parked nearby. It was motionless, as if it was empty, but Bigs knew that as soon as he drove off it would spring back into life.

His mind went back to the force that had saved his life. Once more he thanked the FATHER for watching over him and asked for forgiveness for being such a lowlife. He decided, as he often did, to make the police work for their money and he sped off at a great speed; sometimes driving on the wrong side of the road, in order to avoid waiting at the back of ten cars stopped at a red light.

As he drove at high speed, Bigs began to wonder why was he trying to make people see what they did not want to see. He knew religion was not for him, because once you had chosen a religion and believed in it with all of your heart, you could not admit that it might not be right or true. It was as if, once a person believed in a certain type of religion, they would act as if that religion was the FATHER.

If someone proved something to be wrong in that religion, its adherents would rather disagree or lie than be grateful for being shown the truth. *'Oh, what's the point?'* Bigs thought, as he hand-braked and slid his car around a corner onto another street. Bigs was two streets from home when he decided to look in his rear-view mirror, to see if he had lost the van. Of course he had, but what did it matter? They knew where he lived he thought, breaking out into laughter. He flung the car around the last two corners, with wheels screaming and smoke swirling into the air; the tyres skidded and totally failed to keep grip. Bigs pulled on to his driveway with a skid. Once again as he began to wonder what the point was, his thought was interrupted by the voice.

'There is no point... that is the point,' said the voice.

'Shit! Huh, I know exactly what you mean. People are going to think whatever they want to think; it's their right. Well I think I'm over whatever it was I was trying to achieve or do. I think it's time to see if these three men, who keep wanting to train with me, are really ready to be soldiers for the FATHER.'

Bigs made his way to his front door, still not sure of what it was he had been trying to achieve at the church. A moment of embarrassment came over him as he turned the key to his front door.

As he opened the door, he was immediately greeted by two of his children, Mart and Ric, who were playing in the hallway as he entered. Bigs grabbed them and lifted them into his arms, kissing them repeatedly on their cheeks; as he did he made silly sounds that sounded like ducks. With each kiss the children laughed louder and screamed with joy, as each kiss and sound connected to their silky soft skin. Bigs took in deep breaths as he kissed them, so that their smell would fill his nostrils. He carried them into the front living room, nearly falling over their toys that were all over the hall and front room floor. Michelle was sitting on a leather sofa, breastfeeding their third child, who was a one-year-old girl named Pas.

'Alright Shell?' said Bigs with a smile as he looked at Michelle.

'Yeah we're fine. Are you hungry?' replied Michelle as she went to get up.

'Yeah, but don't get up. I'll get it in a minute.' Bigs leaned over and kissed Michelle and his daughter Pas. Mart and Ric screamed and laughed as they were momentarily thrown upside down in their dads' arms; they exaggerated their position by throwing their heads back and arching their backs as much as they could. Bigs dropped them onto the sofa and they bounced and laughed even more.

Bigs picked up Pas, who had stopped feeding and was holding her hands up in the air for Bigs to pick her up, so that she too could join in the fun. Once in her daddy's arms, she immediately tried to put herself in the same position as her siblings; arching her back and throwing her head back. Bigs obliged her by pretending she was falling onto the sofa. As he did he blew on her neck, making a farting sound which tickled her and made her older brother and sister laugh.

'You farted, Daddy!' they shouted with excitement.

'Oh, no, I didn't,' said Bigs as he chased all three of them around the sofa as they screamed.

'The monster is coming! Quick, hide!' yelled Mart as she ran round the sofa.

Ric did the opposite, making kung fu noises as he attempted to karate chop and kick the monster into submission. Pas being the youngest, followed Mart a bit too closely and bumped into her and fell to the floor unharmed, when Mart stopped abruptly. The three of them found her fall extremely funny and fell on the floor with laughter. Bigs tickled them and they all lay on the floor in a heap. By the time Michelle came into the room with Bigs' dinner, he was sweating and slightly out of breath.

'Okay that's it, time for Daddy to eat his dinner. I'm starving and tired from chasing you lot around,' Bigs declared as he slumped into his leather lazy chair. But his children had other ideas for their dad and started to hit him with pillows.

'That's enough. Let Daddy eat his dinner now,' said Michelle.

'Oh but Mommy, we're playing a monster game with Daddy and he hasn't caught us yet.'

'I've caught you five times,' said Bigs.

'Are you okay?' asked Michelle.

'To tell you the truth, I had a bit of a mad day. I still don't know why I did it, but I went to one of those Christian revelations...' Bigs stopped mid sentence as the doorbell rang. He looked out of the front window to see who it was.

'It's Derrick, Andy and Paul.'

'I'll take the kids in the back so you can talk.'

'No it's alright, I'll tell them to come back later.'

'But I thought you were going to train them?'

'I was, but I lost track of time and then I forgot I was going to train them.'

'Sit down and eat your dinner. I'll let them in before we go in the back room. Come on you lot, Daddy's got things to do. I love you.' Michelle kissed Bigs on his head and smiled.

'I love you all too, and I'll play with you lot later. Behave you two, okay?'

'Yes Daddy. We love you too.'

Michelle opened the front door and went to let Derrick, Andy and Paul in. As she opened the door, Ric saw his chance to get out into that no-go-zone, known as the Street. He made a run for it, his two-and-a-half-year-old legs taking the biggest and fastest steps possible, but Michelle was ready for his mad dash and grabbed him before he could taste freedom. But Ric was ready for her quick response and waited a second for her grasp to loosen. As it did he tried again to wriggle free and take one step closer to the street.

'Hey little man, where are you going? Mommy wants you to go with her... how are you Michelle?' said Derrick, as he stopped Ric from getting any further out the front door.

'I'm fine, how are you guys?'

'We're fit and ready for the boss to beat us up in training.' they all laughed.

'Well, come in. He's in the front room eating his dinner... go straight in.'

'Oh, are you sure? Maybe we should come back later. We don't want to disturb him.'

'No, he was busy and then forgot you were training today, but he'll be finished eating soon. Go through, he's waiting for you.'

'Thanks Michelle.'

'Knock, knock' Bigs turned to the door.

'Come in.'

'Reporting for duty sir.'

'Yeah, I forgot we were supposed to train today.'

'Sorry boss. Do you want us to come back later or something?'

'No, I just got distracted that's all. Come in, sit down... I'll be finished in a moment. You guys ready for training?'

'Yeah always ready boss.'

'Okay. I'm going to build a spliff before we start and let my stomach rest. Anyone else want to build one?'

'No way, not before training for us boss. I don't know how you can smoke weed and train?'

'It's part of my resistance training.'

'So what have you been up to boss?'

'I was just telling Shell, I've had a weird day so far. I went to one of those Christian Revelations.'

'Yeah?'

'Yeah... I walked up on the stage and starting asking questions in front of the whole church.'

'Yeah? What did you say?'

'I asked why they were so selectively blind when it comes to their worship of the FATHER.'

'What did they say?'

'Well, there was only one guy on the stage who was doing all the talking, some supposed man of the FATHER.

He basically repeated scripts from the Bible... the usual bullshit.'

'I don't understand those religious people. If you don't talk scriptures they don't know what you're talking about.'

'That's right. You tell us about the cross and how it's just a weapon used by the Romans, but when I say that to my sister who's a Christian, she says that's not the point. I say it is the point, because if he had been hung like you say Bigs, it would be a rope around her neck instead of a cross.'

'I tried to explain to the people at the church that they were honouring the method by which Jesus was killed, by glorifying the cross, not the man himself. But what I realised today is that there is no point in trying to talk to people who have chosen their religion; they don't want to know because they have found what makes them feel secure, and they don't want anyone to come in and create waves. They aren't looking for the truth... they are looking for something to make them feel good about themselves.'

'But wouldn't you think those religious people would want to know the truth, no matter what?'

'Let me tell you something. Only use the Bible or the Qur'an to find out if what is written in your heart is correct. Never use the books to tell you what is on the inside of you.'

'Why?'

'Because most things on the outside or in this world are corrupt in one way or another. This world's system is designed to keep you as slaves to the system. The FATHER has taught me that the world cannot help itself; it is controlled by wicked minds who would not think twice about mixing their lies into a book that claims to be from the FATHER. In fact, that's the first place they would want to contaminate. It always amazes me, how the people of this world don't seem to connect the fact that it is written that Satan mixes lies with truth, in order to look legitimate. Before I ever looked into this whole religion thing, I spent the best part of my life walking and learning to hear the FATHER OF CREATION inside of me. I'm so glad that I did it this way, instead of reading and learning about religion first.'

'Why's that?'

'Because coming at it this way, I know that it is the FATHER that is talking to me and not the fact that I read a passage in the Bible, and now I'm thinking about it in my mind and thinking it's the FATHER talking to me. Do you understand what I'm saying?'

'Yeah. You know it's the FATHER because everything he told you, you have found in religion... I mean in the Bible or the Qur'an.'

'Yeah, you are right to say "religion". It's like talking to this guy today; he could quote you any passage in the Bible, just like that. But because it was the Bible that he had learnt from, he sees it as the FATHER. So when you tell him something is not right, his first instinct is to defend it. But because I learnt from the FATHER and not the Bible, I take it as a book and understand that once the word from the FATHER leaves them and enters into the hands of men, myself included, it can be misinterpreted or misunderstood. Some of the things the FATHER has told me, have taken me years to fully understand.'

'And there's also the fact that most of the people that wrote the Bible weren't actually there in person.'

'That's right, but the main thing is that you must learn to know the word within you, before you learn the word outside of you; I'll tell you straight out that it isn't easy. And that's what I'm saying; one of the things I've come to understand in looking into the Bible and the Qur'an, is that these people who read and are taught by the Bible and the Qur'an, never seem to see or understand that the people they are reading about never had a Bible or a

Qur'an. What they did have, was the word spoken into their hearts straight from the FATHER.'

'So what has changed?'

'I couldn't tell you, but like I said, I'm glad I learnt the old-fashioned way. Anyway, I'm ready. Let's start training.'

Bigs took the last pull on his spliff and put out the stub in the ashtray. They walked through Bigs' house to the back garden and entered into his gymnasium; it was an extended garage that contained weight machines, punching bags and thick padded floor mats.

They bowed as they entered and took their shoes off at the door. Once they had changed into their training clothes, they knelt on the floor and said a prayer to the FATHER. After they finished they stood and began to train; doing stretching and circuit training, followed by weight training and punching bag work and finishing with mixed martial arts training.

'Fuck, I'm whacked! Shit, I need to fill my lungs with air quickly,' gasped Andy, as he leant forward onto the wall and sweat poured from his heaving body onto the floor.

'I don't know how you can do it Bigs. You just smoked a great big spliff and yet you're not even out of breath.'

'That's because he's iron. My arms are full of bruises,' said Derrick, who was gasping for air.

'Let me ask you something, man. You train with me, and you say you're into the Father and that you want to serve them, like me?'

'Yeah, you know that Bigs. We'll do whatever you say, just name it.'

'I hope so, because I may have a very important job for you to do... but it may involve killing someone. So if you're not down with that, I suggest you don't come back to the next training session.'

'Boy, Bigs... we've killed for money, as you know, and.... well I can only speak for myself, I wish I hadn't. But if what I was, can now be used to serve the FATHER, I'm down for that. I believe you when you say you are a soldier for the FATHER, because I saw what you walked away from and I believe only something like the FATHER could have taken you away.'

'That's why we're all here Bigs, because we believe what you say. More than that, we know you believe what you say. Do you know what I mean?'

'I just want to say I agree with everything they have just said but for me, I have always wanted to know more and be involved in something spiritual. I mean, the life we used to live, let's be honest... you either believe it's luck that you aren't dead or in prison, or you believe it's some kind of spiritual intervention. So when I heard you were giving up the life to seek the FATHER, I knew I had to try and get involved.'

'Yeah, that's what I'm saying Bigs. It's like when you talk about the FATHER and the way we should think and act... I find that guidance so helpful; like when you were teaching us about why we can kill and do the stuff we do, and how we're just misguided. How you tell us that there are millions of soldiers all around the world that are like us, but they're killing for their countries and flags and no one calls them evil or murderers. You say that we're soldiers and our country is the streets we come from. Now, like you say, we shouldn't do that anymore because the bigger war is to save the planet for our children. I honestly believe I'm a soldier and that up until you showed me the truth, I was just fighting the wrong war.'

Bigs leant forward out of his chair. He put his spliff in the ashtray and blew out the blue-white smoke, until there was none left. His eyes were red like fire and the smoke seemed to be never ending. He looked deep into each man's eyes, until they looked away from his fiery gaze.

A shiver ran down the back of each man, as if they had just looked the devil in the eye and were still alive. Their heart rates raised as they waited for Bigs to say something, so they would know that they were alright and not in deep trouble for saying something they shouldn't have. Just as panic was about to set in and they were about to fall on their knees and beg for forgiveness, Bigs began to speak. All the paranoid thoughts left their minds just as quickly as they had entered.

'I hope for your sakes that you are telling me the truth. I swear to you that what I do is not of my own thinking, it is what has been implanted in me from when I was a child. Teach yourself these things and learn to mean them with all your heart:

'One...You are not worthy to serve the FATHER.

'Two... If you get to clean the FATHER'S rubbish bin with your own body and then, like a wet wipe, are thrown in to hell forever; it will be an honour you do not deserve.'

'Sorry Bigs I don't mean to interrupt, but have you got a pen so I can write this all down?'

Bigs got up and took out three crayons and some paper from his children's colouring box. He gave them to Derrick, Andy and Paul.

'Three...You owe the FATHER everything and they owe you nothing.

'Four... You are nothing without the FATHER but if the FATHER is with you, then nothing is impossible.

'Five... You must ask the FATHER every day what you can do for them and not what they can do for you.

'Six... Be prepared to wait for all eternity for an answer to whatever you ask.

'Seven... If you achieve everything in life that you have ever wanted to do, but not one thing you have done is for the FATHER, you must know that your life has no real value or meaning.

'Eight... Never let what you have become be more important to you than the FATHER. Always be ready and willing to give it all up for them.

'If you can get these things into your heart, believe me, they will be worth more than all the gold on the earth. One of the things that really makes me angry, is when people talk and act like the FATHER owes them something.

'Which one of us has paid for the gift of life?

'Which one of us has paid for the planet we live on?

'Who in the world can stand before me and tell me I have paid for the ability to think, to know, to understand?

'Who has earned the right to breathe air?

'Which blind, deaf or crippled person has paid or earned the right to say they deserve better?

'These things may sound harsh to you, but none of us have the right to complain to the FATHER for anything that we perceive to be wrong or inadequate in our lives. No matter what our condition, not one of us have paid for anything better or less. For every moment we live, we must grasp the fact that we did not decide to live, nor did we create the opportunity to exist. What we have is the right to choose how we live and what our heart's desire will be.

'Do not turn to the FATHER for what you want out of life.

'Do not turn to the FATHER because of what you think they are or are not.

'Do not turn to the FATHER because you think they will protect you or keep you out of harm's way.

'Teach yourself to turn to the FATHER, full stop. Or at worst, because they have given you life.

'If you can do this from the heart and know in your heart that they owe you nothing and you owe them everything, you will expect nothing from the FATHER and expect everything for the FATHER from yourself.'

'I don't understand... is it because we can trust in them that we worship them?'

'In this world, that is correct. Most people believe in the FATHER because they expect something back in return. The problem with this type of thinking is that you start to tell the FATHER what to do and before you know it you have forgotten who the boss is, so to speak, and who the servant is. For example, Christians believe that if they pray and speak in Jesus' name, they are entitled to what they have asked for. This thinking is from Satan who wants men and women to make demands on the FATHER, so that if or when the FATHER does not answer their prayers, they will disbelieve in the FATHER. They talk like this because they have forgotten that they serve the FATHER and the FATHER does not serve them.'

'So if you have a problem, should you not ask the FATHER for help then?'

'You should have faith that the FATHER knows your needs and is aware of the situation. Your prayer should be in praise of and thanks to the FATHER. You should talk to the FATHER about your problems and how you can find your way out of them. If they choose to help you out, you should be grateful for their help because you know that you owe them everything already and that this just adds to what you already owe them.'

'So then you shouldn't think that the FATHER'S job is to help you in a time of need?'

'It is not for you or I to say what the FATHER should do. Those who think that way do not know the FATHER OF CREATION, the most powerful being in existence. Only a fool would dare to say or tell the FATHER what to do, trust me on that. This is particularly true when we get ourselves into problems, or when another human being causes us problems. It is not the FATHER who puts us in those situations, it's men and women's free will; that is the reason why we find ourselves calling to the FATHER for help.

'You must learn to know that the FATHER OF CREATION is just and righteous and that we must humble ourselves where they are concerned. If we do, we might be blessed by their presence in our unworthy lives, and then we may be invited into their arms; where all the things we have ever wanted and more will be given to us. But first you must be invited by the FATHER and not by yourself.'

Derrick, Paul and Andy nodded their heads at the same time, as if they were in some sort of hypnotic trance. As they each stared into their own piece of space, the words Bigs spoke floated into their subconscious minds.

'I have one question Boss... I was telling my girl you are a soldier for the FATHER and that I'm hoping to become one. And, well, she said... how can a killer and a gangster become a soldier for the FATHER? I didn't know what to say.'

'You should have told her that it's because you were misled up until now. Isn't that right Bigs?'

Bigs paused for moment before answering.

'When you go home tonight, ask her this: what type of person does she think will be willing to give up their life and do the bloody things we will have to do for the FATHER? Does she think a vicar will, or a preacher? Maybe she thinks the churchgoers will? It is for this reason that we have lived the life we have lived and done the things we have done. It is only if we turn our backs on the FATHER that our lives will have been sinful, evil and of no good. When our work for the FATHER is done, I expect to go to hell; so why not kill for the FATHER? I've killed to save my friends' lives. We are soldiers, but who we soldier for is our choice.'

'I get it now,' said Paul with a grin, still nodding his head.

'Yeah, me too,' agreed Andy and Derrick.

'So, to wrap up tonight's talk. Hope, like you would to win the lottery, that the FATHER will show you favour and invite you into their arms. Do not be like the vain, egotistical and ignorant people, who think they have the right to say what the FATHER can and cannot do. Stay humble gentlemen, and you may know the presence of the FATHER in your lives. And remember, if you make a book your foundation instead of the FATHER, you will be blown left, right, up and down, like a leaf in the wind. With that I bid you good night.'

It was about eleven o'clock pm. Bigs closed his front door as he said goodbye to Andy, Derrick and Paul. He sat down in his chair and began to think about the day; he still couldn't believe what he had done at the church. His thought was abruptly interrupted by the voice.

'You keep saying the FATHER, but to describe them you say "they" or "them" and not "he." Why do you think that is?'

'What do you mean?'

'Do you think that is all they are to you, a FATHER?'

'No, they are everything to me.'

'Are they not your MOTHER too?'

'Yeah, they are like everything to me, you know that.'

Bigs paused for a moment.

'So I should say the FATHER and MOTHER OF CREATION. Sorry, yes it's true; they are my FATHER and MOTHER.'

'This world is corrupt and man has lost the name MOTHER on purpose because it wants to keep women down. But women have helped to do this by trying to act more like men, as if being a man will make them stronger. They have lost their identity, and in doing so they have lost what makes them strong.

'At first, women just wanted to be respected more by men for the great contributions they have made to the world. Women may not have gone out into the world and achieved the same things as men have, but they were the backbone of the family; allowing the men to go out and do the things they did.

'Satan was able to trick women into believing that they should want more than just respect... that they should want to be more like men. Once women took the bait, they were on the slippery slope of falsehood. So as the generations passed, women went from just wanting more appreciation, to thinking that what they wanted appreciation for wasn't worth anything anyway and so the cornerstone of the family began to crumble. Women went from the joys of having a baby to post-partum depression and from being at home to provide a secure, loving and caring environment for her children; to being out as much as the man of the home.

'That meant it was left up to a stranger to provide a secure, loving, and caring environment for the children. But these strangers, called nannies or babysitters, were nine times out of ten only looking after the children for money, not love. This meant that children were no longer being nurtured in a loving and a caring environment, which meant that they grew up much colder; as their hearts were not filled with love. Then as they grew and had children of their own, they too went out seeking for a caregiver; just as their parents did.'

Bigs listened carefully to the voice as it spoke softly to him.

'This has gone on for so long now, that children are now growing in an environment with no adults at home at all; no nannies, no babysitters, nothing. They teach themselves what is important by watching TV, playing video games and hanging out on the street. Women are now truly lost, for what they are they don't want, and what they want to be they cannot have. The home is destroyed because it has lost its cornerstone and Satan's world of TV, video games and the street, becomes the children's secure, loving and caring environment.

'You must not forget the MOTHER, for it is a mother's love, patience and understanding that you snuggle up in. When you mess up and are sinful, it is a mother's forgiveness you look for.

'For out of the FATHER and MOTHER comes all creation. If either one is not a part of the foundation of a thing, there is no solid creation; only something that will eventually break and fall down. No matter what it is, whether it be in the spiritual world or in this world... civilisation, religion, government, men, women, armies, businesses and so on... if it does not understand or appreciate the two forces that make the one supreme force, it will crumble.'

'I hear you,' said Bigs, as he thought about what the voice had just told him. Bigs smoked another joint as he relaxed.

AGENT SMITH

Mist rose through the manhole covers in the middle of the road; red lights shone bright, but the roads were empty. Even the pigeons who normally fill the sidewalks, picking at the discarded and unwanted waste of human life, were nowhere to be seen. The wind blew bits of newspapers up into the air and down again, as if it were playing some kind of game with the paper. There was the sound of rusty metal squeaking, as the wind blew against advertising signs that were hanging off of walls outside of shops and on the posts of street lights; adding an atmosphere of eeriness to the dead of the night.

Suddenly the dead silence of the night was smashed by the sound of car tyres screaming, as they tried to keep their grip on the slightly moist surface of a cold black road. The car sped along, not once stopping at the dozen or so red lights it passed; as it sped through the sleepy streets. It was lucky for the driver that the streets were dead; otherwise the blatant disregard for stop signs would have left them dead instead. Once again the tyres screamed in anger as they tried to keep the car on the road, as the driver turned left and then right; like a side winding sand snake.

Agent Smith looked in his mirror for signs that he had lost his pursuers at last. He checked and double checked the mirror, but he could no longer see the glare from the car lights of his nemesis; this dark shadow that seemed to find him no matter where he went. He had just made it out of the hospital after getting his family checked out, after their terrible ordeal. He knew that if he had left them in there any longer than one night, they would have caught him there.

He was able to get them to his distant relations in this sleepy town, only to find himself being pursued just moments after leaving them with his bewildered second cousins; whom he had not seen since he was a boy. Were they the ones who had called the police? Even if they had, he was sure it wasn't the police he was fleeing from. This smelt like government. There were no sirens or flashing lights, just the muffled sounds of semi-automatic weapons firing their bullets into the night through silencer muzzles.

But who were they? His heart rate began to slow, as it looked like he had once again managed to lose them for now. '*Damn, they were good! Twenty-five years I've been in the FBI and they have made me go almost all the way through twenty-five years worth of owed favours, like a hot knife through butter. Who can I trust? No one, it seems. How about Mike, my boss? I'd better give him a call, see if he can help me... no I can't trust anyone. If only I could crack this damn code for the disk! It's my only ace. Better pull over somewhere nice and secluded... I need to think.*

What am I missing? Pete, if you're out there, show me a sign,' thought Agent Smith.

He pulled into an underground office car park on the outskirts of town, turned off the car lights and looked at the evidence bag for the thousandth time. His mouth was dry and he had nothing to drink. 'Damn!' he shouted, beating the steering wheel with his fist.

'Please LORD, help me. What is it they want and what do I have to do?' Agent Smith sighed; his throat was now getting dry too. He looked at the chewing gum in the evidence bag.

'I don't know why you had gum on you Pete, you never liked the stuff. Maybe you knew I would be in this situation with a dry mouth and throat; so I'm going to make some use of this gum, if you don't mind, in order to get some spit going in my mouth.'

Agent Smith took out three sticks of gum and opened them. He quickly put the three pieces of gum into his dried mouth and chewed.

'Thanks Pete, you're a life saver.'

Agent Smith held the open gum wrappers in the air in front of him in a toasting gesture, as if he were holding a glass of champagne. As he went to put the wrappers down, he noticed out of the corner of his eye, a number written in ink on the inside of one of the wrappers. It was a phone number... 555-6715... and the words, 'The truth will set you free.' He couldn't believe his eyes, and double-checked to make sure he wasn't hallucinating.

'Yes, thank you LORD, thank you!' he shouted.

'This has got to be the password, and the last four numbers of this phone number must be the four digit code. I wonder whose number this is? Hopefully it's a contact number for the priests who don't wish to be found... I've got to get to a phone booth,' thought Agent Smith as he turned on the lights and drove out of the darkness of the underground car park, like a bat out of hell.

INSIDE MOBILE ONE

'Mobile One, this is Sat 1. There is too much cloud cover for real-time imagery. Over.'

'Received Sat 1. How about thermal infrared? Over.'

'Err, that's a negative right now. We're as blind as a bat. Over.'

'Received Sat 1. Let us know as soon as you're back in the operational window. Over.'

The Mobile One operator swivelled in his chair and looked at his colleague sitting opposite him for answers, but all he could do was shrug his shoulders and shake his head.

'Team One. Please tell me that you have a visual on the target. Over.'

'Um, that's a negative, Mobile One. Over.'

'What about you Team Two? Over.'

'Dude, this guy has vanished into thin air. No visual. Over.'

'Team Three? Over.'

'Negative, no visual. Over.'

'Fuck! You know what that means? I have to make the call... shit! This is Mobile One, requesting secure link. Over.'

'This is Pegasus ocean operator. What is your designator and call sign? Over.'

'Bravo, Echo, Delta, 1,9,6,7. Over.'

'Request received Mobile One. Enter code. Over.'

The second man in Mobile One typed a code into a computer key board and pressed the enter key.

'Code received, awaiting verification. Verification complete. Secure link enabled Mobile One. Over.'

NSA COMMAND AND OPERATIONS CENTRE

Assistant Director Collins pressed a button on the intercom system, that put the secure call on loudspeaker. He then told the working agents to be quiet.

'This is Assistant Director Collins. Tell me you've got the target, Mobile One. Over.'

'That's a negative sir. We lost him. Over.'

Assistant Director Collins picked up a phone and pressed one.

'Hold on, Mobile One. Over.'

Director Forbes' internal phone rang; he put down his glass of malt whiskey and picked up the phone.

'Speak.'

'Director Forbes, Mobile One is on the secure Sat link. It seems Mobile Ones teams have lost the target. What do you want me to tell them to do?'

'Wait a moment.'

Director Forbes put down the phone on his table. Taking another sip of his malt whiskey, he pressed his intercom system.

'This is Director Forbes. Patch me through to the Director of the CIA on a secure link now.'

'Patching you through now sir.'

A moment later....

'This is Director Johnson.'

'We had an opportunity to apprehend the suspect and failed. Do you have any teams of your own there?'

'No, I don't. I thought we agreed to let the locals take care of this. What are your units doing there?'

'The suspect took his family to the hospital and used his credit card; his card was red-flagged and we took the opportunity to take care of it in-house.'

'I thought we agreed I would be taking care of the operation from here on out?'

'Yes, we did, but the opportunity changed that. I'm going to give my team seventy-two hours to see what they can do, because they are really close. We are also meeting in three days for the weekend gathering; all of the inner circle will be there.'

'Okay, but I suggest we inform the local police as well and use them to help flush him out.'

'I agree. Do what you have to do, but I have the feeling that forces outside of our control are in operation. If that's the case, maybe we can use them to fish out the other priest or persons involved in this; as I'm sure that's where he'll be heading for answers.'

'I agree. Either way we won't lose, whether we catch him now or later; makes sense to me.'

Director Forbes put down one phone and picked up another.

'Assistant Director Collins.'

'Yes sir. I'm still awaiting orders sir.'

'Tell Mobile One to listen in to the police radios. The CIA are going to put out an A.P.B. for Agent Smith and his car, to the local police immediately. When the locals pick up his trail, make sure our teams are there to pick up the pieces.'

'Yes sir. Will that be all sir?'

'Yes. Call me when you have some progress.'

Assistant Director Collins put down the phone and turned back to the intercom.

'Mobile One, tune in to the locals we're going fishing. Be ready. Over.'

'Received and understood. Mobile One over and out.'

The operator in Mobile One turned to his colleague.

'We're going fishing. Tune in to the locals and advise all teams to be on standby; we're going to let the fish come to us.'

'Good, I like fishing. It means we can get some sleep while we wait for the fish to bite,' said the second operator with a smile.

SKULL AND BONE MANSION

It was a dark and stormy night. Two four-by-four SUV's pulled up outside of a large gated driveway. A blacked-out window rolled down, and a hand stretched out and pressed the intercom. A voice came over the intercom and asked who was calling.

'It's the Secret Service. I'm Secret Agent Carter. We are here to start security checks before Friday's meeting.'

'Okay, could you put your identity card up against the camera, please.'

'Sure.'

'Okay Agent Carter, you know the drill.'

'Yeah okay,' said Agent Carter with a sigh. He stepped out into the pouring rain and tried to cover himself from the downpour with his jacket; as he put his face into a retinal eye scan. The gates opened and Agent Carter quickly jumped back into the SUV, but it was too late; his clothes were totally soaked by the rain.

'Shit, I feel like a fish! It's chucking it out there.'

'I can see from here sir.'

'Oh you think it's funny Williams? You won't be laughing when you're on outside detail later tonight.'

'Hey, it's all part of the job sir. I'll do whatever it takes to keep the President safe.'

'All joking aside, this is your first time at the lodge. After we check the perimeter and all things are in place, I'm going to have to swear you in.'

'I'm ready sir. I've always wanted to be a part of Black Watch, and I know it means being more secretive than we already are.'

'Good, because what you will hear and see here never leaves the Black Watch unit. We are trusted above all secret agents; not even the President's wife is allowed here. We are a part of an elite team of secret agents from all over the world; Black Watch heads them up.

'We are command control and over the next three days we will be protecting not only the President, but ex-Presidents, Vice Presidents, Prime Ministers, ex-Prime Ministers and deputy Prime Ministers. We will guard the world's most rich and powerful men, heads of religion, Generals, Air Marshals, Admirals and the heads of the intelligence services... these are by far the most powerful meetings in the world today and no one outside of the people here today know it is even happening.'

They drove up the twisting gravel driveway, which was covered by trees on either side. The trees swayed in the strong wind and at times it seemed as if the trees were leaning in on purpose to try and grab the SUV's, and drag them into the never ending darkness on the other side of their branches.

The windscreen wipers worked overtime in what seemed to be a futile effort to remove rain from the windscreen. Then out of the darkness of the winding driveway, came a blurred but brightly shining light; it was the light from the mansion. Lightning flashed and lit up the entire sky, for a moment, showing the full grand splendour of the mansion before it disappeared into semi-darkness once again.

'Gee, it's kind of creepy. It looks like one of those mansions in a horror film.'

'What? You're not scared are you Williams?'

'Of course not sir. I'm just observing the surroundings.'

As they reached the front entrance to the mansion, they were greeted by an old man in a raincoat who motioned them to keep on driving along the driveway to the guest house; some six hundred meters to the left of the Mansion.

'Who's that old man?' asked Secret Agent Williams.

'He's Alfred, the head man. He's as old as this mansion; some say he's older.'

'How old is the mansion?'

'Six hundred to a thousand years old.'

'No wonder it looks so creepy.'

'You have no idea, Agent Williams; you have no idea.'

They pulled up outside of the guest house, where another elderly man was waiting with two younger men.

'Now, this could be my lucky day. I don't think I have ever been in a house this fine. I mean, this house alone must be worth, what? A million, at least? And this is the guest house... how many bedrooms are there in this sucker?'

'There are twelve. We will occupy the first four, two to a room, and the rest will be shared amongst our international counterparts. Okay, let's get in out of the rain and we'll get started.'

'What about our bags and stuff?'

'Don't worry about them. What do you think these men are standing here for? Just bring the weapons and tactical bags.'

As they entered the house, they were greeted by a maid who asked them to fill out a card stating what time they would like breakfast, what they would like for breakfast, if they had any allergies and so on.

'You've got to be kidding me... they want to know what I would like for breakfast and what time? No wonder every secret agent is busting their balls to get into Black Watch. Look at this place; plush rugs, fireplace, luxurious leather sofas and widescreen TVs with satellite hook-up.'

'Only the best for Black Watch... but make no mistake, all of this is only available once you're off duty. No sneaking back to watch the game.'

'Of course. Like you said sir, we have to protect the most important people in the world.'

'Okay, let's go to the briefing room and get started on detail.'

'Would you like coffees?' asked the maid.

'Yes, eight cups please.'

Agent Carter laughed at Agent Williams' reply to the maid. 'She'll bring a carafe so we can refill our cups.'

'I'll bring them to you shortly,' smiled the maid, somewhat embarrassed.

Agent Carter led his team of eight men to the briefing and CCTV centre room. They sat around a table and began to draw up the security details for the three-day visit of the VIP's. They checked passports, work permits and any other form of paperwork for all of the staff who were working at the mansion and for all of those who would be working over the three days in which the VIP's would be staying at the mansion.

They made the rota for themselves and for their colleagues, who would be arriving with the VIP's. They checked that all the two-way radios were on the same frequencies and that all radio charges were operational. Then they checked out the perimeters, the fencing and the infrared trip alarms. By the time they had completed all the checks, the sun was beginning to rise. Agents Carter and Williams stood looking over a cliff face, some thousand meters from the back of the mansion; looking at the sun rising up out of the ocean.

'Man, it doesn't get much better than this. Have you ever seen such a view, Williams?'

'Oh yeah, the last time I took my million-dollar yacht for a quick sail around the world sir.'

They both laughed.

'Well, we've put everything in place. Now we get one day to relax and enjoy the perks of the job. Go get some sleep and later I'll beat your ass at basketball.'

It was 2 p.m. and the sun shone down on them with great generosity. Agents Carter and Williams paid it no mind as they clashed and smashed the basketball into the net; as if it were the finals for the NBA itself. Sweat poured off of both men as each refused to let the other get the better of them. Agent Carter, being the older of the two men, was breathing a bit more heavily than Williams, but he tried his best not to show it.

'Okay, this ball wins the game.'

'Bring it on young man... damn, hold on a minute,' said Agent Carter. He took out a handkerchief and wiped his nose as it began to bleed. 'Okay, I'm ready.'

Agent Carter stood with legs apart and moved his arms and hands up and down in anticipation of Williams' next move. Williams bounced the ball left then right, in then out, before stopping dead in his tracks and aiming at the hoop.

Agent Carter jumped with hands raised and reached high into the sky to try and stop the ball in mid-flight, but the younger agent's prayers were answered and the ball flew over Agent Carter's hands and dropped through the hoop without touching the sides.

'Yeah!' shouted Agent Williams.

'Good game, almost let the old man beat you,' smiled Agent Carter as he shook Williams' hand. They grabbed their towels and headed for the showers.

'It's time I explained a few things to you about what you may see or hear whilst on duty tomorrow.'

After they showered they sat down in the lounge and had a light lunch.

'I could get used to this life; maids and freshly cooked food, rather than Big Macs and milkshakes.'

Agent Carter smiled for a moment, then switched off the TV and looked at Agent Williams.

'You understand that although the Black Watch unit is a part of the Secret Service, its duties are separate from those of the normal service?'

'Yes sir I do, and I've worked my ass off to get in here.'

'I know, we've been watching you for some time now. I have to say that you would not have been invited to become a member of this elite unit if we... and when I say "we" I mean the President, Vice President, Secretary of State and myself... did not think you were perfect for the available position. Your record speaks for itself.'

'Thank you sir. I won't let you down.'

'Good. The Unit is different for many reasons; we are the only American Secret Service unit ever to enter this place. Our international counterparts' presence is similarly classified. We call this place the Lodge, and we can be ordered to come here at a moment's notice.'

'Is it true that I will have to go through some sort of test before I can become an official member of the Black Watch unit sir?'

'Yes, we will get to that shortly. You may have heard rumours about us; some are true, others are misplaced gossip. The one thing that is true and we are renowned for it, is our commitment to total secrecy; we don't even talk among other secret agents about what goes on here. This is the biggest and most important point of all.' Agent Carter's nose began to bleed; he pulled out a handkerchief and wiped his nose.

'Are you okay sir?'

'Of course, it's just a nosebleed. Never had one? Well, never mind that. Do you understand what I've just said?'

'I understand sir, and I'm willing to take any kind of oath and any kind of test to prove I'm worthy.'

'Well, that's what we are going to find out today. But first let me explain what is required of you before we go any further. Before you accept the test you must understand that if you fail, you will be dead.'

'What? Are you serious sir?'

'Extremely.'

'Okay.'

'I need to go to the bathroom. While I'm gone think carefully about your answer, I will accept it when I come back; but remember if you say yes, there is no turning back.'

Agent Carter left the lounge and walked along a corridor, but he did not go to the toilets. Instead he entered a secret room where the rest of the Black Watch team were sitting; looking at monitors that showed the whole of the property. They watched Agent Williams as he paced back and forth. Sometimes he stopped, staring into space, other times he seemed to be talking to himself.

'I've got twenty on the kid saying yes but failing the test,' said one agent.

'I'll take that bet. I think he'll say yes and pass,' said another.

'Yeah, well, I've got fifty on him saying no. Any takers?' said another, waving his dollar bills in the air.

'I'll take that bet, he's going to say yes. You can see it in his eyes, he's as crazy as the rest of us.' They all laughed.

'So what do you think, chief? Is he the man or not?' Agent Carter paused for a moment before answering.

'For thirty years I've been the head of Black Watch, and I've seen many come and go in those years. Many have gone crazy and most have died, but one thing we all have is the will to serve to the death if necessary. He will become a member of the brotherhood... that I'm sure of. How long he will last is the bet I'm interested in.'

Ten minutes later, Agent Carter went back to the lounge and sat down next to the fireplace.

'So have you come to a decision?'

'Yes sir, I have…'

'Well what is it?'

'Before I answer, is there any way you could tell me a bit more about the test and what I will be swearing to?'

'Only the very smart ask that question, but unfortunately I cannot reveal any more than I have until you have become a member and are sworn in. If we did it any other way, we would not have a legal right to kill you if you ever attempted to betray us, because you have not yet taken the oath or signed your life away to Black Watch.'

'I understand sir and my answer is… Yes. I wish to become a full member of the Black Watch Unit.'

'I'm glad to hear it. I will inform the President and the Grandmaster. You will be tested tomorrow when the twenty-four members of the inner circle arrive.'

The eight members of Black Watch entered the lounge. Each wore a black jacket and trousers and had an apron tied around their waist, which had a compass and a square ruler across the centre. They each carried a candle and stood in a circle around Agent Williams. All eight agents had nosebleeds, but they did not try to stop them; they simply ignored them and carried on with what they were doing.

Agent Carter left the lounge, and the eight men spoke in a language that Agent Williams didn't understand. They then placed their candles on the floor and one agent told Agent Williams to strip naked. Agent Williams' clothes were placed in the open fire and set alight. Agent Williams was then told to pick up a piece of the burning cloth and light all eight candles without letting go of the cloth; furthermore, he must do it from the centre of the circle.

Agent Williams looked at the burning clothes, then looked at the position of the candles. He saw a suitable piece of clothing that was only partly afire. Agent Williams then took a deep breath, grabbed it, and returned to the centre. He started to light the candles one at a time, but it was not easy because the clothing was flimsy and every time he bent down towards the candles, the heat from the burning cloth heated up his hand. By the time he was on the fourth candle, the flames had reached his hand. He gritted his teeth as the pain became unbearable.

'I can do this, I will do this! Only two to go, the pain is all in my mind, cut it out and focus. But the pain, it's too great; my hand is going to melt. No, come on, keep focused, only one more to go. But I can't, the pain, my hand is shaking, I can't get the candle to light... drop the cloth, it's not worth it. No, I can do it, concentrate! Steady now, last one, no more pain... aaarrr.'

'Yes, I've done it!' shouted Williams in a triumphant voice as he fell to the floor. Agent Carter entered the room, dressed in a black robe with a skull and bone in its centre. Agent Williams was not interested in the robe but in the ice-filled bucket he was carrying.

'Here you go; stick your hand in that. You'll feel better in a moment. Well done, test one over.'

The eight men picked up the lit candles and Agent Williams was told to lie on his stomach. Each man stood over Agent Williams and dropped one drop of hot wax on his back, saying:

'Do you swear to serve the brotherhood until you die?'

'Yes,' Agent Williams replied.

'Do you swear to hold secret all that is revealed to you, no matter what pain you have to endure?'

'Yes.'

While they asked these questions they kept the candles tilted so that the hot wax continued to fall onto the back of Agent Williams.

'Do you swear on the lives of those that you love the most, that all you see and hear, you will never reveal to anyone outside of the Black Watch? Do you accept that if you do, they will surely die a painful death as the price for your betrayal?'

'Yes.'

'Do you agree that from this day forward, if you break any of the promises you have sworn to, you and your loved ones will be slowly and painfully killed, in a manner suited to a betraying pig?'

'Yes... aaarrr.'

Agent Williams' body was red and raw by now, and the bucket that had soothed his hand was now used to cover his back in ice.

'Well done, test two complete. I'm going to tell you something very important, which you must try to remember as you go through the next test. If you can remember the most embarrassing and secretive thing you have ever done, and if you tell me what it is, I will stop whatever test you are going through. But if you lie we will know afterwards, because we will make you take a lie detector test. Now recall whatever it is to your mind, and if you can't continue just say you are ready to tell your secret... but it had better be something that you would not want anyone to know. Do you understand?'

'Yes.'

'Good. Now stand and follow me,' said Agent Carter as he walked through the corridor. Agent Williams followed slowly behind. They walked down a twisting staircase to the basement level and entered a pitch black room. It was only as the eight men entered and illuminated the room with their flickering candles, that it became clear that in the middle of the room was an iron bath filled with water. Some kind of metal plate seemed to be hinged onto the iron bath by a spring-loaded device.

Agent Williams' eyes widened and his heart rate rapidly increased, as his mind tried to make sense of what he could see. Anticipation got the better of him as he screamed out, 'Please, for Christ's sake, tell me what this is!'

Agent Carter turned slowly towards Agent Williams and put his finger to his mouth. Agent Williams began to panic. He fought against it, thinking of all his years training in kidnap scenarios and how the kidnapper always wanted to keep their captives minds in a state of panic, as this made the kidnappers job easier.

'You can and you will do this,' said Agent Williams under his breath.

'Before we start, have you thought of the most secretive thing?'

'Yes.'

'Then there is only one more thing you need to do... step into the bath,' said Agent Carter.

Agent Williams slowly and somewhat shakily stepped into the bath. To his surprise the water was warm. As he went to lie down in the bath, one of the eight men lifted the mechanical device so that he could lie down, whilst the others strapped his arms and legs into place. Now only his head was slightly above the water.

'You must be wondering what this is?' said Agent Carter, pointing to the device above Agent Williams' head.
'You see these two blots on the left and right of your head? They are connectors. As long as this metal plate is touching them, an electrical current is unable to run from this generator to the bath. But once the metal plate is pushed up, it breaks the connection and the generator is free to pump its electricity directly into the bath... all two hundred volts of it. But as you can see, in order for the metal plate to

touch the blots, you will have to submerge your head under the water.

'Every time you come up for air, you will break the connection and deliver two hundred volts of electricity to your body. So it soon becomes a case of what is more important to you; the air you breathe, or not having to endure the jolting pain to your body every time you try to breathe. The generator is on a timer and will switch off automatically after five minutes.

'Oh, and by the way, just something for you to think about; the longer you stay under, the fewer times you will have to come up for breath, but the down side to that is you will have to stay up longer in order to get enough air to fill your lungs... otherwise you will drown. If I were you I would take some deep breaths now.'

As Agent Williams began to take as many deep breaths as he could, the same man that had lifted the device above Agent Williams' head, began to slowly bring it down. Agent Williams gasped for air as the device slowly pushed his head under the water. Holding his breath for as long as he could, Agent Williams heard the generator switch on and the sound of the plate coming to rest on the two blots.

One minute fifty-five seconds came and passed, and Agent Williams had still not come up for air. But as the two minute mark slowly approached, Agent Williams began to pull on his straps and violently jerk his head left to right.

He held on for as long as he could... he had no idea how long he had been under, he was sure he had counted two and a half minutes, but he could not be sure as his mind was constantly interrupted by the thought of the jolting rush of electricity he was going to have to endure... but if he could hold on just a few more seconds, at least he would have made it halfway. He now knew he was going to have to endure a lot of pain in order to refill his starving lungs, just as Agent Carter had said... oh, how he hated that name right now.

'*Here goes,*' he thought, as he braced himself for the jolting pain. Up popped his head, lifting the metal plate off of the blots.

'AAARRR!' screamed Agent Williams, as the pain registered. He gulped for air but took in water instead. It was all too much; the lack of air, the water in his lungs and the jolting pain of electricity that was starting to make his body spasm. '*I'm going to die,*' he thought.

As blackness began to fill his mind he began to feel like he was no longer in water, but rather like he was floating up into the sky. The blackness began to give way to flashes of bright colours that began to merge into one bright white colour; then the light quickly faded and darkness was over him once more.

Now he felt as if he had woken up from some deep sleep, but it couldn't be. He couldn't move, and as he slowly opened his eyes there was nothing but darkness. He turned his head and could only see darkness all around him. '*What's happening?*' he thought. '*Am I dead or am I dreaming?*'

He tried to stand, as he felt as if he was lying down, but he could not move. Agent Williams began to feel claustrophobic; it was as if he was in a confined space. He tried to lift his hands, but they hit something solid... or was he imagining it? The last thing he could remember was drowning. '*Have I died and gone to hell? Is this what hell is?*' he thought.

'Help me, please help me! Is there anyone there? Where am I?' he screamed. He felt like he was going to be sick, and was, turning his head to the side so as not to choke on his own vomit. He then coughed and nearly choked, but as he did he began to cry and laugh at the same time; now he knew he had to be alive.

The smell of vomit filled his lungs; this was a further indication that he was not yet dead. But the laughter soon faded, and the tears and panic grew. If he was not dead, then wherever he was, he was not in a good place to be. He tried to kick at the sides of whatever it was he was in.

Agent Williams began to panic more and more. The air he was breathing seemed to be getting thinner and less fresh, and this could only mean one thing; he was running out of air. His mind raced as it tried to make sense of the situation. Then it hit him like a ton of bricks, he had been buried alive. He had failed by drowning in the third test and he must have passed out; and they had buried him alive. After all, Agent Carter had made it clear that if he failed, it would cost him his life.

'I'm not dead! Please, someone, get me out of here! You've made a mistake, I'm not dead! Please dig me out, I won't tell anyone, I promise. Please, can anyone hear me?' he screamed, but no one came. This was it, a slow death via suffocation. He began to scream but stopped as he realised that screaming was making him breathe more heavily and use up more of the little oxygen he had. He began to cry like a little baby, totally uncontrollably; he realised that by crying he was using up even more air, but he couldn't stop. The more he tried to stop, the more uncontrollably he cried.

'I'll do anything, please help me, I'll do anything. Please, someone help me!'

Agent Williams fell in and out of consciousness and was starting to believe that he was literally taking his last few breaths of life. How could he die this way, who would have thought it... he had begun to think about how he had been so excited about joining the most elite sector of the Secret Service. What a high note to die on, but it wasn't; he was not killed in action saving the Presidents life from a crazed madman, no, he was going to die buried alive by the people he was supposed to call his team members and eventually his friends. He thought of Agent Carter in his robe and how he had told him he might die taking the test; but he hadn't thought they'd meant murder, that's what this was... why not just let him drown in the bloody bath, why torture him this way? Okay, he'd failed, what pleasure did they get out of this? The sick, twisted bastards.

'I would have gladly given my life for any one of you bastards! If you had asked me I would have told you my secrets, because I trusted you all with my life, and look how you have betrayed me.'

Agent Williams wanted to start crying, but he had no tears left.

'I would have done anything for you guys! I know you can hear me! Want to know my darkest secret? I'll...'

'That's it!' thought Agent Williams, he could hardly contain his excitement. He tried to laugh, but he couldn't... his throat was dry and sore.

'I'm ready to tell you my darkest secret.'

He waited to see if there was any response, there was none, and panic began to fill his mind once again as his laughter turned back into sorrow.

'When I was fifteen I watched my mother take a shower without her knowing... I sneaked in and peeped through the curtain and then masturbated. I swear that's the truth. I have never told anyone, no one! Please let me out!'

Suddenly, the darkness that was engulfing Agent Williams turned to an overwhelming bright light and all of the stale air and smell of vomit and urine, was replaced by fresh air that filled the lungs of Agent Williams in seconds. Once again Agent Williams was reduced to tears; for a man who hadn't cried since he was a boy, he had made up for all those years in one day.

'Congratulations Agent Williams, you are now a member of the Black Watch Unit. Welcome aboard, if you wish... or if this has all been too much for you, you can reject the membership and go back to normal Secret Service life. Get some rest and let us know in the morning.'

'What time is it? How long have I been in that box?'

'The time is now 22:30. The last time you were conscious was forty-eight hours ago.'

'What? I've been in that box for two days?'

'No, you were in a bed recovering from your bath. Once the doctors were sure you were okay, you were kept sedated and then we moved you to the box one hour before you would start to come round. You were in the box less than two hours.'

'Shit, what a head fuck! I thought I was buried alive by you guys and left for dead for not surviving the bath test.'

'That's the whole point. We have to make you think that in order to crack the thick skull the service has given you. As for your confession that remains within the brotherhood and you will be able to watch the videos on these guys too.'

'I think I need to take a shower and lie down. The funny thing is I don't feel hungry, even though the last time I ate was two days ago.'

'That's because the doctors have been feeding you via a drip. You've been in the best of hands. Now go and get some rest, and give me your decision in the morning... 0800 hours sharp.'

Agent Williams went back to his room and took a shower. Lying down on the bed, he contemplated his experience over the last two days.

'Shit,' he shouted suddenly. He jumped out of the bed and ran downstairs to the lounge looking for Agent Carter; who was sitting by the bar with a glass of brandy.

'Excuse me sir. But if I was out for two days, then I missed the arrival of the President and the rest of the VIP's... is that correct?'

'No, you haven't missed the President and the VIP's; they arrive in forty-eight hours just as planned.'

'But I don't understand... I thought they were scheduled to arrive at the weekend?'

'Don't worry yourself; just go and get some rest so that you'll be fit and ready for operation when they do arrive.'

'Just one more question sir. Does the brotherhood have a name, other than the Black Watch?'

'If you decide to become a member, all will be revealed then and only then.'

Agent Williams went back to his room, feeling just as bewildered as he had been when he ran out looking for Agent Carter. He lay down on his bed once again and stared into space as he thought about what he had just experienced. The next thing he knew it was seven o'clock and the alarm clock was beeping. He reached across his fresh-smelling bed linen and switched it off. There was a knock at the door.

'Come in, it's unlocked.'

A maid entered with a full English breakfast, just as Agent Williams had requested when they had first arrived at the guest house. The maid put the tray on the bedside cabinet and poured a fresh cup of Brazilian coffee. The smell of the freshly brewed coffee beans filled the room, along with the smell of fresh toast and bacon, and Agent Williams' stomach rumbled and his mouth watered.

'Will there be anything else sir?' asked the maid with a smile.

'No thank you, have a nice day.'

'You too sir. Goodbye for now.'

The maid closed the door behind her and Agent Williams got up and opened the curtains. He opened his window and breathed in the fresh air and looked at the lush green forest in front of him; whilst listening to the squawking sounds of the sea gulls coming from the direction of the cliff face and ocean. '*I'll never smell the fresh air in the same way again,*' he thought, as he sat down and ate his breakfast, fit for a king.

Once again Agent Williams remembered what had happened but for the first time a sense of achievement came over him, rather than the feeling of his stomach dropping to his knees. He realised that it had been hard, but it was all a mental thing and he really hadn't been in any real danger... just discomfort. It was a very clever way of making him feel like his life was in serious danger. '*I wouldn't expect anything less from this level of the Secret Service,*' he thought. He laughed and felt like he was back to his old self. '*Time to get back to work,*' he thought, as he finished his breakfast and went into the bathroom to take a shower.

It was five minutes to eight and Agent Williams was getting ready to go down to the lounge to meet with Agent Carter, when there was a knock on the door.

'Come in! It's unlocked.'

It was Agent Richards; he had come to see if Agent Williams was ready to go down to the lounge. They left together and walked along the corridor to the stairs.

'Well done Agent Williams, so far so good. I've got money riding on you, so don't let me down. When we get downstairs you are going to be a member of Black Watch... you know it's the best job in the whole Secret Service, don't you?'

'Yes... how much have you bet on me?'

'Twenty dollars. I believed in you.'

'Who bet against me?'

'A few members, but don't take it personally. What you went through is a well tried and tested mental breakdown procedure. Some of the best men in our business have failed, and some who made it through the test, like you, have not been able to continue. But I can tell by the way you are dressed and ready, that you have completed the final test.'

'Which is?'

'Understanding that the feeling of near death that you felt was nothing more than an illusion.'

'And what about you?'

'What about me?'

'How did you deal with it?'

'Well enough to be walking down these stairs with you, some fifteen years later.'

They entered into the lounge, where they were greeted by shouts of "well done" and a round of applause for Agent Williams.

'Well done son, no matter what your decision,' said Agent Carter, as he held out his hand and gave Agent Williams a firm hand shake.

'Well, what's your decision?' asked one of the agents, and they all listened attentively for his answer.

'I'll make it short but sweet. I'm in all the way.'

'Knew you would! Congratulations,' some agents said, as they offered their hands to shake, one by one.

'Welcome to the brotherhood. Now, although you were never really in danger while taking part in the test, you have sworn an oath which is more serious than you could ever imagine... and we will carry out our part if it is ever broken. You can never leave the brotherhood until death, do you understand that?'

'Yes sir I do, and I stand by my oath to the brotherhood.'

'Good, because you are now a member of the Freemasons. We are called the Black Watch, and our area of business is the Secret Service. We are in every country in the world and we protect the inner circle. Take a seat, tell me what you know about the Freemasons, and then I'll tell you about the brotherhood.'

'What I know is that... well, what I have heard is that they are powerful and in all areas of the world... from doctors, to lawyers, police, members of government and so on... oh, and they deal in devil worship.'

'Go get a drink and sit down. What if what you just said was true? Would you still want to be a member?'

'Truthfully?'

'Yes, truthfully.'

'What I want is to be a member of Black Watch... that's why I'm here. I had no idea that Black Watch unit was a member of the Freemasons, so I'm not going to lie and say yes; because until just now I was not thinking of the Freemasons.'

'I like your honesty; maybe I should ask it in a different way. Now that you know we are a part of the Freemasons, do you still want to be a member?'

'Yes sir, but I have to be honest and tell you that I do not know what being a member of the Freemasons means.'

They all sat and raised their glasses into the air, and Agent Williams followed suit. But he was unsure of what he was getting into and although he felt slightly uncomfortable; he was sure it was the right thing to do. At any rate, even if it wasn't, it was too late to back out now.

Once again Agent Williams noticed that from the time he had joined Black Watch, all of the team had suffered from nosebleeds on a regular basis. Now, while they were drinking and talking, all of them had to deal with a nosebleed. 'Is there a reason why you guys keep getting nosebleeds?' he asked. There was an uncomfortable silence as they all looked to Agent Carter.

'Here's to the brotherhood,' said Agent Carter as their glasses touched.

'Long live the brotherhood,' said Agent Richards, as they all sat back in their chairs. Agent Carter looked into the eyes of Agent Williams and completely ignored his question.

'What I'm about to tell you very few people know, and I'm not going to waste time telling you about the consequences if you tell another living soul about what you are about to learn. There are many myths about our secret society and most are not true or they're inaccurate…

'In the beginning there was THE MOST HIGH and their WORD and out of the word all things were created… Among the things created were man and woman but these were not the only creations of THE MOST HIGH; more intelligent beings were created long before man became an idea of THE MOST HIGH. Man was given supernatural powers and could talk to the animals that he was master over. He could talk to the air, sea, earth and fire; until the day came when THE MOST HIGH asked man if he wanted to know good and evil.'

The sounds of burning logs made Agent Williams quickly turn around and look at the open fire place. It seemed like the fire was trying to spit out its contents, as the logs popped and crackled.

Agent Williams looked confused and stopped sipping on his brandy. Interrupting Agent Carter he said,

'Don't you mean evil? I thought they already knew good?'

'No, they did not know the meaning of either; in order to know what good is or evil is, you need to know what it is not.'

'But I thought that it was Satan, the fallen angel, who tricked Eve and that she gave Adam the apple to eat?'

Agent Carter smiled and used the interruption to take a large swallow of whiskey; it was as if he was lost in the moment, as it took several seconds after he had swallowed before he spoke. 'THE MOST HIGH doesn't do tricks. What THE MOST HIGH does on earth with man, is to give him the ability to choose. It is Satan that does tricks.'

Once again Agent Williams was confused, but this time he sipped his brandy before talking. Agent Williams was distracted for a moment by the small talk taking place as some agents went in and out, whilst other agents were sitting down watching an NFL match on the big screen.

'But I don't understand... why would Satan want to lie about the eating of the apple?'

'To make you think that he had outsmarted THE MOST HIGH and had caused the downfall of man.'

'But you're saying he didn't?'

'Of course not. Like I said, THE MOST HIGH gave Adam and Eve a choice to be more like THE MOST HIGH and to know good and evil, but it would come at a price. They would lose their connection to their spirits temporarily and once they had gained the knowledge of good and evil, they would have to fight for the rest of their lives to try and reconnect with their pure spirit; which is the only way to get back in line with THE MOST HIGH.'

'But I thought they lost eternal life?'

'No, that's not true. Man, in the flesh, was never put on the earth to live forever. There was never going to be endless life on earth; man was always born to die.' Once again Agent Williams' focus was drawn away from the conversation, to the actions going on in the room. Some of the other agents were jumping up and down and shouting, because one of the NFL teams just scored.

'So you are saying religion has been lying all this time?'

'Of course. Religions are corrupt; their very nature makes them so.'

Agent Williams looked up at the TV to see who had scored and the agents watching the game began to drink whiskey and beer. The excitement of the game, mixed with alcohol, was making them become louder as their emotions began to run high.

'What do you mean?'

'Religion needs to sell itself to the masses in order to fill its churches and collection plates. It constantly has to make changes in order to be in with the times, and the reason for that is because its main selling power is guilt. It sets itself up to be the moral standard, judging the world, and it tells the world that it has approval from THE MOST HIGH to do this; but the standards that it sets are so high that they will always be broken.

'The truth is that the church sets itself against true freedom and sets boundaries so high that man will always be a sinner; and sinners will always need the church to forgive them of their sins. It's quite a good business stratagem; make people feel guilty and then tell them that you are the only legitimate means of release, or they will go to hell.'

This time Agent Carter paused in mid conversation to look over at the TV and the score. This was due to the fact that the agents watching the game began to shout and scream at the TV with total excitement, as the wide receiver was inches from the touch line. Agent Carter took another swallow of whiskey and chuckled to himself before continuing. 'But we in the brotherhood know that man is a free spirit and has the right to do whatever he pleases on earth. At the end of the day THE MOST HIGH will be the judge, not religion; not men who put on a Bishops or Priests clothing and say that they have the power to remove your sins from you.'

The room erupted into shouts of joy as the receiver made a touchdown. The agents jumped for joy hugging one another without a care in the world; for the fact was they were now starting to spill the contents of their glasses on to the floor.

'The world, through its ability to choose, decided not to learn the truth about the words and ways of THE MOST HIGH. Instead the world chose to let another man tell them what they were. Because of their laziness and lack of will, they opened up the door for wicked, greedy and corrupt men to lead them astray... and out of that came religion; which mixes the words of THE MOST HIGH with their lies, in order to look and sound authentic. But religion has never had anything to do with THE MOST HIGH, other than what I just said. It is nothing more than a business that changes form as the world changes; that's why today, just like in the olden times, you can have many different types of religion.'

Agent Williams sat in total silence thinking back to his childhood and the things he was taught in church. It seemed unbelievable, but deep down within he knew that the church was corrupt.

'The true WORD of THE MOST HIGH is the same today as it was yesterday; it never needs to change, because it never needs the people. It is the people who need THE MOST HIGH and the WORD. People like to say that the world has robbed them, but the truth is they have done it to themselves.' Agent Carter paused as a maid entered with a trolley filled with clean bed sheets and towels. She smiled and made her way to the bedrooms.

'If mankind really had the desire to know THE MOST HIGH and the truth, they would be as powerful as the brotherhood; but as mankind came to understand that they truly had free will, they soon lost interest in the WORD of THE MOST HIGH in favour of their own selfish hearts desires. The world fell into war and chaos and the words and works of THE MOST HIGH that were kept as scriptures, were left on the floor like an old newspaper.'

Agent Carter spoke with disbelief in his voice. He thought about how foolish the world had become by not knowing that the scripts that they had treated like an old newspaper, were more powerful than all the armies in the world. He sipped his whiskey as he shook his head.

'Because mankind had fallen so far, even with the scripts they could not ascertain their powers; making the words and works of THE MOST HIGH of no use.

'So mankind became its own judge and its own master and the words and works were almost lost forever. But the Knights Templar knew the value of these scripts, and under the order of the Pope searched the Middle East for them.

'Once they were found, they were taken back to Rome and the Templar were rewarded with the keys to the world. They became extremely rich and powerful, for they knew one of the greatest secrets in the world, known today as the Holy Grail. It was not a cup or anything else you've heard; the Holy Grail is the true words and works of THE MOST HIGH. But the Knights Templar did not give all of the words and works to the Vatican, they gave them portions; whilst hiding a few of the scripts in a place that only they knew and promised that they would never reveal them to the world.' Agent Carter continued to talk as he got up and went to the bar to get a new bottle of whiskey.

'For many years the Vatican tried to persuade the Templar, that it would be in the best interests of all concerned if they had all of the scriptures and kept them safe in their vaults; but the Templar declined all offers of cash from the Vatican. The Templar began to build churches of their own and used the Stone Masons to do this; for they knew the Stone Masons themselves had access to other scriptures containing the words and works of THE MOST HIGH. In joining up with the Stone Masons, their knowledge of the words and works of THE MOST HIGH could surpass that of any other secret organisation.' Once again the room was filled with the sounds of moans and groans, mixed with the sounds of joy.

'So by using the Stone Masons and paying them well for their work, they became good friends and eventually the two organisations would become one. Now, having the knowledge of the scriptures that the Vatican had and knowing the scriptures that the Stone Masons had, the Knights Templar could almost piece all of the words and works of THE MOST HIGH together. But they knew the Vatican would not allow this to happen and that they would eventually come after them; so they built their churches all around the world, and the Stone Masons built secret chambers and rooms for them inside of the churches. The Stone Masons had also built churches for the Vatican and knew that the Vatican might find them to be a threat too, so they made a pact with the Knights Templar and they both hid all of each other's scriptures in places only the other one would know.

'Then the day came when the Vatican, along with the King of France, came looking for the Knights Templar and their treasures. They found the Knights Templar but they never found their true treasures. They killed as many Knights Templar as possible and tortured many trying to find out where the scriptures were hidden; but the Knights never told because they didn't know. People believed that that was the end of the Knights Templar and their secrets, but the truth is that they simply put down their swords, left the known world and joined with the Stone Masons to become the Free Stone masons.'

The fire roared and the clinking sound of bottles touching glasses filled the air, as drinks flowed. The agents were starting to get tipsy; their aim when pouring drinks became less accurate. 'This stuff is a bit too deep for me.' thought Agent Williams.

Agent Williams poured himself another brandy. 'How did the Stone Masons come about?'

'The Stone Masons were born way back, a thousand years before Jesus; they were founded by Hiram, known as the widow's son, who was a master builder and built King Solomon's temple. That temple was later to hold the Ten Commandments and the HOLY presents of THE MOST

HIGH. The building plans for the temple came directly to Solomon from THE MOST HIGH and the plans had hidden divine secrets in them.'

The smell of alcohol and cigars began to fill the room, as the agents watching the game were spilling their drinks every time they jumped up in excitement.

'So what was the secret? Did anyone ever find out?'

'The secrets are all to do with the WORKS of THE MOST HIGH.'

Agent Williams sat up, put his drink on the coffee table and leaned towards Agent Carter. 'What exactly are the WORKS of THE MOST HIGH?'

With a smile, Agent Carter shook his head. 'I'm afraid you can only know that when you become a member of the inner circle, and it takes years of servitude, sacrifice and the building of one's mind, body and soul to reach the inner circle.'

'And how does one achieve that in a way that is acceptable to the inner circle?'

'You must learn the ways of the Freemasons. You will start as an Apprentice, then you will become a Journeyman and then a Master Builder. Then, one day, you may become a part of the inner circle, where you will learn why it is important to learn immortality for your soul.'

'So how did they become so powerful?'

Agent Carter did not answer as he waited for the maid to leave with her trolley, which was now full of dirty bed sheets and towels.

'As time moved on, a new set of thinkers emerged, called the Enlightened. They were mostly made up of scientists and philosophers who were into the teachings of the Moors, who had invaded Europe on and off since the times when Europeans thought the world was flat.'

The shouting continued from the agents sitting watching the big screen; they were now joined by other agents for the last kick of the game and hopefully a touchdown. Agent Williams was starting to feel the full effects of the brandy.

'Who were the Moors?'

'They were Black Africans who spoke to the Europeans about Astronomy, Chemistry and the WORKS of THE MOST HIGH. But most Europeans were not ready for such enlightenment and only a few small intellectual groups could understand what the Moors taught.

'They wrote in books what the Africans taught and talked about the teachings among themselves in their small intellectual groups. As time passed, they began to experiment with what was written in the books... but they had to be careful, as the church would kill anyone dabbling in what was called witchcraft or the black arts. But these small groups became very powerful and as more influential people became members, they began calling themselves gentlemen clubs.

'They eventually took over the Free Stone Masons and became the Freemasons, mixing the secrets from the past with the secrets of the Moors. This made them extremely powerful, so powerful that the church began to see them as a real threat.'

Agent Williams grabbed his head and leant forward. 'I don't understand... why would the church see them as a threat? Didn't the Moors teach that these things came from THE MOST HIGH?'

The football game finished and some agents dug into their pockets to take out the money they had lost in the bet. This did not stop the betting, as a pack of cards had been put on the table and they began to play cards.

'Yes, but that in itself was a problem because by the eighteenth century, Isaac Newton had began to take his understanding of the teachings of the Moors and the WORKS of THE MOST HIGH to the next level. He was the head of the Royal Society and a member of the Freemasons, and he began to explain more mysteries about the universe. The church did not like that, because up until then only the church had known such things, and now these enlightened Freemasons were starting to openly talk in public of their understanding of the universe.'

By now they had all consumed more alcohol than they should have, and it was starting to show in their mannerisms. Agent Carter stood, staggering slightly, then sat down again. 'It's been nice having this chat with you, but it's getting late and I'm well over the limit, so I'm off to bed. Oh, before I forget, you will have an official swearing-in when the inner circle arrive. This wouldn't normally happen, but because you are a part of Black Watch and it is your job to protect them, you will get to see them in person... a great honour, and one that is bestowed upon very few people, my friend.'

INSIDE THE SKULL & BONE MANSION

Agent Carter and the rest of his team were in the mansion going over the security details one last time, as they waited for the VIP's to arrive. They had been joined by their international counterparts and Agent Carter had placed them on outdoor duty, rather than his own team. Agent Richards and another agent were in the CCTV command centre room and the rest of the team, except Agents Carter and Williams, were standing near the doors of the twenty-four VIPs rooms inside the mansion. Agents Carter and Williams stood at the entrance door and were ready to greet the VIPs as they entered; all the agents were in suits and ties.

'Well, how do I look?' asked Agent Carter as he fixed his tie in the grand entrance hall mirror.

'Like a real gentleman sir,' replied Agent Williams, who looked a bit nervous.

'Take a few deep breaths Williams, you look like you're about to shit your pants,' said Carter with a smile.

'I'm glad you find it funny sir.'

'Believe me, I'm not laughing at you. It just reminds me of the first day that I stood where you are now, thinking the same thing as you're thinking; what the hell have I gotten myself into and what are the most powerful men in the world going to make me do next? I couldn't wait for them to arrive and get settled in, so that I could get past this stage and start to do what I loved best; which is to serve and protect. Don't worry, you'll be fine; I have faith in you son.' Agent Carter patted Williams on the back and then quickly put his hand to his earpiece, in order to hear the incoming message clearly.

'First helicopter about to land. Over,' said Agent Richards from the CCTV and command centre.

'Roger that Control. Over. Stand at ease Williams, it's just the military boys; they always land five minutes before the President. They operate on different protocols than we do and will double up on all our positions. No doubt they'll have men hanging halfway down the cliff face.'

Agent Williams laughed, but was interrupted by Agent Carter. 'I shit you not... they are some real hardcore motherfuckers. They sleep in tents while they're here, as if they were at war or something. Don't expect them to talk to you, because they won't.'

Agent Williams looked at Agent Carter surprised. 'You don't believe me? Okay, you'll see...' Agent Carter paused as another message came over the earpiece.

'A1 is en route, ETA five minutes. All teams sound off. Over.'

'Roger that. This is Team One, good to go. Over.' replied Agent Carter. All the other teams replied similarly.

'Okay Williams, this is it son. Relax, all of the hard work has been done. This place is more secure than Fort Knox.'

Agent Williams was sweating slightly, but he was ready. He looked at Agent Carter. 'Thank you sir, for believing in me. I won't let you or the brotherhood down. If I look nervous it's because I want to get this initiation over and done with sir.'

'I hear you son. Don't worry it'll all be over soon and you will truly be my brother.' Agent Carter paused again as he listened to the message coming over his radio on his earpiece.

'A1 has landed. Twelve sticks are being unloaded. Over.'

Agent Williams smiled as he whispered to Agent Carter, 'I can't believe we refer to the President, the Vice President, the Secretary of State and the rest of these people as sticks, sir.'

'I know what you mean, but if anybody happens to be trying to listen in, they won't think we are talking about the President either. Okay, enough bull.' Agent Carter pressed his handheld mouthpiece to his mouth. 'Sticks one hundred meters from door. Team One has taken delivery of sticks. Over.'

'Roger that. Team One has package. All teams sound off. Over.'

The President entered the mansion, followed by his father the ex-President, another ex-President, the Vice President, the Secretary of State, the Secretary of Defence, the heads of the NSA, CIA and FBI, the Joint Chief of Staff, one Admiral and a well-known billionaire and businessman.

Agent Williams could not believe that all of these powerful men belonged to the same secret society that he was about to become an official member of. Fear and happiness hit him almost at the same time. He was happy to be a member, but fearful because it was true that the world had been and was being run by a secret organisation. He was so deep in thought that he did not notice that the

President was holding his hand out to shake. Fortunately for him, Agent Carter was on hand to nudge him in the back discreetly.

'Oh! Err... it's an honour sir.' Agent Williams looked at Agent Carter, hoping to see in his face reassurance that he had not made a pig's ear of his first meeting with the President. Unfortunately, he did not find the reassurance he was looking for; instead, he saw Agent Carter laughing his socks off before stepping in to take control. 'Sir, this is the young man we spoke about. I'm glad to say he has completed the first stage with flying colours, just as you suspected, and he is ready and waiting to be sworn in by the Grandmaster.'

'Good man. We need young men like you, willing to sacrifice themselves for the glory of the country. You should be proud, son; you are about to become one of the true patriots of this fine country of ours.'

'Yes sir, I'm more than proud to serve my country.'

The President then took what seemed to be an urgent phone call and walked with his father up the stairs to his room. The rest of the men paid no mind to Agent Williams; the only exception was the head of the NSA, who looked him dead in the eye with a stone cold expression before saying. 'Tonight your life will change forever. If you do what's right, twenty years from now you could be walking on this side of the line instead of standing there.' Then he too answered his cell phone before walking to his room.

'Talk about whoops! I thought you were going to faint when the President offered his hand to shake,' laughed Agent Carter, slapping Williams on the back.

'A2 has touched down. Twelve sticks on board and ready for delivery. Over.'

'Roger that Control. Team One awaiting package. Package delivered. Team One has package. Over.'

'Received. Team One has package all teams sound off. Over.'

Agents Carter and Williams welcomed the Prime Minister of England, Prince Philip, the Prince of Wales, two ex-Prime ministers, the French President, the President of Israel, the Pope, the head of the European Union Banks, the head of the Builderburg, the head of the Illuminati and a well-known businessman and billionaire.

All of the men went to their rooms and Agents Carter and Williams began their security sweep of the building, before heading to the CCTV command centre. It was almost two hours before the twenty-four men re-emerged from their rooms and made their way downstairs to have dinner.

They were all dressed in black silk robes, which had a compass and square ruler at the top, a cross in the middle and a skull and bone at the bottom. To Agent Williams' surprise, the numbers 322 and a swastika were also printed on the back of the robes; he had always thought of the swastika as something to do with Hitler and racism, so he was somewhat bewildered to see the President of Israel wearing the robe.

'I know what you're thinking Williams, but here it does not stand for what you think. Did you know the swastika was an African and Indian symbol of great power?'

'No sir, I didn't.'

'Of course you didn't. Its true meaning is known by very few, and all were and are extremely powerful people.'

One hour later, Agents Carter and Williams were summoned to a room. The words NOVUS ORDO SECLORUM were displayed above its two enormous doors, which looked as though they had been cut from a massive tree some seven hundred years old, at the least. Agent Carter spoke into his handheld mouthpiece. 'Congratulations Richards! You are finally in charge of operations, the young buck and I are entering the inner circle.' Agents Carter and Williams took off their ear pieces and radio equipment.

Once again Williams had to strip naked and Carter put a blindfold over his eyes and gagged his mouth with a rank tasting cloth. Carter then placed a thick cotton sack over his head. The sack smelt old and of sweat and blood, *'how many times has this sack been used?'* he thought. As if Carter could read his mind he said, 'Every man in this room you are about to enter and every member of Black Watch, have had these things in their mouths and over their heads. That goes right back to George Washington; even the Great Grandmaster, Albert Pike, wore these same things.'

Williams began to shake a little as he began to imagine what might be coming next and exactly what was going to take place, as part of his final initiation. Carter, seeing that Williams' body had stiffened, tried to comfort him.

'Don't worry, you've done all the hard stuff, physically and mentally. All you have to do now is trust the brotherhood and do what you are told. You are about to meet the Inspector Generals, then the whole inner circle and finally the Grandmaster.'

'Just have trust,' Williams kept saying to himself. The head butler knocked on the giant old doors with a wooden staff that had words carved into it in Aramaic, Hebrew and Latin. On the third knock, the doors seemed to open by themselves. Agent Carter positioned Williams and then told him to walk towards the heat. Williams did as he was told.

As he walked the heat grew more intense on his naked body. Williams was overcome with fear, but he controlled his mind and reminded himself that he was to trust his brother Carter and that trust was the only test left to complete. As he walked slowly towards the heat he began to sweat heavily; then a deep rough voice told him to stop and put his hands in the air. He did as he was told, trying to imagine his surroundings.

He must be close to a fireplace. His thoughts were interrupted by the deep rough voice, which told him to turn around six times and repeat the following words:

'My life is no longer my own; my soul is no longer my own; I give them of my own free will to the Prince of the Air.'

'Now turn six times in the opposite direction,' commanded the deep rough voice, 'and say it again.'

When Williams stopped turning, a hand pulled off the sack from his head and placed a knife into his hand. The voice told him to cut his left thumb, Williams obeyed, and as his thumb began to bleed, a cup was put under it and the blood dripped into the cup. Then it seemed as if from every corner of the room, heat began to touch Williams' naked body, and the room echoed to the voices of men speaking in a language that Williams had never heard. '*It must be the twenty-four men,*' Williams thought. He was given the cup that collected his dripping blood to hold... it felt a lot heavier than it should, if it contained just a few drops of his blood. The deep rough voice told him to drink every last drop in the cup.

He waited a moment to see if anyone would lift the cloth from his mouth, but no one did. He was not surprised, because he thought he could taste blood that had been soaked into the cloth... the blood of all the men that had gone before him. He did what he was told and began to drink. Whatever was in the cup tasted like more blood, but it was not all his own; he had not cut himself deeply enough to have provided all that blood.

'*So whose blood is it?*' he thought, and began to feel light headed. He was then told to fall backwards, being sure to keep his hands by his side. Thinking that he could trust his fellow brothers, Williams did as the deep rough voice told him to. As he fell back, he hoped someone would be there to grab him; but instead of hitting the floor, as he had feared, he felt as if he was floating on a cushion of hot air. *'How could this be? When was his head going to hit the floor and smash like an egg?'* he thought, waiting for the impact. Yet it never came, nor did anyone's hands stop him. What was going on? It was impossible to fall backwards for so long, but if he wasn't falling, what was he doing?

MAJOR STONE & WAR HAWK

Major Stone squinted his eyes slightly in order to get an absolute sure shot on the target, which was some two miles away. 'I can't believe this shit.'

'Well you better. Now hurry up and take the shot Major Stone, we don't have all day.'

'Umm, I don't mean to correct you Doc, but actually we do have all day.'

'Okay smartass, I stand corrected. Now would you please take the shot?'

'Okay Doc. Fire in the hole, as they say,' said Major Stone. He was inside War Hawk, a silver seamless craft in the shape of a rain drop; built into this smooth spacecraft was the gun turret. A bolt of plasma, the size of an apple, shot out at the speed of sound and smashed into a target that was a single brick wide, twelve bricks high and twenty foot in depth.

There were a hundred and twenty of them scattered around the open desert target range, covering over two hundred square miles of private and heavily guarded government land. Dr. Goodenberg squinted into the binoculars and smiled with joy, as he watched the concrete pillar explode and smash into millions of pieces.

'Well done Major Stone. Now I want you to take out the next three while heading due south at two steps down, please. Do you copy?'

'Roger that, Doc.'

Major Stone looked south and picked a point; as he did, the supercomputers moved War Hawk towards the spot Major Stone had mentally marked. All that was left for Major Stone to do, was to dictate the speed at which he was travelling. This was done by two foot pedals, similar to a car's throttle and brake. The only difference was that they were electronically operated and moved up and down in steps of one to ten; one up on the left pedal would slow the speed down, and one down on the right would quicken the speed. Two down was used for combat, which meant the craft moved at a speed of fifty miles per hour. Although this might seem like high speed in the world of humans, in the world of E.B.Es, fifty miles per hour was walking pace.

It had not taken Major Stone long to readjust; even though shooting at targets and flying the craft at just above low speeds, had taken him some time to conquer. It was flying by thought that was the most challenging. This involved looking at an area or just imagining it in the mind and then executing the go command; but as humans did not have the mental control that the E.B.Es did, sometimes this didn't work and War Hawk would move to the wrong destination. This was why there had been crashes in the past. This was also why reverse engineering was so important; the military had to find other ways to control the craft, but as the E.B.Es had given them the spacecraft with no other technical input, the military was forced to devise its own system of dealing with humanities inferior mental capacities.

Major Stone was one in a long line of men, who was hoped to have the mental ability to be able to use this technology. It was simply too sophisticated to be used in any other way, even though the military kept trying; and so their hopes were pinned on a man or men who could master their mind enough to fly the craft. Today, for the second week in a row, Major Stone hoped to travel without crashing at step five, which was at the speed of sound.

It was important to achieve this before the next meeting with the E.B.Es, as the general thought in the twilight zone was that the E.B.Es had given their human counterparts the spacecraft, because they believed that mankind would never have the brain matter to use it to its full potential.

Dr. Goodenberg was determined to prove them wrong and since he had become the head of project JAW.67 he had concentrated more on the reverse engineering, rather than on trying to fly the craft they had in their possession. War Hawk had taken twenty years or more of Dr. Goodenberg's life; it was the closest thing he had to a family. It was his child and it was ready for the first time.

He would be able to show the E.B.Es that mankind could use and build upon their technology. All he needed was a damn pilot, and he hoped that Major Stone could be that pilot. Dr. Goodenberg was sure that the E.B.Es had been testing the government throughout time; they had given inspiration to mankind through ideas and had revealed technology to those who sought it.

'Yes!' Dr. Goodenberg shouted, as he watched through the binoculars; Major Stone hit all three targets. 'By GOD I think you are the man, Major Stone.' Dr. Goodenberg smiled ear to ear. 'Okay, it's time for the big one... step five. Are you ready?'

'I was born ready Doc.'

'Okay, then take her up to the correct altitude and begin when you're ready.'

'See you on the other side of the world, Doc,' replied Major Stone, as he raised War Hawk to the upper edge of the atmosphere and began his manoeuvres. It seemed as if Major Stone had been born to fly War Hawk.

He and the craft moved as one, dancing around on the outer limits of the earth's atmosphere, touching the edges of deep space and somersaulting, twisting, and weaving in and out of space and the atmosphere, at the speed of sound. Major Stone was in heaven; it was for him the most exciting time of his life... a dream that could hardly be true, yet somehow was.

'Beautiful, just beautiful! What you are doing, it's amazing! I can't believe how you have advanced,' said Dr. Goodenberg, watching the telemetry on War Hawk as Major Stone put her through her manoeuvres.

'I feel like we are one Doc and I agree... she's beautiful.'

'It's like watching a butterfly dancing from flower to flower. I can't wait to watch it from the data coming in from War Hawk. There's one satellite that's still downloading but I have to say just from reading the telemetry, I know it's going to look spectacular... Hold on a minute... what the hell?' Major Stone did not need Dr. Goodenberg to say any more. He could see what Dr. Goodenberg was reacting to, with his own eyes. 'Good gosh Major Stone, what can you see out there?'

'Shit! Oh, shit!' Darkness engulfed War Hawk and Major Stone.

'Major Stone... Major Stone! Please answer me. What the hell is going on up there?' asked Dr. Goodenberg, whose happiness had suddenly turned into fear of the unknown.

AGENT SMITH AND THE PURSUIT OF KNOWLEDGE

'Hello, hello? Who am I speaking to? Umm... I'm sorry, let me start again. Hello? Are you still there?'

'Yes, I'm still here. Just calm down and tell me who you are and where you got this number from.'

Agent Smith could hardly contain himself... finally he was going to speak to someone who knew what the hell he had gotten himself into; maybe even someone who could lead him to the answers he sought. He took a deep breath and tried to regain his composure before starting to speak once again. 'My name is John Smith... my brother-in-law is...'

The man on the other end of the phone stopped Agent Smith saying, 'Say no more. I will be at the Grand Plaza Hotel in New York in two days time at midday. Wait for me in the lobby, and don't be late.'

'But how will I know who you are, or how will you know who I am?'

'When you enter the hotel, there will be a young girl who sells flowers. Buy a yellow rose and a pink tulip. Hold them in your left hand and take a seat facing the window.'

'Okay but how will I know who you are? Hello?' The line was dead. Agent Smith put down the phone, pausing for a moment while he contemplated the very brief conversation he had just had. He stepped out of the phone booth and as he did he could hear the sound of breaking glass and felt something like small stones hitting his shoulder. As he turned in the direction of what was hitting him, he saw sparks fly into the air; whatever was hitting the phone booths metal frame, was causing sparks to fly. Then it hit Agent Smith like a punch in the nose.

What he was looking at was the effect caused by flying bullets, but as he could not hear any gunfire, it was taking him more than the few seconds it normally takes him to react. Once all of this information had time to penetrate into his mind, he dove for the floor scrambling to his car; as the bullets rained down like rain drops in a monsoon. Agent Smith went into auto mode and fired indiscriminately into the air, trying to open his car door at the same time. He still could not see where the bullets were coming from; all he knew was they were close.

In fact, too close. As he threw himself into his car, the door window rained down on him as the bullets ripped into his door, missing him by centimetres. With the bullet-riddled door still open, he turned the key, and without looking over the steering wheel and out of the window, he floored the throttle and sped off. Glancing up over the steering wheel, he saw he was about to hit a parked car on the other side of the road. He pulled on the steering wheel violently to avoid the parked car, and in doing so almost turned his car over.

While Agent Smith was busy weaving his car left to right, it seemed to the men shooting that he had forgotten they were there; so they put a little more effort into reminding him of the fact, by squeezing the triggers on their semiautomatics just a bit quicker.

In no time at all Agent Smith stopped concentrating on parked cars and got back to the business of trying to avoid their flying bullets. By the time Agent Smith had turned onto the main road, with his pursuers on his tail, the sun was starting to rise and the sleepy little town was beginning to wake up; only to find that its once-safe leafy streets, were now the scene of a deadly pursuit. Shop windows smashed as the gunmen kept firing, while both cars sped around corners at ridiculous speeds.

Agent Smith had no idea of how he was going to lose these men, who seemed hell bent on killing him before breakfast.

'How did they find me again? I drove for five miles before making the call... who the hell are they?' he thought, as he drove at eighty miles an hour down a one-way street, onto a strange back alley. His heart rate was through the roof and his mind was moving faster than the car he was driving; his eyes almost popped out of his head every time

he came to a bend, stop sign, or junction. He was driving completely on instinct.

As he turned to avoid a rubbish collector, he hit the curb and bounced into a back garden. But he kept the pedal to the metal and kept driving, smashing into garden fence after garden fence, ripping through clotheslines and their entire contents of clothing; leaving a blinding trail of clothing on his windscreen. Finally, he managed to stick his arm out of the window and pull them halfway off; as he did, his attention was momentarily taken from watching where he was going and at the speeds he was driving at, that's all it took.

The next thing Agent Smith knew, was the car flipping onto its roof. He and the car slid upside down, smashing through the wide glass doors of a mini mall. By the time the car came to a complete stop, it had reached the escalators to the first floor.

Somewhat dazed and confused, Agent Smith climbed out of the car. He quickly grabbed his gun and ducked down by the side of the upside down car, awaiting the arrival of his unknown enemies who were chasing him; but as he waited he could hear the sounds of police sirens heading in his direction. Instead of hanging around, he headed up the staircase at the side of the escalators and by the time he reached the top, he could hear the police cars skidding to a halt at the entrance to the mall. Searching for the exit doors, he made his escape down a fire escape staircase, until he reached the door to the outside... it was padlocked.

Agent Smith had no choice but to shoot the padlock off, even though it would alert the police and maybe his killers to his location. With the padlock off, Agent Smith wasted no time in opening the door. As he did the alarm sounded and the light outside of the door flashed the location of the breach. Agent Smith was ordered to put down his weapon by the local police, but he paid them no mind as he looked for his next route of escape. When he saw it he went for it, running out the exit and across the open car park.

He attempted to run the hundred or so yards to an eight-story office building directly in front of him. He prayed to the LORD to help him, as the two officers attempted to shoot him down; it was as if the LORD had answered his prayer, because even though the bullets ricocheted off of the floor and smashed windows of the one or two parked cars next to Agent Smith, he was untouched. He burst through the swinging doors and a cleaner screamed as she saw Agent Smith pelting into the building, looking to her like a madman with a gun.

'Please don't kill me, I'm only the cleaner!' screamed the woman.

'Freeze! Don't move!' shouted the security guard at the front desk, who was quickly joined by his partner. Agent Smith looked at the two men and then looked outside to see where the two officers were; they were heading straight for him.

'Look, I'm an FBI agent... I don't have time to explain it to you right now, but it's a matter of National Security that I get to a computer.'

'I said, on your knees! Now!'

'I can't do that... just let me show you my badge.' Agent Smith looked once again to see where the two officers were and it was bad news; they were about to enter the building.

As Agent Smith went to put his left hand in his pocket, he lowered his gun to his waist without knowing it; it was now pointing straight at the security guards. The security guards thought Agent Smith was going to shoot and opened fire. Once again bullets flew everywhere and the glass windows shattered before falling to the floor like a waterfall. Agent Smith dove behind a marble pillar for cover, which began to spit marble shrapnel all over the place as the two security guards fired shots into the pillar; hoping one of the bullets would find its way into Agent Smith.

Agent Smith turned once more to see where the two police officers were and his heart jumped into his mouth as he turned around to see that they were taking aim at him from inside the doors. What was he going to do? If he did not shoot them, they were going to shoot him, but there was no way he wanted to be a cop killer. He turned and went to the other side of the pillar, just in time to see the two security guards take two bullets in the head and fall to the floor. *'What had happened? Were they stray bullets from the police?'* thought Agent Smith, as he looked around to see where the two officers were. They had just moved two steps into the building and were ordering Agent Smith to put down his weapon. Agent Smith wondered what to do, but told them that he could not put down his gun and that he was an FBI agent. There was no reply, so he looked around the pillar, and to his horror he saw the two officers on the floor, dead. Standing behind them were two men in suits, wearing dark glasses. They ordered Agent Smith to come out or they would kill him.

For the first time Agent Smith looked around where he was standing and noticed that the pillar he was standing by was next to a lift. He frantically pressed the buttons and tried to buy some time by asking them to wait just a minute to let him throw his gun out and also by asking them to promise that they would not kill him. When they did, he asked them how could he be sure.

Before they could answer, the lift doors opened and Agent Smith fired off two shots, before stepping into the lift and pressing the button for the top floor. By the time he arrived at the top floor, he could hear the sound of a helicopter circling the building. Agent Smith looked out the window and saw that the road below was full of police. The helicopter pilot saw Agent Smith in the window and ordered him to put down his weapons. Agent Smith shouted back that he had not killed anybody and that there were two men who were chasing him. The problem was, the two men had disappeared.

Agent Smith looked at the situation and began to realise that it was impossible for him to get away. Even if he could somehow escape, it would mean that he would be considered a cop killer and his own colleagues would hunt him down. Agent Smith fell to the floor and covered his face with his hands in despair.

Just then, Agent Smith felt like he had not felt for some time; a cold breeze rolled up and down his body and he felt a cold shiver down his spine. He jumped as he heard someone say, 'Well, well, it seems you have got yourself into a bit of a mess, Mr. Smith.' Agent Smith looked up to see the man who had called himself Death, standing before him. Agent Smith looked all around himself, then to the lift; the numbers above the doors showed the lift to be back on the ground floor and the exit door to the staircase was closed.

'How did you get here? Have you been following me all this time? Did you have something to do with the death of those men down there?'

The man called Death smiled. 'That's a lot of questions, but the question on your mind right now should be... how are you going to get out of here?' The man called Death walked to the window, looking out at the police and the helicopter in the sky. He then turned back to Agent Smith, who had his gun pointed at Mr Death. Mr Death smiled and put his hands in the air. 'What are you going to do, Mr Smith? Are you going to shoot me too?'

'You know I didn't shoot those men, but I swear if you don't tell me how you got up here and whether you shot them, I will shoot you.'

Mr Death put his hands by his side. 'I told you already Mr Smith, when we met in Rome; I believe I said that what you were getting into was going to cause you and your family a lot of trouble.'

Agent Smith frowned and bit his bottom lip. 'Are you here to warn me off? Who are you people? How will you be able to get passed the police down there? If you go near my family again I will kill you, do you understand me?'

'Mr Smith, I hear you loud and clear, but I'm afraid your threats have no meaning to me. I have no intention of hurting you or your family. When it is time for you to die, I will be there.'

Agent Smith moved aggressively towards Mr Death and put his gun to the side of his head. 'If you threaten me again, I will kill you right now... do you hear me?'

Mr Death smiled. 'I have not threatened you Mr Smith, I have merely told you a fact. My name is Death; why do you think that is? Or are you still looking at things through your worldly eyes? Do you think I use that name just to be scary?'

Agent Smith removed the gun from Mr Death's temple and slowly put it down by his side. Once again he felt a cold breeze wrap itself around his body, he shivered and felt the hairs on the back of his neck stand up; he looked around him, but could see nothing. Agent Smith turned back to face Mr Death, but was not prepared for what he saw; he dropped his gun as the shock flooded his body. Around Mr Death was not one, but several entities, just like the one that Agent Smith had seen at his house; the one that had shown him that the killers were on the other side of his bedroom door. They slowly moved around Mr Death's body, as if they were pet monkeys.

Agent Smith stared and filled his memory banks with as much detail as possible. They moved gracefully and had the slight colouration of the bubbles that children made by blowing soapy water through a bubble wand. It was as if he was watching water dancing in mid-air, but they weren't as dense as water. Agent Smith was amazed by what he could see. His mind could not cope with the reality that was before him; even though he could see it, he could not believe it. His mind bent and twisted as it tried to make sense of what his eyes were reporting to his brain.

'Close your eyes Mr Smith. I'm going to help you get out of this predicament you are in.'

'Why?' Agent Smith said, attempting to clear his mind. He coughed and shook his head before asking slowly and somewhat clumsily, 'Why would you help me? What am I to you?'

Mr Death laughed out loud; as he did, it seemed as though he had frightened the entities surrounding him and they darted away like frightened fish. Yet they returned almost instantly, as if realising there was no threat.

'Humans... you always assume everything is to do with you. I do this... I help you because it will make the MOST HIGH and JAW happy, and they will be pleased with me. For what you are about to do and discover, should be... I mean, must be told to the world. Now close your eyes.'

Agent Smith took one last look at the entities around Mr Death. He closed his eyes and then opened them saying 'Please wait one moment.' Agent Smith gazed at Mr Death, for this time he did not want to forget what he looked like. He then closed his eyes and heard the sound of great wind, but he felt nothing on his body. All of a sudden he felt as light as a feather and his whole mind and body seemed to be breaking down into atoms; his closed eyes were filled with a light brighter than the sun, before sinking into complete darkness.

Suddenly he opened his eyes to find himself sitting on a bench outside of the town's local train station. Agent Smith fell to his knees and wept uncontrollably, begging the MOST HIGH for forgiveness. He thanked them for saving him so that he could finish what he had started. He knew now, more than ever, that he would die before letting anything stop him from doing whatever it was he was meant to do.

It was six-forty-five am, and Agent Smith had booked himself on the six-fifty train to Arizona. He ran down the platform with only seconds to spare; the train was just beginning to leave the station. Agent Smith jumped on and made his way to the cabin's compartments. Finding his first class cabin, he entered, closed the door and blinds, and sat down and caught his breath. As he contemplated the past few days and months, he could not believe what had happened. If someone had told him this would be happening to him a year ago, he would never have believed it. Mr Death, the entities... 'Damn it!' he shouted, as he realised that once again, he could not recall the facial features of Mr Death. Still, at least he could remember the entities.

Then he realised that he had still not found out what was on the disk. Quickly, he felt his pocket to make sure it was still there; yes, it was safe. Now all he had to do was to get to a computer. Then he remembered that the man on the phone had told him not to look at it until he had met with him. Or had he? Agent Smith couldn't remember. What if the man was working for the people who were after him? Who were these people? His head began to spin, so he decided to rest and get some sleep. It would be some time before his meeting with the man, and he needed to regain his strength. With that last thought, Agent Smith fell fast asleep like a baby.

INSIDE MOBILE ONE

'I think we've just caught ourselves a fish.'

'What? Where?' asked the second agent inside Mobile One, swinging his chair over to the monitors by his colleague and looking at the data on the screen.

'He's used his credit card again. It seems that Agent Smith has had enough of our little sleepy town and is heading for the desert on a one-way ticket to Arizona. He's also removed two thousand in cash from an ATM.'

'Okay, let's wake up the team. This is Mobile One. Teams One and Two, get your asses in gear. Big Bird, be prepared for takeoff in twenty minutes. Over.'

'This is Big Bird. Dust off in twenty. Roger that. Over.'

'This is Mobile One requesting secure link. Over.'

'This is Pegasus ocean operator. What is your designator and call sign? Over.'

'Bravo, Echo, Delta, 1,9,6,7. Over.'

'Request received Mobile One. Enter code. Over.'

'Code received, awaiting verification. Verification complete. Secure link enabled Mobile One. Over.'

NATIONAL SECURITY AGENCY (NSA) COMMAND CENTRE

'Go ahead Mobile One, this is Special Agent Rodrigo.'

'Yeah sir, eyeball has resurfaced and is on his way to Arizona by train. I have Teams One and Two on standby, and Big Bird is ready for dust off in twenty.'

'What is the source?'

'He used his credit card to withdraw cash and paid for a ticket using his card.'

'How much cash?'

'Two thousand.'

'Now why would he want so much cash? Okay Mobile One, stand by for orders.'

'Received and standing by.'

Special Agent Rodrigo pressed the intercom and waited for a reply. 'Speak to me.'

'The target is back on the map and heading to Arizona by train. He also withdrew two thousand dollars. Mobile One is awaiting a green light.'

'Okay, the old man is away for the week, so let's have something for him by the time he gets back. Get the team on that train before it arrives in Arizona and quietly apprehend the target. Don't let him get away this time.'

'Received and understood sir. We'll get the bastard this time.'

Assistant Director Collins sat back in his chair and hoped that this time they would be able to get their hands on the elusive John Smith; who seemed to be more slippery than a fish. Special Agent Rodrigo stood at the command centre monitors and put on his headset.

'Okay everybody, listen up. Once again we are going to try and catch this one man, who keeps making us look like assholes. Let's not let him do it again. Now let's get busy.'

The officers in the command centre began to work frantically, looking at monitors, typing into keyboards and handing papers to one another.

'Okay Mobile One, you have a green light. Let's get this pain in the ass.'

'Received. Mobile One has the ball. Sat 1, I need a real-time imagery link to my position. Over.'

'This is Satellite Operator Call Sign Sat 1; received and understood. Patching real-time imagery to your location. Be advised, a storm and heavy clouds are heading your way in three hours. Over.'

'Understood Sat 1. Real-time imagery received and looking good. Over.'

'Roger that. This is team leader; all heads up and displays switch on. Over.'

'This is Big Bird. Headings and coordinates loaded on to com, good to go. Big Bird dusting off. Rendezvous with train in one hour ten minutes. Over.'

'Received Big Bird. Uploading headings and coordinates to Sat 1 now. Over.'

'Sat 1 received headings and coordinates. Longitude 10 Latitude 80, sending real-time keyhole visual imagery of train now. Over.'

'Received and crystal clear; all systems good. Over.'

'Sat 1 received, visual testing complete and confirmed good. Over.'

The two men in Mobile One watched the train as it scuttled along the track, heading for Arizona. All they could do now was to wait for Teams One and Two, inside of Big Bird, to reach the train on their monitors. 'It's going to be an hour before we start. I'm going to nap for an hour; wake me when they reach the train.'

'Yeah, well, I'm not going to run the operation while you sleep; so of course I'll wake you.' The two men sat back and while one tried to sleep the other watched the monitors and kept an eye on the storm that was heading their way.

Agent Smith was sleeping like a baby until he was woken by a knock at the door. He leapt up, gun at the ready, but his alarm turned out to be premature as it was the ticket collector, who needed to punch his ticket. After this, Agent Smith did not try to go back to sleep; he looked at his watch and saw that he had been sleeping for exactly one hour. His belly rumbled with hunger, so he decided to go and get a sandwich from the diner cart. As he did, the train began to slow as it pulled into a station. Agent Smith put his gun in its holster and headed for the diner.

Big Bird hovered above the train station and the eight-man team descended to the ground, via ropes, just minutes before the train began to pull into the station. Teams One and Two boarded the train at opposite ends, concealing their submachine guns under their long black leather trench coats. The two men in Mobile One and all those at the NSA command centre, watched the men board the train.

'Sat 1, this is Mobile One requesting thermal imagery. Over.'

'Sat 1 received. Beginning visual test. Thermal imagery maximum resolution, to your location now. Over.'

'Received. Thermal imagery good. Uploading wire frame drawings of train to you now Sat 1. Over.'

'Sat 1 has received wire frame drawings. Over.'

'Okay, according to the drawings the private cabins are situated at the front of the train. The eyeball is in cabin three, four, six, upper deck. Over.'

'Received. This is Sat 1, moving satellite into position over cabin 346, upper deck, and switching to thermal imagery now. Over.'

'This is Mobile One to all teams. Thermal imagery shows us nobody's home. Keep your eyes open; he is supposed to be in a private cabin in the first-class upper deck. He may have gone for food or for a walk, but you must not take him down in public. Wait until he returns to his cabin. Over.'

'This is team leader, deploying two men to upper deck first-class cabin 346. The rest of Teams One and Two will continue stealth recon of train. Eyeball must not be taken down in public. All teams acknowledge orders. Over.'

'This is team leader to Mobile One. All members received and understand orders. Over.'

'This is Mobile One, standing by.'

One hour passed and there had been no sight of Agent Smith; he had not gone back to the cabin. It was quite possible, on a train of this size, that they may have missed him. Special Agent Rodrigo banged the desk as he looked at the big screen in front of him.

'Where the hell is this shit? Okay, Mobile One. I want you to send one of the men outside of the cabin into it and see what you can find. The train is about to enter a very long tunnel and your team will be out of radio contact for forty-five minutes. I want to know what's in that cabin cause I've got a funny feeling.'

'Roger that. This is Mobile One. I need one man to enter the cabin and give me a full report on what is in there. We're going to lose radio contact for forty-five minutes, so get moving. Over.'

'Keep watch while I check out what's in here,' said Agent One.

Agent One entered the cabin and looked around, but there was nothing in there. 'This is Agent One... there is nothing to report. I repeat, the cabin is empty. Over.'

'Did you copy that, sir?'

Special Agent Rodrigo looked at the screens without answering the Mobile One operator.

'Did you copy what Agent One said, sir?'

'Yes I heard you, I'm thinking. Give me a minute. Okay, this is the plan: I want Teams One and Two to do a full sweep of the train again. I want Agents One and Two to keep out of sight but keep an eye on the cabin, and let me know as soon as you come out of the tunnel what's going on.'

'Roger that sir. You want Teams One and Two to re-sweep the train. Agents One and Two to remain in stealth mode and observe the cabin.'

'Mobile One, I want you to gather the data on all cash transactions, for train tickets, within half an hour of the ticket bought by eyeball using their credit card. Understood?'

'Yes sir, but it may take some time. There may be a lot of data.'

'Then you'd better stop wasting time talking to me and get on it.'

'Yes, sir.'

Assistant Director Collins, who was listening to the operation in his office, got onto the intercom and asked Special Agent Rodrigo to come to his office. 'What are you thinking?' asked Assistant Director Collins, sitting back in his leather reclining chair.

Special Agent Rodrigo stood and leant on the table with both hands in front of him, frowning. 'I think he's sold us a patsy.'

Assistant Director Collins clenched his fists. 'Fuck! If that is true then how are we going to know what train he is really on?'

'Well, he has removed two thousand in cash. I'm hoping he needed to get a train to the East Coast, as that's the furthest point from where he is and will cost the most. When Mobile One gathers all the data, we will be able to find out the prices of a ticket to the east and cross-check that with a train that left around the same time as or before the Arizona train.'

'Okay, get going.' Assistant Director Collins banged the desk, hoping that they might just catch him on the Arizona train.

Agent Smith had decided to eat his food in the baggage compartment. He had shown his badge to the baggage crews and made up a story that the FBI were running a test to see if it was possible for a man to hide on the train, without being found by their agents.

He told the baggage men that members of the FBI may be coming onto the train at the next station and if they were to see the agents they could not alert them to where he was, as that would interfere with National Security.

The men agreed not to say anything and Agent Smith ate his food in peace, but his legs had become cramped because he had been in there for so long. He thought it would be a good idea to survey the train for enemies; they wouldn't be hard to spot and if they had somehow found out what train he was on, by now they should be having second thoughts and starting to doubt whether he was on the train at all.

The train pulled out of the tunnel and the team leader immediately radioed Mobile One with a status report.

'Teams One and Two have not been able to locate eyeball sir, and it is impossible to find any link with the cash... there's just too much data. Too many people have used cash on all of the train routes, going in all directions.'

'Okay, how about surveillance footage?'

'We sent a team in, but the train police won't play ball, and we can't get a court order as this op is black sir.'

'Is there no Internet link usage with their surveillance system?'

'You're kidding. Their system is still in the Stone Age. They still use VCR's to record and none of the stations are connected to one another.'

'Shit. Okay, stand by.'

Special Agent Rodrigo went back to Assistant Director Collins' office to report, but unfortunately Assistant Director Collins had already heard the conversation. 'Get them off that fucking train and get their asses back to base immediately!' Collins shouted.

Special Agent Rodrigo, with only one foot in the door, immediately turned around and went back to the command centre.

'Big Bird, prepare for immediate evac. Teams One and Two, get your asses to the roof of the train and prepare for open parachute evac. Over.'

'Roger that. Okay you guys heard him, onto the roof. Get parachutes on your backs, we're going to fly off the train like butterflies in a seventy-mile-an-hour head wind.'

'Yee-ha! I love this shit! What a rush,' shouted one of the agents. The team began to make their way to the back of the train.

Agent Smith slowly walked back to his cabin, with no idea whether he was heading for a head-on collision with the bad guys; but he had to stop and use the toilet. '*All that time I was in a toilet and now my bladder decides it needs to release its load,*' he thought to himself, stepping into the bathroom.

Teams One and Two continued to make their way to the back of the train. The agent in front just caught sight of the back of a man entering into a toilet, and wondered for a second if he could be their man. But as he walked up to the door, a team member stopped him to tell him that his parachute pack was not closed properly; by the time they had fixed his parachute, the agent had forgotten about the man in the toilet.

Together the agents made their way to the back of the train and began to climb up onto the roof.

Agent Smith finished using the toilet and walked back to his cabin; keeping his eyes wide open for the first sign of any trouble, and was relieved that he didn't see any. He entered his cabin and sat down, hoping that he would be able to make it to his destination undiscovered. He placed his gun under his newspaper and sat back in the chair by the window; with the movement of the train gently rocking him, he soon dozed off to sleep again.

Meanwhile, Teams One and Two were on the train roof and had secured safety lines on the roof using suction pads, to keep them from flying off of the roof before they could pull their chutes; it would be one minute until they reached the designated area that had the correct clearance for such a manoeuvre. The operator in Mobile One was almost ready to give the command to deploy the chutes, when he noticed that the satellite thermal imagery was showing that somebody was now sitting in cabin three four six.

'Shit, abandon deploy! I repeat, abandon deploy and head for the cabin immediately. Target spotted on thermal imagery. Over.'

Teams One and Two used the safety lines to slide back to the end of the train; making their way as quickly as possible without drawing any attention to themselves.

Assistant Director Collins jumped up out of his chair, as he heard the operator announce that the target was showing on the thermal imagery. He ran into the command centre to watch it on the big screens and to take over the operation; he was not going to lose the son of a bitch this time, as it seemed that once again Agent Smith was in grasping reach.

Special Agent Rodrigo ordered the teams to secure the whole area of the upper deck and allow no one to enter or leave. He then gave the go-ahead to the team leader to breach the cabin door and stun Agent Smith with a non-lethal electrical charge. Assistant Director Collins then made it clear to all involved, that he was going to take direct control of the operation from here on; adding to the order that deadly force was only to be used if it looked as though the target might get away. As Agent Smith slept, blissfully unaware that Teams One and Two were about to kick down his cabin door, he began to snore as he fell deeper into sleep.

'This is team leader. We are in position and ready to breach door. Over.'

'Roger that, team leader. Thermal imagery shows target sitting by the window, dead ahead of you. You have green light... go, go, go! Over.'

The team leader pulled the pin on a flash bang grenade, that was used to disorient a target with a flash of light and a loud bang. Agent One kicked open the door and the team leader threw in the grenade; both men then stepped back and turned away from the door, so that the flash and bang would not affect them. Immediately after the grenade went off, they re-entered the cabin and the team leader was able to fire the darts into the stunned target.

All looked well at the command centre and Assistant Director Collins and Special Agent Rodrigo sighed with relief, as the thermal imagery showed the team leader and Agent One, standing over the target.

'Yes! We got the son of a bitch,' shouted Assistant Director Collins, thumping Special Agent Rodrigo on the back.

The storm that had been on its way had now arrived and communications, via Sat 1, were about to be lost.

The thermal imagery was the first to go, as all the screens showing it in the command centre snowed out. Mobile One then lost communication with the command centre, via Sat 1, but Assistant Director Collins wasn't too bothered; they had got their man and he knew Teams One and Two would bring him back to the command centre. Special Agent Rodrigo tried to confirm that all was well, but the eye of the storm had moved straight over the trains area and all links were temporarily down.

INSIDE THE SKULL & BONE MANSION

Williams felt a burning sensation across his eyes, it was as if the blindfold was burning; then the sensations became less, as if the blindfold had completely burned to nothing. He still couldn't work out what was happening to him, as he continued to fall backwards without hitting the floor. Deciding to see if the blindfold had in fact burnt away, he opened his eyes. He could not believe what he saw, but once he had closed his eyes and opened them again, he was forced to acknowledge that what he saw was real and began trying to make out the details. It was as if the room he had entered was actually a burning inferno, but he was sure that when they had stood outside of the room, it had been a room inside the mansion. Yet there was no way that what he was looking at could be inside of a building because there was nothing but fire; there were no walls, just a wall of fire.

He realised two things in that very moment. The first was that he was lying down but he did not know what he was lying on, because when he put his hands by his sides to push himself up into a sitting position, there was nothing underneath him. It was as if he was floating in midair, just as he had thought when he began to fall backwards.

The second thing he realised was even though he was in a room that seemed to be completely on fire, he himself was not burning; he wasn't even very hot. He was sweating but that seemed to make it more confusing because his sweaty state told him the fire was real; but that didn't make sense, because if it was real he should have melted like a stick of wax thrown into a fire.

'Arise,' said the deep rough voice.

'I can't. I already tried,' replied Agent Williams, somewhat confused and scared.

'Arise,' said the deep rough voice once more. Agent Williams tried to get up again and to his surprise this time he was able to stand, but he jumped as high as he could when he saw what he was standing on; it was fire, and as he landed he tried again to jump, until the deep rough voice told him to stand still and look up. Agent Williams was confused and disoriented; he looked up slowly and as his mind registered what was before him, he completely forgot the fire below him. His jaw dropped and his eyes widened until they seemed as though they might pop out of his head.

The twenty-four men were kneeling with their heads bowed and their robes covering their heads, and their robes seemed as if they were on fire but they did not seem to be bothered by this. It was not this that had Agent Williams' mouth opened as wide as possible, it was the beast sitting in an enormous golden chair right in front of him.

Its eyes were like fire and its nostrils breathed out fire and smoke. It had two straight horns, about twelve inches high, sticking out of the front of its head and two upward curving horns, about three feet high, sticking out of the left and right sides of its head.

Its horns looked as if they were made from diamonds and sapphires, and great flashes of coloured lights sparkled from them. Its face resembled that of a dragon and its neck was like the scales of a giant snake. Its body was of fire and smoke, but the fire and smoke had a form like that of a body builder on steroids. Out of its body protruded four fiery muscled arms and at the ends of each arms were four clawed hands, sharpened at the tips and razor sharp. The beast had two legs with clawed feet that were the same as the hands and horns.

The beast stood up from its great chair, it was about fifteen feet high from head to toe and then it opened its wings which were made of fire and smoke; they were twelve feet or two meters wide from tip to tip and hot molten ash fell from them.

Agent Williams vomited and collapsed to the fiery floor. The beast raised his lifeless body without touching him and while Agent Williams' body was suspended in mid-air, the beast revived him and made him stand. Agent Williams' whole body shook and fear such as he had never felt before filled his mind and heart; as the beast stood in front of him in its full splendour. The beast spoke to him, showing sharp diamond-like teeth: 'You have freely given your soul to your brotherhood, and your brotherhood has freely given it to me. For I own the brotherhood, and all that comes freely to the brotherhood comes freely to me,' said the deep, rough voice of the beast. Agent Williams was paralyzed to the spot in which he stood in sheer terror, and could not have spoken even if he had wanted to. He was so afraid that he lost control of his bladder; a small amount of steam rose as his urine hit the fiery floor.

Then from out of the beast's belly came six entities that looked like white smoke; they circled the beast before hovering in front of it. Then one entity rose into the air and flew straight at Agent Williams without warning, covering his entire face in a cloud of white smoke. This made Agent Williams cough and with every intake of breath the entity entered his body.

Once Agent Williams began to realise his body was being invaded by the entity, he tried holding his breath... but the entity seeped into his body through his eyes, ears, and nostrils, turning Agent Williams' eyes to a painful-looking bloodshot colour. As blood began to drip from his ears he screamed, 'GOD, help me!' But it was too late. He had given his life and soul freely to the brotherhood and the beast *was* the brotherhood. He screamed as the entity took up residence in his body and although he struggled to hold on to his mind, body and soul it was too late; Agent Williams was now truly a brother.

Only the twenty-four did not share that fate, for they served the beast willingly and were rewarded with great power on the earth. They were the wicked men of the world.

Agent Williams was now a full member of the brotherhood, but his life was never going to be his own again. He would now share his body with the entity and the entity would have 99 percent control over his body; yet the entity could not control Agent Williams' thoughts, but this did not matter to the entity, because it would still be able to control his body and make it do anything it wanted. Agent Williams screamed from within himself but the entity did not allow his mouth to scream and so no one but Agent Williams and the entity knew he was screaming. The entity made Agent Williams' body bow before the beast and the beast said, 'Rise, my son, and protect the twenty-four men;

make sure no harm can come to them, so that my plans on earth can be fulfilled.' Agent Williams rose and tried to stop the entity from walking out of the room but it was no use, he could not control his body's movements anymore; when he tried really hard to speak or go against the entity, the most that would happen would be that his nose would bleed. That was the only sign of the agonising and frantic fight Agent Williams was putting up within his body.

Agent Williams shut the doors behind him, and as he and Agent Carter stood on guard, they turned and looked at each other for a long time. As they did so, both of them got nosebleeds.

The beast sat back in his chair and the twenty-four men sat at a table that appeared out of nowhere. 'We need to make changes to the laws all around the world. The Antichrist is becoming self-aware and we need to be ready. I want you to begin to make the people of the world feel more insecure. I want more CCTV; I need to be able to see as much of this world as possible,' said the beast.

'Yes, our Lord.'

'Why is it taking so long to bring the whole of the world into chaos? Have I not given you the powers of the supernatural world and of the demonic angels?'

'Yes Lord, but the powers of the MOST HIGH and of the Angelic angels are everywhere, and although against man your powers can work wonders, against the MOST HIGH'S powers they have no effect whatsoever. It would seem that they are keeping us from completing our work, because he is growing. We have tried to kill him a thousand times from his birth; we even made his mother birth him prematurely. Every time we try to kill him, his angels kill thousands of our soldiers in return; in this world and in your realm. We have had to pretend that most of the dead soldiers in our world have died in wars overseas, and so we will not try to kill him again.'

'My Lord. We are having success in poisoning the air, waters and soil. We are cutting down the rain forests as quickly as possible; almost all of Africa has been deforested. The polar caps are starting to melt faster and the currents of warm and cold air around the world's oceans are changing. As you know, we have even had success in creating a hole in the ozone layer; many did not believe we would be able to do that, but with your guidance and power we have been able to do it. Our scientists say that in ten more years, we will be past the point of no return.'

'Yes Lord. We are also selling more guns and weapons of mass destruction worldwide than ever before and more people are dying. We are able to starve millions while we supply them with guns and tell them that they should kill in order to gain the wealth of the land; and while they kill one another, we take over the land and its wealth.'

'Yes Lord. We have control of all the natural fuel supplies and are pumping it out of the earth more quickly than ever. Those countries that do not allow us to get our hands on their natural fuels, are plummeted into civil war through our work; we assassinate their popular leaders and replace them with brutal dictators of our own choosing. Things are looking good, even though we have not yet gotten to the level you desire. Believe us Lord, the world has never been so bad, not even in the times of Noah. Please, do not be angry with us.'

'Yes Lord. The people of the world are kept under control by subliminal messages in their TV programming. We feed the desires of their flesh and of their carnal minds, with big dreams of all the material things of this world and in the meantime we take the world right from under their noses. They are all too busy trying to be the next
Millionaire, to really care what's happening to the planet they live on.

'They're so stupid, they don't even realise that if they ever did become millionaires, they soon won't have a planet to spend it on anyway. And as for those with a little more soul, the religions you created a long time ago are still sucking them in like lambs to the slaughter; our only real problem is him Lord.'

'I need you to step up the terrorist training and start preparing them for something big. Give them a name that will be remembered and a leader you can never catch,' said the Beast.

'Yes Lord. The terrorist groups we formed from the earlier part of this century are still going strong, and we have been able to find and control all of those in the world who wish to cause us harm. There are very few extremists left in the world that we do not know about or who do not have a terrorist organisation to join.'

'The people of the world are so stupid Lord; they have never worked out why they are the ones who die when a so-called terrorist organisation strikes and never us, the leaders of the world.'

'No. I want a new organisation, something that can bring all of the extremist groups under one main body; so that we can centralise the entire terrorist groups activities.'

'Yes Lord, but what if they won't join this new organisation?'

'Kill every member that doesn't join you. We'll tell the world that they are the real terrorists. Kill many innocent people in your part of the world and blame it on those in the other parts of the world, who have not bowed to my ways. Go into the parts of the world that have not bowed to my wishes and destroy them all. It's time we used terrorism against our deadly enemy, to gain access to those parts of the world that have natural fuel resources we have not been able to get our hands on.'

'Yes, our Lord,' replied the twenty-four men, as they stood up from the table and knelt in front of the beast. Then without warning the beast, the great chair that the beast sat on, the table and chairs that the twenty-four men sat on and the fire that had engulfed the room, were gone. The twenty-four men then left the room, via a door that led into a candlelit room.

The mansion floor was covered in words written in goat's blood. There was a goat tied to an altar and its throat had been cut. The blood trickled down a groove in the altar to a golden bowl and the blood in the bowl had been used to write the words on the floor.

The twenty-four men in black silk hooded robes, stood in a circle with their heads bowed. They spoke in an ancient language, summoning the beings of another dimension to come forth and to let them see and know what they knew. The room was filled with burning candles and incense filled the air. Suddenly there was a rush of air and all the candles went out. The room was filled with the sound of rushing wind and then the room became completely pitch black. Still talking in the ancient language, the men tried to keep their footing as their black hooded robes flapped violently in the swirling wind.

Candlestick holders began to fly through the air, smashing into the walls. The golden bowl was hurled into a wall and the blood inside of it splashed violently all over the room; the men were covered in goat's blood, but kept talking as if nothing was happening. The goat, with its throat cut, began to rise into the air; from the altar, it moved into the middle of the circle of men and exploded into pieces. The men were covered in bits of blood and guts from the goat, and once again they acted as if nothing had happened and kept talking in the ancient language.

Then, as suddenly as it had started, the wind stopped and all of the candles that remained standing in their candelabra relit themselves. The room began to reappear from out of the darkness and as it did, in the middle of the men a force became visible; it was see-through, like a mass of air. For the first time, the twenty-four men stopped chanting in the ancient language, staring at the force from another dimension. The men then linked arms and one of the men spoke to the mass of air in the ancient language.

'Oh great force from the spiritual dimension, tell us what we need to know and let us see what we need to see; for it is written that your knowledge is for those who seek it and your wisdom is for those who know how to possess it. We know there is only one ruling force and that they are THE MOST HIGH. We know that all living things are under them and belong to them. We know all may call upon the forces of the universe by knowing the word. Enter us now and reveal to us that which we seek.'

The unseen force rose almost to the ceiling of the room, some twenty feet high, and began to glow brighter and brighter. Soon it was so bright that the men had to cover their eyes and bow their heads. They began to sweat as the room got hotter and the candles melted and withered to nothing. Then the force exploded into twenty-four pieces, flying at great speed into each of the men and the men were thrown to the floor. This was then followed by the sound of rushing wind leaving the room, until it was dead silent.

Taking a deep breath, the Grandmaster asked, 'Is everyone okay?' They all answered yes, although they were clearly somewhat dazed. They removed their robes and then four at a time, they went into a shower room at the side of the room and washed themselves; glancing into the mirrors on the wall to make sure they were completely clean. When they had all cleaned themselves, they walked down a long corridor and entered a room.

They sat at the old oak table, and servants brought in tea and coffee and light refreshments for them. They ate and drank without speaking.

When all of the servants had left the room, they began to write on notepads on the table. Some moments later they all finished and then passed the notepads to the Grandmaster.

After reading each notepad, the Grandmaster stood up and spoke. 'Agent Smith will be meeting with the priest in New York, in two days. He has the disk, but he still does not know what is on it. We must take appropriate action to rid ourselves of these men once and for all, and bury these things forever.'

AGENT SMITH'S CABIN.

Agent Smith woke suddenly to the sound of a bang at his door. He grabbed for his gun, but it dropped from his hand as his cabin door began to open. *'How could they have found me? Who are these people?'* thought Agent Smith, grabbing for his gun blindly as he stared at the cabin door. It was too late; the newspaper used to conceal the gun was now getting in the way. The door was half open, and Agent Smith decided that instead of trying to grab his gun, he had better try to stop the door from opening any further. He bolted for the door like an Olympic sprinter off of the blocks, in the one hundred meter dash.

NSA COMMAND CENTRE

Assistant Director Collins and Special Agent Rodrigo watched the screens as the rest of the staff worked frantically to regain communications with Sat 1, Mobile One, and Teams One and Two.

'Damn it, I need confirmation! Get these links up and running as soon as possible,' shouted Special Agent Rodrigo.

'Don't worry, think positive. I'm sure we got our man,' said Assistant Director Collins. Just then a young, slim and pretty lady, came running up to Assistant Director Collins and whispered something in his ear; he immediately turned and headed for his office. As he went, he told Special Agent Rodrigo that he had to take an important phone call, but that Special Agent Rodrigo was to let him know as soon as all links were back online.

Assistant Director Collins entered his office, taking a deep breath and composing himself before picking up the phone.

'Hello sir, I hope your time away has been enjoyable; we have everything under control. You'll be glad to know we have apprehended the target and should be getting confirmation any minute now.'

'I doubt that very much, and I do not have time to waste. Get your men to New York as soon as possible.'

'I assure you sir... I know the target has been very slippery up until now, but we have watched his capture via sat link.'

'Whether that is the case or not, I still need your men in New York to apprehend an accomplice. Be there within twenty-four hours, at the Grand Plaza Hotel; the meeting is in two days. We will use the target to lead us to this accomplice, is that understood?'

'Yes sir, but what if my men have already caught the target?'

'Get your men to New York and stop wasting my time with irrelevant questions.'

Assistant Director Collins put down the phone and poured himself a glass of whiskey. The screens blacked out, then lit back up with the pictures of thermal imagery.

'This is Sat 1. We are back online. Do you receive, command centre? Over.'

'This is Special Agent Rodrigo, receiving loud and clear Sat 1. Thermal imagery is back online and is clear. Mobile One, do you copy? Over.'

'This is Mobile One. Receiving you loud and clear, command centre. Over.'

'Sat 1, thermal imagery is back online. Do you

copy? Over.'

'This is Sat 1. Receiving you, Mobile One. All links are good. Over.'

'Mobile One, this is Special Agent Rodrigo. What is the status of Teams One and Two?'

'We are trying to regain link now sir. Give us a minute and we should have communications back online with Teams One and Two.'

'This is team leader... can you hear me? Over.'

'This is Mobile One. Yes I can hear you. Can you hear me? Over.'

'Yes Mobile One, receiving you. Over.'

'What's the status on the target, team leader? Over.'

'Bad news sir... It's not the target. Over.' Team leader bowed his head and waited for the abuse to start.

'Say again, team leader? Over.'

'It is not the target. It's some young man in his early twenties who decided to sneak into one of the first-class cabins. I think he has gotten more than he bargained for sir. What are our orders? Over.'

Special Agent Rodrigo put his hands on his head and screamed. 'Stand by, team leader.'

The operators in Mobile One looked at each other in disbelief.

Special Agent Rodrigo walked along the hallway to Assistant Director Collins' office, knocked the door and entered. 'Did you hear all of that sir?'

'No, I did not. This little shit is really starting to do my head in. The old man was just on the phone and we have new orders. Get your team to New York pronto and have full surveillance of the Plaza Hotel... I'm sorry, I mean the Grand Plaza Hotel. We will be able to pick up the target there, along with another target. I'm guessing that wasn't the target on the train then?'

'Yes sir... I mean no sir, it wasn't.'

'Close the door on your way out, and do not disturb me until everything is ready in New York.'

'Yes sir.' said Special Agent Rodrigo, his head and shoulders drooping forward. He went back to the command centre and relayed the new orders to his team.

Agent Smith apologised for the second time to the member of the refreshments staff, who had brought Agent Smith's complimentary first-class light refreshments. This consisted of a bowl of soup, two slices of bread and butter, a chocolate mousse and an apple and banana; all of which were now all over the poor young man delivering it.

Agent Smith explained that he had not heard the young man's first three knocks and must have just heard the last one, which made him jump to his feet; and that he had tripped over his bag and slammed the door in the young man's face. The young man was clearly upset, but as he was dealing with a first-class passenger, he thought better of saying what he really thought.

Gritting his teeth he asked Agent Smith if he would like a replacement. Agent Smith quickly refused and closed the door; he was somewhat embarrassed, but mostly relieved. He knew that if it had not been the young man, it would have been his life that he would have lost, not his pride.

He picked up his gun and put it in his holster. Looking at the time, he decided to go to the diner and get a stiff drink to calm his nerves. As he walked, he felt his inside pocket for the disk; there it was, safe and sound. Then he tried to remember what flowers he was supposed to buy... '*one red rose and one yellow tulip, I'm sure that's it*,' he thought, rocking from side to side with the movement of the train. He glanced carefully at every person he passed, trying to spot if they were overly interested in him; but he felt in his gut that he was safe for now. It was seven-forty in the evening and he was sure that if they knew where he was, they would have made their move by now. Finally he made it to the bar and asked the bartender for a large whiskey, which he drank as if it was the last drink he was ever going to have; then he ordered another one.

MAJOR STONE & THE EXTRATERRESTRIAL BIOLOGICAL ENTITIES

Major Stone stared into the darkness. Although he was constantly attempting to reach Dr. Goodenberg via the radio, it was of no use; wherever he was, there was no way of communicating with the Professor. He checked the systems on War Hawk... they were still fully operational.

He switched the searchlights on, but although the beam of light swept into the darkness until it could not penetrate the dark anymore, it showed nothing of the place in which he was in. Major Stone began to take readings of the atmosphere outside of War Hawk such as Density, psi, temperatures, radiation, Uranium, Plutonium, toxic chemicals and most importantly oxygen levels. The radar readings showed him that he was on solid ground, not on or in water, and the atmosphere readings suggested that he was in an atmosphere similar to that on earth.

Major Stone charged up his weapons. Switching to thermal viewing, he began to search his environment for any heat sources which might give away the position of the capturers, that he believed were observing him. There was no sight of any heat anywhere, so he switched to echo location radars; those too showed nothing. He tried sonar, but the result was the same. 'This cannot be, how big is this place? I can't even get a reading of the size. None of the radars are coming back, that means they are not bouncing off of any walls; which means the surroundings of this place are so far away the sound waves don't ever reach them,' thought Major Stone.

Major Stone could not think straight, nothing was making sense. All he knew, was that he was somewhere in space in what he believed to be a spacecraft and from what his readings were telling him, it was a gigantic spacecraft. 'What should I do? Come on, think,' he thought to himself. He switched to outside communications and spoke into his microphone. 'Hello, is there anyone there? Do you understand English?'

'What the fuck am I doing? As if they are going to speak to me,' he thought.

Two hours passed and Major Stone had not done anything else, since speaking into the darkness; instead, he waited for the enemy to come to him. Whatever it was they wanted, he was not going to be a lab rat for them. So he closed his eyes and pretended to sleep, although he was not that convincing because every five minutes or so he would open his eyes to see what was happening in the pitch-black darkness that surrounded him.

The answer was a frustrating 'nothing.' Then what seemed to be some sort of force field window began to open, about four hundred meters in front of War Hawk. The view was of space and the earth, which glowed bright blue like a circular neon light; it looked beautiful but was quickly getting smaller. Using War Hawk's massive computers and laser beam systems, Major Stone used the ever-vanishing earth to work out what speed the craft was flying at. To his surprise, he found that the spacecraft was flying at over five thousand miles per hour.

As it whizzed past the moon, to Major Stone's Astonishment it was joined by six other crafts; they caught up to the craft he was on in a matter of seconds and then they maintained their speed and distance just behind the spacecraft he was on. This allowed Major Stone the unbelievable and mind-blowing chance to observe the crafts in great detail. They looked like lights, changing colours from blue to yellow-white to red; as they approached the craft he was captured upon, at great speed.

As they approached Major Stone took readings of the speed the crafts were travelling at. They were travelling at a mind-boggling nine thousand miles per hour and as they reached within a hundred feet of the spacecraft, they immediately slowed to five thousand miles per hour. As they slowed down, they suddenly took on definite forms, except for one that remained a yellow-white orb.

Major Stone took out a pencil and note pad from his space suit. Removing his somewhat cumbersome gloves, he made quick sketches on his pad for personal recollection, while War Hawk's digital scanners took more in depth pictures and readings.

The first craft he sketched looked like a typical flying saucer. The second, which was shaped like a cigar, was silver in colour and the top and bottom halves each rotated by turn. The third was triangular in shape, but there was nothing connecting the bottom part of the triangle; its lower section was black, and the rest of it was a light blue silver in colour. The fourth was diamond-shaped; its metallic bottom half kept spinning at great speed, while the glass-like top half did not spin. The fifth was a boomerang shape and was gold and silver in colour. Lastly, the sixth was the orb with a yellow-and-white glow all around it. None of the crafts had visible windows or doors, and Major Stone could see no jets or propellers, nor were there any vapour trails; a fact which Major Stone found particularly hard to comprehend, as the crafts were flying at such fast speeds.

Suddenly all seven crafts leapt into hyper speed, which War Hawk had no ability to read. Then the six crafts that he could see so clearly just seconds ago, appeared to be no more than coloured lights.

Major Stone had remained calm throughout this earth-shattering experience, but his heart missed a beat when he looked for the big blue earth and found that he could no longer see it anywhere. The craft then slowed back down and took on a definite form once more. Major Stone forgot to breathe when he saw in front of him a spaceship the size of America and getting closer and closer.

He gasped for air and began to hyperventilate. But the suit he was wearing was designed to pick up on such events and mixed the level of air he was breathing to slow down his heart rate and make him breathe more deeply and slowly. Major Stone regained his composure and shouted, 'No, please don't!' Then as the force field's window closed, he was once again plunged into darkness.

One hour had passed and Major Stone began to cry, though he did not understand why. Was it frustration? He had been trained for most things, but this was beyond anything he could have ever conceptualized. His mind seemed to go from composure to extreme fits of panic and then back to composure again. His breathing and heart rate were just as erratic, and he was also slipping in and out of consciousness.

Then out of the darkness came a brilliant light that blinded him and then disappeared immediately. Major Stone did his best to pull himself together and as he did a second burst of brilliant light came rushing into the darkness; this time it remained. Major Stone needed several minutes to re-adjust his eyesight to the near-blinding light that now filled War Hawk and the spacecraft.

As his eyes adjusted, three blurry images began to take form in his sight; eventually resolving into three black shapes, tall and slender. As he regained more focus, he could make out the shape of their heads, which resembled those of a praying mantis, and their long slim arms, bodies and legs. It seemed as if they wore no clothes, but he could not be certain; then his eyes finally became fully adjusted and his mind screamed in terror. They were like humans, but at the same time they were inconceivably different.

Their heads had the shape like that of a praying mantis, but their features resembled those of humans. They had two eyes in the same place as human eyes, although theirs were large and black with no visible pupils. Their noses were in the same place as humans but they did not stick out, they were more like holes in the head. They had mouths in the same place as humans and had two arms and two hands, two legs and two feet.

Their skin was blue-green in colour and the texture was like that of a dolphin's skin. Major Stone did not bother to try and count their fingers and toes, as his mind was too busy dealing with the overwhelming feeling of being in some sort of hallucination or a delusional state of mind; it was so, so, surreal. All that he had read and learnt about E.B.Es while at Area 51, had not prepared him for what was now in front of him; the unequivocal proof that man is not alone in the universe. With that thought, Major Stone passed out.

AGENT SMITH AND THE PRIEST

Mobile One took up its position in the hotel underground car park; having linked itself illegally into the hotel surveillance system. Teams One and Two were on rotating shifts and were covering all entrances and exits, while Team Leader and Agent One took turns observing the lobby and lift areas. Sat 1 was providing phone-tapping capabilities and multi-linking of digital and audio feeds to all involved in the operation, and Big Bird was providing aerial support. Operator One in Mobile One made a phone call to the Metro Police pretending to be a Federal Marshal and asked all CCTV camera operators to be on the lookout for the man whose picture he was about to send them. If they spotted him, they were not to arrest him; instead, they were to call the number on the bottom of the photo immediately.

As usual, Assistant Director Collins and Special Agent Rodrigo watched and listened from the command centre. They were a little more on edge than normal because they expected Director Forbes and the head of the CIA, Director Johnson, to be joining them shortly. Normally this would not have been a big deal, but Agent Smith had so far made them all look stupid and incompetent.

Agent Smith had to find out what the status was concerning himself; did the police suspect him of the murder of two officers and two security guards? Was this why he had made it to New York without interference? Were they waiting for him at the hotel, as they had been at the hospital and when he made the phone call from the phone booth? Paranoia gripped Agent Smith as the train pulled into the station. Would they be waiting there on the platform, or were they just going to let the local cops arrest him? Or worse, would his own people from the Bureau do it?

Agent Smith did not know what to do. Should he get off the train or stay on the train? Phone his contact... no, phone the Bureau? It was easy to organise and plan whilst on the train but now that he had reached the station, actually carrying out that plan was so much harder; because paranoia was getting the better of him. *'Shit, what should I do? Oh come on John, we haven't come this far to stop now. Anyway, I'm sure Mr Death is out there watching and he'll help me if things get sticky, as he wants to impress the MOST HIGH and JAW, whoever JAW is,'* he thought. As he thought he felt less afraid, remembering what had happened at the offices. *'Nothing is going to stop me; I'm on a higher calling. Let's go,'* he thought.

He decided to phone his boss and long time friend Mike; if there was anyone he could trust to be straight, it was Mike, but it was risky. If Mike has been made to believe that Agent Smith had killed those two officers, their friendship would mean nothing. In that case, Mike would do everything in his power to get him, even if it meant using their friendship. Agent Smith knew he had to be really careful.

He now truly believed that the people who were after him were government agents of some kind... dirty to the core but nevertheless, still government... so they would be listening and watching all possible links to him. Agent Smith walked off the train and headed for the phones at the end of the platform.

He picked up the phone and began to dial, but hesitated before pressing the final number. He knew that if they didn't already know where he was, then they would as soon as he made this call... but he had to. *'I've Got to find out what the enemy is up to. Keep it short and sweet, listen out for any telltale signs that Mike thinks you're a cop killer,'* he thought, as he looked at his watch to mark the time that the call was answered. He pressed the last number and the phone on the other end began to ring; a woman answered.

'Federal Bureau of Investigations how may I help you?' said the operator.

'Patch me through to extension 355-187.'

'Hold the line please, while I put you through.' Agent Smith looked up as he heard a helicopter overhead and then he immediately looked all around him; his heart began to speed up and his mouth felt dry. 'Come on, hurry up Mike. Where the hell are you?' he said down the phone as he looked at his watch.

'Hello, how can I help you?'

'Well, that is what I'm trying to find out.'

'You know, I wondered if you'd call. If you hadn't I would have started to believe the rumours going around about you.'

'I don't know if I can explain, and even if I did, I don't know if you'd believe me anyway.'

'Look, this line is not secure, and I don't want to be involved in this... but your sister called me the other day and asked me if you were okay. I told her yes, as far as I knew.'

'Okay, I'm sorry to have bothered you. I thought you were an old friend. Thanks for telling my sister I was okay; I'll give her a call when she gets in from work around five. Like I said, sorry to have bothered you.'

'We were friends once, but from what I hear that friend died a long time ago. It's out of honour for that old friend that I'm going to give you a head start before I come looking for you.'

'You say that like you've already found me guilty.'

'If you're innocent then come in, we'll treat you like one of our own... but if you keep on running, what do you expect me to think?'

'Sometimes Mike, it's not that easy. I wish you would trust me.'

'How can I trust you when you haven't trusted me? What the hell is going on John? You haven't been yourself for some time now... everybody has noticed. Now the NSA and the CIA are saying this is all to do with spying. They say you've been selling secrets to our enemies for years and you killed two agents at your home. Do you have any idea how long I've been trying to get a hold of you to try and help you? So don't talk to me about old friends, because that is bullshit.'

'I'm sorry Mike, I know how it looks.' Agent Smith put down the phone, his worst fears realised; they were blaming him for the killings of the two cops and two security guards. *'Of course they would, they had to ruin my credibility just in case I make it to the finish line... textbook CIA,'* thought Agent Smith, who was starting to get a clearer picture of who he was dealing with.

It was twenty-five minutes to twelve, and Agent Smith had a ten-minute walk ahead of him. He looked up to the sky, and under his breath he asked the LORD to be with him and somehow provide a way out of the situation he was about to enter into.

He could see the Grand Plaza Hotel dead ahead; although he was sure that by now he was under surveillance, he kept walking towards the hotel. Drivers impatiently beeped their horns at the cars in front them, as the streets were almost at a gridlock. Agent Smith dodged in and out of the slow-moving traffic, half expecting a black van to pull up beside him and hijack him. As he reached the kerb, this time he dodged in and out between the slow-moving pedestrians, who were almost at a standstill; and again, he half expected a gunman to jump out of the crowd and shoot him in the back.

He entered the hotel and although he pushed the rotating door as hard as he could it seemed to move sluggishly and his shoes sounded like a tap dancer's shoes as he danced his way through the crowd; which seemed to be moving in every direction but the one he was going in.

It was five minutes to twelve, according to the grand clock face that was set in marble above the enormous, polished reception desk. Agent Smith looked to his left and saw the seats by the window, graciously flower-embroidered in a material that looked like silk; these were the type of chairs and seats you could sleep in for a week, without getting uncomfortable. This was definitely the high end of the hotel business, but where was the flower shop? After a second or two, Agent Smith saw it to his left and made his way there.

He bought one yellow rose and one pink tulip. As he paid for the flowers, the woman at the stand gave him back his change and at the same time put a note on the inside of the two one-dollar bills she had given to him. Agent Smith took his change and the note and sat down facing the window; he checked his surroundings for possible hidden cameras and microphones, but then soon realised that the contact had not picked this position lightly. It was impossible to plant any devices that would be useful as it was an open area; no lights above just a stained glass roof that blended into the marble ceiling. The only way anyone could see the note that he had, would be to sit down next to him or stand behind him. He put the note in his hand and picked up a newspaper from on top of the table in front of him. He pretended to read the newspaper while he read the note. It said:

'The enemy is close and is watching you right now. But don't worry, they will want to see if you will lead them to anyone else. If my employers are involved in this, and I believe that they are, they will not make their move until we are both together, and they will want to get the other two priests as well. We must use this to our advantage, for it is our only chance of escape.'

Agent Smith felt as if someone was looking over his shoulder. Nervously, he put the note under the next page and pretended to read the newspaper. He looked around to see if anyone was there, there was no one; so he began to read the note once more.

Assistant Director Collins and Special Agent Rodrigo had been joined by their boss, Director Forbes, and the head of the CIA, Director Johnson. They watched the screens intently, which were showing the hotel lobby's security cameras' view of Agent Smith, sitting down next to the window and reading a newspaper.

'Team Leader, get closer and give me a visual via your coat button cam. I want to make sure it is a newspaper he is reading and if it's not, I want to know what it is and what it says. Over.' ordered Special Agent Rodrigo.

The Team Leader put his hand to his mouth, as if he was coughing, and spoke into the handheld mouthpiece. 'Roger that. On the move. Over.'

The Mobile One operator had to adjust the

frequencies on one of the machines inside of Mobile One, in order to get a clear picture from the Team Leader's button camera; as he negotiated the crowd of Japanese tourists who had just come into the hotel. This cost him crucial time, but he eventually made it to the back of the chair in which Agent Smith was sitting. The picture was not that good, but it showed Agent Smith reading the paper, with no sign of any note or anything else unusual.

'Okay, back off. I want all teams to move into lock down positions now. Copy.' ordered Special Agent Rodrigo. The Team Leader moved back to his position, while all the other members of Teams One and Two moved into lockdown mode. They took the safety catches off of their 9 millimetre hand guns, put their fingers on the triggers and waited for the next command, while covering their exit and entry points.

'Remember, I do not want anyone to make a move before the eyeball has rendezvoused with the other target or targets. Is that understood?' asked Director Forbes.

'Roger that sir. No one is to make a move without your say-so. Over.'

'Where is this asshole?' said Director Forbes, speaking off-air to the men in the command centre.

'Be patient, he'll be there. He needs what Agent Smith's got, just as much as we need him; besides, Agent Smith has nowhere left to go. From listening to the phone call we just intercepted via Sat 1... my team have done their job... it seems that not even his old friend and work colleagues at the FBI believe in him. It sounds very much like they believe he's a cop killer and a traitor. This guy is starting to lose the plot; he was on the phone way too long. Everybody will know where he is now, and we have the surveillance tapes from the offices. No guns were found on the scene and all witnesses to the murders are dead... so like I said, he's got nowhere to go but jail or death,' replied Director Johnson.

Suddenly Agent Smith received a phone call; it was the man he was supposed to be meeting. Sat 1 intercepted the call so that everyone could listen in.

'It's me, the priest... Listen... don't say anything, just listen. We don't have much time. I need you to take the elevator to the sixteenth floor and head to room 1002. I won't be in there, so once you get inside just wait for twenty minutes and then put the disk in the envelope that I have left in the room. Then call for room service and ask them to come up immediately and collect a package for the front desk. If I think it's safe... or, should I say, when I think it's safe... I will come and get the package, and then I will call you and tell you what to do next.

'I'm sorry to mess you about like this, but it is in both of our best interests to play it as cagey as possible. Anyway, I'm sure a man from the FBI is used to this sort of stuff.' Agent Smith put down the phone without saying one word and got up and headed for the elevator.

'Okay Team Leader, he's on the move. Plant the tracking device on him,' ordered Special Agent Rodrigo.

'Roger that. Moving into position now. Over.'

'Okay, we've got twenty minutes before we can intercept this disk and change it for a fake one with a tracking device in it. I want a man on that front desk in ten minutes; use your Federal Marshal badges. Mobile One, make a call to the hotel, speak to the manager and tell them we have a fugitive inside the hotel and we need to put a man of ours on the front desk; then intercept all calls from room 1002. I don't want any calls of his making it to the front desk. Hold on one moment... ' said Special Agent Rodrigo as he turned to Director Forbes. 'Sir, do I have permission to stand the men outside the exit doors, in order to make this guy feel safe? I don't want any of our men to spook him.' Director Forbes turned to Director Johnson and they discussed the situation with one another; then Director Forbes turned back to Special Agent Rodrigo and said,

'Okay stand them down, but make sure the tracker is in the fake disk. We have to find out where the priest is going with that disk.'

Team Leader moved towards the elevator and waited next to Agent Smith for the lifts to come. As the doors opened, Team Leader moved in first and stood at the back of the lift; then Agent Smith moved in, along with five other guests at the hotel. Team Leader watched Agent Smith, who was oblivious to Team Leader's presence.

As the elevator stopped at the first floor, Team Leader said 'excuse me' as he pushed his way from the back of the lift to the front, to leave. As he did, he planted the tracking device on the back shoulder of Agent Smith's coat.

The lift doors closed, and Team Leader radioed in that the tracking device had been planted. The operators in Mobile One swung into action and started to follow Agent Smith as he walked through the hotel. Unknown to the hotel staff and Agent Smith, the agents had placed scanners on every floor, as well as in elevators and stairwells. This, along with the tracking device on Agent Smith, allowed them to know exactly where Agent Smith was in the hotel.

'Target is on the sixteenth floor and is exiting the elevator now. He is moving along the corridor and has stopped at door 1002. He has now entered. Over.'

Agent Smith locked the door, then looked around the room quickly before heading to the balcony. He headed back into the sitting room, put his coat on the chair and looked up to the ceiling; but his mind was looking much further than that and he fell to his knees. 'I thank you for saving my life so many times and I thank you for not doing what you should have done a long time ago; which was left my sorry behind for not being grateful enough for all the times you have saved my life. Please, help me now. I have no one else I can rely on and I never have; I'm sorry it has taken this long for me to realise that.' Agent Smith stood and looked at the time; there were seventeen minutes to go before he had to make the phone call. He tried to prepare himself by saying, 'Here we go.'

Mobile One had made the call to the hotel management and they had agreed to let them place their man at the front desk; they were also all too willing to provide hotel clothing. Director Forbes, Director Johnson, Assistant Director Collins and Special Agent Rodrigo, all watched the digital clock count down the seconds and minutes. 'Okay, front desk, check.'

'This is front desk, ready and waiting sir.'

'Team Leader, you're looking good in the bellboy uniform. How's the fit?'

'It's a little tight in the crotch, if you must know sir.' There was a little snigger and laughter from all the team... that was until Director Forbes, with a stony face and even colder attitude, reminded them of the seriousness of the job at hand; telling them that if they did not complete this mission successfully, they would all be digging shit in the North Pole.

Teams One and Two had retreated to Mobile One, but Agent One and another team member were on the roof; Big Bird was circling the hotel.

'Mobile One and Sat 1, we're getting some kind of interference on the hotel security feed. Can you see where the problem is coming from?'

'This is Sat 1, roger that. I'm on it. Over.'

'This is Mobile One. There's no problem from this end. Over.'

'Okay, we're reading the tracker as stationary in the sitting room. Can you confirm that, Mobile One?'

'Roger that. The tracker has not moved from the chair and no one has left or entered the room. Over.'

'Okay, all systems checked. Two minutes till phone call.' Special Agent Rodrigo turned to Director Forbes and told him that everything was in place. Director Johnson asked, 'Are you sure there are no other ways for him to get out the door, without being seen by us?'

'The only way he could leave is through the window, and he would need a very long rope to do that.'

'But do we have it covered?' asked Director Johnson.

Assistant Director Collins pointed a laser light at one of the big screens, 'This one's showing the wireframe imagery and computer graphics of the hotel's layout. There is a balcony, which is here, but it's inside the hotel's inner square. There is a small garden at the bottom, but the doors are locked and can only be opened by a security guard's swipe card or five digit code.

'The garden is not in use, it's just there to add some colour for any of the guests that decide to stand on the balcony and we have surveillance of the garden... it's these cameras here. On top of that, any time the doors are opened, a security alarm light comes on at the front desk, alerting the reception and security staff. The only other way out is through the door he went in.'

Director Forbes asked the front desk to confirm that the garden area door's alarm light, had not gone off at any time. 'No sir. No alarms of any kind have gone off here... Sorry, the only one that has gone off was the roof alarm, and that happened when Agent One went onto the roof. Since then there's been nothing, sir.'

'Okay, it's time. Look sharp people, we're about to go into action. Team Leader, are you ready to collect the package?'

'Yes sir.'

'Front desk, are you ready to exchange Package One for Package Two?'

'Yes sir.'

'Agent One, is there anything to report?'

'No sir, everything is quiet up here.'

Ten minutes passed, and there was still no phone call. Director Forbes banged the desk and demanded to know what was going on, but Assistant Director Collins and Special Agent Rodrigo had no answers.

'What do you want us to do, sir?' asked Assistant Director Collins of Director Forbes, who once again looked like he was going to explode. Special Agent Rodrigo stepped in, saying, 'I think we should send Team Leader up to the room. Have him pretend to be room service, or say that he has come to change the sheets or something.'

Assistant Director Collins said 'I don't think that will work. Everybody knows it's maids who change the sheets.'

'I don't care if everybody knows! Get him up there now and in that room under whatever scenario,' shouted Director Forbes.

Team Leader knocked on the door to room 1002 and waited for an answer... and waited, and waited.

'No one is answering... what do you want me to do sir?'

Special Agent Rodrigo looked at Director Forbes.

'Use the master key and get the hell in there and tell me what's going on.'

'Maybe he's fallen asleep sir,' said Assistant Director Collins, shrugging his shoulders. '*If looks could kill,*' thought Special Agent Rodrigo, watching Director Forbes' response to Assistant Director Collins' theory.

Team Leader entered the room, stating he was the bellboy sent up to collect some broken glass from the bathroom. But there was no acknowledgement from anyone in the room. He could see the coat on the chair, which still had the tracker on its back, and there were two empty mini-bottles of brandy on top of the compact fridge. Director Forbes, Director Johnson, Assistant Director Collins and Special Agent Rodrigo, watched all of this via Team Leader's button camera. Once again Team Leader made himself known, and once again there was no reply. He looked in the bedroom to see if anyone was in there sleeping, but there was no one there.

'I guess that puts an end to my theory,' said Assistant Director Collins under his breath but not quietly enough as Director Forbes heard him and fixed him with a steely glare.

Team Leader made his way into the bathroom and checked behind the shower curtain, but there was no sign of Agent Smith anywhere. Everybody was mystified.

'Would someone tell me how the hell he has disappeared into thin air?' shouted Director Forbes.

Team Leader made his way to the balcony, and as he did his button cam view made everybody take a deep breath in disbelief. For a second no one said or did anything, they just simply stared at their screens.

Then Special Agent Rodrigo sprang into action.

'Get down that ladder and show me where it goes! Teams One and Two, get your asses to all exit points immediately! Agent One, get down to the fifteenth floor. Mobile One, put the surveillance cameras on playback from twenty minutes ago and show me who and when someone came out of the room below and where they went; if they got into a cab or walked on foot. The traffic is jammed solid out there, so they can't have gotten far. Big Bird, scan the area for clues until I have an update for you. Let's move it people, go, go, go!'

Team Leader began to climb down the rope ladder, which went down to the next floor's balcony. Team Leader descended down the rope ladder and entered the room on the next floor; as he did, he tripped on a wire that was attached to a smoke grenade safety pin. The pin shot out, setting off the grenade. Smoke filled the room and set off the fire alarms and sprinklers, which soaked Team Leader and eventually put his button cam. out of action.

People swarmed out onto every floor of the hotel and into the lobby; pandemonium broke out, and the hotel became a mass of bodies moving down the stairs and out of the hotel onto the street. Agent One had no choice other than to move with the crowd, and Teams One and Two could not break through the sea of flowing people rushing onto the street. It was impossible for any of them to get to their exit points.

Mobile One reported back that none of the surveillance cameras showed anyone leaving the room below, in the last twenty minutes, so they must still be in there; but added that they had lost live feed to the hotel.

Director Forbes grabbed his head, shouting 'Not again!' Special Agent Rodrigo asked Team Leader for a status report as his cam link had gone down, but there was no reply. Big Bird was now looking for a needle in a very giant haystack, as the bodies continued to flow out of the hotel and mix with the already crowded streets of everyday shoppers.

When the dust had finally settled, Teams One and Two were able to get back into the hotel to find out what had happened to their Team Leader. Once they had made their way up to the fifteenth floor, Teams One and Two burst into the room... only to find their leader tied to a chair, his mouth covered in duct tape. Once they had removed the tape, Team Leader began to give his account of what had taken place after he had stepped into the room and set off the smoke grenade.

Just after he was overwhelmed by the smoke, he had been hit over the head; the next thing he knew, he was being tied up by two or three men. He was left facing the window and couldn't see what they were doing, but he knew they had left some ten minutes after the fire alarms went off. To make matters worse, Mobile One could not check any of the cameras to see if there were any clues as to what they might have been wearing. All they knew was that Agent Smith and the priest had set them up to believe they would still be in the hotel, making phone calls from room 1002.

The truth was, the note that Agent Smith had received from the flower shop girl had told him that he would have to go up to room 1002 and then climb down a rope ladder to the next floor. The note added that before he got up to leave the lobby he would be receiving a call, and he was to play along with what was said. Once Agent Smith reached room 1002 he put his coat on the chair, checked that the rope ladder was secure, and then took off all of his clothing and shoes and left them under the bed; changing into the clothes left for him by the priest.

Once he had climbed down the ladder to the room below, he was met by the priest and his son who introduced themselves: first the priest, whose name was Philip and who looked like he had seen better days. He was very thin and gaunt and was about six feet tall, with a face that was covered by his overgrown silver hair and his appearance made him look more like a hippie from the sixties rather than a priest.

His son's name was Mark, and he too looked as if he had been living in the wild jungles of Africa, but he was in very good shape and his hair was cropped short; he also had a full-grown beard. Philip explained that his son had been a Delta Force operative for ten years and was a Sergeant Major; the only reason he had left the force was because his dad had told him that he was in great danger and that he needed his son's help to avoid certain death. It was his son who had made the plans they were now following.

Mark told them that they would now wait for the enemy to realise that something was wrong and to begin investigating where they were; then they would set the trap, which was the smoke grenade. Agent Smith wanted to know why they just didn't get out of there straightaway, and why they needed to hang around until they set off the smoke grenade.

'Because if we leave now, they will pick us up on their surveillance cameras. Even if they don't spot us right away, when they find out it was all a setup they will look back through the tapes and spot the three of us leaving, and we don't want to give them any information on us whatsoever.

Secondly, I want to find out who we are up against. Are they military or agents? That will tell me a lot about their tactics and equipment capabilities. We will use the smoke alarms to create mass panic and slip out in the crowd because for all we know they may have air support, or worse, satellite capabilities as well.

So we need cover for when we are in the street and in the open. We'll use a trap wire so we don't risk being seen by the operatives, who will come down the ladder looking for a gun fight. The smoke will subdue them for a moment and I'll use that to disarm them, hopefully with non-lethal force. Finally Agent Smith, I want to confiscate their communication equipment so I can eavesdrop on their chatter. That will tell us an awful lot about them, too much for me to mention now. So let's get in the bedroom and wait.'

MAJOR STONE & THE EXTRATERRESTRIAL BIOLOGICAL ENTITIES

Major Stone slowly opened his eyes and what he saw frightened the life out of him; three E.B.Es were standing over him. They were what had come to be known as the "little greys"... about four feet in height, with large heads, big black eyes, skinny necks, arms, bodies and legs. Unfortunately, Major Stone could count the amount of fingers these E.B.Es had, because they were using them right under his nose, literally. They had three fingers, and the little grey standing over his head was using them to put a long thin flexible metal rod up his nose. Major Stone tried to get up from whatever he was lying on, which happened to be a steel operating table with small holes in it. The holes allowed body fluids to fall through the table onto a grid-like floor, which collected the body fluids like a drain system collects the rain.

Major Stone's eyes widened and then filled with water, as the instrument was pushed into his nose. He kept trying to get up, but was paralysed... except for his mouth, which worked well to express his pain. He screamed when the pain registered in his brain.

'What are you doing to me? Why... I come in peace,' he cried out, as tears streamed down his face. The little greys showed no emotions whatsoever, they were clinical in their acts; as if everything they did had a greater purpose, than just simply causing him pain. They put a machine over his head and two long pointed needles... as thin as cotton thread, but as strong as steel... descended from out of the machine; both were pointing straight towards the corners of his eyes. The needles slowly moved down towards his eyes, and as if to add insult to injury, they stopped just mere centimetres above the corners of his eyes; allowing Major Stone just enough time to contemplate the pain he was about to feel... and then it was no longer a thought, but a horrible reality. Once more his mouth worked beautifully in expressing his pain, and without blinking their large black eyes, the little greys paid no attention to his pain. It was almost as if they did not know what it was.

Major Stone had trouble seeing for a while, but it did not stop him from feeling the pain of whatever it was they pushed up his rectum and penis shaft. By the time Major Stones eyesight had returned, his mind had been overly compensated with vivid pictures sent to it via his nervous system; registering every agonizing touch of the little greys cold metallic instruments. After the little greys had finished with Major Stone, it looked to him like they were comparing notes. Then a humanoid-looking E.B.E. came into his view and seemed to be communicating with the little greys. As they all stood over him, the humanoid left the sight of Major Stone.

The next thing Major Stone knew, he was in a room that had no windows but was warm and reasonably comfortable. He jumped to his feet, realising he could now move, and tried to find a door; but there was none to be found. The light in the room did not make any sense, as he could not see where it was coming from. The floor and walls were made from some sort of soft but firm material and the bed he got up from was also made from some sort of fabric. All the things in the room were like nothing that he had ever seen before.

Suddenly, out of the wall appeared one of the three E.B.Es that he had first seen while he was still in War Hawk; it was at least six and a half feet tall, if not seven foot. Although it kept reminding Major Stone of a mantis because of the shape of its head, it also reminded him, confusingly, of a human being; especially when it began to speak.

'How are you feeling? A little confused, no doubt?'
'What do you want with me?'
'To know.'
'To know what?'
'If you have a spirit or not.'
'How can you tell if I have or don't have a spirit?'
'That is what my brothers have being finding out. I'm sorry if it is painful to you and to all the other humans they have done it to; there is no other way to know.'
'Why do you need to... No, fuck that, who gave you the right to find out? Who gives you the right to treat me like a lab rat, you fucking animals?' screamed Major Stone. Spit flew out of his mouth as he shouted and vented

his anger. 'I'm a human being, not an animal. How dare you violate me like that?'

'You mean like how you violate those beings that you consider to be less than you?'

'Don't you dare try to make a moral issue out of what you have done to me and everyone else; who after suffering what you have done to them, have to go back into a world that ridicules them and calls them freaks or impostors and liars.'

'I do not try to make a moral issue out of it; I'm simply asking you if it is a moral issue to you. Like... what did you say earlier? Ah, that's it... "like a lab rat", is that right? Do you think a rat has fewer rights than you do because it is less intelligent than you?'

'I don't care about a fucking lab rat! If you're here to do more tests for my soul then you'll have to kill me first.' Major Stone made a fist and began to swing at the E.B.E.

'I have come to talk with you Major Stone, and to find out what your intensions are regarding War Hawk.'

'Why would I tell you anything?'

'Because if you want this nightmare to be over, you will indulge my curiosity.'

'What is it to you what we do on earth? Why are you interested in what we are, or if we have souls?'

'I am not interested in whether you have a soul... that I already know. What we were looking for was a spirit Major Stone,' replied the alien.

'Why? What does it matter to you if I or anyone else on earth has a spirit? Is this what you do, go around the universe checking out who has spirits?'

'We do it because... like you Major Stone... we have our orders. We are extremely professional soldiers and carry out our Master's orders exactly.'

'Who is your Master? Satan, I take it?'

The E.B.E. put up its hand. As it did Major Stone was lifted off of the floor and flew back against the wall, hitting his head with a considerable force. As the E.B.E. kept its hand out, Major Stone was kept in midair; pressed against the wall as if the impact was a continuous thing. He began to choke and suffocate as the force seemed to be pushing the life out of him. Just as he felt as if he could take no more, the E.B.E. put down its hand and Major Stone fell to the floor, gasping for air.

'Be careful how you talk concerning my Master, for I would burn all the worlds in the universe to serve them. They are the owner of all living things, you included,' snarled the alien.

'Okay, I'm sorry for insulting your master... but you are in the middle of torturing me, and this is how we human beings react. When we are in pain, we lash out at our enemies,' coughed Major Stone.

'I am not your enemy, nor am I your friend Major Stone, and there is nothing you can tell me about human beings that I do not already know.'

'Then what are you and what do you want with the people of earth?'

'I am a soldier of the MOST HIGH, and I myself want nothing from the people of the earth.'

'So what does the MOST HIGH want with us? I know you've said you're a soldier, I know you are following orders, but what are your orders?'

'What they have always been. To defend the universe for, by and under the authority of the MOST HIGH.'

'So it's true, you are the angels of our Bible? But why does the Bible make you look like humans, and why does the government deny your existence?'

'You must ask yourself and your government these questions, for it is you and your people that have done these things you speak of... But let me share with you what I have seen since the first-begotten son last left your world. Dark, wicked and unclean forces, have been in control of mankind like they have never been before. This is because the ruling men of the world have an extreme case of pride, ignorance and vanity. You have taken the images of all things original, that are unlike you in the western and European world, and have made them to look like you; not even the sons of the MOST HIGH have escaped your whitewash. In doing so, you have made lies of the truth and have condemned all of those who believe in your false and graven images.'

'But that was not all of mankind that did that... the majority have been lied to and don't know they are following a lie. Does that mean you will kill all of us who didn't know any better?'

'That is not for me to say, but I have a question for you. Do you believe that if they were told the truth, they would leave the lie for the truth?'

'I hope so, but I don't really know without knowing what the truth is.'

'The truth is something that the ruling men of this world, along with the European and the western world, cannot handle.'

'Please try me. I would like to know the truth, no matter what it is.'

'Okay. What if I told you this world was not created for mankind, but for the sons and daughters of the MOST HIGH, and that you and the rest of the people on the planet were there to give them something to do? What if I told you that you were put on the earth to sing praises and glory to the MOST HIGH for allowing you to exist, and that heaven is none of your business? What if I were to tell you that the earth, your physical body and your soul do not belong to you, and that the only thing that is yours is your mind and the choices it makes?

'What if I told you the truth is that Jesus, Moses, Abraham and all of the other people in your Bible were black? And that all the things I've just mentioned were taught by all of them to mankind, but mankind is proud and vain and wants to be more than just praise bearers to the MOST HIGH; just like the story that Satan Lucifer Devil wanted to be more than a bringer of the praises and glory to the MOST HIGH. You have filled your minds with such vain thoughts, you have made yourselves into gods, you have lied to yourselves and have said that the earth is yours and that you are the rulers of your lives and the owners of your bodies.

'You say that you are above the angels and have taken our place as the sons of the MOST HIGH, which is funny because we were never the sons of the MOST HIGH; only the begotten are the sons and daughters of the MOST HIGH. But that really doesn't matter to you, just as long as you believe that you are at the right hand of the MOST HIGH. The actual facts of whose place you have taken are not relevant because vanity, ignorance and pride are what motivate you, not the truth.

'Do you want to know what we angels find funny? If you were above us, you would know that without the MOST HIGH you would be nothing. If the MOST HIGH wishes you not to exist, you will be no longer. If you were above us, you would know that it is impossible to know what the MOST HIGH knows, and that life and death will always be beyond your understanding.

'You would praise the MOST HIGH for being alive for just a moment, because you would know you did not create yourself. Mankind has been given free will and the ability to choose its own destiny; and what have you done with that free will? You have chosen to give that free will to a few men and have given them the power to have all the control over the world; and you have let them decide and make the world you live in. And then you keep asking the

MOST HIGH why the world is the way it is. You do not own this world but for now you do have control over it and you have given that control over to wicked men whose only interest, on the surface, seems to be money and power.'

'You say "on the surface"... what do you think is going on underneath?'

'I do not think Major Stone, I know. They have made a pact with demons.'

'Please, tell me... what is that pact?'

'In exchange for power, riches and control of the world and mankind, they will destroy the earth and kill as many people in the Third World as possible. The wicked men will kill them by way of starvation, war and germ warfare.'

'Please forgive me for interrupting, but if they have made a pact for those things you speak of, why would they then destroy the earth once they have gotten their power, riches, and control?'

'Because they know the earth does not belong to them and that one day, no matter what they do, it will be taken away from them by the begotten of the MOST HIGH. The chosen will be elevated to the next heaven, after the first death.'

'Sorry, but what is the first death and the next heaven?'

'Believe me Major Stone, with every answer I give you there will be a next question you have to ask. Such are the ways of the MOST HIGH. One level of consciousness and knowledge leads to a level of consciousness and understanding, and that leads to a level of consciousness and wisdom; which then leads to the next level... let's call it level two of consciousness and knowledge, understanding and wisdom. These levels go up into infinity.

'Let me just finish by telling you that the wicked men who have power over the earth, can never get to such a level as eternal life. Satan Lucifer Devil and demons can only show them how to trick mankind into giving them the control of the earth, nothing more. So mankind has sold its power over itself and the earth, to a few wicked men for next to nothing; and they will keep mankind under their control for as long as they can. They will keep up their end of the deal and will keep on destroying the earth with the power you have given them; until the earth is no more or until the first-begotten son of the MOST HIGH comes. Or until you, the majority, decide to take back the world from the wicked men and make it a better place for all to live; so that the first-begotten son does not have to do so. So do you now wish to change your beliefs to what I have just told you, or does the lie that you can all go to heaven seem more comfortable to you?'

'So you are saying only the sons and daughters of the MOST HIGH will go to heaven, no one else? If that is true, then why do religions lie about it?'

'The sons and daughters of the MOST HIGH will always return home Major Stone. For the rest of mankind, only those who have found favour with the MOST HIGH might make it there. The reason that religion lies is because religion is a part of the government, and both of them are a part of how the wicked men have tricked mankind into giving them power. Religion and government were given to them from Satan Lucifer Devil, and they are needed to keep the majority in check.

'Do you know if the whole world were to live like you do in the western and European world, it would run out of resources in no time at all? The wicked men have to keep at least a third of the world below the poverty line in order to live their glutted lives and to allow you who live around them, to have a much smaller piece of the pie. Here's something to think about the next time you have a Big Mac Major Stone: the billions of people in the Third World who will pay for that Big Mac for you... the billions who are hungry, at war and are being killed.'

Major Stone did not know what to say or think. On one hand it sounded like it was probably true; if the government he knew was anything to go by. All of the stuff that he had read in the JAW file, also suggested this to be true. Still, he had to play his cards close to his chest and not let on to what he knew; so that he could find out what the E.B.E. knew.

'I can agree with you on the government side of things, but the church? I always believed they were the messengers for the MOST HIGH.'

'Do you believe in Christ, Major Stone?'

'Yes, of course I do.'

'And who was it that taught you about Christ?'

'The church... I mean the Christian church.'

'What if I told you they had not only lied about Jesus' race, but also about his name?'

'But why would they do that? It's written in the Bible. Everybody knows there is a Jesus Christ. Okay, let's say they have made a mistake or they changed his last name... what would that really mean? They still tell the story about him.'

'Let me put it this way and try to keep up. There is no Jesus Christ, because Christ means 'chosen one'. Jesus was not chosen by the MOST HIGH, he was born out of the MOST HIGH.

'To be Christ means he was chosen, and to be chosen means he had no birthright. To have no birthright would mean he was not the son of the MOST HIGH.

'If he were not the son of the MOST HIGH, that would mean he was from somewhere else. To be from somewhere else would mean he was not the original son.

'If he were not the original son, this would mean he is not the truth. If he were not the truth, this would mean he is a lie and a copy. To be a lie and a copy means someone removed or replaced the original son.

'To remove or replace the original son means that someone is telling a lie, and a lie is the opposite of the MOST HIGH.

'To be opposite the MOST HIGH means Christ, which means chosen, came from and was chosen by someone opposed to the original son and the MOST HIGH.

'To be opposite the MOST HIGH means Christ came from and was chosen by Satan Lucifer Devil, for he is opposite the MOST HIGH, and the wicked men of the world are his puppets.

'And that's why a name is important: it tells you whom you are dealing with Major Stone. Tell me, do you know the last name of the real Jesus?... Don't try to answer; I already know the answer.

'Religion and your Christ tell you that heaven is for everyone because it wants you to look to the sky for your power and riches; while the wicked, knowing the truth, take from the earth now instead of waiting for the afterlife.

'Religion and your Christ tell you not to fight, but to love instead and that your fight is not with the flesh, but with evil spirits. But tell me... when was the last time you saw a spirit kill anyone in this dimension? Man has the power and the free will to kill or not to kill. No spirit has the power to make man kill or not kill, none, and while you try your best to fight spiritual wars, which is no more than just saying no to things you know to be wrong and unjust; the wicked take the wealth of the earth and kill all they can.'

This was more than Major Stone could take in, under the circumstances. Right now he was more concerned with what was going to happen to him, than with the woes of the world.

'What is going to happen to me now?' he asked. The E.B.E. smiled. 'I'm going to ask you again: what is your intention with War Hawk?'

'I don't understand. Why do you ask me something you must already know? You can read my mind, can't you?'

'Yes, I can read your mind, but I want you to speak. It is the words you speak that I am interested in.'

'Why? What good are the words if they are lies and do not speak what is in my mind?'

'Because then I will know how much of your spirit lives and how much is dead. Then, Major Stone, you will be free to go; for I will have completed my orders.'

'I don't understand. Why do you need me to tell you? Can't you find out how much of my spirit is alive some other way?'

'Very good, Major Stone. Even though your life may be in danger, you still try to find out vital information concerning your so-called enemies.'

'I don't understand. What do you mean?'

'Oh, come now, Major Stone. You are trying to find out how much I know and if I know what the real mission of War Hawk is.'

'Okay, let's start again. How many people have you checked to see if they have spirits, and how long have you been checking?'

'To this point in time? Many billions of years and several hundred million people.'

'But if you have checked that amount, then why is it that only a small number of people have any idea that they have been abducted?'

'Let's just say that some people have an ability to retain information, even when it is removed.'

'And what about those people who think they have been used for breeding purposes?'

'They may well have been.'

'So what you are saying is, you don't know?'

'Like I have already told you, I am a soldier of the MOST HIGH. What concerns me is whatever I'm told to do. Unlike you humans Major Stone, I don't think of myself as being able to understand everything. I have been blessed with knowing the MOST HIGH and having a function that is useful to them.

'No one but the MOST HIGH can understand the ways of the only perfect being in existence.

'When you get home, look out of your window and look at the vastness that you are in. Ask yourself how could you ever understand such an enormous and complicated thing, as the universe and life. If you don't learn to have faith and understand how little you truly are in the universe, you will be like your scientists, who find out one thing and begin to boast that they know how the universe was made; only to find out another thing and another.

'What they don't admit to you is that they will never know enough to tell you how the universe got here, it's just too big; and they always want to pretend they know everything. The last people on the earth we would want to make contact with are your arrogant and obnoxious scientists, because what they have learnt are the minutest of things in the universe of the MOST HIGH.

'So stop thinking like you should understand everything and just listen and learn. The ways of the MOST HIGH are beyond your reach.

'Now, I have a question for you. What are your government's intentions concerning War Hawk?'

'Okay. The truth is they want to show you that they can build a machine from the technology you have given to them; if necessary, they will use it to defend our planet.'

'So they have made another machine for destroying things, rather than using the technology for something good. There are a million and one good things the technical information we have given them could be used for, and there are only a few bad things it can be used for. Yet you have only been able to find the bad things.'

'Yes, but if you wanted us to build the good, why didn't you say so?'

'Because it is your choice; that is the law the MOST HIGH has set on the earth and the law concerning mankind.'

'But why doesn't the MOST HIGH just stop man from doing the things that are bad?'

'Imagine if you were a spirit that dwelled in the place of the MOST HIGH, the most powerful and frightening being in existence. Do you think you would dare to do anything that they did not like?'

'No.'

'So a place like the earth and flesh exists, to allow a spirit to be their true self and make choices about what they choose to believe in; rather than because they are in the presence of the MOST HIGH.'

'I don't understand. Are you saying this flesh that I'm in and the earth that I live on, are here just to find out what a spirit is really all about?'

'Yes, that is one of the reasons... and before you ask I will explain this one thing; because there are many reasons, but you don't have the brain capacity to understand them all.

'Always remember that you are smaller than an atom in the scale of the knowledge and wisdom of the MOST HIGH, so such things as life and death are hard for you to understand. Yet to the MOST HIGH, they are the smallest of equations.'

'So is it true that you have come to destroy the earth and take control of it?'

'The earth belongs to the MOST HIGH, and therefore no being could take it for themselves... a lesson mankind is still struggling to comprehend. Secondly it is mankind that wishes to destroy the earth, and you are doing a very good job of it. When my General awakes he will take the earth away from the wicked men and will watch over it; until mankind has learnt that it is not meant to be the owner of the earth, but the gardener who cares for the earth and all that live in it.

'If mankind could learn to do that, the MOST HIGH would not have to send his first-begotten son to clean up your mess. But the truth is mankind is so blind from pride, ignorance and vanity, that when the first-begotten son of the MOST HIGH comes to the earth, you will hate him and want him dead.

'You kill, starve and lie to one another and then ask, where is the MOST HIGH? How can such wicked things be allowed to happen? Yet it is you who do these wicked things.

'You want freedom and choice, but you don't want to be responsible for your actions. You kill the earth everyday in a slow and painful strangle, sucking the life out of her, and when she retaliates with earthquakes and tsunamis, you cry out again saying where is the MOST HIGH and how could they let this happen; and you willingly forget that *you* have the power of choice over your actions.

'And when the first-begotten son of the MOST HIGH comes and rules over mankind with an iron rod, you will hate him and resent his authority. And the wicked of the earth will say to you, "We must come together to stop the son of Satan from ruling over us; he is not our Christ, because our Christ is only about love. How can the son of the MOST HIGH kill us and be righteous?" You will join with them saying you do it for the sake of freedom and democracy.

'And when the first-begotten son of the MOST HIGH kills and slays those who come against him, you will say how can that be right, it is he who is the evil one not us; for what has mankind done to deserve such a thing, and you will not believe that he is righteous. You will side with the wicked and plot to try and kill the first-begotten son of the

MOST HIGH, and he will kill and slay all those who try to come against him.

'Then *you* will say he is not our Christ, because our Christ is only about love. How can the son of the MOST HIGH kill us and be righteous? And you will say we reject him and curse him. And you will side with the wicked men and say let us kill him, just like the wicked men say; because you will have become like those which have already been killed and slain.

'The war will go on and on until only the righteous are left, and then the first-begotten son of the MOST HIGH will put down his sword and peace will be upon the earth. The earth will be healed from the works of the wicked and will suffer no more from the hands of the ungrateful child.'

Major Stone did not know what to say. He had now lost his fear of this E.B.E, which he now thought of as an angel, and now he wanted to know as much as he could. For the first time in his life he was willing to betray the government. He wanted to be on the side of the angels, not because they were more powerful than mankind, but because they sided with the real truth. This angel had taken time to try and elevate his dumb behind, and for the first time Major Stone felt like he understood things about his own world; things that had been kept secret from him by the very people he was supposed to trust.

The angel opened a force field window and to Major Stone's surprise, they were underwater.

'What planet are we on?' asked Major Stone.

'We are on your planet. This is the Pacific Ocean, and we are some three miles down.'

As Major Stone looked into the darkness, he saw lights in the far distance and as the craft got closer, he could see that it was a City under the ocean. It was not until the craft was some half a mile out, that Major Stone could truly appreciate the vast size of the city. In fact it was more the size of a country, reaching into the darkest depths of the ocean; as if it had been built in a canyon bigger than any he had seen on the earth's surface. It seemed to go on and on, as if it did not stop until it reached the centre of the earth.

'How far down does this place go, and what do you call this place?' asked Major Stone, feeling sheer disbelief at what he was looking at.

The craft began to slow and manoeuvred itself into position, to dock with a porthole. Major Stone stared into the canyon and was mesmerised by the country under the sea. It was as if he was in an aeroplane looking down at America at night, with all of its lights glowing from its many different cities; such was the size of what he could see.

'This is my home from home, Major Stone, my country. I have lived here for thousands of years and will do so until the MOST HIGH says no more.'

The craft docked and the angel asked Major Stone to follow him through the porthole and into the country under the sea.

AGENT SMITH AND THE PRIEST

Agent Smith sat down at the dinner table and had breakfast. He, Philip and Mark were staying at a safe house in Canada. It was a small two-bedroom apartment that looked like it had not been decorated since the sixties; the wallpaper had orange and white swirling patterns, the blinds were made out of fake bamboo and the chairs looked like oranges with the middles cut out.

Agent Smith could hardly finish his breakfast quickly enough; today was the day he would finally find out what was on the disk.

24 hours had passed since they had reached Canada. Philip, who had asked Agent Smith not to refer to him as Priest or Father Shane at any time, had taken the time while

they travelled to their new home to explain to Agent Smith what had happened to his old friend Father O'Brian.

The same people who had presumably killed Agent Smith's brother-in-law, who was Philips old friend Pete, had somehow found Father O'Brian. Philip could only imagine what they had done to him, in order to make him give up Philip's whereabouts. Philip had just managed to escape, with the help of an unknown person who called himself Death. Once he had made good his escape, he knew that if he was to have any chance of staying alive, he had to contact his son. Mark was the only reason he was still alive, not forgetting the help from Mr Death of course.

Mark had been following Agent Smith from a distance, but he was not going to make contact until he had a chance to watch the enemy at work and get an idea of their operational tactics. This meant that they had used Agent Smith as bait, but it had been necessary in order to be able to plan and set up their escape from the hotel and their flight to the safe house.

Philip and Mark had gone in to town to pick up some stuff they were going to need. Agent Smith was not sure what that meant, but at the time he was too tired to ask. Now, with a full night's sleep behind him and a belly filled with a hearty breakfast, he was ready and waiting to ply them with a list of questions once they returned.

It was a little after ten o'clock when Philip and Mark returned. They entered the safe house with bags of food and boxes of equipment. Agent Smith recognized some of the equipment such as two-way radios, binoculars, cable wire, shotguns, bulletproof vests, ammunition,
pickaxes, shovels, wire cutters and so on. But there were other things they brought in that he had never seen before... things like little black boxes with switches on them and small boxes with aerials sticking out of them.

Before Agent Smith could ask what they were, his attention shifted to the disk. Philip reminded him of it by switching on the computer in his bedroom and asking Agent Smith to come and take out his disk and put it in the computer.

Agent Smith was like a puppy dog who had just been given a bone; he hurried to the bedroom and gave the disk to Philip. Once the disk was in the computer, Philip asked Agent Smith to enter the code... 'The truth will set you free.' Then Philip told Agent Smith that he had the four-digit code, and entered it: '6706'. Agent Smith smiled shaking his head, and said 'So without you, I would have never cracked this code.'

Philip pressed the enter key and the computer came alive with the information on the disk. Philip explained that the disk didn't just have the information on it that their enemy was looking for; it had a code on it, that they had put there. What their enemy did not know was that they had hidden the code among the information; this code was the exact location of the evidence that proved that what was on the disk was true. And when the time was right, they may be able to use the information to trade for their lives or to honour the death of their family and friends, Pete and Father O'Brian, by releasing the evidence to the world.

'But I don't understand. Why don't we just use whatever is on the disk? Isn't that enough? After all isn't it that, what is making these people come after us?' asked Agent Smith.

'Yes... only because they do not know that we have cracked a secret code that they have spent the last hundred years trying to decode. They think we are trying to reveal their secrets about the coming of the first-begotten son of the MOST HIGH, about the existence of aliens, and about the truth about their secret order and its secret agenda. They know we only have a copy on a disk; it's an embarrassment to them, or an unwanted spotlight at best. If we take this disk to the media, it won't prove anything by itself; not without hard evidence to back it up. But that, by the grace of the MOST HIGH, is what we have found.

'If they knew what we had discovered, they would have sent all of the armies in the world after us. Don't get me wrong, there is information on this disk that they don't ever want to see the light of day, because it in itself will create questions and discussions and thoughts and ideas, that are dangerous to the establishment.'

'Like what exactly?'

'Well, I thought you would want to read them for yourself... but for example, there is an entire side to Jesus that has been deliberately left out of the Bible. That's why from his birth to age 12 and from age 12 to age 33, there are big gaps. Have you never wondered why no one can tell you the last name of one of the most famous people ever to be spoken or written about in the history of the world? Everyone seems to believe it's Christ, but it's not and never was; we have been lied to and the powers that be say it is for legitimate reasons. The only problem is, they can't tell anyone outside of their little secret organisation why that is; other than it is a threat to National Security. And that, John, is closer to the truth than you know.'

'Why?'

'Have you ever stopped to think how or what it would be like to be the son of the most powerful being in existence? If not, let me try to help you. You would have powers inside of you, of overwhelming ability. You would have the power to heal, which the ruling powers on earth don't mind telling you about; but you would also have the power to destroy on nuclear levels and higher.

'What would you as the all-conquering Roman government do, when the son of the MOST HIGH came to town? Would you try to make him submit to your rule of law, like you had done dozens of times before to whole continents?

'What do you think he would do? Would he submit himself to the law of the invading Romans? And if he did not submit himself to your rule of law, what would you attempt to do to him? Kill him? Would he then slay those who dared to come against him? Don't forget, he had to wait 33 years until he was to be killed.

'This is the side that the Romans destroyed from all of the text that went to make up their Bible, and they did a good job of it. But they made one vital mistake and overlooked one important area... that was the records kept by the Romans themselves. They somehow overlooked their own paper trail; maybe it just was a simple case of habit. You see, the Romans kept records on everything... it was part of what made them so efficient, organised and powerful.

'Anyway to cut a long story short, all the evidence of the full nature of Jesus, had been tailored down to a level that the Romans and any following power would like. You must understand that the people who stand to lose the most from the return of the first-begotten son of the MOST HIGH, are the people in power such as Presidents and Prime Ministers.

'Most ordinary people think the Pope will be the first to run to Jesus and kiss his feet in gladness that he has returned, but that's not the truth. The Pope and all previous Popes before him, have gotten used to people kissing *their* feet and when the first-begotten son returns, they will no longer be the head of the church. But worse than that, they know that they have been involved in blasphemy and have committed murder in the name of Jesus.

'Do you know that in the 16th century, the churches sold indulgence slips of paper that absolved the buyers of their sins... making the church and the Popes a fortune? There has always been corruption in the Vatican. This is why the church and Rome had to kill Jesus, but no matter how they tried... and believe me they did in the early days and somewhat less in the latter days of his life... it was not until he said he was ready to die, that they could finally achieve their goal. Then once he was dead they buried, as best as possible, the true life of Jesus; yet even though they had killed the man, they could not kill the legacy.

'Did you know that the Romans took the teachings of Jesus, watered them down and then gave them back to the people? However it didn't work because the people who had followed his teachings, remembered what he had taught. There were not many of them who still dared to follow his teachings but the small number who did, kept having success over the legions of Roman armies. So then the Romans created Christianity, sending in their man Paul who used to be named Saul.

'Now they say it's all in a name and this is a good example of that saying. You see, for Saul to become Paul meant that he had left the followings of Abraham and had converted to Roman beliefs. A Jew would only change his or her name from a Jewish one to a Roman one, if he or she had no intention of ever being recognised as a Jew again. By Jewish law, changing one's name was a sin and once you did that you could never go back. So Paul then claimed to see Jesus in a vision and suddenly Christianity was born.'

'Dad, we don't have time for this. Please bring me the coordinates.'

'Sorry son, you know I get carried away... Anyway, to make a very short story shorter, all was forgotten. The Christian faith was in place and it claimed to follow Christ and promoted peace and love. In truth, this was something that Jesus also promoted, but it was not the only thing; as you will find out when you read the information on the disk.

'Anyway, George Washington had been given the records of Pontius Pilate and of the Emperors before and after him; these extremely sensitive documents were handed down to him to be hidden in the city of Washington. This was because Washington and his side of the secret order, were planning to completely lock the church out. They believed in science, reason and geometry, and they wanted the people to be ruled by that, rather than by what they saw as an outdated religious system.

'These records that were kept by the Romans were more accurate and were extremely detailed, compared to the scriptures. The records described the true teachings of Jesus, along with a list of his family members and a full physical description of Jesus. When the power struggle finally broke out between the church and the Freemasons, many years after the death of Washington, the codes that the two head families had that were the key to the location of the records, were lost forever. Each organisation thought they could crack the other's code, but neither was able to do so. However, as long as the other could not crack it, they would be able to share the control and power.

'As time went on, the fact that the information had been kept highly secret and that the records were essentially lost, meant that they all felt more secure; believing it would now never be found. This also allowed them to keep their own bloodlines in power.

'Well, let's just say that if I told you any more, I would ruin what is going to be a fascinating read.'

Philip scanned the information and every now and then he wrote a number in a small black book. Once he had gotten all of the information he needed, he turned to Agent Smith and told him to sit down and take his time reading the information on the disk; however, he warned him that it might be more than he could handle. He then explained that he would be in the next room pinpointing a position on a map of Washington DC and then he and his son would be planning their next and final mission. He also said that if they all managed to live to see the end of the mission, the world would finally be told the truth. He looked at Agent

Smith sincerely and then went into the next room to join his son.

Agent Smith sat back in the chair and began to read the title page.

J A W 1967 THE ARMAGEDDON CODE

TOP SECRET FOR YOUR EYES ONLY

JAW are the initials of the first-begotten son of the MOST HIGH. The name must never be written in full at any time. Nor should the real teachings of JAW be copied, published, shown, read or spoken about at any time, to any persons below the level of triple A for-your-eyes-only clearance. Such writings are kept only for the purpose of verifying and identifying the authenticity of any person making such a claim, as to be the first-begotten son of the MOST HIGH.

Therefore, from the time of the rule of the Emperor of Rome, there has been a decree that the first-begotten son of the MOST HIGH shall be referred to as the only begotten son of GOD. Furthermore, the full name JAW must be changed to JC or Jesus Christ. This must be maintained, for it is imperative that any false messiahs are able to be easily identified.

Case material: Records of Pontius Pilate, summary overview

Description of information: The below text is a summary and a version, from the Vatican's version of what is written in the original records kept by Pontius Pilate; as well as the governors and emperor who preceded him and those who came after. The text below comprises of snapshots of the full text, which has been condensed for practical purposes; some are official records, while others are personal notes.

The actual text itself is said to be some thousands of pages long. Its whereabouts are still unknown.

Governor's Personal Daily Report
What am I to do with this boy? His age can be no more than 15. How can a mere boy mock the imperial armies of Rome? He is said to be responsible for the death of two legions of Rome's most hardened soldiers; his thirst for the blood of Rome seems to know no end. Soon the Emperor will hear of his exploits and my life will be near crucifixion. Curse this land and all that it has brought forth.

Governor's Report to Rome
The rumours grow that this boy has been sent to save the Jews and their land from Rome's occupation. It is not quite clear how many men follow this boy in his terrorist campaigns across Nazareth. I have sent in extra troops to quell the unrest, but I fear I will need more soldiers from Rome; all this because of a boy who will not die and his band of outlaws! How can it be that they say this boy is divine, when he lives with prostitutes, robbers and thieves?

Governor's Report to Rome
It is getting to be beyond a joke now. It has been two years and now the boy is 17; he walks around killing Rome's soldiers as if they were flies. He makes no attempt to hide and has been quoted as saying he is protected by some GOD called the MOST HIGH, and that Rome is not his master.

Governor's Personal Daily Report
They call him Jesus, and it would seem he has several brothers who are a part of his terrorist organisation. The emperor grows restless with the unrest that this boy brings; he will be the death of me.

Governor's Report to Rome
It would seem this Jesus has offended more than just Rome and his enemies go beyond Rome as well. King Herod, the Pharisees and most in the Jewish community, do not like what he has to say and what he does. Maybe if we join forces we can get rid of this rebel once and for all.

Governor's Personal Daily Report
I have increased the taxes and have made it clear that as long as this Jesus continues to murder Roman soldiers, the people of this cursed land will pay. The Pharisees have been to see me today; they say the people are getting upset with having to pay the price for this rebel's ways.

Governor's Personal Daily Report
Now he is in his twenties and he is still the thorn in Rome's side. Because of this Jesus, two of my predecessors have been killed by Rome for failing to bring this terrorist to justice. Caesar's fury grows. I have been sent here to end this insult to Rome; may the Gods be with me. It would seem that this Jesus refuses to call himself any religious name, saying he has no religion but to serve the MOST HIGH, whom he now calls his FATHER and MOTHER. I must use this to further the rift between him and his own people.

Governor's Personal Daily Report
This Jesus is telling the people not to be afraid of Rome but to be afraid of his GOD the MOST HIGH. He tells them to rise up against Rome and remove them by the sword. He has killed too many legions of Rome's finest warriors. Those who have seen his terrifying anger in battle say he is invincible and talk of him as if he can fly or has wings and eyes of fire; obviously battle fear has taken hold of them. It has become almost impossible to find soldiers

willing to go wherever he is and fight him in the name of Rome. I have hired outlaws from around the world to kill this Jesus and have paid them handsomely for the task. I will send my own spies to the battlefield so that they can watch this Jesus in battle from afar and return to me alive so that I may find out what his secret is.

Governor's Personal Daily Report

The world has stopped in its tracks to hear about this man, aged no more than 32 years, who has been killing Rome's finest soldiers for more than a decade... and who, it is said, cannot be killed. Rome has offered the biggest reward ever, to the man that can kill him. My body grows cold with fear. I cannot tell the Emperor what my spies have told me; it is madness.

The Battlefield

It took place in a valley that is half a mile wide and surrounded by rocky cliffs. The river that once ran through the middle of it has long since dried up, it's like a desert; the soil is like red brown dust, baked in the heat of the midday sun. Little life grows or lives here, except for the odd fox or wild dog and the few rodents that survive on underground plants and fruit. Lifeless and barren, harsh and unforgiving, the place is strewn with dead bones scattered across its face; from animals foolish enough to think this valley would forgive them their trespass. But today the valley is filled with the sounds of horses and men
marching; their body armour, swords, spears and shields make music, as they tap against one another in rhythm with their footsteps.

Outlaws, warriors and Goliaths from across the globe, renowned for their skills and fearless hearts in battle, march side by side with Roman soldiers. There are more than twelve thousand men here, ready to battle to the death. On the other side of the dried-out river bed, Jesus and no more than a thousand men, make camp at the foot of the valley's cliff face.

The next day, Rome's trumpets sound out and echoes across the valley basin; Rome's soldiers move to attack position. First the horsemen ride to the right and left, to flank Jesus and his band of outlaws; while Rome's foot soldiers, carrying spears and shields, come straight ahead to attack Jesus from the front. Its Archery division sends its fire-filled arrows overhead, to rain down on the heads of Jesus and his men. Behind Jesus, the outlaws, warriors and giants descended the rock path with swords, clubs and spears drawn from all angles. Jesus and his men are under attack from an army of more than twelve thousand strong; surely death is imminent for him now... and if not for him, at least for his men.

Insert by Priest: This is where the wise and the foolish part, for only the wise know that the flesh by itself is nothing and that the world that cannot be seen is something. Those who can only see with the eyes of the flesh, will see twelve thousand soldiers going up against one thousand. Yet those that can understand the ways of the MOST HIGH will see twelve thousand unclean spirits going up against one thousand clean spirits and they will know that the twelve thousand are doomed; for the man who gives his life freely to the MOST HIGH will never fall or die in battle.

This is what Rome would never be able to see for arrogance, vanity and pride, will always blind a powerful nation that does not recognise the hand of the MOST HIGH. The spies told Pontius Pilate, that on that day they saw the hand of the MOST HIGH as Jesus went into battle. His eyes became fire and white wings appeared from out of his back, his face glowed so brightly that it made seeing his face impossible, and the whole of his body glowed as if it were on fire.

He drew his flaming sword and within half an hour he had killed twelve thousand soldiers in all directions, by way of the sword. He left the survivors to his band of men, who had to chase them down as they fled, screaming for their lives. When they had killed them all and none were left, they regrouped and prayed to their GOD, the MOST HIGH. They gave the victory to the MOST HIGH saying aloud 'there is none higher, mightier, greater, wiser, holier, more righteous, more faithful, more forgiving or more true than the MOST HIGH... the only living Supreme Being, creator of the universe and all living things; without whom all things would cease to exist.'

It is said that at no other time, but in battle, would Jesus transform into what he did on that day; nor did he transform at every battle. Only once did men ever live to see it, and that was the time when the spies watched on behalf of Pontius Pilate. It was said that if you did see it, you would die if you were not one of his band of men. Some say the only reason that the spies did not die was because they were not in the battle.

Governor's Personal Daily Report

No one has seen or heard from this Jesus in thirty days. The rumour is that he has been hiding in the wilderness. My spies say he has gone there to put down his anger as well as his sword. Only time will tell. I pray that it is true, for I don't believe Rome will tolerate my failure much longer. I fear that I will meet the same fate as my predecessors.

Governor's Personal Daily Report

My spies inform me that this renegade has put down the sword and has become a preacher of the word of the MOST HIGH. I dare not believe it... have the Gods of Rome heard my pleas and saved me from the fury of the Emperor?

Governor's Personal Daily Report
My joy has turned to sorrow; this Jesus' words are as sharp and as deadly as his sword. The Pharisees are extremely angry. They approach me daily, saying that what he preaches is blasphemy. They ask me repeatedly to do something about him, as they cannot. I have made it clear to them that they must deal with this Jesus; he is no longer Rome's concern. The truth is that Rome washed its hands of this man the day he stopped killing Roman soldiers. There is nothing more we can do.

Governor's Personal Daily Report
King Herod now comes to me saying that Jesus and his cousin, known as John the Baptist, are meeting daily. He says that John the Baptist has been teaching Jesus the ways of Abraham and Moses and that John is an extremely dangerous man who is filling Jesus' head with ideas; telling him that he is the first-begotten son of the MOST HIGH and that he is here to show the lost sheep the way.

The Pharisees come to me again saying that if something is not done about this man, Rome will face an uprising such as it has never seen before.

The Spoken Word of Jesus
'Man should pray to the MOST HIGH and give praise, glory and honour to the MOST HIGH and no one else. For the precious gift known as life, has been given to them from no one but the MOST HIGH. All men should learn to live in love and in harmony with one another and live life to the fullest, because no man knows the day of their death; life is a gift from the MOST HIGH, not a guarantee.'

Governor's Personal Daily Report
He has infuriated the Pharisees, they beseech me to do something about this man. I tell them he is not Rome's problem anymore; they say he is teaching men and women to rebel against them and Rome. They say this Jesus is now teaching.

The Spoken Word of Jesus
'The Pharisees lie when they promise man everlasting life through the church. You waste your time asking the Pharisees to speak on behalf of man with the MOST HIGH; for they are no more righteous than any other man, and all have sinned. You will not find my FATHER and MOTHER in a church building, for their church is in the mud, in the seeds, in the grass, in the flowers, in the trees, in the birds and the bees, in the air all around you, in the rain, in the clouds, in the stars, in mankind and in *all* living things. Your church is inside you and all around you, no matter where you are. No man can tell you heaven is yours, for no man knows that he will go to heaven unless the MOST HIGH tells him.

'Understand me; the MOST HIGH does not need to buy you with promises, nor do they need to explain to you the nature of the universe they built. For the MOST HIGH needs you not, you need the MOST HIGH. So when a man promises you heaven, for going to their church or for being a part of their religion, say to them "you know not what the MOST HIGH knows about me and the universe, therefore you cannot know who will or will not go to heaven."

'Understand this as well; eternal life is not for everyone it is only for a few and these few will only die in the flesh because they have spirits and will return to the spiritual realm.

'But, although they have spirits and return to the spiritual realm, that does not mean they will be in the presence of the MOST HIGH. Very few ever get to be in the true presence of the MOST HIGH and those that do, are either known as the begotten of the MOST HIGH, Archangels, or the chosen ones. The rest of mankind has been given the precious gift of life, and when it ends they will go back to the dust they came from.'

Governor's Personal Daily Report
This Jesus goes too far. Once again, the Emperor of Rome will not like his teachings. Rome has made itself a god and has promised many everlasting life for their support of Rome. Once again he has managed to anger his own people by telling them that they are less worthy than the begotten, the archangels and the so-called chosen ones.

Governor's Personal Daily Report
Now not only do the Pharisees come to me daily, but they bring large crowds with them; all wanting the head of this Jesus. They say he regularly enters the churches and causes trouble among the sellers; even if they are selling the word of their GOD. It would seem that he is turning back to his old ways, but now he seems to be focusing his renowned anger at his own people; even the church is no sanctuary for them. My spies tell me he continually wrecks the churches and runs everyone out of the church, saying that it is his for the worship of his FATHER and MOTHER and not for the sale of their goods.

There is hope that the gods of Rome have heard my prayers. My spies tell me this Jesus has said... Please read underneath:

The Spoken Word of Jesus
'I will give my life, so that the begotten and the chosen ones do not have to suffer for their sins. For I am the first begotten and I have also sinned. For we are born into iniquity and must know sin so that we can reject it, just as the prodigal son returns to his FATHER and MOTHER.

I also do this to show you, the begotten and the chosen ones, that death is not to be feared; it is only a door to another dimension. The fear of death is the biggest and greatest sin for the begotten, as it shows that we have left our spirits locked in the flesh and we have forgotten who our FATHER and MOTHER are; and now we fear the world more than our FATHER and MOTHER. Fear of death shows that we have lost faith and trust in them and for this sin, I come to take away the bitter taste of death.'

Governor's Personal Daily Report

My spies tell me that a large amount of people believe in him because he does not condemn them but tells them... Please read underneath:

The Spoken Word of Jesus

'Try not to do anything to a person that you would not want done to yourself. Even though it is true that many of you will not go to heaven, you should praise the MOST HIGH continuously for being given life. Before I knew who I was, this is what I prayed: "What can I do for you, the MOST HIGH, before I die and go to hell?"'

Governor's Personal Daily Report

This Jesus continues to anger the people and causes great unrest among most, because he refuses to talk to anyone but the lost sheep. Many come to speak with him and hear the word, but they are rejected by him and his outlaws. Only once did he break this refusal, saying... Please read underneath:

The Spoken Word of Jesus

'Mankind has free will and can choose how he wishes to live out his life on earth. The MOST HIGH will not tell mankind what they can or cannot do, nor will they make them do what they do not want to do because if the

MOST HIGH did that, they would break the law that they had put in place; which is free will for all mankind. Only when a man dies will he know what awaits him. Likewise, do not feel down because I say you are not all begotten or chosen, be happy for your power is in free will. Satan cannot hurt you nor can bad things happen to you, unless you choose to let them hurt you.'

Governor's Personal Daily Report
He continues to tell the lost sheep... who I assume must be the begotten and the chosen ones... that they must not fear death, nor should they fear or bow to Rome or any religion. He tells them that they should only bow to the MOST HIGH, who is their master. He claims... please read underneath:

The Spoken Word of Jesus
'All of mankind has a soul; it is not flesh, nor is it spirit. It is ultimately the desires of the spirit world and the heart and the influences of the flesh, that struggle to control one's choices in life. If all are equal and unwilling to bow to one another, war will begin until one is the victor.

'If the spirit is the victor, in this case the heart and flesh will bow.

'If the heart is the victor, in this case the spirit may die; if the desires of the heart are for the things of the world, then it and the flesh will overpower the spirit. But if the desires of the heart are for the things not of this world, then the flesh will die.

'If the flesh is the victor, and the desires of the heart are for the things of this world, the spirit will die; if the desires of the heart are for the things not of this world, the flesh can defeat the spirit and the desires of the heart, with the help of unclean spirits.

'This war, known as the war of self, can last throughout a person's entire life and can continue to the grave without resolution. Torment is the end result for the person; they will suffer all the days of their life, never knowing why they cannot find peace within themselves.

'At this point, into their lives will flow many unclean and unseen spirits, for people who cannot make up their own minds can easily have their minds made up for them. Now their life will plummet into the world of darkness and they will be led by things they cannot see and do not know. These unclean, unseen spirits will fill their minds with pride, ignorance and vanity, blinding the person to the truth; for the further from the truth a person becomes, the more likely they are to become lost and to be filled with the teachings of the unclean, unseen spirits. For the desires of the heart contain the written word of the MOST HIGH, and the desires of the flesh are from the world.

'There are only a few members of mankind who have a spirit. The majority of mankind are spiritless, and their war of self is between the desires of the heart and the flesh. Those who have a heart that desires the world are capable of extremely wicked things; such as world domination through war, pestilence and starvation. They have no problem with the killing of hundreds of thousands of innocent babies, children, women and men.

'They will live for the pleasures of the flesh and will care not for the world or the earth. Pride and vanity will rule their lives and they will sleep well at night; for pride and vanity have a friend called ignorance that follows them wherever they go, and ignorance is bliss. As long as that person gets what they desire, they will not care how they got it or who may have suffered.

'With ignorance comes selfishness, and with selfishness come lies and deceit. By the time that person dies, their soul may contain thousands of unclean, unseen spirits, and their soul will be taken to hell. Now that I have taught you what you have forgotten, I will prove these things to you by letting the Pharisees and the Romans kill me. Do not cry for me, for my suffering is just and will be but a moment in the sands of time.'

Governor's Personal Daily Report
My spies tell me that this Jesus is about to ride into town as the King of Kings and Lord of Lords. This latest insult has driven the Pharisees near to madness; they say that by doing this he mocks the Emperor directly, by challenging his sovereignty over the land. I dare not tell them that this one man has Rome by the throat.

Governor's Personal Daily Report
It seems as if the gods of Rome have finally heard the cries of Rome. My spies tell me something I dare not believe. They say this Jesus has had a last supper with his disciples and is preparing to hand himself over to Rome. I will not let my excitement get the better of me... I will be cautious, for it may be a trap. He may have finally grown tired of being a so-called prophet and may have gone back to the sword; or he may be planning to enter into the main Roman compound to slay us all.
My spies come to me and tell me this Jesus has sent Judas to the Pharisees telling him... Please read underneath:

The Spoken Word of Jesus
'Judas, go tell the Pharisees and the Romans they can come and get me at the garden. Tell them I won't kill them and that to prove it I have sent you, Judas, one of my most trusted men. For I must now complete my mission here on the earth.

'I must prove to the begotten and the chosen that I will lay down my life for the MOST HIGH and that the MOST HIGH will pick me up again for a short time; so that they may see that what I have told them is true. My suffering at the hands of my enemies must not blind you my friends, nor the begotten or chosen ones.

'My pain, suffering, humiliation and death at the hands of my enemies, will be a bittersweet experience for them. For in killing me they will complete the prophecy that will send me back to the right side of my FATHER and MOTHER; giving them all praise and glory. I will return to you and only you, and the begotten and the chosen ones will bear witness to the truth. For in the times to come, the Pharisees and mankind will hunt you down and will kill all of you who say the MOST HIGH is their master. You will all need your faith in the times to come.'

Governor's Personal Daily Report

I cannot believe it. The great Jesus stood before me today, battered and bruised, but I still stand on the side of caution. I have told the Pharisees, in front of him, that Rome has no fight with this man and that they had better take him to King Herod who killed his cousin John the Baptist. If this Jesus wishes to shed blood, then standing before the man who killed his cousin, good friend and teacher; will surely unravel his true plot and unleash his renowned fury.

If it is true and he is willing to lay down his life for his GOD, then the egotistical, bloodthirsty, sexually deprived King Herod will kill him just as quickly as he killed John the Baptist; for the mad king believes this Jesus to be the reincarnated John.

Governor's Personal Daily Report

This cannot be happening. The Pharisees and Herod have failed to make good on their anger towards this Jesus, and they have not killed him. He stood once again before me; only the journey has not been good to him, as he has bruises upon bruises.

I truly believe he is going to let Rome kill him, or anyone who dares to do so, for that matter. I have spoken in length with him today and he admitted that he is willing to let me kill him. The Gods of Rome have finally heard my cries and have given me this Jesus, to do with as I please. It will go down in the records of Rome and the world, as my finest hour, and I will be glorified like a God.

The entire world will know me as the slayer of the mighty Jesus, and history will portray me as a mighty governor and soldier. Rome will once again be victorious over all its enemies, and those who think that they can come against Rome will tremble and hide under the rocks; for it will be Rome that writes the history that is in the making here today. For the Gods of Rome are truly the greatest of all.

Governor's Personal Daily Report

Today I will know if this Jesus is really willing to give his life for his GOD. I will have him tortured, for he must be made an example of. His death must be slow, humiliating and extremely painful; and must occur in the full view of all the people. He will be put on the cross, for this is a fitting demise of such a thorn in the side of Rome. I fear it will take some years before this Jesus' legacy is forgotten.

The first thing I will do once he is dead, is go into the land and slay all who knew him and all that have followed him; none will be left who ever saw this man in the flesh. Once that is done, I will send word to Rome that some decades from now, a man must be sent into this land; though he must not come from here, for the people will be wary. This man will have to investigate what the people know or remember about this Jesus, for I will not rest until all that know him or believed in him, are dead.

Governor's Personal Daily Report

Today was a great day, I could not believe my eyes. I know the Gods of Rome have applied justice to this Jesus, who mocked them and Rome. He was first whipped and beaten within inches of his life but this almost spoiled what I had in store for him, and I had to allow him a day's grace so that he could carry his cross to Skull Mountain.

What kind of man is he? He believed so much in this GOD that he called the MOST HIGH, that not even the pain could make him disbelieve. What a waste. This man could have been a great asset to Rome... but these blacks are a foolish people; so strong and yet so weak because of their belief in this MOST HIGH. Rome could not be beaten forever by this black Jew and his outlaws. It is written that these blacks are beneath us and must be conquered and ruled, for they do not know the value of their land and how rich its soils are. This Jesus eventually had to fall to the far superior Gods of Rome.

Today was a mighty day for Rome. Jesus, stripped naked for all to see, was marched to the place of crucifixion carrying Rome's instrument of death on his back. Today the cross has become an icon of Rome that will be remembered forever, just as I will be. The mighty Jesus is no more and it was the mightier Rome that brought him down.

How could this black thing believe he could make Rome bow forever? Now I will kill all of his people and erase all of these damn black Jews from the face of the earth. Some say the great earthquake happened because of his death, but I say that if he were so great he would have gotten down from the cross or stopped us in the first place. I believe his black magic had run out and he knew it. And this MOST HIGH who supposedly made the earth shake in anger... where was he, and why did he not stop the killing of his son?

35 years After the Death of Jesus

Rome has sent an investigator to the region to find out what impact the death of Jesus had on the people. The investigator was charged with discovering if the people still remembered what he had taught, if they still believed him, if they would dare speak of it in public, if they would proclaim themselves to be believers and if they would tell his story to strangers.

To Rome's horror and shock, belief in him is even stronger than it was when he was alive. Moreover, many who had hated him for what he had preached, now honoured him for dying for what he believed in. Lastly, because of the brutal way in which Rome killed him and so many black Jews, Rome is hated more now than then.

Governor's Report to Rome

The almost indestructible nature of the black Jews is hard to fathom. No matter how many we kill, they still seem to breed like rats; and even though we have killed almost all that dared to stay in this cursed land, they still exist in large amounts in regions to the east. Furthermore, it has been almost impossible to get them to follow Rome's gods over this one GOD known as the MOST HIGH. I think it may be better to make a hybrid religion from their religion and change their thinking from within, rather than to continue with the methods used to this point. These black Jews are rebellious and will not bow, no matter how many soldiers attempt to control them.

Rome's Reply to Governor

Rome has read your report. Unbeknownst to you, we had already made such decisions to attempt to reach these savages and teach them the ways of Rome from within. We are already building a religion from the core of their beliefs, and have called this new religion Christianity. Our only problem to date is the fact that you did not kill off Jesus' brothers and sisters, as you reported you had. The only reason Rome has not had your head for this is because it has turned out that killing them would have been more damaging to Rome's efforts to quell the hearts of these savages. His brothers and sisters have been able to keep the focus on the teachings of their brother; this has not been a bad thing, because his teachings are no match for Christianity.

Our man Paul is spreading the new word and it is being received well among the black Jews. We have changed such things as A: Join Christianity and you will go to heaven and B: All who join our new religion will be reborn with a new mind and spirit and become joint heirs with Jesus, the head of our new religion Christianity. To combat Jesus' brothers and sisters, instead of killing them and making them martyrs like Jesus, we will offer the people what they don't offer and we will offer more than they do.

Paul will tell the people that he has received word from Jesus the GOD in heaven, not from Jesus the man. The man's new name is Jesus Christ, and he has told Paul to spread Jesus' new word from heaven... that all are to become Christians and share in the glory of heaven, standing by the right side of Jesus. Only if they become a Christian will this be possible and if they do, they will become the new sons of GOD and will be higher than the angels.

We will rid from the followers of Christianity, the curse of the begotten; we will say that Jesus is the only begotten and that we the people of the church of Christ will become his body, as he is the head of the church.

In short, we will take his teachings and give them to the entire world, not just those he came to speak to. How dare he claim that Rome is not good enough to hear the message he brought? Christianity will be made into a world religion and the cross will become our symbol; and the world will idolise it and Rome. For it was Rome's cross that killed the mighty Jesus and all will be made to remember this, lest they suffer the same fate.

I do not believe that the teachings of Jesus that have been upheld by his family, will be able to compete with what we will offer the people through Christianity. As long as we don't kill them, they will slowly become less of a threat; we will beat them through the mind rather than through war.

It was Caesar who said that you must hide in the last place your enemies will think to look, and so it will be with Christianity. Rome will keep itself distanced from this religion until the black Jews have been made passive.

We will also introduce this new religion around the world. However, we will have to change the image of Jesus and the followers of the MOST HIGH to look like me, the Emperor, and like the people of Rome; rather than those black savages. And the MOST HIGH, will now be called GOD. Rome will send another investigator into the region in another 35 years, to see if our new religion has been successful in distancing these savages from their long-held beliefs. We will take this black religion and make it suitable for our people. We will make it our own.

Known Family of Jesus

Mother Mary, Father Joseph. Last name removed.

Brothers of Jesus; three names, not relevant apart from James who is against Christianity.

First cousin: John the Baptist. Killed.

Marital status

Wife: Mary Magdalene
Children: Five, names unknown
Whereabouts of wife and children unknown

<u>Analysis with Facts and Hindsight:</u>

The true teachings of Jesus are harder to swallow than the teachings of Christianity. The real Jesus didn't teach that we must turn the other cheek. If someone was to hit him on the cheek, he would have given them a beating, at the very least. He lived by the law 'an eye for an eye and a tooth for a tooth'. If you treated him with respect and love, he would treat you likewise. However, if you came to him with the sword, then war you would get.

It is good for governments to maintain the status quo, as teaching the people that Jesus accepted revenge against one's oppressors, would lead to greater anarchy on our streets. Rome shared this view and decided it was best to view Jesus in GOD form, and to keep the focus off of his human nature. One must remember that Rome was finding it difficult to keep that part of the world under control and Jesus before becoming a preacher, had been a champion among the people and a legend throughout the region.

Once he had let himself be killed, the people in his community lost hope. Rome tried to capitalise on this, but the people still would not adopt to the Roman culture or its many religions.

It was recognised that if they used the name of Jesus and then slowly grafted it into Roman theology, over a long period of time, the people would begin to believe that Christianity was in fact the religion of Jesus and was a part of divine authority. In fact, the people had been tricked into following just another Roman religion, which portrayed itself as righteous by associating itself with the word 'Christ'... as if that name had come from and was a part of Jesus. This grafting system took over twenty years and many hundreds of thousands of people had to be killed in order for it to be completed.

It is quite clear that although Jesus lived like any other man; he was also part angel and spirit. Rome and its religious leaders deliberately focused on a heavenly Jesus, made perfect and without sin. But it was clear that Jesus was not perfect and at no time did he claim to be so.

The claim that Jesus did not have sex also seems to be false and its purpose seems to come from the same thinking. Rome was portraying Jesus as Spirit only, rejecting his human nature. The idea that Jesus could not have sex because he was the son of the MOST HIGH does not make any sense, as sex is not a sin in the eyes of the MOST HIGH, who created it as the form for creating life. But the people seem willing to accept whatever they are told.

Jesus had sinned throughout his life and was no different from any other man in that aspect. What made him different was that he was the son of the MOST HIGH, and he made it clear over and over again that no man, himself included, went to heaven because of what they did or did not do.

Once again the thinking by Rome was to tell a story about the GOD Jesus, not the man Jesus. When referred to by a man as a good preacher, Jesus replied 'why do you call me good?' If he was without sin, to call him good would have been an understatement but Jesus made it very clear none were good on the earth, himself included.

If Jesus was without sin and was made to pay such a heavy price for a crime he did not commit, it would be true to think that a great injustice had taken place. For us as humans know it is not right to charge a man with a crime he did not commit, therefore, it would not be foolish to assume that the MOST HIGH would condemn his son for something he had not done; as they are without doubt the most intelligent and righteous of all beings.

Also man has free choice; this in itself removes any possible blame being put on Jesus' feet. Moreover, his death was meant to prove a point, not to remove man's sins. If it had been meant to remove man's sins, then there would be no Judgment Day to come for anyone...

It is quite clear from the records that JAW did not come to speak or to promise heaven to everyone. It is clear, even from the Roman times, that if the masses are to be kept under control, a large majority of them need to believe that they can live after this life on earth.

Therefore, it has been a decree from the Roman times, that the teachings of JAW be changed to state that not only the begotten and the chosen may enter heaven, but that everyone may. Also, it is in the interest of the present-day governments that religions keep on operating to pull in those people who need such comfort; therefore, JAW's teaching that no man needs religion will be changed to read, that without religion no man can get into heaven. This will allow the government to maintain control of the majority easily.

Statement 1: Those who wish to pretend to be the Messiah will use the name Jesus Christ, because their agenda will be to fool people into following them. Those false prophets who claim authority will also use the name JC.

Statement 2: The real Jesus will not call himself JC, because that is not his name and because he does not care if people follow him or not.

Statement 3: When referring to JAW, the term 'they' is used because JAW is a triple being: part supernatural spirit, part angel and part flesh.

Statement 4: The return of JAW is not certain and their birth place will be hard to determine. They must be born into the flesh and will be unaware of who they are for a period of time; this time span is unknown to man. They will live among us like any other person until their time of awakening, which may occur at any point between twelve and sixty years of age.

Statement 5: JAW will be the complete opposite of most of the text written about him in religious books. He will have a great hatred for any religion that does not put the MOST HIGH in a position for all praise and an even greater hatred for any religion that uses his name or any other name, to take away or reduce the amount of praise that should go to the MOST HIGH. He will hate the cross and those who worship it or pay homage to it, or any other idol.

Statement 6: To all future Presidents, Prime Ministers, and rulers of the world: the name JC and the identity provided from Roman times will only allow you to know who the false Messiahs are. Not even the real Messiah will know who they are until the time of their awakening, which will be ordered by the MOST HIGH themselves.

Statement 7: Therefore, it has been the decree from the time of rule of the Emperor of Rome that it be written in all religious texts, that the title of the first-begotten son of the MOST HIGH will become the only begotten son of GOD, and JAW will become Jesus Christ.

Statement 8: The begotten are not created by the MOST HIGH. The MOST HIGH gave birth to the begotten and they are therefore part MOST HIGH. No man knows how many children the MOST HIGH has. When trying to comprehend such matters, remember that giving birth and having children is not an idea, desire, or design of mankind; nor was it created by mankind.

Agent Smith sat back in his chair and tried to comprehend what he had just read. He could not, so he read it again and again; even though he still had many unread pages ahead of him. Eventually he decided to let the information he had just read digest in his brain before carrying on reading. He went into the next room, where Philip and Mark were sticking pins in a map. Agent Smith stood there, half watching them and half contemplating what he now knew.

'The whole world has been lied to,' he blurted out. Philip and Mark stopped what they were doing and immediately turned to Agent Smith.

'Come John and sit down. It must be quite a bit of a shock... that is, if you believe what you have just read?'

'I don't want to sit down, thank you. Yes, it is a shock and yes, I do believe it. What do we do now?'

'Well, Mark and I have almost finished pinpointing the exact whereabouts of the records. But I'm shocked you have read all of what was on the disk so quickly.'

'I... I haven't finished. I just had to stop for a moment to try and take in what I've read.'

'Believe me John, when my dad told me what was going on... and I believed my dad, because I know he's not a liar... it still took me a while to come to terms with it. But we are about to uncover the actual documents, which will not only prove what you have just read, but will tell us the real name of Jesus.'

'And then what? Do we tell the world his real name? I mean, if we tell the world, how will anyone know who the real Jesus is? After that every nut will change their claim from JC to JAW, whatever that means.'

'That John, is the question your brother-in-law Pete and I had to decide, once we had stumbled onto the Vatican's coded version of the records. Who has the right to say who knows what, or how much? We decided that if it is the word of the MOST HIGH, then everybody has a right to know the truth and to make up their own minds as to what they want to believe. That's why Pete gave his life. He, more than any of us, was willing to give his life so that the world would know the truth. Where Jesus is concerned,

I think we'll know when the time is right who the real Jesus is.'

'You guys are getting way ahead of yourselves. We're going to need some help if we're going to get into what I think is going to be our point of entry,' said Mark.

'Oh of course, I almost forgot to ask you John. Is there anyone in the FBI you can trust?'

'Yeah... Mike, my boss; I spoke to him already. Shit, I forgot to contact him. We went to the training academy together and we've been friends for a very long time. We made a code that if at any time one of us got too deep into something to handle it alone, and we needed the other's help, we would talk a certain way. That would tell the other one that the shit had hit the fan, without tipping off any eavesdroppers. Basically, Mike spoke as if he didn't believe me; he said he thought I was guilty and implied that he would be coming after me himself. That told me that it was not safe to talk on work, mobile or home phone lines. I have a number here to call him on after six. When I last spoke to him, I was so upset that I'd been made out to be a cop killer, I almost forgot about our code. What time is it now?'

'Six-forty.'

'Okay, I'll give him a call. What do we need?'

'Plans for the part of the sewer system that runs dead centre between the White House, the Capitol, and the Jefferson and Lincoln Memorial Buildings. Plus, we'll need information on any access tunnels and alarm systems that may be in operation, and security details as well.'

'The whole nine yards. Shit, Mike's going to love me for this.'

'Is it possible to get all of that?' asked Philip, almost as if he suspected the answer would be no.

'With Mike's level of clearance, it shouldn't be a problem. I mean, if we needed to go in under any one of the buildings, it would be near-impossible, but you want to go in the middle right?' asked Agent Smith.

'Yes. If my dad's decoding skills are as good as he says, then it would seem that instead of sticking this stuff in a box in an underground safe under the White House, they have decided to hide the records in the middle of all four buildings. Why is that, Dad?' asked Mark.

'There was great mistrust at the time between the church and the Enlightenment, otherwise known as the Freemasons. Both sides knew that if they could get rid of the other side, the remaining one would have all the power. Thus, a code was set up, as I told you before. Sometime after that the Freemasons, under the leadership of Albert Pike, went right down the dark road and began to practice in satanic rituals, worshipping the god Virgo who is said to be the queen and bride of Satan. But many of the members did not wish to follow such devilish ways.

'The other version of these events, and believe me there are many, is that this group of Freemasons thought Albert Pike wielded too much power. For this reason they tried to break away and attempted to steal the records from their original resting place; which was actually under the White House in a safe. Ultimately, however they did not succeed. Albert Pike, using the unseen forces, knew their every move. He had them all killed and then re-housed the records in a location that he alone knew; this is the latest code, which today's Freemasons couldn't crack.

'You have to understand that these secret organisations are made up of fragmentary groups within the one organisation. You have the Illuminati and the Builderburg who are very powerful organisations in themselves and there are many others, as well as individual persons of great wealth and power. All are kept under the umbrella of the oldest organisation, the Freemasons.

'There are so many egos to control within this one secret sect, that wars constantly erupt inside the inner circle; which is divided into many different factions. So codes are made, things are moved, secrets are divulged, power moves are made, and continents and countries are won and lost all around the world. And all of this happens to suit these twenty-four men, whose only desire is to be as rich and as powerful as possible, for as long as possible. Yet the world and mankind's offspring must pay the price for their greed.'

'But how have they kept power for all these hundreds of years?' asked Mark.

'Bloodlines, my son, bloodlines. They groom their children to be heartless from kindergarten to boarding school,' replied Philip.

'But don't some of them rebel and refuse to be like their parents?' asked Mark.

'Before you answer him Philip, I'm going to the phone booth to make the call. I'll be back shortly. To tell you the truth, I could do with stretching my legs and getting some fresh air.' Agent Smith made his way to the phone booth, his mind bouncing from one revelation to another. As he walked down the thirty or so steps to reach the bottom, he looked back at the apartment and studied its design.

'All those steps to walk up and down... so narrow and they're the only way in and out. I must tell Mark I think he could have picked a better building; if they were to find us here, we'd never be able to get out. I wonder who lives underneath? Maybe we'd be better on the bottom floor; at least then we could jump out of a window,' he thought. He stepped into the phone booth, closed its door and dialled the contact number for Mike.

'Hello Mike, it's me.'

'*What the hell took you so long?* You were supposed to call me the next day! I thought they had either caught you or the phone numbers were somehow different and you'd been trying to call me on a different number; are you okay?'

'I'm fine Mike but this shit that has hit the fan, is nothing like anything we ever imagined we'd be using this coded system of ours for…'

'Listen, you don't have to tell me John. What I'm about to tell you, only me and one other person knew about; and somehow these same people that are after you have got to them. I don't know what I'm going to do.'

'What do you mean Mike?'

'I had a man on the inside of the Freemasons, it took me years to set up. Just before I became head, I was approached by a clandestine organisation asking me if I wanted to become a member. They knew everything about me and said it would be the right thing to do, now that I was going to be the head of the FBI. I told them no, and they said I was making a mistake.

'The next day I got a phone call from the President, telling me that I had to be at a mansion in the middle of nowhere. To make it worse, I got official letters telling me the same thing. It was all carried out under National Security and I was obliged, by my employment contract, to remain silent about the whole thing.

'I mean, this was the norm, it wasn't even special. Once you made it to this level in the government, you're sworn to secrecy on things like this. So I did as I was told and was basically told whose toes not to step on; and they weren't all government people, not by a long shot. I mean, you had the usual heads of departments, Presidents and Vice Presidents and their friends; but there were also high-end religious people, global corporations and terrorist organisations.'

'What? Are you serious?'

'You better believe it. I never got in that deep; they knew I was not one of them, but they knew I was a company man and would do as I was told. And if I didn't, well, let's just say it would be a fool that got on the wrong side of them. I mean every President and Prime Minister, before their inauguration they have to go and sit before these people, who then decide if they become president or not.'

'Are you shitting me? Aren't we the ones who vote who's in office?'

'John these people... well it's not the people, it's the organisation they become a member of. You see Presidents, C.E.Os and heads of religions come and go; but the secret organisation, well, they are there forever. This organisation has built the entire system that runs every major country in the world. I mean, they control it all. When you and I and the dumb fucks of this world go to vote, we take it for granted that the system is not rigged. We half-brainwash ourselves into believing this because we want to believe that the country we live in is free and a democracy.

'It's easier for us to look at China and Iraq and say aren't we lucky we don't live in those countries? But the truth is we have no idea about the system we live in. It's always been run by a few, they've just removed the ugly-looking dictator in the bad suit and replaced it with a complex system. If you decide to try and find out why something is, you will soon be confused or pissed off at all the red tape you will have to go through, just to get a simple answer.

'They sell us a dream and while we watch the dream they fuck us all from behind. The average man and woman in the street know that the way we live right now is not good for us or for future generations, but the organisation won't change how things are run. Every year they have committees telling them things are getting worse and what do they do? They schedule another meeting with the same committees for the same time next year and then it happens all over again. It's the biggest con and we're all going down with these people who have sold their souls for power.

'So I sent a man in undercover, to find out who exactly sits at the table at these meetings. When I was sworn in, they were all wearing masks and black hooded silk robes with markings on them, and no one showed their face at any time. But I have no idea what's gone wrong; my agent refuses to contact me... it's as if he has become a completely different person.'

'What was his name, if you don't mind me asking?'

'It doesn't make a damn bit of difference now because he's become one of them. His name is Williams and I picked him myself because I thought they would not be able to get to him but I was wrong, I should have known better; but I did get pictures from him before they turned him around and the people on those pictures are bad news.

'When it came down to us from the NSA and the CIA that you were a spy, I knew then that you were the only other person I could trust. These people and their organisation are in everything. They are the USA, UK, Russia, Europe and any heinous dictatorship anywhere in the world. They are the billion-dollar businesses and they are the military companies that feed the constant conflicts all around the world. I truly hope that whatever you have, whatever it is that they are willing to kill you for; can bring them to their knees John. If not, your kids and mine are going to inherit nothing but contamination.'

'I'm glad you said all of that Mike, because I wasn't sure what it was I was doing this for anymore. I've heard so much that has told me that my life is one big lie; that almost everything other than GOD and my family that I believed in, is false. This is so above my head that I don't know why I haven't drowned yet... No, that's not true; I do know why I haven't drowned yet. It's because of the MOST HIGH... and yes Mike, what I have *will* bring this organisation to its belly, never mind its knees. Now here's what I need from you in order to do that.'

Agent Smith returned to the apartment. Climbing up its steep stairs, he knocked on the door with a *ratta-tat-tat*, so that Philip and Mark would know it was him; that was the coded knock.

'Everything is set. I have to phone Mike back tomorrow to confirm a drop off point and time, for the information required.'

'Excellent. I think with the help of the MOST HIGH, we will pull this off. We'll tell the world the truth and avenge the killings of our friends,' said Philip, hugging Agent Smith.

'Well, I'm going back now to read some more. I'll see you in a moment,' said Agent Smith. He turned slowly and walked out of the room, almost as if he were in a trance. Philip looked at his son, who looked back at him. They said nothing for a moment, then turned back to their flags and map.

Agent Smith slowly sat back down into his chair and looked at the computer screen. As he did, he began to feel cold and a shiver ran down his spine. Immediately he spun around in his chair but he went a bit too fast, as his turning momentum lifted the chair onto its right back leg and Agent Smith tumbled to the ground with a bang.

Philip and Mark ran into the room to see what had happened, Mark had his gun drawn as he entered.

'Oh my Lord,' said Philip as he stared in amazement.

'Move back towards me John,' said Mark, aiming his gun in front of him.

'It's okay Mark, put down your gun. This is a friend of mine who has saved my life.'

'What is it?' asked Philip, as he stared at the see-through entity.

'I don't know, but I see it every now and then.' Mark put his gun to his side and asked Agent Smith to think back and try to remember what happened when he saw it. Agent Smith tried, but could not really concentrate; he was so in awe of the entity that every time he saw it he just wanted to look at it.

'John I need you to think, is this good news or bad news?' shouted Mark.

'There is nothing to fear. If it is frightening you then maybe you should go back and get on with finding whatever it was you were looking for.' snapped Agent Smith, who just wanted to be left alone so he could take in what he saw as the entity's beauty.

Agent Smith turned to Mark telling him to leave and as he turned back, he just caught sight of the entity as it moved up towards the ceiling and then vanished.

'Damn!' shouted Agent Smith. 'Look what you've done, it's gone now and I didn't get as much time as I could have because of you!' Agent Smith picked up the chair and sat back down on it with a thump. He looked at the screen, but didn't read anything.

Mark mumbled something to himself as he turned and went back into the other room. Philip remained standing in the doorway for several minutes, repeating the words *'That was amazing.'* Eventually he looked at Agent Smith and asked him again, 'What was that?' But Agent Smith did not reply, and eventually Philip went back into the other room as though he were in a trance.

It took Agent Smith half an hour of sitting in his chair, trying to make himself go cold and get a shiver down his spine, before he gave up and admitted to himself that he would now just have to hope that the entity would return.

He thought about its very faint light rainbow colour; it was like the others, but he realised that they all had slight differences. This one had a very faint rainbow colour effect running through it, while another one had a light blue effect; he was certain that they were not all the same, as he had originally thought. What that meant, he was not certain, but he felt as if he were getting to know something about them, and for some reason that made him feel warm inside. He looked at his watch and was amazed to see that two hours had passed since the entity had left and he still hadn't started reading. He scrolled onto the next page.

JAW 1967 The Armageddon Code

TOP SECRET FOR YOUR EYES ONLY

Case material: Angels and Demons and Their True Identity and Purpose

From the beginning of recorded history mankind has reported on beings not of this world, known as angels and demons. There are many cave paintings depicting angels, demons and lights in the sky. In modern times, the Bible is probably the place most associated with angels and demons. In the Bible, angels are often mistaken for stars or else are called stars; this would suggest that angels, in the physical realm, can shine bright like the sun and can be viewed from a great distance. This also means that they can fly.

In ancient times, mankind made gods of these beings that did not look like mankind; there are many sculptures and paintings to prove this. Many of these ancient worlds saw these beings without having any communication with them.

It is believed that these were angels and that they would only speak to the people to whom they had been sent to by the MOST HIGH. However, it has been known to our organisation that all worshipped beings were not angels; most made themselves known to ancient mankind and deliberately promoted the worship of themselves, and these are known as demons.

Those who are with Satan are not angels; they are beings who were created by the MOST HIGH but who, like so much of mankind, have rebelled against praise to the MOST HIGH. They have seen their own intelligence as all-powerful and wish to make themselves gods.

Mankind believes that these demons are looking to wage war against the MOST HIGH, with Satan as their leader; but this couldn't be farther from the truth. Satan has no desire to wage war against the MOST HIGH, simply because they know they could not win.

Only the foolish can entertain such a notion and not even demons are that foolish. Satan understands who the MOST HIGH is better than all of mankind put together and knows that the MOST HIGH is the foundation of all creations. This means that if *they* do not exist, then nothing in the universe of all realms can exist. To kill the MOST HIGH is to kill oneself.

These demons are actually creations on the run from their own planets. They are more advanced than mankind and have travelled vast distances to reach a safe place from the terror that pursues them. This terror is known as JAW and the angels of war. These beings have found a safe haven on earth for thousands of years, but their very nature is mischievous at best and totally evil at worst. Hence, they are pursued by JAW and the angels of war.

These beings have been safe here on earth because mankind is a young seed in the creation of the universe and has only developed the ability to leave the earth in the last century. This is not by chance; the so-called demons who are beings, E.B.Es or aliens, have been dictating the pace of mans development so that it will run concurrently with their own agendas.

They have fooled mankind into believing that they are angels and gods, when in fact they are just a creation of the MOST HIGH who are more advanced than mankind; they were given free will and their own planets in their own solar systems, just like mankind.

It is our organisation's decision to keep the fact that these are just beings on the run from JAW a secret and to let mankind believe they are demons associated with Satan. It is in the best interest of our organisation that these beings identity be kept secret from mankind, as it will undermine our authority if mankind is made aware of their existence.

However, as for the angels of the MOST HIGH, a policy has been in place from the days of the Roman Empire, that these beings should have their appearance changed to look like humans with wings; rather than the beasts that they truly look like. Mankind thinks angels are humans with wings; we have been able to turn the real angels into aliens or E.B.Es, which they are.

The difference between these beings is not how they look but how they operate. Angels operate on a higher knowledge level than the E.B.Es; the authority in which the angels operate under is more restricted but never-the-less it is still way higher than the E.B.Es. Angels function directly under the orders of the MOST HIGH, like soldiers, to create positive and negative choices and much more.

Both are creations of the MOST HIGH, however, angels work to maintain creation values and balances and checks and stops, in the physical and spiritual dimensions; whereas E.B.Es, like humans, work to serve their own interests. This is why E.B.Es have been able to lie to mankind and pretend that they are angels and even gods; so that they can get mankind to do their bidding. The other thing to understand is that some E.B.Es live in the physical and spiritual dimensions.

To sum it up, E.B.Es are like a con man who'll put on a police uniform and pretend he has the right to tell you what to do. Angels are the real police force of the universe but the authority of the MOST HIGH which they operate under, is removed.

It is important we keep mankind guessing about the end of our world, they must not know that the end is drawing near; although mankind does not know that when physical angels can be seen, it means the coming of JAW. It is still a good idea to keep mankind under the assumption that they are looking at alien beings rather than angels. We must try to make them unsure that they are looking at anything at all; just in case any unforeseen situation may arise, in which mankind became aware of the real meaning of the sighting of angels in the physical world or strange lights in the sky.

It has not entered into the minds of mankind what terrifying creatures angels really are. Mankind does not comprehend the work that these creatures were created for. They are the soldiers of the MOST HIGH, and they are at the top of the food chain. They will kill an entire galaxy without question or remorse, and have done so on many occasions. Their life is dedicated to serving the MOST HIGH without question, and their purpose is to destroy all that does not please the MOST HIGH.

Mankind cannot deal with the knowledge that such beings do exist and are above the authority of mankind. It has been advised that such sightings should be disclaimed by the government and that at no time should any sightings be connected to their true identity.

Therefore, mankinds image will take the place of the angels, meaning all pictures of angels will now be a picture of a human being with wings; whilst all sightings will be classified as UFO or alien and the real angels will be known as aliens that do not exist.

Even though not all angels kill, it has been the norm from Roman times, to make angels look like mankind; this gives mankind the impression that they are the centre of the universe and that they are the MOST HIGH's crowning glory.

If we were to admit that the angels are beings on a higher level than ourselves, we would be admitting that rather than being the crowning glory of the MOST HIGH, we are just another creation; one that is not as high as many of the other species out there. This must never be known to mankind as it will open Pandora's Box and we would have to divulge too much information about mankind and its true place in the universe.

So to clarify: angels, who are the soldiers of the MOST HIGH, are known today as aliens; in whom people are encouraged to disbelieve.

The truth is that angels are a creation made by the MOST HIGH, just as mankind was created. However, they are far superior to mankind and they exist on two realms at the same time. One of these realms is the physical, which is the realm in which mankind exists, and the second is the spiritual or non-physical.

There are many types of angels. Some live mainly in the physical but can go from one realm to another, while other certain types live only in the physical and others only live in the spiritual. Their functions are different. Some interact with the physical world without ever being in the physical realm, while others interact with the physical world from within the physical realm. Some interact with humans indirectly, while others interact directly with humans. Those that interact with humans directly, do it in different ways; some will appear as humans, even though that is not their real physical appearance, others will appear in their true physical form and there are those that will remove their interaction with humans from the humans minds.

Some come to harm mankind mentally, physically, or both. Some come to help, guide, or both. Some are physically superior to mankind, but all are mentally superior and have mental abilities that man cannot even dream of. All have a function, and whether it is to the good of mankind or to the detriment of mankind, that fact remains true.

Even Satan has a function. He is an angel with a job to do, not the great enemy of the MOST HIGH as he is made out to be in the Bible. The reality is there are no enemies of the MOST HIGH. None have the power or capability to become anything more than an extremely minor irritation to the SUPREME BEING. They would be crushed like a bug underfoot if they tried to challenge the MOST HIGH, Satan included.

This is where religion comes in. It allows mankind to think that it is, at the least, on the same level as beings such as the angels. In fact certain religions, usually the more popular ones, allow mankind to think that they are on a higher level than beings such as demons. This is necessary in order to reduce the levels of anxiety in the population, because if these are high it will lead to unrest, mass hysteria and a breakdown of law and order.

The angels who are of most concern to our organisation, are the angels under the General JAW. Their function is the destruction and occupation of worlds in the universe. The lifestyles of the inhabitants of these destroyed and occupied worlds, are offensive to the MOST HIGH; or are at risk of causing intergalactic offence. This means that what they are doing on the planets that they are dwelling on, will eventually affect other creations of the MOST HIGH on other planets or galaxies.

It is believed that JAW and his armies deal with creations of the MOST HIGH on a prioritized scale. Firstly they are dealt with according to their offensive nature to the MOST HIGH and secondly according to their threat level. For example, in the last few thousand years mankind is believed to have become highly offensive to the MOST HIGH... however, that time has passed in a matter of seconds in the MOST HIGH's realm. Although to the foolish it may seem as if mankind is getting away with its actions, that is the result of a lack of comprehension on the part of mankind.

As to the second consideration: mankind is considered to pose a high threat level, because mankind has discovered space flight. It is believed that mankind has already, in the short time since it invented spacecrafts, dumped thousands of tonnes of space debris without any concern for where it may float or to what it may come in to contact with.

JAW is the first-begotten son of the MOST HIGH and is the General of the angels of war. An ancient text refers to them as the locusts of living beings, which devour all flesh in the physical realm and torture all unclean spirits and souls in the spiritual realm. This same text reports that there is no escaping JAW and his Hades, but that many beings have tried and that some have made it to earth; however, when they have reached the earth they have heard the wind of the oncoming JAW and his angels of war. As earths time is now up, it has entered into the sights of JAW.

It is believed that these beings, which are part of the cause for mankinds doom, will use their mental abilities to cause as many as possible of mankind to offend the MOST HIGH; so that JAW is kept busy on earth while they make their escape and hide deeper in the universe. They have promised to take us with them so that we may avoid Armageddon, on the condition that we keep delivering as much of mankind as we can to the worship of false idols and gods; which will rack up the numbers of people to be dealt with. The more offensive we can make mankind, the more time JAW will spend dealing with them while we escape.

Excluding the MOST HIGH, there are none more powerful, terrifying, skilled in warfare, torture, death and destruction of the physical, spiritual or any other realms or beings, than are JAW and the angels of war.

It is believed that over the past two thousand years in the physical realm, JAW and his Hades have been systematically going from galaxy to galaxy, solar system to solar system and planet to planet; and that they have wrought death and destruction on all creations unpleasing to the eyes of the MOST HIGH.

This is the true function of JAW; a well known saying of his is 'My heart's desire is to rid all unpleasing things from the sight of the MOST HIGH, and I will not rest until there are none left.' The angels of the MOST HIGH have a saying as well, which is 'It is our hearts desire to do the unpleasing works of the MOST HIGH, so that the MOST HIGH may sit back and relax and enjoy their heavenly creations.'

J A W 1967 the Armageddon Code

TOP SECRET FOR YOUR EYES ONLY

Case Material: Spiritless Mankind

We must make sure that mankind never knows the truth, if we are to stop them from ever having any chance of saving themselves. We must continue to brainwash them into believing that the religions we have given to them, dating back to the times of the Romans, are authentic and originate from God. Jesus Christ must be made out to be their saving grace, and they must believe that all that come against him are devils. This must be done in order to fan the flames of fury of JAW when they are awakened.

Mankind must never know that Jesus sinned only in one way, which was that for a time he did not believe in the word of the MOST HIGH. Whilst growing up, he said he did not believe the MOST HIGH existed, but he repented of this talk.

The MOST HIGH forgave him, but told him that he would have to die one day for the sake of his brothers, sisters and the begotten of the MOST HIGH; who would act in similarly foolish ways whilst they were growing up. As he was the eldest and because he had committed this sin first, he would have to show them what they would come to forget; who they were and who their FATHER and MOTHER was.

Mankind can never know, that apart from the above sin, no matter what Jesus did, he could not sin. Mans laws were not the authority that governed his life.

Mankind must never know that it was us who made the laws and the Ten Commandments, not the MOST HIGH. Only guidance and advice is offered to mankind from the MOST HIGH; they will not make laws and commandments as that would break their own law of ensuring free will to all mankind.

The JAW codes tell us that Jesus will not know who he is, as this is the law written by the MOST HIGH. He will grow in the western world under Satan's philosophers, which is us and our world system; as he grows up, he will reject our world system through his own free will and choice.

The JAW codes also tell us that he will see himself as nothing and will reject communal prayer, to spend time alone in private prayer; begging the MOST HIGH to use him for whatever they please until the MOST HIGH is done with him and then throw him away into hell. He will think he is not worthy of heaven or the glory of being used by the MOST HIGH.

He will praise the MOST HIGH for the gift of life and will remember every day that he has not paid for the gift of life and is in eternal debt to the MOST HIGH. Therefore, he will be unwilling to ask the MOST HIGH for anything else, other than to be used by the MOST HIGH for whatever they wish.

He will hate all religions, as he will know that they are the work of Satan and the spiritless mankind.

The conditions on the earth have been made perfect. His hatred for the church will make mankind believe he is a devil and once he is awakened they will believe he is the Antichrist. In fact he will tell them that is who he is but mankind will never work out that the reason he is the Antichrist, is because Satan is the ruler of this world by the choice of mankind; who have chosen Satan's religions, the new testament and Paul, over the old testaments and Abraham.

Modern mankind must never know that it is the child of Satan. It must never know that Satan went before the MOST HIGH and asked for a people who were not as close to the MOST HIGH, as the people in the ancient times were. Satan complained that he would have no chance to sway the ancient people away from the MOST HIGH, because the MOST HIGH had made themselves known to them and fear kept their hearts pure; they were obedient out of fear and not out of true love for the MOST HIGH. So the MOST HIGH removed themselves and allowed Satan to make his own philosophy, which is our world system and religions.

Mankind must never know that the MOST HIGH did this because mankind was given free will and choice and had to have two opposites to choose from. Mankind must never know that Satan is doing his job by providing opposite thinking to the MOST HIGH, so that mankind can have a choice. They must believe that when they choose Satan, they are choosing a being that is challenging the MOST HIGH for control and that will kill the MOST HIGH and their angels.

This will fan the flames of JAW's anger and growing in the world he will know that those who choose Satan's way, believe this to be so.

We, the spiritless of mankind, have been able to convince the world that our way is the best way. All of the so-called chosen ones and spirit-filled people have followed us; they have taken to our religions and long for our dead things, over their living things. They have sold their spirits to us for worthless things.

We have led almost all of them astray and have delivered them to our gods and they, like lambs to a slaughter, will sacrifice their lives for us and our gods. In return our gods will take us up in the Rapture, to a new home deeper in the universe. Mankind has even bought into our Rapture and have come to believe that it is from the MOST HIGH, even though they know the MOST HIGH has never spoken of such a thing.

We must make sure that mankind never knows that Adam and Eve had a choice as to whether they would know good and evil. Mankind must never know that the MOST HIGH did not command them to not eat of the tree, but explained to them exactly what it would mean if they chose to know such things. The true meaning of Adam and Eve's choice to know good and evil was spiritual death.

They must never know that death from knowing good and evil actually meant that Adam and Eve had their spirits removed and became flesh and soul only, never to birth children with spirits. They must never know that from then on, 99% of mankind would be born without spirits. It must not be made known that they must fight the flesh and the world of the spiritless mankind, looking instead to the MOST HIGH for guidance.

Mankind must never know that Jesus came to explain this to the begotten, who are born with a spirit on earth but do not know who they are and will not be told until an unknown time that is set by the MOST HIGH.

Only the chosen ones, who are born without a spirit but have fought against the flesh and have desired the MOST HIGH over all else, are given a spirit by the MOST HIGH. They will see themselves as JAW saw himself whilst growing, not knowing who he was. They will call themselves unworthy of the MOST HIGH and will reject our religion; which says that we are something so great and important, that we have become the children of the MOST HIGH and are higher than the angels and that we are worthy of heaven and of standing at the side of JAW and THE MOST HIGH.

Never forget that it is our duty to keep the number of people who become chosen ones, as low as possible.

Mankind must never know how vain and proud they have become, nor must they know how angry this will make JAW and his angels of war. They must never know that by thinking and saying these things, they have automatically removed themselves from any hope of ever being favoured by THE MOST HIGH. For it is written and is known that those that think and say they are first will be last, and those that think and say they are last will be first. We have not hidden this from them but they still choose to think that by being a part of our religion, they have the right to call themselves joint heirs with Jesus.

They must never know that JAW was born not knowing who they are and believing they are nothing... seeing themselves as "last". They must never know that only those who think and do likewise will become the chosen ones.

Mankind can never be told that they are pieces in the world's most sophisticated video game and that most will live and die being at best, praise bearers to the MOST HIGH and at worst, nothing more than scenery; like a crowd in a video game.

Never forget that we owe it to our ancestors to keep these things secret and kept away from public knowledge.

We must never forget the tireless, hard work that our ancestors put into destroying the knowledge of JAW from his people. We must not forget the continuous work of our forefathers in Africa, who for four hundred years and more made slaves of the people of the MOST HIGH, destroying their land, heritage and history.

Only in our organisation today are they known to us as the black Jew. They know not who they are, and they know not that they are the original Jews; the chosen people of the MOST HIGH. It took great effort on the part of our forefathers, to rid the black Jew of the knowledge of themselves and to kill all who remembered who Jesus was; but today we can truly finally say that they do not have a clue and that the whole world believes the original Jew looked like a European, not an African.

We have completed the work of our Roman forefathers and have completed the transition from black to white. We have made the world hate blacks and have made their colour come to mean everything wicked and ugly, while our white colour has been put above theirs and has come to mean everything good and beautiful. All of heaven is now white not black and the world will not believe in a black Jesus, or aliens for angels. Without mankinds knowledge and with little effort, in the deepest parts of their subconscious minds we have planted the idea that black is evil and so any Black humans with supernatural powers who claim to be Jesus, will be rejected as evil and will therefore be believed to be of Satan.

Our religions have made it be known that in the last days Satan will come to destroy the earth. Mankind is so dead, that it cannot see that this world is so wicked that if Satan were not already here, when he eventually came there would be little left for him to do. Yet millions buy into our religions that say Satan is still yet to come.

We have not hidden from them that the greatest trick Satan has ever played, is convincing the world that he does not exist and yet they still choose to believe in what we tell them. This is because mankind, without a spirit, will always need a book to tell them what they should be feeling and thinking on the inside. Our forefathers have taken full advantage of the knowledge given to them from our gods, the beings who are on the run from JAW; and we must continue to do so.

Mankind can never know that we have made the Bible only using the teachings we want to use. They truly believe that the MOST HIGH needs books to explain things to them, and therefore they believe that the Bible must be correct. They are truly dead and have not understood that mankind has free will and choice; and therefore can choose to lie or distort the word of the MOST HIGH. They cannot understand that the MOST HIGH writes in the hearts of the spirit-filled mankind. But we have made it so, that they will always reject the spirit-filled mankind and their teachings from the MOST HIGH, in favour of our teachings in our books.

Mankind can never know why the Bible does not have any books called Jesus.

They must never know that Satan will stand before the MOST HIGH and say: "We never lied to mankind. We told them that Paul is the author of the New Testament and that Matthew, Mark, Luke and John are not Jesus; they just told a story about Jesus and it was mankinds choice to believe that they are apostles and disciples of Jesus.

'We did not hide it from them that Paul, Matthew, Mark, Luke and John did not know Jesus personally, or that they came from Europe and not from the land of Jesus. Mankind has chosen to think of them as Jesus' disciples and has chosen to believe that their teachings are true. They have chosen to believe the fact that because they called him Jesus Christ, means that was his true name.

'We did not hide from them the fact that Jesus did not leave his land to tell the world his teachings, and we did not hide it from them that he told his disciples not to go where the Gentiles are. We did not hide from them that he only came to speak to the lost sheep, and that it was Paul who said the New Testament was for the whole world.

'We did not hide from mankind that it was Rome that decided to canonise the Bible or that it was man, not the MOST HIGH, who decided what was to be in the Bible and what was to be left out."

Mankind cares not that the Bible has been written in so many different versions; each version was made to suit the ruler of its day and different versions were made for rulers in different countries. Each ruler decided what scriptures were in and what scriptures were out.

Satan will say to the MOST HIGH: "What a foolish and slothful people! They cannot be bothered to know about the man who ordered the canonised Bible, Constantine Emperor of Rome, nor to learn about how all emperors are vain and proud and call themselves gods. They are foolish and cannot be bothered to understand that Rome is known for many religions and that all of them are an offence to the MOST HIGH; as all of them have idols that are worshipped, such as the cross."

Satan will say to the MOST HIGH: "What a false people! They pretend that they care not for themselves but for the glory of the MOST HIGH; but they love Jesus only because they believe he came for everybody and that because of him they can go to heaven. It has not entered into their hearts or minds that if that was really true, no one would have killed Jesus because what he said would not have offended anyone."

We have told them to call themselves Christians, rather than calling themselves believers and lovers of the MOST HIGH; they do not understand that in doing so, they have replaced the MOST HIGH with their religious name. Yet we have not hidden it from them that no name should be held above the MOST HIGH; they chose to do this with their free will.

Satan will say to the MOST HIGH: "We did not hide it from them that the cross was used to publicly kill the enemies of Rome, as well as rapists and murderers; or that until Jesus was killed by the cross, alongside rapists and murderers, it had nothing to do with him. We did not hide that this was done to insult and humiliate the so-called King of the Jews; by killing him in a way reserved for rapists, paedophiles and child murderers."

Imagine how JAW will feel when he sees half the world worshipping our symbol of strength, power and domination: the cross.

Imagine how JAW will feel when he sees half the world bowing on their hands and knees before the cross; the thing we used to cause him great humiliations and even greater pain and suffering.

Imagine how JAW will feel when he sees half the world now looking to our cross for guidance and protection, as if it were a God.

Imagine how JAW will feel when he sees half the world wearing our cross around their necks and kissing it; knowing that it makes them feel good, when they know it caused him such pain.

JAW will utterly destroy them, and we will make good our escape. It is now all in place; now all we must do is await his awakening.

Agent Smith sat back in the chair once again and very slowly shook his head in disbelief. He looked at the next page.

J A W 1967 the Armageddon Code

TOP SECRET FOR YOUR EYES ONLY

Case material: Satan Lucifer Devil.

Satan Lucifer Devil: this is the full name of Satan, who is not the enemy of the MOST HIGH; rather, he is an archangel. Mankind must never know that Satan Lucifer Devil is not the enemy of the MOST HIGH, but is the enemy of man.

The MOST HIGH chose Satan to sit at the opposite end of the universe and to play the MOST HIGH in a universal game of chess. It is correct to say that Satan did not want to play this game, as it meant that he would be going up against the MOST HIGH and ultimately would lose. However, he never desired to become a true enemy of the MOST HIGH and challenge them for the throne.

Satan's function is to supply mankind with constant knowledge of evil and to provide mankind with constant choice; as mankind is born into a world of good and evil. Mankind must decide, not Satan, what choices it will make. Mankind believes that Satan is an enemy of the MOST HIGH, believing that Satan is opposed to the MOST HIGH through rebellious choice and not because the MOST HIGH has given Satan this function. Yet if Satan were opposed to the ways of the MOST HIGH and were an enemy wishing to kill the MOST HIGH, if he continued to live, then he would have to be so powerful that the MOST HIGH could not kill him.

Mankind have chosen to believe this.

Mankind must not know that Satan is nothing more than a doorman. He does not try to get mankind into heaven in order to destroy heaven; he stands before the MOST HIGH and tells the MOST HIGH what he was able to get mankind to do on earth. The truth is that Satan is an enemy of mankind and is only a danger to those who choose to follow him instead of the MOST HIGH. He will lead all who choose to follow him into hell.

Also contrary to common belief, Satan does not live in hell. He lives in the first and second heaven in the spiritual realm. He is an archangel who interacts with the physical realm but cannot enter the physical realm. When a man or woman enters the spiritual realm they are less than Satan, but in the physical realm, man and woman are more than Satan because of free will. The saying 'The devil made me do it,' is a lie. Satan cannot make mankind do anything; mankind must choose to do it.

Agent Smith stared at the screen, he was stunned; not at what he had been reading, but at how easy it was to believe. The only thing shocking him was the way the minds of those who wanted to control the world worked. It all made sense... their lack of care for the planet and the fact that they never seemed to be rich enough; that no matter how many billions they had, they always wanted more and more.

Agent Smith looked at his watch and then got up to stretch his legs. He had to look at his watch again, as his mind had not registered the time when he first looked at it. He was torn between wanting to read to know more and wanting to take time to try and understand what he had been reading so far. However, the thing he now wanted to know, more than anything, was what Jesus' full name was. He decided that the best thing to do was to talk with Philip about what he had just read and to try and put it all into context in his mind.

As he entered the room, Philip and Mark were standing over the map on the floor, looking down at it intensely.

'John, take a look at the black flag in the middle of the map. That flag represents the biggest cover-up in human history. What we will find, if we make it, only the MOST HIGH knows,' said Philip.

'You look a bit pale are you all right?' Mark asked John.

'I really don't know. I think I'm okay, though a little shocked at what I've read so far. But I'm sure it hasn't sunk in yet,' replied Agent Smith.

'Well, it's a lot to take in John. How far have you got?' asked Philip.

'I'm reading about Satan, but to be honest with you it was all getting a bit too much... and then it started to make sense. To be truthful, I think I'm in shock right now. How could the church lie to people like they've done?'

'It's quite simple really John. We as people sometimes forget that no matter who the people are that we are dealing with, whether it be the Pope or the President, they are still human beings. We forget that too often and look at certain institutions as infallible, like the church or the government. We forget that they are all run by people, who, in the privacy of their own homes, are just like you and me,' replied Philip.

'Oh, come on! These people are nothing like you and me! These people are truly evil and we must take them down,' shouted Agent Smith.

'As soon as we get this information from your man Mike, we'll do just that,' said Mark.

'So what should I call myself Phil?'

'What do you mean?'

'This whole religious thing... I mean it's a lie, from what I've read so far. This whole religious thing... or should I say Christianity?... came about because some emperor didn't like the fact that Jesus, or should I say JAW, was black and he didn't want to teach the Romans his religious beliefs. So the Romans made Christianity and changed everything in heaven to white just to get back at this dead JAW, who only came to teach the begotten and chosen ones,' Agent Smith tried to stop a tear from leaving his eye, but he couldn't.

'I know John. It's hard for men like us who have believed in religion with all our hearts growing up and who were told that the one thing we can trust in is the Bible. But try not to confuse things; the MOST HIGH is real and JAW is too.

'If we had sought the truth instead of religion, we would never have settled for Christianity, because we would have needed to know why there were obvious inconsistencies in our chosen religion. But we didn't, because the truth was not what we sought; it was comfort we sought, something that told us that no matter what we did, we would be all right.

'That is how the wicked are able to snare us in their trap; they tell us what we want to hear. Isn't it funny how a rumour becomes fact... take Christianity. All Christians believe that they are following the teachings of Jesus Christ, who is the only begotten son. Well, we now know that's not the real son, but let's pretend we didn't. If I asked you to go up to Jesus and say 'Hello, I'm a Christian,' would Jesus answer with:

A: Hello my follower, bride and body, you faithful servant of mine? Or would he say:

B: What does that mean, I'm a Christian?

'If you asked that question to any Christian in the world today, they would wholeheartedly tell you every single time, that the answer is A. Yet the people involved in the lie didn't hide the fact that Jesus never said he was a Christian. He had no idea of the religion called Christianity... how could he? He was dead by the time it was born. Skilful storytelling, slowly manipulates your mind into believing that it is his religion... and we all believed it, because the truth was far scarier.

'JAW did not come to the earth concerned about how we would take the truth. He only came to tell the truth no matter what we thought of him, because the MOST HIGH has nothing to sell; it is man who has something to sell and who needs a buyer. Did you know that ordinary people were not allowed to own the Bible? The church did not want the people of the earth to have it in their possession. Why? So that the people would have to come to the church,' said Philip.

'I didn't know that, but I know what you say is true. How can they do these things in the name of the Lord and not fear the MOST HIGH? It just seems so unbelievable,' said Agent Smith. As he looked to the floor, another tear fell from his eye.

'There have been so many versions of the Bible and so many interpretations. Scriptorium insular 12th century epistles written in Latin. Glossy ordinaries commentary of scripture from the Augustine journals. John Wycliffe translated the New Testament and was expelled from his professorship at Oxford university.

'The Bible was outlawed between 1408 and 1530. Imagine... the church outlawed the Bible, the word of the MOST HIGH; just because they wanted the people to have to come to them, in order to have their sins removed. The church put itself between the MOST HIGH and mankind, they changed the name of JAW to JC so that mankind would never be able to pray effectively; that's the whole point of Jesus Christ. And we accepted what they told us; these same people who banned their own book from being in the hands of the people.

'There was a guy called John Bunyan who wrote a book called the Pilgrim's Progress. It was the most popular book in England after the Bible in 1679, so the church told him to say that they had authorised the book; he refused, and they put him in jail for twelve years.

'There was the Geneva Bible. Queen Elizabeth did not like the version of her time, so she made her own version called the Bishop Bible. The Bishop Bible was used by the church and the Geneva Bible was to be used by the people. That's right, two Bibles with different texts were used at the same time; meaning the common man had to live by one version, while the church and the queen lived by another. These things are not hidden, but we choose not to know them. We follow these same people who would make one Bible for themselves and another for you and me, and who then banned the Bible before they had made the changes for the common man,' said Philip, frowning.

'Did you know that Mary Magdalene was not a prostitute? The church did not like the fact that a woman had such an important part in the life of JAW; so they made it look that way so that they could keep her Gospel from being in the Bible. She was the wife of JAW... very few people know that. It was for this reason that she was such a threat to the church. The Gospels of James and Thomas, JAW's brothers, aren't in the Bible. Nor is the Gospel of Philip, or many others. They didn't line up with what the church wants to sell, and so they were excised. It took over a thousand years for them to admit the truth and these are the heads of the church we believe in, and the controllers of what we read in the Bible.'

'But why not tell the people the truth and let us decide our own fate?' said Agent Smith.

'Control the truth, and you control the people. The truth will set you free, and those that wish to control you and me will not allow us to be free. They have made a pact with these beings who are on the run from JAW; we used to say they had made a pact with the Devil, but that's not true,' smiled Philip.

'We've got to put these sons of bitches in hell, even if it means chaos on the streets; the truth must be told,' snarled Agent Smith.

'It's late, I think we should all get some sleep,' said Philip.

Agent Smith agreed, somewhat reluctantly, and

looked at the map before going back to the bedroom to switch off the computer. As he did, he began to realise how he was feeling... 'surreal' he thought. Philip smiled saying, 'Sometimes it's best to sleep on things of this nature; let yourself get used to what you now know. We've got such a long journey ahead of us, that we will have plenty of time to talk. Well, good night John.'

Philip closed the door behind him and Agent Smith walked to his bed and fell on top of it, back first. He stared into space as his mind threw thought after thought, back and forth, until he fell asleep.

The next morning Agent Smith woke to the smell of fried eggs and bacon, making his stomach rumble and his mouth water. After brushing his teeth and throwing water on his face, he headed straight for the kitchen.

'Good morning John, I hope you slept well?' said Philip, with a big grin on his face.

'You must have slept well, you look like you've won the lottery,' replied Agent Smith.

'Sit at the table. I've cooked breakfast, as you have no doubt gathered.'

'Where's Mark?' asked Agent Smith.

'Superman is out running his daily ten kilometres,' said Philip as he sat down with two plates of fried eggs, beans and bacon.

'Get this down you, food fit for kings,' said Philip, passing a plate to John.

'You know from the day I met you, despite all the things we've been through and the people we've lost, you have never ceased to amaze me with your jolly self. How can you remain so happy, knowing the truth? The church and the government, whom we both trusted, have lied on a huge scale to the whole world. Why aren't you angry as hell about this?'

'If I were to allow myself to get angry, what would that change?'

'Nothing, but at least you would get it off of your chest.'

'When we reveal to the world what we know, I will have gotten everything off of my chest John. Anger does not solve one's problems; it just adds to them.' Philip smiled at Agent Smith and continued to eat his breakfast. Agent Smith finished his breakfast and went to phone Mike at the phone booth. As he walked to the phone booth, Mark came jogging by. He said 'hello', but he did not stop as he jogged back to the apartment.

Agent Smith put down the phone after talking with Mike and headed back to the apartment. As he walked up the stairs, he looked behind him and saw two black SUV's heading towards the apartment. He quickly ran up the last few steps, and for a moment was taken aback by how fit he had become over the last few months. He knocked on the door, and before he could say anything Mark quickly pulled him in.

'Get your bag and stuff together quickly,' said Mark impatiently. 'While I was jogging, I was doing my usual recon of the area and I saw two SUV's parked two clicks south of here in the woods. Eight men were flown in by helicopter and judging by their baggage they weren't here for the scenery. They're ex-military, I have no doubt about that, and I have no doubt they're here for us. We've got five minutes before they'll come bursting through the door.'

Agent Smith got his things together before meeting Philip and Mark in the bathroom. Mark closed the door and as he did, there was a knock at the front door. A man's voice shouted, 'Package for a Mr. Smith.' Thirty seconds passed and the man outside said again, 'Package for a Mr. Smith, is there anyone home?' Then, without warning, the front door was blown to pieces and two stun grenades were thrown into the room. Seconds later there was a loud bang, followed by a brilliant flash of white light.

'This is Agent One, we are now entering the apartment. Over.'

With their MP5 submachine guns pointing every which way they looked, four men entered the apartment and looked around all of the rooms. Agent One slowly opened the bathroom door but it was empty, he checked behind the shower curtain but there was no one there.

'This is Agent One, no sign of life here. Over.'

'Hold on Team One, we're scanning for a heat signal now. Copy.'

'Copy that, awaiting your order. Over.'

Sat 1 typed codes into the computer, ordering the satellite to show thermal imagery.

'It's fucking impossible. They were in the bathroom two seconds ago,' said Operator One in Mobile One.

'Stand by Team One. Team Two, check your perimeters; they must be on their way out. Team One, check the apartment next door, and I want two men downstairs right now to check the apartments below. Move it,' said Special Agent Rodrigo.

'I don't get it, they were there two seconds ago,' said Operator One to his colleague.

'How long did that cloud cover the apartment for?' asked the second operator.

'No more than a minute, tops. We were without satellite visual for no more than that. Where could they have gone?' said Operator One.

'Bring me up on screen two, all sewer diagrams for these apartments. Quickly!' shouted Special Agent Rodrigo. Diagrams of the sewer system came up on a large screen in the command centre. 'Got you, you little bastards! I know how these rats work now. Team Two, get your asses to the bottom apartment to your left and search the bathroom floor for a manhole cover. It's probably been painted the same colour as the floor. Team One, get to a road called Mirage, there's a manhole cover there and we'll cut them off. Team Two will flush them out, so Team One hurry up and get down there and wait for them. Mobile One, get ready to receive downloads of these diagrams I'm sending you now, and send them on to Teams One and Two. There's no escape this time,' smiled Special Agent Rodrigo as he stared at the diagram.

THE WORLD UNDER THE SEA

Major Stone could not believe what he could see before his eyes, as he left the spacecraft and walked into the world under the sea. As the angel led Major Stone into a courtyard, the angel was joined by three other angels. Two looked the same as the angel leading Major Stone, but the third was totally different; it looked extremely fearsome. Its skin was pale brown and lizard like, it was around seven feet tall and well-built and sticking out of the top of its head were seven tips that looked like imperfect arrowheads; they ran from the top of the head to the nape of the neck.

Major Stone looked around as they walked through the courtyard, he noticed that the floor was made of glittering diamonds or crystals; it was quite beautiful. Colours shot out from the floor as they walked... blues, greens, reds, yellows and many more. Above them was a see-through force field and beams ran through the middle of it; they were made from a white silver metal that gleamed as brightly as if someone had spent an entire day shining them.

Major Stone called to the angel he had been following, and then realised he did not know its name.

'What do they call you?' he asked.

'You may call me Demon Destroyer,' replied the angel.

'Is that your real name, or is that what I can call you?'

'My real name is unpronounceable by human vocal cords, but it means the same thing,' smiled the angel.

'Are demons the angels that betrayed the MOST HIGH and joined Satan to war against the MOST HIGH and you angels?'

'Satan Lucifer Devil is no match for the MOST HIGH. It is true he was found to have bad thoughts in him and wished he could be the MOST HIGH…You may find this hard to believe or understand, but such thoughts are not unnatural. All of us who know the MOST HIGH are, how can I say this, obsessive fans. We are so deeply in love with the MOST HIGH and the works that they do... we marvel at their creations and are blown away by their ideas. We live to serve them and admire their brilliance; we are blown away by their awesome power and abilities and stunned by their compassion and understanding. They could destroy all of us in an instant and start again, but instead they show great patience. We all want to be like the MOST HIGH, like any child that has the greatest Father and Mother in the world. We idolise them and yearn to be close to them. They are our everything, and we are not worthy of knowing them.

'It's just that Satan Lucifer Devil acted like the mad fan who gets a bit too carried away with their idol and tries a bit too hard to be like them. His punishment was that he would have to play against the MOST HIGH in a game and would have to spend some time away from the MOST HIGH. A portion of angels were also found to have the same, let's say, lack of emotional control and they were sent to help Satan Lucifer Devil.'

'So why do you wish to kill them? That's what your name means, doesn't it?'

'Demons are not angels. They are beings, or should I say creations, who have what you would call supernatural abilities. They are worse than your wicked men and they too are now on the earth, helping the wicked men to control mankind. Satan Lucifer Devil uses them to complete his work on earth in the game he is playing... but the demons, well let's just say, they are living on time they do not have.'

As they walked to the other side of the courtyard, two enormous golden doors opened and they entered into the first city under the water.

There were angels of all types coming and going. Some were flying, some were walking and others seemed to hover; as they went about their business in the underwater world. Major Stone began to feel very scared, and tried to keep as close to Demon Destroyer as possible. The city was made up of homes in the rock, that went up and down the canyon for miles in all directions; lights shone out of the rocks, which must have held thousands of homes. The streets were made of the same crystal or diamonds as in the courtyard, and the brightness of the beams also acted as lights; lighting the whole city up and making the floor glow in rainbow colours. It was possible to see many homes under the floor as they walked; it was as if they were suspended above a sheer drop that went down for miles, adding a surreal kind of light that took some getting used to. Spacecrafts flew in and out of the darkness of the sea and could be seen through the force field.

They reached a force field door and went through; now they were inside the mountain. Its floors were made out of gold and the corridor walls were made out of light blue and white crystals, that glowed and gave off light. They entered another courtyard, but this one had a force field as the floor. Major Stone looked down at it and jumped with fright; he could see blue and white lighting that went down for miles like a cylinder. Once he had realised that he was not going to fall straight down, he looked up and saw the same thing going up for miles.

Angels stood on force fields that sped by, going up and down, and before he knew it he was feeling his stomach trying to come out of his mouth; as they dropped down on a force field at great speed. Then suddenly it stopped at an even greater speed and Major Stone was sick... but to his amazement, his sick just disappeared as if it had never been there.

As he looked up from his bent over position he saw the fearsome angel, whose name he did not know and whom he was too afraid to ask, leave the force field they were standing on. The fearsome angel looked back at Major Stone who, even though he was afraid to look back, found himself staring at the arrow like bones sticking out of his head. He then saw the teeth as the angel smiled, which made Major Stone even more fearful... they were razor-sharp, like those of a shark. Major Stone quickly looked away from the angel as his heart began to beat faster.

The angel turned and walked through a force field door and then without warning, the force field they were standing on flew upwards at a great speed; this time sending Major Stone's stomach into his feet. Major Stone fell to the floor and did not try to get up. He felt like he was in an out-of-control jet aeroplane, flying at mark two. He tried to look less ridiculous to Demon Destroyer and his two companions, but they looked at him sprawled on the floor and laughed. Lights flew by as the force field went through more sickening gyrations in many directions; then suddenly they stopped.

'How much more of this, I mean, how much further do we have to go? I'm feeling pretty weak right now,' said Major Stone, who looked like a child who had thought that he could handle a roller-coaster ride, but had thrown up at the first dip.

'This is it Major Stone, we get off here,' replied Demon Destroyer.

As they walked along a corridor, every now and then they would pass over or under a see-through force field, that allowed Major Stone to see lights in the canyon and spacecrafts moving to and fro. Major Stone began to take a little more notice of the hundreds of different types of angels, going about their everyday business. It seemed unreal to Major Stone, who every now and then expected to wake up in bed, back at area 51.

'Demon Destroyer, are all these beings angels too?'

'No, not all. The MOST HIGH has more creations than you could ever imagine or count,' said Demon Destroyer, as he stopped at a force field door.

'This is your resting place for now, I will come for you in ten hours. Food is being prepared for you now and will appear on the table in ten minutes. If you are not hungry, leave it until you are, and then say 'food warm up' then it will be ready to eat.' Demon Destroyer put his long arm out in front of him and pointed to the door.

Major Stone stepped into the room and the door turned to rock. Major Stone thought he was locked in and went to bang on the rock, but as he did it turned back to a force field door and he fell flat on his face... at the feet of Demon Destroyer, who smiled. 'You are not a prisoner, but it would be advisable for you to stay in your room and get some rest until I come for you.'

The floor was a mix of diamonds, gold and crystal and the walls were like waterfalls; on one side of the waterfall wall, was a force field window which looked out into a valley. Major Stone put his hand into one of the walls and it felt like warm water falling down, but at the same time it was somehow solid. Major Stone pressed against it and his body was half covered in the falling water, but he could not go any further and when he stepped back from the wall, his clothing was completely dry.

Major Stone jumped when out of nowhere appeared a full course dinner, on what could only be described as a force field table. The dinner looked delicious: chicken, potatoes, vegetables and rice, in a sweet smelling gravy. At this point Major Stone realised that he had not eaten for some time and without further ado he scoffed down the dinner, which seemed to melt in his mouth. After he had filled his belly and moved away from his force field chair and table, the food, the chair and the table disappeared and a bed materialised out of nowhere. Major Stone laid down and before he knew it he was fast asleep.

When Major Stone woke up he was feeling rather thirsty, so he cautiously said 'Water please,' not knowing what to expect. Then from out of nowhere water appeared, floating in mid-air. Major Stone did not know what to do... it was just there in mid-air, and there was no glass or cup. He stared and wondered what to do. If he tried to drink it, would it fall to the floor, or worse, all over him. He looked for the glass from the night before, but his thought was interrupted:

'Just drink it,' said Demon Destroyer as he entered the room.

'I thought it might fall on me if I did that,' replied Major Stone, as he put his lips slowly next to the mass of water. He sipped hesitantly at first but soon relaxed and began to find it rather weird but nice. The water tasted like none he had ever tasted, and drinking it straight out of mid air was so refreshing; so much so that Major Stone said 'water please,' three more times before he had enough.

'We have taken the War Hawk apart and put it back together again. Very impressive, if I was looking to start a fight with someone, but apart from that it has no good use whatsoever and will only bring more pain and suffering to those it is supposed to protect,' said Demon Destroyer.

'The people who built War Hawk, think that it will make you think twice about attacking us,' replied Major Stone.

'Major Stone... these people are blinded by power. They have forgotten the lies that they have told and now believe in them as if they were true,' sighed Demon Destroyer.

'They think that if they can make enough War Hawks and find enough dummies like me to operate them, we'll be able to put up a fight that could win. On the other hand, there are those who see their future in escaping JAW and the angels of war; while the other idiots and I, fight to the death for a flag that they don't really give a damn about... why are you smiling?' asked Major Stone.

'Do you remember when we first began talking and you did not understand why I was so interested in what came out of your mouth, knowing that it might have been lies?'

'Yes, and I can see what you are saying now. I guess that I have come to trust in you, over my own government,' replied Major Stone.

'You no longer feel the need to lie and protect something, just because you think it's patriotic; that's how the wicked men of the world fool you. They give you a flag and tell you to die for the flag because that's being patriotic, but the truth is, it's nothing more than dying for a flag. You did not come to understand right and wrong because someone showed you the American flag... these are virtues written inside of you by the MOST HIGH themselves. Wicked men and demons then stole them from you and gave them back to you wrapped in a flag. They told you to defend the flag and your country, not the MOST HIGH or the earth. Once they have you fully brainwashed into that type of thinking, they can then send you anywhere in the world to kill anyone they say threatens that flag and country.

'The truth is that it's a few men in high places who are threatened, and even though deep down inside of you something doesn't feel right, you will still do what is asked of you for the flag and country,' said Demon Destroyer.

'So how can we protect ourselves if we don't build such things as War Hawk? As much as I believe in what you say, the minute you start to invade the earth and want to kill me or my family, we'll want to protect ourselves... people all around the world are going to feel the same way,' said Major Stone.

'If you think you can protect yourself from JAW, then it is already too late for you. Listen like you have never listened before to what I'm about to tell you.

'Nothing can stop him, nothing but the MOST HIGH can stop or defeat him. He is born out of the MOST HIGH to destroy all who wish to come against them. He is born to be invincible. He is born to slay. He is unstoppable and knows no mercy. He controls the gates of hell and the bottomless pit. He is the MOST HIGH's war machine and once unleashed he will bring hell to earth or to wherever he is awakened. He is the right hand man to the MOST HIGH and their love for one another is renowned; for he is the first child born out of the MOST HIGH and their bond can never be broken.'

'But why doesn't the MOST HIGH just make man stop doing wicked things? I know we have choice and free will, but when it goes too far why not just make it stop? Why bring JAW into it?' asked Major Stone.

'The MOST HIGH has given mankind all the signs in the world Major Stone; along with all the chances. Global warming, destruction of the rainforest and wildlife, wars, famine, disease... you have even managed to destroy the ozone layer.

'Do you really think this has all been done by accident? The MOST HIGH warned mankind to change, but they have not forced mankind to change; therefore mankind believes it is because the MOST HIGH can't. There is no such word to the MOST HIGH as can't... they can do all things good and evil, both, if they choose. This is why we angels love them so much, because they choose not to do evil. That is why all praise is due to the MOST HIGH, the only ruler of the universe,' said Demon Destroyer, with a proud tone in its voice.

'So JAW is now coming to punish mankind for not hearing the MOST HIGH's warnings?' asked Major Stone.

'You asked why the MOST HIGH doesn't stop these wicked things... JAW is that stop Major Stone and they will now be coming to the earth. So you are getting what you have asked for and you don't like it. After all the times mankind has asked why the MOST HIGH doesn't intervene in the problems of mankind... now all of mankind will know what it means when a creation stops listening to the CREATOR and makes them intervene.'

'So is that it? Is there no other way to save mankind?' asked Major Stone intently.

'You cannot save them with War Hawk if you use it for combat,' replied Demon Destroyer.

'What about all those people who have been believing with all their hearts and soul, that Christianity was the way to show praise to the MOST HIGH? What of those who believed in his son and honestly believed his name was Christ? Are they going to pay because the church lied to their preachers and the preachers then lied to the people?'

'Only the MOST HIGH can answer such things. What you must understand is that JAW was born into your world just like everybody else and he grew with no knowledge of who he really was. This world did as much as possible to make him feel as if the MOST HIGH had forsaken him; just as it does to all who are not a part of the wicked mens bloodline. Everybody takes rejection in their own way; some become Muslims, others Christians and others take it as a challenge and become professionals in their chosen areas. But the one thing that ties them all together, like an interweaving piece of string, is choice.

'JAW chose to search for the MOST HIGH wherever he could find them, never believing he would be anything but another spirit on its way to hell; he honestly believed that and he did not try to be perfect or to gain his way into heaven by calling himself a religious name. He did not try to make the MOST HIGH accept him into heaven, because of mans own ideas about the law of dogma. He refused, saying that it was he who owed the MOST HIGH, not the MOST HIGH who owed him.

'Though all the time he longed in his heart to die for the MOST HIGH, he never understood why. He could have chosen to reject such thoughts, because he really believed he would not get any redemption from the MOST HIGH; and Satan Lucifer Devil did everything in his power to make sure JAW believed hell was going to be his resting place. But JAW did not care if he went to hell, because he did not believe that he was worthy of heaven. What mattered to him more than anything, was to be of some use to the MOST HIGH before going to hell. He looked for no reward and wanted none.

'That's what JAW had chosen to do in his life. He spent every day, not just simply repeating prayers, but training and teaching himself hand-to-hand combat. He asked the MOST HIGH every day what he could do for them, saying, 'Please know I'm here, willing to serve you in whatever way you see fit.' And do you know what he always said at the end? He said, 'Because you are righteous, you should not have to do a thing. I am the unrighteous and should only be used to wipe the bottom of your feet; like a towel that is thrown away after use.' Can you imagine those preachers in their thousand dollar suits and flashy aeroplanes, saying such a thing in the privacy of their own homes; without an audience to praise them for their undying love for Christ? In fact, could you imagine them saying that at all? No, for they are filled with pride and vanity.

'Do you know the church uses things like sex to make people feel guilty, so that people will always need to go to church; even if it is just at one particular time a year? They say Jesus Christ never had sex, nor did he ever marry or have children... because if he did have sex, this would mean that there was something wrong with him. Yet all of the preachers who tell you this, were born as a result of their parents' having sex, and they themselves have wives and have children. Yet Christ, for some reason, was banned by them from ever having sex or a wife.

'Major Stone, be very careful who you follow and what you read. It was the MOST HIGH that created sex, and JAW will indulge in it like any other human being. That is really why they are so hell-bent on maintaining the stance that the son of the MOST HIGH will never have sex, because they know that the real one will, with the full blessing of the MOST HIGH; and that he will have children and adore them. Only the wicked would wish to refuse someone the right to choose to have a family, which is the second greatest gift after life itself.'

'So what you're saying is that by not knowing who he is and by thinking in the way that he has, he has set the bench mark and only those who think likewise will be saved?' asked Major Stone.

'Only the MOST HIGH can say. Man must know sin before he can reject it and the only way anyone can truly know anything, is to become it. It is not sin that leads to hell, it is the unrepentant mind. If you have never sinned, you cannot say you have rejected it; you cannot say you have turned away from it and are walking in the way of the MOST HIGH, because you did not know it to walk away from. Every being is tempted and seduced by sin, and no matter who you are, there is always a sin out there that will be tempting.

'Jesus sinned like anyone else, but when the time came to make the choice between wilfully sinning and repentance, he rejected sin and overcame it. In this way, all of mankind can overcome their sinful ways. Whether they have one sin or a thousand, whether it be silly and small or serious and big; it takes the same amount of effort to overcome any sin, big or small.

'Satan Lucifer Devil used pride, vanity and ignorance, to gain the minds of the western and European worlds. He taught them to go into the ancient world and kill and enslave as many as they could, because the MOST HIGH had not been fair to them by giving all of the knowledge to that part of the world. He told them how to make the people of the ancient world their slaves and then told them to paint everything in the world, even the MOST HIGH, in their image; he used jealousy to achieve these things. The western and European worlds must understand this and reject what they have been taught by Satan Lucifer Devil and the wicked men, and must be willing to see the colour of truth, not lies; for by changing the colours and images they have become believers in lies.'

'So is there any truth in the saying that we fight not against the flesh but against spirits in high places?'

'The first war is the war of self. This is where the spiritual warfare takes place, but when the war is in this world instead, we fight against the flesh.' replied Demon Destroyer.

THE SEWER RUN

Agent Smith joined Philip and Mark in the bathroom and was amazed to see a hole in the bathroom floor. All the time Agent Smith had been there and he never knew that Mark had dug a hole... he had covered it so well that unless he had told you about it, you would have never known it was there. The hole allowed them to drop into the apartment below, which Mark was also renting under another name. He had secured a rope ladder to the hole and they climbed into the sewer system.

Agent Smith admired Mark's thinking and

planning; he never seemed to leave anything to chance. He had brought gas masks and night vision goggles for the duration in the sewer system; not to mention the petrol quad bike and trailer that Philip and Agent Smith were sitting on.

'They train you guys well,' shouted Agent Smith.

'What?' Philip shouted back.

'Never mind,' shouted Agent Smith, as they bounced along.

Mark, riding the quad, was oblivious to the fact that anything had been said, and was concentrating on controlling the quad at speeds of forty miles per hour. He made it look easy because he had done practice runs several times.

They made it to the manhole cover, some two miles away from the apartment. Mark switched off the safety catch on his gun and removed his gas mask. He told Philip and Agent Smith to wait at the foot of the ladder, but not to climb up it until he returned. Agent Smith took his gun off of safety, and he and Philip watched Mark slowly climb up the ladder and remove the manhole cover; he then climbed out, his gun pointing forward. Agent Smith and Philip watched with great anticipation, praying that Mark would not come to any harm.

Back at the apartment... Agent One and his three-man team jumped into the SUV and waited for the diagrams to be sent to them; then Agent One entered the street name into the satellite navigation system and waited for the route to come up. As soon as it did they sped off, only to find a mile later, that it had led them to a gated dirt road.

'This is Agent One. The sat.nav. has brought us to a dirt road, that it claims is a short cut. The gate is locked... should we proceed? Over.'

The operators in Mobile One looked at the road map on the screen, as did Special Agent Rodrigo and his team. They all hurried to find the best route, and all decided that the route set by the Satellite Navigation System was the quickest. Agent One shot off the chain on the gate, and they began to drive as fast as the dirt road would let them; kicking up dust and gravel like a long brown tail behind them, as they bounced from side to side.

Team Two were coughing their guts up; they were about three hundred meters into the sewer and the smell of raw sewage was extremely potent. They weren't able to run, as the floor was just too slippery and uneven and they had also lost radio contact with the surface; yet they kept on walking in the direction given to them before they had entered and could see where they were going through their own night vision goggles.

'Take it easy fellers, we don't need you crashing. I'm getting readings from Team Two from their trackers, and they aren't moving too fast; which means the targets must be moving at the same pace. It must be difficult down there. Over.' said Sat 1.

'Do we have any radio contact with Team Two?' asked Special Agent Rodrigo.

'That's a negative sir, we have lost all contact,' replied an operator in Mobile One.

'Then let's not assume anything. Team One, drive fast but safe. Do you copy?' said Special Agent Rodrigo.

'Driving fast but safe sir. ETA five minutes. Over.' replied Agent One.

'Copy that, Team One. Sat 1 we need a visual of the target area. Copy.' ordered Special Agent Rodrigo.

'This is Sat 1, attempting real time visual over target area now. Over.' answered the operator.

As the pictures came up on the big screen, it was clear that they would lose sight of the target area in a matter of minutes, as a cloud formation was being blown in from the west.

'Shit. How long until estimated incoming cloud

cover, affects visual? Copy.' asked Special Agent Rodrigo.

'Weather readings indicate less than two minutes to arrival and loss of visuals in five minutes, max. Over.' replied Sat 1 operator.

'Team One, how long to arrival?'

'Three minutes sir. Over.' answered Agent One.

Rodrigo sat back in his chair and watched as the clouds slowly moved over the target area.

Back at the manhole cover... The manhole cover shifted and as the light of day shone into the darkness of the sewers, Agent Smith and Philip were blinded momentarily. Agent Smith pointed his gun blindly into the light.

'Is that you Mark? Answer now or I'll shoot,' shouted Agent Smith.

'Okay, don't shoot. It's me, Mark. Come up here now, we don't have much time,' he ordered.

'After you. Come on Philip let's get out of this rats hell,' said Agent Smith, as he offered his hand to help Philip up from behind the quad bike.

The two men climbed out of the sewer and were glad to breathe in some fresh air. Mark led them across the road to his SUV and they got in as quickly as possible; then he went back down the ladder into the sewer alone. He jammed the throttle and started up the quad bike, then placed it in to first gear and watched the quad bike and trailer wander off aimlessly down the long dark tunnel. He climbed back out of the sewer and put the manhole cover back in place, got into the SUV and began to drive to the Canadian border; constantly looking over his shoulder for the enemy.

Team One made it to the manhole cover just seconds after Mark had pulled off, but they didn't see him, due to the bend in the road. They slowly pulled the manhole cover off, all their guns pointing into the darkness.

'Team One ready to enter the sewer system now. No sign of targets above ground. Awaiting orders to confirm entry. Over.' said Agent One.

'Proceed with caution. We are unable to make contact with Team Two, so watch out for friendly fire. Copy.' replied Special Agent Rodrigo.

'Received and understood. Proceed with caution. Watch out for Team Two. Entering now. Over.' said Agent One, as he motioned to his team to begin the decent into the sewer.

'Switching to night vision now. All team members proceed with caution, as Team Two is somewhere down here,' said Agent One to his team.

As they reached the bottom, they could hear a low rumbling sound, off in the distance.

'What's that sound?' asked Agent One.

They listened intently.

'It sounds like a lawn mower,' said one of the team members.

Then they all turned suddenly, as they could hear the sounds of men walking in the distance. The echoes were quite loud and must have been travelling some distance, because Team One had to wait ten minutes before the men who were making the noises, came into sight. Agent One recognised the outline of the men coming towards them; it was Team Two.

'Hold your fire. This is Agent One and Team One,' he shouted into the dark.

Team Two stopped in their tracks and hugged the walls in an attempt to make themselves less of a target.

'What's your call sign, and what's ours?' shouted Team Twos leader, who wanted to make sure it was really Team One and not an ambush.

'We are Papa Charlie X-ray, and you are Hell Fire Beta,' shouted out Agent One.

'Okay, we're coming up. Have you got them?'

asked the Team Two leader.

'No, but we can hear something in the distance; if it isn't them then they've got out already,' replied Agent One.

They moved on down the tunnel towards the low rumbling sound. The two teams were having problems keeping their footing, as the gradient began to slope almost at a 25-degree angle; soon it was too late and they began to slide instead of walking. Then one man slipped and they all fell, in a domino effect. When they reached the bottom, they landed on top of the thing that was making the rumbling noise.

'Fuck! This means they have moved on by foot and could be at least twenty minutes ahead of us by now, or else they never came this far in the first place,' shouted Agent One, firing off a round into the distance.

'That's the good news. According to the diagrams, we now have to get back up that slippery slope and walk back to the manhole cover... and that slope is going to be impossible to climb up with all that water coming down. Which means we'll have to continue on down this sewer for another two miles, before we come to the next manhole cover. Oh, and just to put the cherry on the cake, we won't be able to contact Mobile One until we get out; which means Rodrigo is going to kick our asses,' said Team Two leader.

Special Agent Rodrigo got out of his chair and began to pace up and down. The Sat 1 operator had fed all the trackers of the two teams into the command centre and now it was the only thing that Special Agent Rodrigo had, to tell him his teams were still alive and moving. Big Bird was en route from refuelling, after having dropped the teams to the SUVs in the woods by the apartment.

'Big Bird, I want you to sweep by the diagrams first sewer manhole. Make sure Team Ones vehicle is there, then follow the road heading towards the border and give me a visual via your cameras. Copy.' said Special Agent Rodrigo.

'Yes sir, but... what about the team?'

'Fuck them! I should make them walk back to the USA... Just do the sweep first, then the recon. It will take them at least five hours by car to get to the border, so I want some pictures of any cars on the road to look at. Then you can go and pick up them assholes from the second manhole, once they've reached the surface and made contact. Copy.' said Special Agent Rodrigo.

'Received and understood. Starting sweep now sir. Over.' replied the helicopter pilot.

Meanwhile... Mark tried to keep the SUV within the speed limit but kept finding himself speeding up, as his actions began to mirror his mind. They were so close and he knew more than anyone, that meant the going was going to get tough... really tough. He felt exposed driving like this, but he had done his planning and this was the quickest way.

'I hope we're doing the right thing. Will white people see us as traitors, or will they be like us and want to know the truth? I really hope you're right Dad and that we'll get more of that divine intervention you talk about,' he thought as he looked at his Dad in the back, talking with Agent Smith. They were deep in conversation and looked like two men on an outing. 'Looking at them you would never think that the powers of the world were trying to kill them,' thought Mark, as he turned down the radio to hear what they were talking about...

'Adam and Eve, once they had decided that they wanted to know both good and evil, fell asleep. At that time their spirits were removed.'

'Sorry to interrupt, but what are you two talking about?' asked Mark.

'Your dad is telling me about an old scripture that the Vatican has in its vaults... continue please,' said Agent Smith, curious to know more.

'Yes, well where was I... oh yes, they had their spirits removed and when they awoke they knew good and evil. However, up until then they had only done good but now, with their little evil selves and no spirit in them, there was no stopping them. They slaughtered many of the animals and plants, turning the rivers red with blood. Harmony between man and beast and all things was removed from the garden and Adam and Eve began the mighty struggle to regain just the smallest bit of their supernatural powers.

'You see, before I read this, I had always struggled to understand why Satan had not made them eat from the tree of life before. According to what we were taught, once he had told them to disobey the MOST HIGH and eat from the tree of good and evil, he would have made them evil for all eternity. This just seems like the logical thing to do if you are Satan and you are trying to cause maximum problems for the MOST HIGH. But of course, we now know why he didn't do that; because it's all been a lie. Satan was never there in the garden and never tricked Adam and Eve into doing anything.

'Adam and Eve made their first choice and exercised their free will. We may not like that, but that's what they did the day they ate from the tree of good and evil. You see, they couldn't just read a book on evil; they had to become it to truly know it.'

'I don't understand why they had to turn that into a lie. Why not just tell it, like how you just told it?' asked Mark.

'Think about it... who does that sound like? Killing animals, destroying plant life and turning rivers red... maybe it points the finger too closely to that side of the family that still wishes to remain evil. It's quite a good measuring stick, don't you think? Will we measure ourselves against the Adam and Eve with spirits, who looked after the animals and plants and did not contaminate the rivers in any way? Or will it be the Adam and Eve who fell asleep and had their spirits removed; ruling the world, making animals extinct like there's no tomorrow, chopping down rainforests as if they hated them and turning the rivers red, not just with animal blood but also human blood... It's a bit too close for comfort. It sounds better if it's all to do with Satan tricking them.

'The other lie religion tells is that Eve was made from Adams' rib. The MOST HIGH made them both at the same time. Adam was physically and mentally stronger, while Eve was biologically and intellectually stronger; and together they were a powerful force. Yet when they were apart or against one another, they would simply cancel one another out,' replied Philip.

'So all those women who call me a bonehead and believe in women's lib, must be right,' remarked Mark sarcastically.

'Ah, no, not exactly. The head of the union was Adam, he was the first human creation and Eve was the second.'

'I'm confused. I thought you just said they were made at the same time?'

'Yes, but like twins Adam came out first then Eve; however, it's not just because of that. You see the MOST HIGH had to make one be submissive to the other, in order for harmony to work and they did this by giving women more intelligence than men. In other words, they made them smart enough to know how to run a smooth home. A true woman knows this and therefore knows that looking after her somewhat less intelligent man is not putting herself down but rather it is caring for him; just as she would her children, who also depend upon her understanding and wisdom of caring, to grow strong,' said Philip.

Suddenly, their attention was caught by a low-flying helicopter overhead, which was heading towards the border.

'That looks like our enemy,' said Mark.

'What are we going to do?' asked Philip.

'Nothing, it's on a recon mission. If we turn around or do anything out of the ordinary, then we'll stick out like a sore thumb. They won't know what car we're driving, so my guess is they're going to analyse the pictures sent back from the helicopter, and try and guess if we are in any of the vehicles. It's a good sign, because it means they don't have a clue where we are; they just know we must be going back into the States,' said Mark.

'Yeah and they won't know we have state-of-the-art false identities, provided by my good friend Mike,' said Agent Smith.

'So what you're both saying is that there's no need to panic,' smiled Philip.

'Hey dad, you're the one who keeps telling me to have faith,' replied Mark.

'That I do son, but it's what you have faith in that is the true meaning.'

'Speaking of that, what would you say to the people who put their faith in the cross?' asked Agent Smith.

Philip thought for a moment.

'I would say, take a good look at the people who knew Jesus personally and loved him. Look at how they acted towards the cross before, during and after his death; it has no meaning to them... not any good meaning anyway. When he was dying on the cross, they saw it not; all they saw was a man they loved deeply who was dying. After his death, not one of his disciples could be found referring to the cross, calling it a symbol of faith, or making the sign of the cross.

'Then if you take a look at the people who did not personally know Jesus but said they loved him, look at how they acted towards the cross after his death; it has more meaning to them. Look at Paul, the Romans and the Christians, they look pass Jesus and see the cross; they praise the cross and in times of trouble they make the sign of the cross. Jesus loved the MOST HIGH. Yet today we love the cross and say we love it in addition to loving Jesus Christ. How many times do we say we love the MOST HIGH? Jesus only ever mentioned the FATHER and MOTHER as his true love,' said Philip, as a tear ran down his face.

'It's okay Philip, we're going to make the world know the truth and then let them decide what they want to believe,' said Agent Smith.

'Did you know that John the Baptist taught Jesus about the laws and the ways of Abraham, because Jesus did not know them? When the MOST HIGH sent an angel to tell Jesus it was time to become a Messiah, he had to go into the wilderness and bury his fury deep down inside him. It took him forty days to do that before he could even think about serving his FATHER and MOTHER. Then he needed to learn from John the Baptist, how to be a preacher. You see, it had been a long time since he had been a little boy who would go into the Temple and talk with the people. He had spent most of his life fighting the invading, pagan Romans; who were an insult to the MOST HIGH, in his eyes,' said Philip. They continued to talk randomly of the different aspects of Jesus and the corrupt world, going from one topic to a complete other.

The low-flying helicopter flew past again, this time heading back in the direction of the manhole covers. Unknown to Agent Smith, Philip and Mark, the helicopter was on its way back to pick up Teams One and Two; who had finally made it out of the sewer system and were enjoying the fresh air while they waited for Big Bird to arrive.

Special Agent Rodrigo was speaking to Director Forbes and Assistant Director Collins, giving them an update of the situation.

'Well, your teams can try to stop them anything up to a hundred miles out from the border, if you can identify the vehicle. But after that we've got to do it officially and use the border police on both sides, plus an official FBI team. Don't worry, they've already been briefed and they're on their way to the border now. Either way we will get them, dead or alive. They won't be able to pull any of their disappearing acts here,' said Director Forbes with a smile.

Special Agent Rodrigo had his office team scanning the pictures for any telltale signs. There were two lots of data coming to them; one was live video feed and the other contained still pictures of all the vehicles on the road, heading to and from the freeway.

Big Bird had finally picked up Teams One and Two and was back on its way towards the freeway; sending a constant live video feed to the command centre. Teams One and Two polished their guns and got ready to take out the three men who had put them through so much shit..literally.

'I've got something,' shouted out one of the Agents at the command centre.

'What is it? Bring it up on the main screen,' ordered Director Forbes.

The Agent put it up on the main screen and pointed out an SUV driving towards the border with three men in it. Special Agent Rodrigo then began to manipulate the image using the high-powered computer system, which calculated the colour and facial description of the vehicle's occupants after a few minutes.

'Yes,' they all shouted, as the computer flashed the words POSITIVE MATCH across the screen and then showed the three faces of Agent Smith, Philip and Mark. Then, while Director Forbes, Assistant Director Collins and Special Agent Rodrigo discussed the next manoeuvre, an Agent brought up the license plate.

Special Agent Rodrigo begged for the last chance for his team to finally get Agent Smith and his colleagues. Director Forbes agreed, making it clear that they only had ten miles in which to do it; as the SUV they were in was almost a hundred miles from the border. He wasted no time in downloading the images to Big Bird that specified what vehicle to look for and told them that Agent One was to stop them by making them pull over. If they didn't do that straight away with only one warning, then Agent One was to shoot the driver, pick up the pieces and be out of there.

'This is Agent One. We are one minute away from contact with target vehicle. Over.'

'Copy that, all systems good to go. Proceed as ordered. Over.' replied Special Agent Rodrigo.

'Received and understood. We have green light. All orders are green for go. Over and out.' replied Agent One.

As Big Bird got closer to the target, it flew overhead for half a mile and then slowed down and hovered fifty feet in the air, watching for the target. When the target came within four hundred meters, it dropped to no more than five feet off of the ground. Traffic swerved to avoid it and cars hit cars in the other lanes... the traffic was not at rush hour levels, but there were enough cars on the freeway to cause a small pile up a few hundred meters behind Big Bird.

Mark slammed on the brakes as he saw the helicopter hovering some three hundred yards in front of him, but he was hit from behind. The SUVs rear end flipped into the air and shunted them at a left angle, to within two hundred feet of the helicopter. The helicopter then moved to within fifty feet of the SUV.

'Get out with your hands in the air! If you do not comply immediately, I have orders to shoot,' said Agent One through the PA system.

'What do we do now Mark?' asked Philip timidly.

Mark did not answer. He tried to start the engine which had cut out when the SUV was hit from behind. The engine spluttered into life, then Mark found drive and punched the gas.

Agent One calmly aimed at the head of Mark and took the shot. Mark swerved the SUV as he began to pick up speed, and the first shot from Agent One hit the windscreen.

'Everybody down, *now*,' shouted Mark.

Agent One took aim again and tried to anticipate Mark's swerving action. Thinking he had them in his line of fire he took a shot, but just as he did the helicopter began to climb in order to avoid being hit by the speeding SUV. The helicopter ascended just in time, as the SUV barely squeezed underneath. As they drove under the helicopter, the air in the SUV began to fill with the smell of petrol and just as it looked like they may have made it to an off road some two hundred meters away, the SUV began to splutter to a lifeless stop. Smoke began to fill the SUV and they all began to cough.

Big Bird had turned around so that Agent One could get a fix on the target. This time he was making sure he did not miss by using a rocket-propelled grenade.

'Keep her steady, target acquired, tone good, taking the shot. Fire in the hole,' shouted Agent One as he pressed the trigger.

The rocket hurtled towards the SUV, leaving a trail of white smoke as it went.

'Come on Dad, get out now!' shouted Mark, pulling violently at his dad's arm and almost dragging him along the ground. Agent Smith began to run towards the side of the road; as he did, he turned and saw a black object coming towards them with a white tail of smoke behind it.

'Shit! Get down now. *Down*!' shouted Agent Smith to Mark and Philip, who were a few hundred feet away from the SUV. Mark instinctively did as he was told, pulling his dad with him. As all three of them hit the ground, the RPG hit the SUV and exploded. Shrapnel flew everywhere; pieces of the SUV smashed into car doors, and the engine block smashed into the ground just feet away from Mark and Philip. They were covered in flying tarmac and concrete, cutting their heads and arms as they tried to cover and protect their heads from the flying shrapnel.

A hot piece of metal from the explosion, smashed into a van. It passed through the van as though it weren't even there and buried itself into the bodywork of a coach; slicing electrical cables, and worse, the fuel line. The fuel line immediately caught fire, and like a trail of lit gunpowder, a flame snaked its way back to the main fuel tank. It exploded up into the air like a mini-atomic mushroom, lifting the coach up into the air and smashing it back down onto the van. Agent Smith had been hiding beneath it, but he just managed to scramble twenty feet away as the ball of fire, that had once been a coach, came crashing down.

Agent Smith covered his head with his hands. Curled up like a baby, he closed his eyes and prayed he would survive the onslaught. Glass rained down on him like rain and then he felt the heat, as a wave of hot air passed all around him. Smoke filled his lungs and he decided it was time to get up and run before he died of suffocation. He gingerly opened his right eye, then his left and was amazed to see the burning coach balancing on the van; then the smoke became too thick to see anything and he got up. As he did, he heard Philip calling to him from the roadside and headed towards him; but stopped when he began to hear a new sound.

'What was it?' he thought, and without thinking he jumped to the side of the road. He did not have time to warn Mark and Philip, and could only hope that they had gotten out of the way too; as the second RPG hit the burning coach and obliterated it. Luckily Agent Smith was now a few hundred feet away from the coach, whose already-mangled body shattered into pieces. The sound of flying metal once again filled the air as more smoke billowed out.

Agent One scanned the area to see what damage he might have caused to Agent Smith, then reached back to pick up another grenade. As he did, his teammate sitting next to him slumped forward, lifeless. Smoke curled up out of a nine-millimetre hole in his head. Mark took aim again, this time at Agent One, who was in the middle of reloading the RPG.

'Oh, shit!' he shouted, as a red light from Mark's MP5 submachine gun took aim... not at Agent One, but at the grenade he was about to push into the launcher.

'Bingo!' said Mark as the laser-guided aim shone on the grenade. He squeezed the trigger.

All Agent One could do was close his eyes as the bullet hit the grenade and Big Bird exploded into a million pieces. The sky was filled with fire and smoke as the helicopter hurtled towards the ground, exploding once more before it hit the ground and then again when it made contact with the cold black tarmac. Agent Smith looked just in time to see the helicopter explode in the sky, then he tried to see where the shot had come from. Mark was to his right, fifty meters in front of him, but he could not see Philip. Beginning to panic, he sat down on the freeway and tried to get his breath back. Mark came running over to see if he was all right.

'Where's your dad, where's Philip?' gasped Agent Smith.

'He's okay. I put him in the bushes over there. Are you okay?' asked Mark.

'Yes, I'm fine. The explosion's just got my heart rate a bit too high. What happened?' asked Agent Smith.

'It seems once again I was able to use you as bait, only this time I didn't mean to. They want you dead more than me and it seems the idiot was trying to kill you with an RPG, which allowed me to get two free shots... The funny thing is I missed the guy with the RPG with the first shot... he leant back and I hit his mate; but as he sat up I saw the rocket grenade in his hand and that was that,' smiled Mark, using his hands to describe an explosion; then he went to check on his dad.

Police sirens could be heard in the distance, so Mark grabbed his dad and told Agent Smith to find a working car among the vehicles lying abandoned on the freeway all around them. It looked as though World War Three had taken place in a phone booth and the seven hundred meters around the booth showed the fall out.

'I've got one,' shouted Agent Smith to Mark and Philip.

Philip was in a complete daze and was totally disoriented. Mark had to hold and help him into the car.

Agent Smith tried to bring Philip back to reality as Mark drove them towards the border. They soon joined other vehicles that had stopped to look at the wreck from the explosions. Police helicopters flew overhead and the police sirens that they once heard in the distance, soon passed them by; heading for the many pillars of black and grey smoke rising in the air.

'Hopefully this will work for us; with the SUV we were in gone up in smoke and the bad guy's dead. Let's hope all that mess keeps them busy and allows us to slide through unnoticed,' said Mark, in an upbeat kind of way.

'We've made it through all they've had to offer so far; it would be ironic if we failed because of the Canadian border control,' smiled Agent Smith.

'Are we there yet?' asked Philip.

'Not just yet Dad, but your divine intervention is working well so far.'

Mark pulled over at a gas station some fifty miles before the border, and all three used the toilets to clean up; wiping the blood and dirt off of their faces. In the trunk Mark found some cowboy shirts and a couple of cowboy hats; they changed into them and even though the owner must have been a very wide cowboy, they all managed to make the shirts look half decent. It was becoming dark and they hoped that the ground zero they had just left, would still help them as a distraction at the border. So with cowboy shirts and hats on, they went for it and approached the border.

Back at the command centre...

'Shit! No, it can't be happening!' shouted Special Agent Rodrigo, as all of the screens in the command centre went blank.

'Sat 1 give a visual of the area. Copy.' said Special Agent Rodrigo.

'This is Sat 1. Visual of area up, linking now.
Over.' replied Sat 1, as the screens in the command centre switched to an overhead view of a gun battle scene.

Smoke rose into the air from several burning cars. There were small craters in the road and twisted metal and concrete fused together in the heat of the blast. There were dead bodies scattered over the entire area; some were only pieces of bodies, while others were missing arms, legs and heads. Some people were barely alive, others walked
around completely in a daze and others dragged themselves as far as they could, not knowing where they were going to. The mangled body of the helicopter could be seen clearly;

bodies hung out of it and continued to burn, as did the helicopter itself.

'Teams One and Two, do you copy? Over.' asked the operator in Mobile One, but there was no reply.

'This is Mobile One requesting immediate clearance to send in cleanup crew. Over.' said Operator One.

'Green light, proceed immediately Mobile One. Over.' replied Assistant Director Collins.

'What shall we do now sir?' Special Agent Rodrigo asked his boss.

'We make sure the FBI teams stay at the border,' said Director Forbes.

'Don't you want them to go to the scene and ascertain what has happened?' asked Assistant Director Collins.

'No, that's exactly what they'll hope will happen; if they're still alive. And if they are... I want those sons of bitches,' said Director Forbes in a stern voice.

'Okay Rodrigo, shut down the project. It's in the hands of the official FBI team now; they'll be handling this as one of their own turned traitor. We will of course step in once they're in custody and will take full control,' said Assistant Director Collins.

Agent Smith's phone rang, it was Mike. 'Bad news buddy; we've been ordered to arrest you guys at the border on some trumped-up charges of treason. I'm amazed you still have this phone after what just took place,' said Mike.

'You know already what happened here? What's the situation like at the border? We were hoping that the mini-war we just had might have gained us some distraction time?' said Agent Smith hopefully.

'I'm afraid not old friend. My men have got orders to wait at the border... and before you ask, yes, that means I'm not running the show. The NSA are running this one behind closed doors, which means the minute we get you into custody, they'll swoop behind closed curtains and no one will ever see or hear of you guys again. Those bastards do it all the time,' replied Mike angrily.

'Any suggestions?' asked Agent Smith.

'Sorry buddy, done all I can do... Wait a minute... I may be able to get one team to look out for a truck or something based on some bogus Intel (intelligence), but that's about it. These people want it to be done officially, so that any chance of inside help will stick out like a sore thumb. It's best if you don't rely on me or anyone else. Good luck. If you're held I may be able to get you to Washington before the handover by using some red tape, but it won't hold. When the NSA want something, nothing stops them. Well once again, good luck. I'm sorry I can't be of more help to you.'

Agent Smith put down the phone and thought for a moment before telling Mark to pull over, some ten miles away from the border.

'That was Mike. The fake passports are worthless and the FBI won't be leaving the border anytime soon. We're up shit creek without a paddle,' sighed Agent Smith. Mark put his hands on his head and groaned.

'So what are we going to do?' asked Philip. They sat in the car in silence, searching for an answer. In the distance they could see four helicopters flying up and down the sides of the border, covering at least six miles either way.

'You guys, what I think we should do is drive a little closer; I'll go ahead on foot and do a recon mission and find out what the situation is, and if there's any way we can get across,' said Mark.

'How close do you want us to drive? And should we turn round or just wait where we drop you?' asked Philip nervously.

'About two miles out, and then wait there.' answered Mark.

'It doesn't matter; I can tell you now the FBI will run the full book on this one. They will make it so impossible that we'd have to go back ten miles into Canada just to find a place they haven't covered. We're fucked,' sighed Agent Smith. They returned to pensive silence.

'Let's do that. Let's go back into Canada and rethink our strategy; there's no point in giving in now. Mark, you can find us another safe house, can't you?' asked Philip, somewhat desperately.

'No, we've used up all our money setting this phase into operation. This is it, we've passed the point of no return. We don't have the money to go back and come forward again; we can only use what's left to go forward,' answered Mark, as he put his head back and blew out a long sigh.

'What if we take a train? I saw a station a few miles back,' said Philip.

'No, they'll have any means of entering the USA covered,' replied Agent Smith.

There was silence for several minutes.

'How long do you think we can sit here for?' asked Philip.

'Until we get caught or the car runs out of gas,' replied Mark, less than enthusiastically.

'What's your point?' asked Agent Smith half-heartedly.

'Maybe we should just stay here until daybreak. Maybe they'll think we're dead or that we slipped through their fingers. What do you think?' asked Philip.

'If they don't find us dead at the war zone back there, and if we don't cross the border, they'll assume we are on foot and they will begin a manhunt from the border back to the war zone,' answered Agent Smith.

There was silence once again, but this time it was broken by a search beam from a helicopter that was coming towards them.

'Everybody, get as low as you can in the car. *Now!*' shouted Mark.

The helicopter hovered at the side of the car while the searchlight peered into the car. Mark, Philip and Agent Smith held their breath as they lay flat on the floor, hoping they could not be seen. It seemed as if the helicopter had spotted something, because it began to circle the car.

'They've spotted us; we should make a run for it!' panicked Philip. He tried to get up, but was held down by Agent Smith.

'Let me go John, I can't breathe,' shouted Philip.

'I can't do that Phil, we don't know if they've spotted us; it may be just the pilot making sure no ones in the car,' snarled Agent Smith as he tried to keep Philip from bolting.

'He's right Dad, just calm down. If they don't leave in a minute or two then we'll know something is up, but if we run we're not going to get far. Save your energy and do as John tells you, please,' begged Mark, still slumped down on the floor in the front.

The helicopter continued to hover over them, circling the car while its spotlight focused on them. Then the light went out, but the helicopter remained, hovering in circles.

'Oh good, the light's gone out. That means we're okay, right?' asked Philip, hoping the answer would be yes.

'No, it means they've found us or they know someone is in the car,' replied Agent Smith.

'They've probably switched to infrared and thermal lights to make sure and to count how many people are in the car. I think it's time to run; we all know where we need to get to,' said Mark.

'What, you want us to split up?' asked Philip.

'Yeah, Mark's right. We need to give ourselves the best possible chance of getting to the records,' agreed Agent Smith.

'No, no, we have to stick together!' shouted Philip.

'I think me and your dad should create a diversion for you Mark, and you try to slip by. We'll tell them you were killed in the gun battle,' said Agent Smith.

'No!' shouted Philip.

'Look, it's the only way. If we run together, we're all caught. If you and I run first and draw the helicopter away from the car, then it will give Mark the chance to disappear into the night!' shouted Agent Smith.

'Mark, I love you son, and I know you will make me proud. Give it your best,' said Philip, as he realised it was their only chance.

'I love you too Dad. I'll get you out, I swear!' shouted Mark, holding back his tears.

'You have to concentrate on finding those records. That's how you can save me and John,' replied Philip.

'Are you ready to do this Mark?' asked Agent Smith.

'Just take care of yourselves. You never know, it may be you that have to save me,' smiled Mark.

'Okay Philip, let's do it. One, two, three... let's go!' shouted Agent Smith, and they scrambled out of the car and ran towards the field.

The helicopter's search beam came back on and followed the two men as they ran for the field on their right. As they made it to the bushes, the helicopter followed and kept its beam of light on them. Mark took his opportunity and ran across onto the other side of the freeway. Agent Smith and Philip scrambled through the bushes, tripping over roots and shrubs as they went.

'This is pathetic John; we won't get far at this rate, and I'm already feeling tired. The cold is making my legs go numb,' moaned Philip.

'Just keep moving forward. Try to remember that we're doing this so Mark can make a decent run for it,' gasped Agent Smith.

The helicopter pilot switched on his PA. 'Give yourselves up now. There is no point in running, you are completely surrounded,' he said.

Philip slipped and banged his hip and arm badly. He screamed out in pain and lay on the wet, muddy grass and sobbed.

'Come on Philip. Don't give up now!' shouted Agent Smith.

'Go on. It's better if we split up now. I can't go on John, my hip and arm are badly bruised. I'm not made for this sort of thing. I'm sorry John,' moaned Philip, as he tried to fill his lungs with much needed air.

'I understand Philip. In the movies they always make out that in these times and situations, one finds superman like strength.' said Agent Smith, who every so often would have to stop talking to regain his breath.

'The truth is, if you're not trained for such things the nervous energy works against you, and instead of giving you strength your adrenalin saps your energy. So trust me when I say you can make it. You have to think positively and not give up.'

Agent Smith didn't know what to do. He tried to pick Philip up and carry him, but every time he tried he slipped over on the muddy ground. He took one last look at Philip and then began to run at a steady pace. He cut his face several times on tree branches, tripping and stumbling, but he kept on going. The helicopter pilot tried to stay on both men by increasing the size of its circles around the two, but as Agent Smith continued to run, the distance became too wide and the pilot decided to stay with the man who was not moving anywhere.

Police were soon on the scene and Philip was arrested and taken to the border control holding cells, before being interviewed by the FBI.

Agent Smith had no idea where he was running to, but he thought that as long as he could keep the attention on him, Mark might be able to get away. The helicopter tried to find Agent Smith, but he had made it into a forest and the tree cover was dense. Agent Smith stopped to catch his breath and looked up to see if he could see the helicopter, as he could hear it hovering somewhere over head, but the trees were too thick to see through.

Then Agent Smith heard a sound that made his heart drop down to his socks. It was the sound of dogs barking back in the distance and he could see the flicker of flashlights heading his way. He sucked up as much air as he could and began to run again; he was impressed with how fit he had become, and he had a fleeting thought of how unfit he had been before he went to Rome to see his brother-in-law Pete. But he soon came crashing back to reality when he tripped over a tree root and fell down a small creek, landing in the middle of a small river.

He quickly got to his feet and began to run along the river, back downstream. It was risky; if the dogs didn't stay close to the trail, they might pick up his scent as he passed them. He hoped that the river would help to conceal his scent as the water got deeper; he began to half swim and float down the river. His heart stopped when he heard the dogs directly next to him, but they were on the other side, some eight hundred meters or so away. It seemed like it was working; the dogs were sticking to the trail he had taken before falling down the slope into the river.

The dog handlers scratched their heads as the dogs stopped at the foot of the river, seeming a little unsure of where the scent went. Was it down-river or up-river?

Agent Smith thought he was going to make it, but he didn't know where he was going to make it to. He was lost, heading downstream in a river and he had no idea where the river went. Then, out of nowhere, his body began to shake violently... it was out of his control. He nearly drowned but managed by blind luck, to make it to the river's edge. He was too weak to climb out of the water; he turned onto his back and looked up at the stars before passing out from hypothermia.

CANADIAN AND USA BORDER CONTROL CENTRE AND HOLDING CELLS

Three men peered through the one-way looking glass at the man sitting on the other side; his arms were on the table and his head was bent over, his face almost touching the table.

Lead FBI agent Tony Campbell... a six-foot-six, ex-college football running back, whom his FBI teammates had nicknamed the 'Black Rock' because of his black skin and a rock-hard body... looked at Philip. Holding up a document file containing Philips' entire life history, he said, 'So this guy's a priest?'

FBI agent Ray Johnson, whose smaller frame seemed dwarfed next to Agent Campbell's, answered him. Johnson was white and middle-aged, of average build and his blond hairline was rapidly receding at the front.

'Yes sir, it seems strange for a priest to be involved in such a case. What is the connection between him and Agent Smith?'

FBI Special Agent Paul Clifford, a well-built man of Mexican race and in his early thirties replied, 'I think the connection is his son, Mark. We have him in cell three. Now he's a piece of work. Ex-Delta Force, served in Iraq, Afghanistan, Bosnia, Somalia and almost every other place on the planet that's suffered an extreme conflict in recent years.'

'Yes, this Mark... It seems Special Forces have not taken kindly to our holding him. They're sending some hotshot General down from Washington to take him into military custody,' said Agent Campbell.

'This whole thing is weird, don't you think, sir? I mean, the NSA are just using us as some sort of PR stunt because this whole thing has happened in Canada, and yet the charges are against one of our own: Agent Smith, who after twenty years service has become a spy and a cop killer. Now he's linked to this priest and his Special Forces son. Does this make sense to anybody?' asked Johnson.

'No, none of it does... but who do you think will win over custody of Mark; the NSA or the military?' asked Agent Clifford.

'Not forgetting, our boss has ordered us to bring them to Washington before any handover to the NSA or military. How's our boy Smith doing?' asked Agent Campbell.

'He's okay. He had a slight case of hypothermia when we found him, but the doc says it was really exhaustion and the coldness of the river that knocked him out,' replied Agent Johnson.

'Okay, let's put them altogether and see what they'll tell us about what is really going on here,' ordered Agent Campbell.

Agent Smith, Philip and Mark were placed in a larger room, and the three FBI agents began to observe them from behind a one-way looking glass.

All three laughed when they were, one by one, put into the larger room and saw each other for the first time since trying to make a run for it.

'Mark my son, how did they catch you? I thought you would be on your way to Washington by now, but I'm glad to see you alive and well. And you John... I thought when the helicopter stayed with me that you would have used your FBI training to avoid capture. Oh well, at least we're all alive,' smiled Philip, reaching out to his son and his friend. The three men stood in the middle of the room and hugged for several minutes before releasing one another. Philip shed a tear of happiness and gave thanks to the LORD.

All the time the three FBI agents watched and listened; with DVD machines recording their every word and movement.

'Do you know what the funny thing is?' asked Agent Smith, laughing.

'No,' replied Philip and Mark.

'They're going to take us to Washington now for a full-blown interrogation.' Agent Smith began to laugh, and so did Philip and Mark.

'You mean to tell me, that all this time, all we had to do was get arrested?' laughed Philip.

'Yeah, they will drive us straight into Washington… Hey, you guys in there! I know you're listening to us and watching us; do you want to know what this is really all about? It's about the lies this government and religious leaders have been telling us for all of our lives. You guys are being lied to right now!' Agent Smith stopped what he was saying and walked up to the mirror and looked straight ahead; as if he was not looking at himself but at someone behind the mirror.

'So it seems like these men want to get to Washington, but what for?' said Agent Campbell, who was standing in front of Agent Smith on the other side of the mirror.

'How long before we fly them out sir, and should we inform our boss that they want to go to Washington?' asked Agent Clifford.

'No need to inform the boss at this stage. He was adamant that they be brought to Washington due to the nature of the charges; and the fact that it's the only way we'll get any time to interview them ourselves before the NSA takes them away. We leave in two hours for the airport, so let's leave them together and see what else they have to say,' answered Agent Campbell.

The two hours passed and the FBI agents heard two hours worth of unbelievable statements and inquisitions from Agent Smith, Philip and Mark.

As they prepared to leave the border holding cells, the three FBI agents were uncomfortable about what they had just heard. It was far-fetched and sounded like it was out of a movie, but in a weird way it explained why an FBI agent, a priest and a Special Forces soldier were all wanted by the NSA and Military. In a bizarre way, it made more sense than the idea of Agent Smith being a spy. Agent Campbell looked at his two colleagues and shook his head.

'Do you believe what they have just said sir?' asked Agent Clifford.

'Oh come on, they've been telling us fairy tales because they know we're listening in,' said Agent Johnson.

Yet despite Johnson's scepticism, Clifford couldn't shake his gut feeling. 'Okay, if that's a load of lies, why the hell is a priest involved in all of this? And why is the NSA hiding behind us?' asked Agent Clifford.

Johnson broke out into laughter. 'Oh, come on man, you don't buy into all this horseshit, do you? What! Aliens are fucking angels, something named JAW is coming to get us all, like the fucking bogyman... come on Paul, tell me you don't buy into this shit. Look, for all we know the priest may be the mule; he may be the one that gets the information that Agent Smith is selling to the enemy, and this Mark is the contact for the overseas buyers!' said Agent Johnson in a raised voice.

'Now, that to me, is the bullshit,' intervened Agent Campbell.

'But sir, come on! You don't believe this shit do you?' asked Agent Johnson, somewhat confused that his teammates did not see how unbelievable it all was.

'I'm not saying it's the truth, but it's what they believe. What they just discussed was not bullshit to them. Play back the discs while we're en route and listen carefully; they're talking about things they believe to be true. Plus, it's true that Agent Smith and this priest knew the priest who was killed in Rome. Now, I've looked at that file and believe me, whatever these priests are into, it has international consequences. There's something going on here that's more than spying, that's all I'm saying. Can't you feel it in your gut, Ray?' asked Agent Campbell as he packed up and got ready to go to the airport.

'That's exactly what I'm saying; something in my gut says this is big. And what they have said, no matter how far-fetched it sounds, seems to me like it's in the right area,' added Agent Clifford.

'I think you two need a vacation,' replied Agent Johnson, with a nervous laugh.

They began the journey to the airport. One police vehicle with four armed police officers led the way, followed by Agents Campbell, Johnson and Clifford in their SUV. Agent Smith, Philip and Mark were transported in a police van that was followed by another police vehicle, with another four armed police officers inside. Agent Campbell was still interested in what the three suspects might have to say, especially if they thought no one was listening. He hid a small listening device in the back of the police van and listened to the conversation the men were having on their way to the airport.

He was shocked to hear the men still talking in the same way that they had been in the holding cells; but was even more shocked to hear that the three men believed that they had been in a fight with government agents, who belonged to some secret organisation. Furthermore, they still believed that these agents would attempt to take them into their custody or kill them.

Agent Campbell opened his laptop and brought up a file on Director Forbes, Head of the National Security Agency. He found nothing out of place. 'What did you think you were going to find? If this guy *is* dirty, he has the power to hide it better than anyone else,' Agent Campbell thought.

As they made their way along the twisting, tree-lined road towards the bridge, Agent Campbell saw a flash of light in the night sky. It looked like a blue-yellow ball of light, speeding towards the trees in front of him; and then he could no longer see it, because of the trees. 'It must have been a reflection of a streetlight,' he thought.

Bang! There was a sudden explosion in front of them, and their SUV smashed into the police vehicle. The police car was on fire, and nothing remained of it but a twisted piece of unrecognisable metal. The only reason Agent Campbell knew that it was the police car, was because its flashing blue and white lights were still flashing; even though they had half melted into a lump of plastic. Agents Clifford and Johnson were greeted by two exploding air bags and a shower of glass, as their SUV hit the half destroyed police vehicle. The SUV toppled over the police vehicle, landed on its side and slid to a dead stop.

The police van behind the SUV skidded to a stop just before the burning police vehicle. The driver tried to radio the situation to his control centre, but his radio would not work. The police vehicle that had been behind the van stopped but as the four officers began to get out to find out what had happened, a blue-yellow bolt of light hit their car and their police vehicle exploded, just as the first police vehicle had.

Agent Smith, Philip and Mark were certain this was the work of their enemies, coming to finish the job that their colleagues had failed to achieve. They couldn't see what was happening outside, as there were no windows in the police van. They shouted to the driver and the police officer in the front to tell them what was going on, but there was no reply, so they nervously waited for their turn to be blown up.

Agents Campbell and Clifford were unconscious. Agent Johnson was dazed and was trying to undo his seat belt, but could not get it unbuckled. As he struggled to free himself, he glanced through the sunroof and caught sight of a helicopter landing on the other side of the trees. He couldn't see it properly, but it looked like no normal helicopter. In fact, as he strained to see, he realised the only reason he had thought it was a helicopter was because it had hovered over the ground. But as he kept trying to reposition his body to get a better look, he couldn't see any rotating blades, nor could he hear the familiar sound that helicopters make. However, the trees obscured his view so that he could not get a good look.

Finally he managed to undo his seatbelt and check if his colleagues were okay. Feeling both unconscious agents pulses, he could determine that both of them were still alive. He tried for several minutes to wake them, but to no avail.

Agent Johnson was then distracted by the sounds of gunshots coming from the police van; then he heard the two police officers shouting at the person or persons, 'Stop, or we will shoot!'

He pulled himself out through the sunroof and although he was still somewhat dazed by the crash, he managed to pull his own gun out of its holster; but he dropped it and had to bend down slowly to the floor to pick it up. As he did, his head throbbed and he became a little unsteady on his feet, so he crouched to the floor and tried to regain control of his movements.

Agent Smith, Philip and Mark, upon hearing the gunshots and the two police officers ordering whoever was outside to stand still, thought that their time was up. This was it, they were going to die this time... who could save them now? They certainly couldn't save themselves as they were handcuffed and unarmed. This was it, their enemy had finally won; the only thing left for them to do now, was to find out how they would die.

They all decided to die like men and not to beg for mercy. They braced themselves as the gunfire stopped, and there was an eerie moment of silence. Then, suddenly the doors on the van began to crumple like foil and the sound of twisting metal filled the van so loudly, that they had to cover their ears with their hands. Philip fell to his knees as the sound of twisting metal intensified; it sounded as if a hundred fingernails had been scraped along a blackboard all at once. The doors flew off and the three men looked at one another for the last time.

Previously outside the van.....

'Don't come any closer or we *will* shoot!' said the police officer who was driving the van.

Agent Johnson looked up from his crouching position to see a two-legged being walking towards the van. 'But it can't be,' thought Agent Johnson, trying to refocus his eyes and mind, but they both still saw the same thing; it was an alien. Agent Johnson fell onto the floor from his crouched position, he didn't know whether it was the knock from the crash or the fact that he was actually, truly looking at an alien, but his mind went to pieces. He sat on the floor and watched as the two police officers in the van tried in vain to shoot the alien dead but it kept on coming towards the van; even though the two officers pumped all of the rounds in their guns into the alien's body. The bullets had no effect.

Once the alien reached the van, Agent Johnson watched the alien suffocate the officers without even touching them. They dropped to the floor and Agent Johnson watched in sheer disbelief as the alien, once again without making any physical contact, began to open the doors to the back of the van; but because the doors on the police van were locked, the alien made them crumple up like tin foil, removing them without even touching them.

Agent Johnson tried to get to his feet, but couldn't. He tried to aim his gun at the alien, but he was paralysed. All he could do was watch in disbelief.

Back inside the van..... The van doors flew open.

'Hello Agent Smith and Philip. I always seem to find you two in the most unforgiving circumstances,' said the alien with a smile.

Agent Smith, Philip and Mark, looked at the being and wondered what it meant. They looked at one another confused.

'Sorry, but do I know you?' asked Agent Smith cautiously.

All three men moved slowly towards the back of the van, not sure what this alien had in mind for them. 'Was this one of the beings that the wicked men worked for?' they thought.

'I'm so sorry,' laughed the alien. 'I forgot how I look... You see this is the real me and because we didn't have a lot of time I forgot to change my image to the one that you are used to,' said the alien.

The three men still had no idea of what the alien was talking about... until, in front of their very eyes, it shape-shifted into a form that Agent Smith and Philip had met before.

'Let's start again, shall we? Hello Agent Smith and Philip. I take it this is your son Mark. We have not met, so I can understand your confusion Mark... Well, aren't you two going to say hello?' asked the alien with a smile.

This time Agent Smith and Philip ran out of the van and hugged the alien. 'Oh it's so good to see you!' shouted Philip. 'You can say that again!' Agent Smith added.

'I can't believe it. You mean all this time, this... well I mean, that is how you really looked? Like an angel? We know what your kind really are,' said Philip, not sure if he had said what he had meant to say correctly.

'Would someone please explain to me how this man, or alien, just changed from an alien into a man?' asked Mark, completely confused.

'Sorry son, this is my... Well, I don't mean to be impertinent, but this is my guardian angel. He has saved me and John from these sticky types of situations many a time now,' said Philip, before he was interrupted by Mark.

'Oh, I know who you are! You're Mr Death,' said Mark.

'The one and only,' shouted Agent Smith.

'I'm afraid this is the last time I can help you... and if I'm being totally honest it wasn't really me that saved you, it was the pilot of that spacecraft over there; he's inside waiting for you. Hurry up now and get on board, you have things to do. Take care of yourselves and I hope you succeed in your mission,' said Mr Death.

Before they could say another word to Mr Death, he vanished into thin air.

Agent Johnson watched it all in disbelief. He still couldn't move and he didn't want to; he just sat on the floor in complete awe of what he had just witnessed. He didn't even try to stop the three fugitives as they ran across the road towards the helicopter, as he perceived it to be; because even though he knew it wasn't a helicopter, he didn't know what else to call it.

Agents Campbell and Clifford began to regain consciousness and moaned for help. Agent Johnson ignored them, watching the helicopter take off and head into space at an alarming rate of speed. His teammates called for help again, and this time he responded. Getting to his feet, he headed the couple of feet back to the SUV, stopping momentarily as he realised he was no longer paralysed.

'Help!' shouted Agent Campbell.

Agent Johnson peered in through the side window of the SUV, which was still on its side, and stared at Agent Campbell. However, he didn't try to get him out.

'Get me out. Why are you just standing there?' asked Agent Campbell angrily.

'You're not going to believe what I just saw!' shouted Agent Johnson excitedly.

'I don't give a shit. Just get me out of this damn car!' shouted Agent Campbell in response.

'Okay, yes sir. I'll have you out of there in a minute... but I've got to tell you, those three guys weren't lying. I saw it with my own eyes!'

'Saw what? Have you bumped your head and gone mad, man?'

'Yes... umm, no. I mean I have bumped my head and I was a little dazed, but I haven't gone mad, I swear. Just let me try to explain.'

'Just get me out of this car and check if Paul's okay,' shouted Agent Campbell.

INSIDE WAR HAWK

Agent Smith, Philip and Mark sat in their seats, which were just behind Major Stone. They marvelled at the speed at which War Hawk took off and how quickly they entered space. Looking at the earth from such a great distance was mind blowing to all of them. They stared out of the window like children taking their first plane flight.

'Isn't she beautiful?' said Major Stone as he too looked down on the earth.

'She's more than beautiful, she's our home. She was given to us to protect and care for, and in return she would do the same for us,' said Philip as he filled his eyes with the splendour of the earth's colours, shape and textures.

'I'm Agent Smith, this is Philip and Mark. We thank you for joining with Mr Death and saving us, but who are you and why did you save us?' asked Agent Smith.

'My name is Major Stone and this is War Hawk. We are both a part of the JAW.67 project and we're supposed to be the last line of defence against JAW and the angels of war. I have no idea how much you know, but I do know that if I don't help you to uncover and make known the truth, we are all going to be dead,' replied Major Stone, looking at Agent Smith sincerely.

'So how do you know what we are trying to do? Who told you where to find us and who we are?' asked Mark.

'Let's just say my eyes have been opened to unprecedented levels. I have seen a world under the sea that is as old as the earth itself and that is more advanced than our world, and I have met soldiers who don't question their Commanding Chief, known as the MOST HIGH, or GOD to you and I.

'Like Mr Death, they have powers we can only fantasise about, and yet they do not have any of the ignorance or vanity that the people in our world have, who have less than one percent of their power. They showed me what is going to happen to the world and why... and it's all our fault. They showed me that you three men were the last hope for mankind. They showed me that whether you fail or succeed, it will not prevent the coming of JAW, but it may save many from his fury; and all those who had been lied to but who wished to know the truth, may have one last chance to make the right choice.

'But they also showed me the heart of mankind, and how it was vain and ignorant. They showed me that many, if not almost all, would reject the truth because they believe in their hearts that they are much more than what they really are. Because of this, they would much rather live the lie and see themselves as being higher than the angels and more important than the sons and daughters of the MOST HIGH, and they'd rather be the centre of the universe rather than know the truth and become bearers of praise to the

MOST HIGH; like the millions of other creations who were created by the MOST HIGH. So even if you do succeed, don't be surprised if mankind hates you rather than loves you, for telling them the truth. Don't be surprised if they reject your truth for the lie,' sighed Major Stone, beginning to move War Hawk back into the earths' atmosphere.

Agent Smith, Philip and Mark said nothing as they gazed into space and stared at the approaching earth. As they moved closer and closer to earth, they began to see the lights of the cities and towns.

'So I take it you have broken the code on the whereabouts of the records of Pilate. How did you manage that? The government has being trying to crack such codes forever,' said Major Stone.

'Well, the truth is that it was quite simple once we had all the facts. Because we were all priests, we had access to documents that most will never even know exist, never mind see. Then one day, years ago, we all met by accident and through conversation we realised that we were working on different texts, that when you put them all together they actually described a very big picture,' said Philip.

'But I don't understand. Why wouldn't this type of thing happen all the time?' asked Major Stone, as he flew War Hawk into Washington DC and switched War Hawk to stealth mode.

'Well, you see the church never allows anyone but its highest members to read any document, scripture or record in its entirety. It always splits up the reading of such important documents, giving the pieces that are to be read to individuals all around the world. Furthermore, no one knows what anyone else is reading,' answered Philip.

'This is what makes me so mad; even the church doesn't allow the truth to be known to its own priests. And then we the people are supposed to think that they are ambassadors for the truth. It's all lies,' said Agent Smith.

'So once you were all together, how did you break the code?' asked Major Stone.

'It was quite simple. As I've said, George Washington was a Freemason and he hid the documents under the White House... but those documents were fake. I only decoded this bit of information minutes before we were attacked at our apartment in Canada. The real documents were in a picture of George Washington, his wife, daughter and son; they were all pointing to the same place in the picture.

'You see, when unravelling something to do with the Freemasons, first you have to know their inner secrets, as that is how they truly operate; through smoke and mirrors. Simply put, they tell a lot of lies and mix the truth in with it, but the outer defence is all lies; which means that if you take the first things you are told or hear about as the truth, you will be on a path to nowhere. You have to know how many layers cover the truth,' said Philip.

'It sounds awfully complicated to me. I get lost at the first story you tell me,' said Mark as he scratched his head.

'That's the whole point. You have to tell the whole story, even if it is a lie, to get to the truth.' Philip knew it wasn't making sense out loud, not in the way that it did in his head, so he stopped trying to make them understand. 'That's the power behind the Freemasons. Everything's a code and if you don't know the code it would just seem like a true story, when in actual fact it would be a lie; and the true story would seem like a lie,' he thought to himself.

They hovered twenty feet above the streets of Washington D.C., and the people below had no clue they were there. Mark directed Major Stone as to where to go, and they stopped almost in the middle of the White House, Lincoln Memorial, the Capitol, and the Jefferson Buildings. They were some four hundred meters behind the National Museum of American History.

'Well, this is as far as I go gentlemen; the rest is up to you,' said Major Stone, as he opened the bay door on War Hawk to let the men out.

They thanked him once again for saving their lives and shook Major Stone's hand. Then, one at a time, they left the War Hawk and headed for the manhole cover that was their destination.

UNDER THE CAPITAL

Mark lifted the manhole cover, and the stench of the sewer greeted him with all of its foulest smells; he nearly threw up, but managed to keep his stomach contents down. Agent Smith passed him a gas mask and each man put one on, then they climbed down into the darkness of the sewers; closing the manhole cover behind them. Mark led the way, following a map given to them by Mike, Agent Smith's boss and long time friend.

Mark suddenly stopped and opened a pocket on the rucksack that he was carrying. He took out some wires with clips on the end and then asked Agent Smith to take out an ultraviolet light out of his rucksack and to switch it on. Agent Smith did as he was asked and when the light was switched on he could see laser lights running across the pathway they were walking on. The laser lights went from one side of the wall to the other and covered the eight-foot by six-foot tunnel they were in. It was impossible to pass through the tunnel without cutting the beams of light.

What Mark was going to attempt to do was to bypass the laser lights, by attaching wires to the sensors and then sending a charge via a battery pack, so that when they walked through the beams of light the sensors would think that nothing had happened; as the voltage from the beams of light to the sensors would not be broken. But if he did not connect the wire properly or if he broke the beam before the connection was made, it would be all over as the silent alarms would be triggered and Washington's finest would be on the scene in minutes. According to the layout on the map, he had to do this ten times on the way to the destination and then ten times on the way back.

Mark began to sweat as he slowly made each connection; he had to stop several times in order to control the shaking in his hand and arm. He concentrated so hard that his eyes began to hurt and once again he had to stop to refocus. The sweat and coldness of the tunnels made it hard for him to grip the small clips at the end of the wires; he lost his grip on the clips a few times and once the wire fell almost cutting the laser beam, but he managed to swing it away before it did.

They made it past the first five laser beams before Mark stopped in his tracks once more, as he surveyed the tunnel ahead. He reached into his rucksack and pulled out a powerful crossbow. Putting a special arrow onto it, he fired it some ten meters ahead onto the tunnels ceiling. The arrow slammed into the concrete ceiling and wedged itself half a meter in. Mark pulled several times on the rope that was attached to the arrow, to make sure it had a strong enough hold and then he placed a sharp pointed bolt with a hook on it, into the crossbow. He fired this into the ceiling directly above his head, then attached a pulley to the rope and tied the rope firmly to the hook. This had to be done because the floor just in front of them was pressure-sensitive and could tell the difference between a rat or a cat crossing over it; therefore it would certainly register a grown man. There were another three pressure-sensitive floors that they would have to cross on their way.

Each man had to pull himself over the pressure-sensitive ground, by attaching a harness around his waist onto the pulley. Philip found the ten meters a little hard to do and had to rest halfway along; as he stopped he almost dropped his rucksack to the floor, but just managed to grab it as he rested in midair. Mark decided that at the next pressure-sensitive point, he would attach a second rope to Philip and pull him over.

They finally made it over every pressure-sensitive point and laser beam light trap. Now they faced the CCTV cameras which rotated in such a way, that if they timed it correctly, a person could move in between the cameras into their blind spots and make it the twenty-five feet to a coded door. This door would then have to be decoded, opened and closed in under twenty seconds, in order for the person not to be seen by the last CCTV camera.

Mark would go first, decode the door and leave the door lock enabled, so that when the camera turned towards the door it would look closed. But this meant that they would all have to get through the door within thirty seconds, because after that the door would show up as opened in the CCTV control room. Mark showed Agent Smith and Philip the rotating cameras. As they watched the movement, Mark explained at which point they had to run under the camera, and then under the next one and so on. Agent Smith and Philip watched the cameras movements and practiced running under them at the right times, over and over again in their minds; until they were certain they could do it in reality. They were all very nervous as they knew that this was it; if they made a mistake, it would be over for all of them.

Mark got ready to go first, Agent Smith and Philip checked their watches and the movement of the cameras one last time. Sweat began to cover all three men as their heart rates accelerated. They had calculated that it would take Mark ten seconds to decode the door lock, and so they were all going to move straight away, one after the other; which they hoped would give Agent Smith and Philip ten spare seconds standing under the last two cameras.

They began. Mark moved under the first camera and waited a moment before moving under the second. Agent Smith then moved under the first camera and waited a moment before moving under the second. Philip then moved under the first camera and just then their watches began to beep, which meant that they could not move out of the blind spots they were now in. If a foot or arm were one centimetre out of place, it would be picked up by the cameras. So each man held his breath and hoped that the information and calculations were correct.

Their watches beeped again and they continued to do the process all over again until they reached the door... but as Mark used an electronic decoder on the door, it was taking more time to break the code than they had anticipated. Agent Smith counted down from ten and as he got to three, it was clear it was going to take more time. Mark left the electronic decoder in the card swipe slot, so that the decoder could continue, and placed its main unit on the floor next to the door; then he jumped under the camera with Agent Smith. This was not part of the plan, and now all they could do was hope that the man or men in the CCTV control room, did not spot them or the device on the floor next to the door.

Mark and Agent Smith began to sweat even more as they tried to make themselves as thin as possible, to them it felt as if they must have stuck out like a waving red flag. Philip was sure the game was now up and that at any moment the tunnels would be flooded by armed officers intent on shooting first and asking questions later. After all, they were now all cop killers and the body count was rising.

It was at that moment that Philip saw the whole picture for the first time and his mind and heart filled with dread. He had been so focused on exposing the truth at any cost, that he had not actually counted the cost; but now suddenly that cost had slammed itself into his mind like a sledgehammer into sand.

He was no longer seen by the police as a priest or a man of the cloth; he was now known to the police as a cop killer and he would never be able to prove any different. His knees gave way as he began to slide down the wall to the floor; as he did, the camera began to pan back towards him, just as his knees and lower legs moved out of the blind spot.

Mark saw what was happening and his heart jumped out of his mouth. Everything then went into slow motion as Mark's mind attempted to calculate the movement of the camera, the distance and time needed to get across to his dad, pick him up, and move him back into the blind spot before the camera could see them. But before Mark could even make a move, Agent Smith had done so; grabbing Philip and pulling him up to his feet, just as the camera was about to have him in full view.

Philip sobbed and Agent Smith slapped him around the face and told him to get a grip. Philip mumbled something as he sobbed, but Agent Smith couldn't understand what he was saying and told him that whatever it was it would have to wait, as they were almost home. Their watches then beeped and they saw, with relief, that the electronic decoder had finally unlocked the door. They all ran through the door, closed it, and gave a big sigh of relief; they weren't there yet, but for the moment the pressure was off.

Mark told Agent Smith to guard the door and gave him a submachine gun to hold, while Philip sat on the floor and tried to regain his courage. Mark then measured out a point on a wall in the room they were in, which was full of cable boxes that were connected to thousands of cables, fuse boxes and control switch boxes.

He placed a shape charge on the wall, which would only blow a hole as big as a window in the wall, then they all crouched in the corner some fifteen meters away and covered themselves with a heavy-duty cover; Mark then pressed the detonator button. The explosion wasn't that loud and they were only covered in dust and small bits of bricks and mortar.

When the dust settled, they could see a room on the other side of the wall that had been untouched for a very long time. They grinned and broke out into screams of joy and laughter. They had done it! They had found the room that had been bricked up and hidden to all mankind, from the times of the construction of Washington DC and the founders of the Declaration of Independence! Slowly Agent Smith and Philip crawled through the hole and stood with lamps in their hands. The lamps lit up this room that had been in darkness for hundreds of years, and they looked around in amazement.

The hidden room had given Philip back the strength and courage he had lost... in fact, he felt as though he had never lost it. Mark, on the other hand, slumped to the other side of the wall whilst still in the cable, fuses and control boxes room; guarding the door whilst getting his breath back. As Agent Smith and Philip stared at the objects in the room, they couldn't believe their eyes; it was like a treasure room full of paintings, golden swords, shields, coins, knives and forks, cups, goblets, candlestick holders and miniature statues. There were marble statues, pearls and diamonds in many trunks.

'This is just like the Freemasons,' Philip laughed.

'It's mind-blowing. I didn't even think about the possibility of us finding such great riches,' said Agent Smith, somewhat subdued.

'But this is nothing John. Remember what I told you about how the Freemasons work? This is for the lucky bastard who might accidentally come across this place; all of what you see in front of you would make most people forget to wonder if there might be greater treasure to be found. But believe me John, this is just the surface. Look for a switch that does not look like a switch,' said Philip.

'How do you find a switch that doesn't look like a switch? Are you sure this isn't it? There's an awful lot of stuff in here Philip. A man would be rich forever on the stuff in here,' said Agent Smith excitedly.

'You see, that's what I'm telling you! You have fallen for the trap and by the sounds of things, you've forgotten why we are here and what we are looking for… You see all these riches and think you have hit the big time, but this is nothing; this is for the fools and those who only seek wealth.

'What we seek is buried much deeper with more riches than you can imagine, because the Freemasons know that true power and wealth is in the truth, the knowledge of truth and the wisdom of truth,' replied Philip.

Suddenly Mark shouted, 'We've got company!' and then the sounds of gunfire came through the blown hole in the wall and went loud and clear into the ears of Agent Smith and Philip.

'Shit, I better get back there and help Mark!' shouted Agent Smith.

'No. If you want to help him, find the switch. It's our only hope!' Philip shouted back.

Mark opened the door slightly and sprayed bullets into the tunnel, then closed the door. He was answered by a barrage of bullets that hit the closing door and made the door look like a large page of Braille writing. A small hole developed in the door as the back-and-forth gunfire continued; bullets began to fly into the room and ricochet off of the walls.

'You guys need to hurry up and find the records. I need some help out here if we're going to have any chance of making it out of here alive!' shouted Mark.

'Just keep them from coming in here for a few more moments!' replied Philip.

Mark looked through the hole in the door quickly, and then ducked back down as a swarm of bullets entered the room through the small hole.

'What did you say?' shouted Mark.

'Just keep them back for a few more minutes!' replied Philip.

'Keep them back? That's not my concern. How we are going to get out, is!' Mark shouted back.

Once again he took a quick look through the small hole, which was starting to get way too big for Mark's comfort. He had to do something, but what? He tapped his gun against the wall as he thought. Bullets kept on flying into the door and room and it became quite clear that the aim of the police or security firm, was to blast bullets into the door until it crumbled to nothing.

'Okay, stop shooting. I give up. Do you hear me out there? Stop firing, I give up!' shouted Mark.

The gunfire stopped and a voice shouted, 'Throw your weapon out, then open the door slowly and walk out backwards until I say stop.'

Mark had to stall them and buy more time, but he did not know for what. He crawled up to the hole in the wall and told Philip and Agent Smith that they needed to use this time to get back on his side of the room before the shooting started again.

'I said, put your gun through the hole in the door and walk out backwards!' shouted the voice.

'Okay, but how do I know you won't kill me?' asked Mark, trying to buy some more time.

'Ah, I've found it!' shouted Philip, as he shone his light on a brick in the wall.

'How do you know that's it? They're all bricks, why is that one special?' asked Agent Smith.

'It's what's on this brick. It has a pattern on it... a compass and square ruler, the sign of the Freemasons. I suggest you stand next to me John, while I press it,' said

Philip. Once Agent Smith was next to him, Philip shouted to Mark telling him to get here, as they were going into an underground temple and would make their escape via another exit.

Mark crawled through and was overwhelmed with what he could see. Like Agent Smith, he took a moment to regain focus on what it was they were down there for and he too was also willing to settle for what they had found, and had to be persuaded by Philip that the greater riches were with the records they were looking for.

Philip took a deep breath and pushed the switch, but nothing happened. Once again Agent Smith and Mark believed that what they had found was the true treasure and that they should now think of a way to get the treasure in front of them out, rather than worrying about hidden temples. If the records were not there, then at least they had tried, and they could use their newfound wealth to hire the very best lawyers and get the charges against them squashed. Philip became very angry, telling his son and Agent Smith that he was ashamed that they had forgotten what it was they were here to do.

'You have one minute to come out, otherwise we will start shooting again and won't stop until you're all dead!' shouted the voice, which was somewhat muted from the treasure room they were in.

There was a sound like old rusted chains and cogs beginning to move after a lifetime of stillness. The sound continued until part of the floor began to separate like a jigsaw puzzle. As it opened fully, a spark lit a fuse, which lit a lamp, and the lamp lit a drain pipe that was filled with paraffin. The flame ran along the drain pipe as it spiralled down a staircase, and as the flame ran along the drain pipe, it lit up more lamps as it went.

Agent Smith and Mark couldn't believe the depth of the staircase; it looked as though it went down two hundred meters or more. An old sand timer, just under the opening of the floor, had begun to run down.

'What does that mean?' asked Mark as he pointed to the sand timer.

'It means it's time to go,' said Philip as he began to carefully walk down the stairs; he was followed by Mark and then by Agent Smith. The staircase was old and creaked with every step, but it seemed to be secure.

Back upstairs..... One minute had passed and the police and security firm officers began to open fire again on the room and the door. They decided not to waste any more time, so they used shotguns to destroy the door quickly.

Back on the staircase..... When they were twenty feet down the sand timer ran empty and the hole in the floor immediately began to close up again, like a jigsaw puzzle.

'Well, there's no turning back now,' said Agent Smith.

'Believe me, there never was,' replied Mark as he thought about the sounds he could hear in the distance, coming from the cable room.

Halfway down they could see, for the first time, the size of the room they were in. It was like a temple, some three square acres in size, and it was filled with treasures from all around the world and from as far back as the Roman Empire times. The drainpipe ran along the walls, and the flame continued to light up lamps all over the Temple. They all stopped walking halfway down, weak at the knees because of what they were seeing.

It was as if they had entered Aladdin's cave; there was a hundred times more wealth than there had been in the room that they had just left. There were Roman chariots and solid gold statues of everything; from life-size horses and eagles to Egyptian kings. Hundreds of trunks were filled to the brim with gold, silver and bronze coins; cases of gold bullions, diamonds, rare paintings, marble statues of Sphinxes, and so much more. They slowly walked down the stairs and along the middle of the floor, staring in amazement at the riches before them. They spent the next twenty minutes just looking around, picking things up and looking at them in detail. They were spellbound by what was before them and had totally forgotten what they had just left behind; let alone the police who were hunting them.

Meanwhile up at the room..... After the smoke had settled down, the police and security officers were sure that they had killed the intruders, however, as they entered the room they found nobody there. Then just as soon as they had discovered the hole in the room and cautiously peered into the darkness to see where the intruders had gone, the NSA took over the scene. Swiftly they ordered all police officers to the surface and told all the security officers to go back to the staff room for interviews.

With the crime scene now under the control of the NSA, Director Forbes, Assistant Director Collins and Special Agent Rodrigo stood in the command centre. They watched on the big screen, via Sat 1, as members of Teams Three and Four prepared to enter the room that was on the other side of the hole in the wall, in the cable room. Mobile One had been reassigned to England to take over full-time surveillance of Target One and air support was now carried out by Eagle Eye.

'This is Agent Three. Ready to commence operation Toad in the Hole. Over.'

'You have a green light Agent Three. Copy.' said Special Agent Rodrigo.

'Copy that. Teams Three and Four, begin operation Toad in the Hole. Over.' said Agent Three.

'Yes sir,' replied a team member as he threw a couple of flares through the hole, followed by two flash bang grenades. Another two team members each fired a clip through the hole in the wall and sparks danced off of the walls inside the room; as the bullets made contact with the walls and objects in the room. Two other members then crawled through the hole into the room and they were immediately frozen to the spot as the flares showed them the treasures that now surrounded them.

'Is it all clear?' asked Agent Three, somewhat impatiently.

'Sorry sir, yes... it's all clear, but you have to come in here right now,' replied one of the men.

Director Forbes could not believe what he could see through the head cameras of the two team members, who were now inside the treasure room. He smiled for a moment, and then told the two men to start looking for a switch that would not look like a switch. Special Agent Rodrigo looked at Director Forbes and wondered how his boss knew such things.

INSIDE THE TEMPLE

Agent Smith and Mark went from treasure to treasure, not quite believing that they were standing right next to such riches. Philip, on the other hand, showed little interest in the treasures and was busy looking for another hidden switch. He searched top to bottom and side to side and could not find the switch. He knew it had to be in there somewhere, but where? Agent Smith and Mark were like kids in a sweet shop. They had found a diamond-encrusted crown and were both taking turns putting it on, as they sat in a chair obviously made for a king.

Philip had to remind them that they were not out of danger yet, and that they had still not found the records. This meant there had to be another secret room somewhere, and they needed to find it before the police or FBI found them.

'I doubt the Rent-a-Cops will have any idea how to get down here,' said Agent Smith.

'Have you forgotten that the people we have been up against have had unlimited resources up until now? They have not stopped pursuing us and they have the power to influence the FBI into doing their dirty work for them!' shouted Philip.

Agent Smith and Mark got a hold of themselves and began to help Philip search for the hidden switch.

Back upstairs..... Teams Three and Four were now all in the smaller treasure room, looking for the switch that did not look like a switch, but they were having no success.

'This is Agent Three. Is there any more info that you may be able to give us, on exactly what we are looking for? Over.'

'Look for anything with the markings of a compass and a square ruler on it. Copy.' replied Director Forbes.

'Err.. copy. I need a bit more detail. What does this square ruler look like? Over.' asked Agent Three.

'Get me diagrams of a square ruler and compass and send them to Teams Three and Four,' Special Agent Rodrigo ordered his operations staff in the command centre.

In the meantime down inside the temple..... 'I think I may have found something,' shouted Mark, as he signalled for Philip and Agent Smith to come over to him.

'What is it son?' asked Philip.

'Well, it may be nothing. It's just that I've been looking at the lamp-holders, and this one is the odd one out. The distance between all of the other lamp-holders on this side is the same, until you get to this one; there seems to be an extra one in between these two... can you see?' he asked, as he pointed out the difference in the size of the gap between them.

'Yes, I see it. This could be it. Shall we find out?' asked Philip, as he reached forward to grab the lamp-holder. He pulled it and the piece of the wall that the lamp-holder was on immediately opened.

THE SMALL TREASURE ROOM

'This is Agent Three. I have received the diagrams of the compass and square ruler and am now proceeding to find any such markings. Over.'

'Send in Teams Five and Six to retrieve all properties in that room, and have a team of archaeologists ready to examine all artefacts back at HQ. Make sure nobody outside of our teams know anything about this or where they came from,' said Director Forbes to Assistant Director Collins.

'This is Agent Three. We think we have found the switch... can you see what I'm looking at sir? Over.'

'Yes, we can see it. Press it or pull it and see what happens. Copy.' said Special Agent Rodrigo.

'Copy that. Pressing it now sir. Over.' replied Agent Three.

In the command centre, they watched as Agent Three pressed the brick with the pattern of a compass and square ruler on it; the very switch that Philip had pressed an hour ago. Yet when Agent Three pressed it, nothing happened.

'It's gone in, but nothing has happened sir. What should we do next? Over.'

'Be patient,' said Director Forbes.

Then the sounds of chains and cogs could be heard, and the floor began to open. One or two of the team members were caught by surprise and they suddenly fell to the floor when their feet and legs had nothing to stand on. Their teammates tried to grab them and pull them up but one man fell, and as he did the floor opened up enough that his body fell all the way through and crashed onto the staircase. The staircase was too old to withstand the sudden force and weight put on it and after a single creaking second, the sound of breaking wood could be heard as the staircase at the top began to pull away from its wall brackets. Splintering sounds could be heard as the beams underneath it began to give way; abruptly, the first spiral collapsed, sending the agent tumbling to his death while the other team members looked on helplessly.

Just minutes before the agent fell to his death, Philip had pulled the lamp-holder and the piece of the wall that the lamp-holder was on, had opened immediately. The opening was about as big as a door, and the three men wasted no time on entering.

They lit a lamp on the side of the wall and once again a chain reaction was set into effect; lighting up the staircase in front of them. This staircase sloped straight down and was made of stone; unlike the spiralling wooden staircase that had just claimed the life of the agent. The wall closed, and they began the descent down the dungeon-like staircase. Its dampness and coldness reminded Agent Smith of the staircase he had walked down, when he had met Mr Death for the first time. They followed the staircase all the way down, which took them some ten minutes and at the bottom they were greeted by a gap of about thirty feet before solid ground could be reached; the gap itself looked like a drop into the abyss. Mark picked up a stone and dropped it into the abyss; he had to wait a very long time before hearing the upward echoes of what sounded like a splash into water.

'So how do we get across this gap from hell!' shouted Philip.

'Does this ever end?' growled Mark.

'We have no special arrows left, do we?' asked Agent Smith.

'No, we left them in place for the journey back,' answered Mark as he grabbed his hair in frustration.

'Then that's it. We're fucked,' said Philip, which made Agent Smith and Mark forget the problem they faced, as they looked at Philip in shock.

'Dad!' said Mark, surprised.

'Philip, I don't think I have ever heard you swear the entire time I've known you,' said Agent Smith, even more surprised.

'Well, believe me I have my moments and now is one of them,' replied Philip.

'We're going to be stuck here forever if we don't think of something. So unless you want to starve to death, we'd better get our thinking caps on,' said Agent Smith.

'Look!' shouted Mark as he pointed to an engraving on the wall *'Only the strong and wise can pass.'*

THE SMALL TREASURE ROOM

Dust filled the small treasure room as the broken staircase finally came to rest, some twenty-five feet below the opened floor.

'Agent Three, what the hell just happened? Over.' cried Rodrigo, as the screens in the command centre filled with the pictures of dense dust and fog.

'We lost one of the team and the staircase structure is compromised sir. Over.' replied Agent Three, as he coughed and tried to clear his lungs of the dust.

'Give us a visual. Copy.' said Special Agent Rodrigo.

'Copy that. The dust is starting to clear; give me a second on that visual,' replied Agent Three, as he bent over the opened floor and looked down to survey the damage for himself and give a visual through the head camera. They all looked down at the distance to the staircase that was still standing.

'It doesn't look like the main structure is damaged, just the first two or three spirals,' said Director Forbes. Assistant Director Collins and Special Agent Rodrigo looked at one another.

'We won't know that until we send a man down there sir, ' said Special Agent Rodrigo.

'Well, stop wasting time and get a man down there,' replied Director Forbes.

'Agent Three, get out your grapnel and abseiling kit; we need to know if we can still use the staircase. Copy.' ordered Special Agent Rodrigo.

'Err.. that's a negative sir. Over.' replied Agent Three.

'What's the problem, soldier?' shouted Director Forbes.

'There's just one problem with that sir... we didn't bring any abseiling kits. Over.' replied Agent Three.

'How long will it take to get some sent there?' Special Agent Rodrigo asked one of his staff.

'We could have sent some with Teams Five and Six, but they'll need what they've got for the extraction of the artefacts. Perhaps we could delay the removal, and give priority for use of the rope and pulleys to Teams Three and Four?' answered the staff member.

'No!' shouted Forbes. 'Just use what you've got and get down onto that staircase; it's only about a ten-foot drop. Lower a team member down, now! That's an order,' snarled Director Forbes.

'Copy that sir, deploying a man now. Over.' replied Agent Three.

The team members did a quick rock-paper-scissors match, to find out who was going to be the unlucky man who would have to risk his life to find out if the staircase was still safe. A few seconds later, Agent Three and the other team members slowly began to lower the unlucky team member down as far as they could and he would still have to drop another ten feet or so before landing on the next level of the spiral staircase. They let the man go and held their breath, hoping he would land on solid ground. He hit the wooden structure feet first, with a bang; dust rose and the staircase creaked and buckled slightly, but it held his weight, if somewhat precariously. The team member made the sign of the cross and then kissed his hand, as he looked up at his fellow teammates who were looking down at him.

'I don't know how many times it will handle that kind of impact, sir. The brackets on the wall look like they don't have much life left in them!' shouted up the agent.

'Did you copy that sir?' Agent Three asked Special Agent Rodrigo.

'Yes we heard. Hold on for further orders,' replied Special Agent Rodrigo.

'So what do you want me to tell them sir?' asked Special Agent Rodrigo.

'Continue to deploy the men until they cannot get any more men down there,' answered Director Forbes.

'If I may sir?' asked Special Agent Rodrigo.

'Go ahead, speak,' replied Director Forbes.

'It may be better and safer if we send the agent on the staircase down to check out the rest of the structure, and then send the other men down one at a time. This may help us to keep the integrity of the structure in place for as long as possible sir.'

'That will take too much time Rodrigo. I know you are concerned for the safety of your men but in times like these I expect all agents to be willing to take a risk. We cannot afford to let these men get too far ahead of us. Losing them now is not an option,' replied Director Forbes.

Reluctantly Special Agent Rodrigo ordered his men to be lowered one by one, but he told them to keep on moving down the staircase and not to wait for the next man to come down. As the fourth agent, out of the now seven-man team, landed on the staircase, the agent who was lowered first had just reached the bottom and was dumbstruck by the treasures before him. However, the three agents that were still on the staircase heard the gut-wrenching sounds of wood under too much pressure and they began to run down the stairs as quickly as possible, but this did not help, as in doing so they added more impact and pressure to the already weakened structure.

As the second agent reached the last segment of the way down, the staircase buckled at the top and began to fall down like a house of cards. The last agent onto the staircase was the first to be engulfed into its exploding and splintering wooden grasp. The dust hid the agent's impalement, as the wooden staircase collapsed and sent shards of razor sharp wood into his body. Then all four agents video displays blacked out, and Special Agent Rodrigo screamed '*NO!*' as he watched another team that he had trained, being killed like ants underfoot.

Back at the gap..... Philip read the engraving on the wall. *'Only the strong and wise can pass'*, he repeated and he began to study the walls surrounding the gap. He stood at the edge of the floor and looked down into the abyss and then looked up at the ceiling, some eight feet above them. Looking at the walls, he saw that the distance between the two sides narrowed over the gap to about four feet apart, and then on the other side of the gap it widened back out to about eight feet. He also noticed that along the sides of the wall, which were over the gap, certain bricks stuck out by about six inches all the way across.

'Do you want to know the good news or the bad news first?' asked Philip, as he turned back round to face Agent Smith and Mark, who were both slumped on the floor with their heads in their hands.

Both men immediately looked up and in unison said, '*Good news first!*'

'I have found the way across.'

'What is it?' asked Agent Smith.

'The key is in the engraving: 'Only the strong and wise can pass.' It means that if you are old or physically weak, you will not be able to cross.'

'Because?' asked Mark.

'Because to cross you need all your strength. Do you see how the wall narrows in over the gap on both sides?'

'Yes.'

'And do you see how certain bricks, every so often, stick out all the way across?'

'Oh yeah, I can see it. Can you Mark?' asked Agent Smith.

'Yes, I can,' replied Mark as he and Agent Smith began to understand and see what Philip could see.

'That's because to cross you must use the bricks like stepping stones,' said Philip, somewhat downcast.

'Yes, well done. You are the man, Dad!' shouted Mark, as he began to size up the crossing.

Agent Smith and Mark laughed as they stood and looked at the bricks that stuck out, and then suddenly Agent Smith stopped laughing.

'So what's the bad news? You said you had good and bad news. What's the bad news Philip?'

'I'm not going to be able to go any further with you,' sighed Philip.

'Don't be silly you can do this. I know it looks hard, but trust me Dad, you can make this,' said Mark reassuringly.

'You have come too far to start giving up now Philip. Shame on you,' said Agent Smith.

'I honestly do not think I will be able to make it. I just don't have the strength.'

'Look, let me go across first and make sure it's safe; then I'll come back and tell you if I really think you can make it or not. Okay Dad?' asked Mark.

'Okay son,' answered Philip.

Mark began to cross the gap, stepping onto the bricks that stuck out. They were spaced about two feet apart from one another and were a bit slippery. Mark braced himself by using his arms to support him and by holding onto the wall as best as he could. He was now about halfway across and distributing his weight as evenly as he could by using his arms, as he moved carefully from his right foot to his left and then to his right again. Then just as he put his left foot onto the next brick, out of the blue Philip shouted out 'Are you alright?' causing Mark to almost fall into the abyss. Mark caught his breath and shouted back 'Don't ask me again until I have made it to the other side, please! And the answer to your question is I was alright until you asked me.'

'Sorry!' said Philip, then Mark smiled and refocused. He continued his slow careful progress, but as he neared the other side he stepped on a brick that must have had a crack in it and as he shifted his weight the brick broke and Mark began to slip into the abyss.

He pushed on the sides of both walls using his arms as brakes, in an attempt to stop himself from sliding any more, but the walls were wet and slimy and it was very hard to find the grip that he needed to stop his falling momentum. Philip cried out... *'No!'*... and Agent Smith prayed Mark would regain his footing. Mark scrambled desperately to get a grip, but it was too late; he was slipping more and more into an intolerable position for his arms and legs to hold on to. Yet it was this intolerable position that saved him, as it wedged his body into the four-foot gap. He was in pain but happy to still be holding on, even though he was more or less balancing on his neck and spine; he began to untwist himself by placing all of his weight back onto his right foot. He took a second to recompose himself and without looking back he shouted, 'I'm okay but the brick on the right... sorry, on the left, has broken,' He stopped as the pain from the bruising on his left side began to make its presence felt.

Mark became extremely shaky, so much so that Agent Smith told him to stop and take a breather.

Philip slumped to the floor and knew this was the end of the line for him. 'A slow death by starvation,' he thought.

Mark felt weak, but he thought of how his dad must be feeling watching him struggle and how it must be making him doubt even more that he would be able to make it across. From this thought, Mark found the strength within to enable him to keep on going. His problem now was he had no left foot hold, which meant that he would have to twist his body so that his left leg could rest on the brick on the right side; but it was too much to ask of his body and near impossible to do.

He would have no other choice but to reach with his left leg right across the broken brick and step onto the next left one. He stretched across the broken brick, hoping the next one would be all right. He brought his left foot down onto the brick, almost having to jump in order to make the extra distance. As he began to transfer his body weight onto the left foot, he thought that he could hear the sound of the brick snapping under his weight, so he clenched the wall as tightly as possible to prepare himself for another slide. His heart could not beat any faster and his head throbbed with anticipation, as he tried to correct the fall before it even happened; but it was all in his mind and the brick did not break. He was fine, although he did not feel fine. 'Anything but that,' he cried, as he realised what it was his Dad was trying to tell him about the crossing.

Once he was on the other side, before he could even turn and face his dad, he fell to the floor unable to care that he was breathing in the damp and dust off of the ground. How could he tell his dad that it would be okay? He couldn't bring himself to even think about going back across; as he had originally said he would.

Instead, he slowly raised himself to a sitting position and took several deep breaths, before he realised that all the time he had been lying there, his dad and Agent Smith had been calling to him to see if he was all right.

'I'm going to go next Philip. I know it looks like it's impossible for us two old men to do it, but I know that it's always the hardest for the first man who has to take all the risks. Watch me. I'm going to take it nice and slow, and if you do the same I promise you, you'll make it,' said Agent Smith as he held Philip by the arms and looked him straight in the eyes.

Mark jumped to his feet and shouted across.

'It's not as hard as it looks. That brick caught me by surprise, that's why I fell and then the bruising I got made it look really hard for me to cross. All the other bricks felt really strong though, and I don't think you'll have a problem.'

Agent Smith took a deep breath and began his crossing. He put his right foot onto the brick in front of him and then transferred his weight onto his right foot, as he brought his left foot across. He then pulled his upper body forward using his arms and then transferred his weight onto his left foot, as he brought his right foot across; as he did this, he looked down into the deep darkness beneath him. Distracted, he almost misplaced his right foot and only placed half of what he should have, onto the brick. His heart pounded as his mind screamed *'no, please!'* and then he began to feel the sliding motion that Mark had felt when the brick broke under his foot.

Agent Smith pushed his arms against the walls instinctively and scrambled to hold on with his arms and to regain his footing. Philip broke down and cried, he could not take much more and he asked the MOST HIGH to help him. Mark watched as Agent Smith clawed to hold on to his life and then his right foot finally got the standing it needed. He stood still as his heart banged against his chest, as if it was trying to break out and be free of this madness. Agent Smith felt a pain in his left arm. He wanted to sit down to let it pass, but he couldn't; sweat poured down his face and his entire body. His hands, arms and legs began to shake; he tried to control it, but the more he tried the more violently his body shook. He could not hold on much longer and knew he was about to die. '*No!*' he shouted in his mind, '*we will make it!*' and without further thought he began to step across the bricks one by one.

'That's it, you can do it!' shouted Mark, as Agent Smith got closer and closer.

'It's a miracle' thought Mark as Agent Smith seemed to have found the strength he needed. Agent Smith knew he could not cross slowly and that he had to keep on moving because the shaking was getting more and more out of control and stopping only made it worse. He walked across as if he had been there before.

His legs were shaking violently, but because he kept hopping from one leg to another, he was minimising the problem. He was just about to reach the halfway mark and he smiled at Mark, as he could now see the whites of his eyes. Mark smiled back and shook his fist as he shouted 'Come on, you can do it!'

Agent Smith looked straight at Mark with a smile and kept shakily walking across.

Then Mark's smile turned to a frown as he realised the point at which Agent Smith was at, and he began to shout at him to slow down and to look down.

'Stop! You're about to come to the place where the broken brick is!' shouted Mark, as he waved his hands and arms frantically at Agent Smith.

Agent Smith was one step away from the broken brick and stopped just in time. Mark blew a sigh of relief, saying, 'I thought you were a goner!'

Agent Smith smiled and looked back to see Philip. He said, 'It's been great knowing you. I wouldn't have made it this far without you.' He then turned back to Mark.

'We've only got a small distance to go John. Why are you telling my Dad that? Now just stretch over the broken brick!' shouted Mark, but he did not realise that Agent Smith was shaking like a junkie without a fix.

The fact that he had stopped to miss stepping on a brick that wasn't there, was not as good as it had seemed. Agent Smith was now shaking like a leaf and had no way of controlling himself. He looked at Mark and smiled again. Mark shouted to him to hold on, saying that he was going to come out there and give him support. But Agent Smith just shook his head saying, 'I have completed my mission and the men who killed my brother-in-law are dead. Tell my wife I love her and that I found the killers of her brother and killed them with your help. I wish you were my son; I know you will finish what we have started.'

Agent Smith screamed in frustration as he struggled to control his shaking; his eyes widened as he looked at Mark and began to lose his grip. Philip screamed out 'No!' and Mark began to step out towards Agent Smith, who screamed out 'Oh GOD!' as he tried to hold on; but the walls were slimy and lacking in grip.

Agent Smith's left foot began to shake itself away from the brick it was standing on and as it slowly slipped off, Agent Smith gave up trying. He fell into the abyss.

Mark and Philip, who were still on opposite sides of the gap, broke down and cried uncontrollably; only pausing slightly as the horrible sound of Agent Smith's body could be heard smashing into the sides of the walls and then splashing into the water below. Philip could go on no further; his mind collapsed and he fainted.

'John, can you hear me!' Mark shouted into the abyss over and over again, but there was no reply.

Mark called across to his dad, who was slumped over himself in a sitting position. Then Mark began to hyperventilate and to black out but it was just for a moment as his mind had been trained to deal with such stress; even if he didn't want to. He stood up, although he was very unsteady, and held onto the sides of the wall to hold himself still.

'Dad are you okay? Please answer me!'

NSA CONTROL CENTRE

Special Agent Rodrigo covered his eyes and held his breath.

'Damn. I guess I was wrong. Never mind. Take two men from Team Five and use whatever ropes and pulleys are needed in order to get down there; and find the men responsible for the death of all our agents. Use your anger positively,' ordered Director Forbes.

Special Agent Rodrigo gave out the new orders and went to the bathroom. He smashed the mirror on the wall and almost destroyed three toilet cubicles, before his rage could be brought under control.

When he had finished, he washed his face in cold water, took several deep breaths, composed himself and went back to the command centre as if nothing was wrong.

'Team Four, give me a visual on the staircase. Copy.' asked Special Agent Rodrigo.

'Copy that sir. Providing visual now. Over.' replied Agent Four.

The screens in the command centre showed a bleak picture. There were no connections left standing between the stairs, the ground floor and where Team Four were standing.

The only way down now was to abseil. The four agents from Team Three, who had gone before Team Four, were splattered all over the floor. Teams Five and Six took a peek at what had happened, and then got on with the work of removing the treasure.

Team Five had lost two men to Team Four, so they were now a two-man team having to work as a four-man team, which did not make them or Team Six happy; they would have rather been going after the men who had killed so many of their colleagues. Director Forbes heard their mutterings of discontent over the radio, and warned all of them that their job was to serve and to take orders, not to question why.

Team Four made it to the ground and stepped over their teammates dead bodies, as they began to search the treasure temple for the whereabouts of the enemy;
however, they found no signs. They stared in amazement at the treasures before them and even put bits of the bounties before them, in their pockets.

Director Forbes told them to look for switches or levers, as there had to be another hidden room. Everyone at the command centre tried to spot the switch or lever, as they watched on the big screen.

Director Forbes then had to leave on important business, but would want a full report when he returned.

OVER THE ABYSS

Philip began to come round and slowly began to hear his son's voice calling to him. As he awoke, the pain came crashing down upon him once again. He had not known Agent Smith very long but they had shared more meaningful moments in their short coexistence together, than he had done with most of the people he had known all of his life.

'Dad speak to me!' shouted Mark, over and over again.

'Yes son I'm all right. I'm all right,' Philip shouted back as he tried to stand up.

'Please LORD give me strength, fill me with your Holy Spirit,' Philip said to himself as he stood. Then it was as if his prayer was answered immediately, as he was filled with strength in a way that he could not explain. Philip wiped his eyes.

'John, are you okay? Can you hear me?' shouted Philip over and over, but there was no answer.

'We must do this son; for all the people who have died and for all the people who wish to know the truth and nothing but the truth. Last but not least, we must do this for our dearly departed friend, Agent John Smith,' shouted Philip to Mark.

'Okay, but take your time. Let me come back across and we'll cross together, because I'm not going to lose you too!' shouted Mark.

'No, no, you must stay there. Listen to me son, you don't need to come across. I should have paid more attention to it.'

'What? Paid more attention to what?'

'The wording. It says 'Only the strong and wise can pass.' There are two types in that saying: we concentrated on the physically strong, but not on the wise. Look around you... is there anything that can be pulled or pushed?'

Mark began to look around. He walked down the tunnel and got as far as another set of stairs that went downwards at a slight curve. To the right was a lever marked 'for the wise'. He fell to the floor and cried out, 'I've found it!' As he pulled on it he thought of John, wishing with all his heart that he had only looked around before John had made his attempt to cross. Mark picked himself up and walked quickly back to the gap, struggling to process his emotions.

Mark looked across at Philip and Philip looked back at him. Suddenly the ground underneath them began to shake, as from out of the wall on the right, over the gap, three slabs emerged and slid across and rested on top of the bricks that stuck out on the left.

A pang of mixed joy and grief struck both men as they thought that if only they had taken just a little more time concerning the gap, they would have been standing there with John; yet they were happy that once again they had overcome the obstacle before them. Philip did not hesitate, he crossed straight away as if he had lost his fear of death; and he and his son hugged as if they had just met for the first time in many years. They cried until they had no tears left and then began to walk down the staircase into the unknown.

When they reached the bottom, they found a door made out of solid stone, with no handle. Mark pushed on the door and tried to move it left then right, but it did not move, not even a little.

'I don't believe this!' shouted Mark.

Philip laughed. 'Well, we've tried the strong; now let's try the wise. Mark, do me a favour... go back up the stairs to the lever you pulled and put it back to its original position for me.'

Mark smiled and did as he was asked. As he returned the lever to its original position, the concrete slabs over the gap slid back into the wall and the abyss was opened once more.

'John, can you hear me?' shouted Mark one last time, hoping for the impossible to become the possible. There was no reply. After looking into the darkness for a moment, Mark returned to his dad to see if his dad's wisdom had triumphed over his strength.

MAIN TREASURE HALL

Team Four had to be brought back under control as the treasures in front of them began to get the better of them; they tried to stuff so much of it into their pockets that it became blatantly obvious that they were trying to steal as much treasure as they could.

Special Agent Rodrigo reminded the team that theft of government property was a Federal offence and that when they were found guilty of treason, the death penalty was likely to be their sentence. On hearing such things, coupled with the name Forbes, was more than enough to bring them to their senses and they reluctantly replaced the items they had stolen.

Special Agent Rodrigo told Agent Four to pan back to his left and hold. Special Agent Rodrigo looked hard at the lamp-holders and then it became clear what it was that had caught his eye.

'Pull on that lamp-holder in front of you. No, not that one, the one in the middle,' ordered Special Agent Rodrigo.

ARK OF THE COVENANT

Philip and Mark walked slowly into the room. As they did the solid stone door closed behind them and they were thrown into complete darkness. A light began to shine in the middle of the room, which was barely enough to pierce the darkness in the middle of the room; leaving the surrounding areas still in complete darkness.

Philip and Mark walked to the light. As they got closer they could see an altar and on that altar was a richly embroidered tent. Inside the tent was a golden Ark and behind it was a very old cross; like those that had been used in Roman times to kill Jesus. As they got closer, they saw another golden box; this one was inscribed with Aramaic words.

'What is that golden box with the wing like things on it?' asked Mark as they stopped at the end of the altar.

'This is something I never thought I would see. I can't believe it. This can't be real. Do you know what we are looking at? Take off your shoes, bow your head with me and fall onto your knees,' whispered Philip as he fell to his knees. Mark did likewise but wanted to know why his Dad was showing so much respect to the tent.

'Is it the cross behind it that you are praying to?' asked Mark, bewildered.

'No. Just close your eyes and let me say a prayer for the both of us,' replied Philip.

> *'We make a joyful noise to you LORD, in all the lands!*
> *We serve you LORD with gladness!*
> *We ask to come into your presence with singing and praise!*
> *We know that the LORD is the MOST HIGH!*
> *It is you that made us, and we are yours;*
> *We wish to be your people, and the sheep of your pasture.*
> *We are glad to bring praise to you!*
> *We give praise and thanks to you, for we have life because of you!'* prayed Philip.

Philip lifted his head and nudged Mark, who was still bowing his head; then they both stood.

'This glorious tent, my son, is known as the tabernacle. 'The box with the funny wings on it,' as you put it, is the Ark of the Covenant and it is supposed to hold the Ten Commandments. But as I have taught you, there were no Ten Commandments... so what is inside it I don't know. That cross must be the one they killed Jesus on.

'This box has words in Aramaic on it and the words say, 'Only the righteous can know what lies within.' Shall we?' said Philip as he walked up the steps towards the golden box.

As they reached the top step, they could see another box that looked like a Roman chest box.

'Do you think that has the records in it?' asked Mark.

'We will soon find out,' replied Philip, as he stood over the first golden box.

He looked at Mark, then at the box and then he slowly reached down and pulled on the top lid; as he did, a suctioning sound could be heard... then, with a puff of dust, the lid opened. As the lid opened, the floor rumbled slightly and a faint sound, like that of an explosion, could be heard; which seemed to come from the darkness in the room.

'What was that? Was that because you opened the box or did that come from somewhere else?' asked Mark as he stared into the box.

'I don't know. It sounded like it came from behind us, by where the door is I think... I'm not sure; it could just be the echo in here. I felt the ground underneath me shake and then I heard a sound like a small explosion,' replied Philip.

Looking into the box, Philip and Mark stood in awe of what shined out at them. It was almost as if the sun had been allowed to shine from out of the box. They looked down at the glowing orb, which was on a chain; its light was soft but brilliant at the same time, and it changed colours continuously. It mesmerised both men and they stared at it for so long that it seemed as if they had no concept of time. Both men wanted to pick it up and put the chain around their neck, but were too afraid.

Eventually, after almost an hour had passed, Mark tried to pick up the orb of light, but as he did an unseen force field came out of the orb and he was blown from the middle of the room back into the darkness; where he came crashing down onto the floor.

'Mark! Mark are you okay?'

'Yeah Dad, I'm fine. It looked worse than it was. The force just threw me back like an explosion; but without the force that rips you apart. Actually it was quite fun.' said Mark as he dusted himself off and walked back to the middle of the room.

'Well, I don't think I'll try that,' said Philip.

'No... I think you should. It probably won't do that to you,' replied Mark, because in his mind he knew he was nowhere near being righteous as he had killed too many innocent people, such as women and children, as a Special Forces soldier. All his years in Covert Operations had meant that he had done many things for his country he was not proud of.

So Philip moved towards the chest, which he believed to be the treasure they were most looking for. With sweaty hands, he looked at Mark and slowly began to open the chest. He closed his eyes as he did not dare to look into the chest straight away; just in case he was to find nothing. But after a few seconds, he plucked up the courage and opened his eyes and he was not disappointed, as before him were scrolls of records in Latin; just how he had imagined them to look. Philip let out a sigh of relief and cried out in joy. Picking up the first scroll on the top, he carefully unravelled it and began to read out loud the records of Pontius Pilate.

Meanwhile..... Team Four had made it to the gap and were awaiting orders. Assistant Director Collins and Special Agent Rodrigo were studying the gap with their staff, and soon realised that the only way across was by using the bricks that stuck out. They paid no attention to the writing on the wall, and soon Team Four found themselves at the lever before the slightly curved staircase.

'What should we do sir, push the lever?' asked Agent Four.

Without the direction from Director Forbes, who had left the building a few hours ago on important business, it was now left up to Assistant Director Collins and Special Agent Rodrigo to try and work out the puzzles in front of them.

'Leave it for now, we don't know what it may do; it could be unfriendly. Continue down the stairs and find out what's there,' ordered Assistant Director Collins.

The agents finally reached the stone door and tried to open it using brute force, but to no prevail.

'Okay, now send a man back up to that lever and pull or push it and see what happens,' ordered Special Agent Rodrigo.

One of the agents went back upstairs and pushed the lever. The ground under his feet began to shake, and the agent quickly grabbed his semiautomatic weapon and began pointing it in every direction. Then he watched the slabs come out of the wall to the right and come to rest on the bricks that stuck out on the left.

'Son of a bitch! You mean we all scrambled across that gap for nothing?' said the agent, and then he went back down the stairs to tell his colleagues what the lever did.

Assistant Director Collins and Special Agent Rodrigo shook their heads and ordered the team to try and blast their way through. Agent Four held the remote detonator and counted down from five, before pressing the button. Rubble flew everywhere, and all of the team were covered in dust. It took several minutes for the dust to settle before Team Four could assess the damage done to the door, but the prognosis was not good; they had hardly scratched the surface, removing no more than a foot at best from a door which was at least four foot thick.

'What now sir?' asked Agent Four.

'Do it again and again, until you either break through or run out of dynamite!' shouted Assistant Director Collins.

'Okay. And... what then sir?' said Agent Four without doing anything.

'Don't tell me you used up all the dynamite you had on one go?' asked Assistant Director Collins in disbelief.

'I'm afraid so sir. We weren't packing high-level stuff in the first place, just some shape charges.'

Assistant Director Collins and Special Agent Rodrigo looked at each other for answers, then told the team to await orders. They began to replay the digital information from the head cameras, looking for any clues on how to get the door open.

Back inside the room..... After a couple of hours reading, Philip smiled and shouted out, 'We did it! We finally know the full name of Jesus!' He hugged Mark and they both let out a long sigh of relief. Mark put the records in the rucksack and then turned and looked at the Ark.

'What about that one? Are you going to look inside it?' asked Mark.

'You better believe I am!' shouted Philip, full of joy.

He stood over the Ark and looked for two buttons on the sides. When he had found them, he pressed them and the top of the Ark slowly began to lift. As it did, the room began to shake and dust and small bits of the ceiling plaster began to rain down.

A wind like sound could be heard, lightning flashed above the men's heads as they cowered towards the floor, and a whirlwind began to form over the Ark. Philip and Mark held onto one another, as the whirlwind began to suck them in towards the Ark. More lightning flashed, and the whirlwind began to reach up towards the ceiling; making a hole in the ceiling and continuing out into the city and up to the sky.

Black winged figures seemed to fly around the whirlwind dancing in and out of it as the lightning continued to flash and the ground relentlessly rumbled under their feet. A crack began to run along the centre of the floor in the middle of the room, stretching from one side of the room to the other.

As the ground opened, tormented humans in the millions stacked one upon another like sardines in a can, could be seen on one side of a great gulf. Next to them were beings that were not human, who were also stacked one upon another, and then next to them were other forms of beings, stacked one upon another in their millions. This went on as far as the eye could see. The human beings and beings on that side of the mighty gulf, were crying in one voice in utter pain and sorrow; as their bodies crushed one another mercilessly. Their cries and screams were continuous, and were so loud that Philip and Mark did not know how long they could bear it.

Out of the deep of the mighty gulf a black cloud rose; this was no normal cloud, it carried in it lightning and fire. It moved with purpose and direction as it rose and moved in and out of those squashed and stacked one upon another; causing them great pain as its lightning gave off massive amounts of shocks and its fire consumed their flesh. The black cloud rose out of the mighty gulf, and as it reached Philip and Mark it stopped as if to look at them. It towered over them like an enormous giant.

The black cloud's lightning disappeared and its fire went out; then suddenly, without warning, it wrapped itself around Philip and Mark, holding them to their spot with a grip like an anaconda. They could not move and the black cloud made them look down into the mighty gulf.

In the middle of the mighty gulf were thousands of angels of war. They would pluck and pull out humans and beings at their will and would take them deep down into the gulf, beyond the sight of Philip and Mark; but the cries that came up from the deep were more horrifying than the cries of those squashed together.

Then Beast like creatures rose up from the deep and sprayed their fiery breath over those who were squashed and stacked one upon another. Their flesh sizzled and burned and the sound and smell of burning flesh filled Philip's and Mark's senses; until both men fell to their knees and emptied the contents of their stomachs. The black cloud forced them to watch the burning humans and beings, who cried out even more as their skin melted and fell from their bodies like melting wax from a candle; leaving only muscle and bone.

Then different beastlike creatures flew over and sprayed out from their mouths sand and salt, that completely covered those squashed and stacked one upon another; filling their stripped and extremely raw flesh with pain not imaginable to mankind.

Thousands of angels of war plucked and pulled them out as they pleased, and took them down into the deep where their cries would magnify; and then the angels of war would bring them back and take some more and then bring them back and take some more; repeating the process over and over again.

Then those squashed and stacked one upon another re-grew their burnt skin and flesh, as if it had never been burnt. Then different beastlike creatures rose out of the deep of the mighty gulf and out of their mouths they sprayed flesh-eating locusts, totally covering those squashed and stacked one upon another. And the locusts fed well and the cries of those they fed on rose up out of the mighty gulf, and Philip and Mark wept until they could weep no more. They tried to turn away, but the Black cloud would not let them and the black cloud said to them,

'Those whom you look upon are the evildoers of mankind. Murderers, paedophiles and those who practice wickedness, deceit and lasciviousness; those possessed of the evil eye through such sins as covetousness, jealousy and envy. They are the two-faced, the proud, the vain, the ignorant; they are blasphemers, idolaters, atheists, devil worshippers, lovers of inequity, lovers of religion and wicked souls. These things have been chosen over good by those who love wicked and evil things, and they will never know they have become these things because of the very nature of these wicked and evil thoughts.

'The angels of war take them into the deep and practice their torture techniques on them. These things go on day and night and never stop.'

The black cloud then covered that side of the mighty gulf, and Philip and Mark could see them no more; then it turned their heads and bodies to face the other side of the mighty gulf.

There they saw human beings in the hundreds of thousands and beings of all types in their millions, standing in a field full of all the things in the garden of Eden, and they could look across and down into the deep of the mighty gulf and watch the fate of the sinners who cried to them to help them; but they could not offer help.

And they could eat of all of the wonderful fruits in the garden, but they still could not eat of the tree of life, nor did they eat of the tree of good and evil. The angels of the MOST HIGH had taught and showed them things still yet to come and had filled their hearts with good things, which would lead them to everlasting life, and the black cloud then said 'These are the righteous.'

Then the black cloud let go of Philip and Mark and returned into the deep. Its lightning returned and its fire burned like a furnace and as it descended it smothered those squashed and stacked one upon another, and they cried out in great pain.

Then the crack in the ground closed up and the whirlwind ceased, and the figures of winged beings disappeared. The whirlwind descended out of the sky until it reached the Ark, and then it disappeared as the lid on the Ark closed. Philip and Mark looked up and saw that the whirlwind had left a hole in the ceiling, that reached right back up to the surface; and it had left the hole at an angle so that the men could easily climb out.

When Philip and Mark reached the surface, they were standing where the big Christmas tree would normally stand in December, in Washington DC. But as they stood up, a fire lit up all around them and they could see the wicked twenty-four men standing in a circle around them too. Director Forbes walked up to Philip and Mark; he was dressed in his black robe with his hood on, so they could not see his face properly.

'If you could look down from the sky, you would see that you are standing in the middle of a pentagram inside of a circle; the fire marks out its lines,' said Director Forbes.

Philip and Mark looked around and they could see cars in the distance. Philip shouted out for help, which made Director Forbes laugh out loud.

'Oh, I'm afraid no one can hear you, we have blocked off this entire area. Our Secret Service men and women are the best in the world, so you can be sure we are not going to be disturbed,' gloated Director Forbes.

'We know the truth. We know who you are!' shouted Mark.

'Yes, and now you know the real… or, should I say the full name of Jesus. And now you wish to tell it to the whole world and let them know the whole truth? I don't think so. Hand over the records and I will let you live,' said Director Forbes.

'How can we trust you not to kill us the minute we give them to you?' asked Mark.

'Without the records, you are just two madmen who have killed several law enforcement officers; who sooner or later will be picked up by the locals and arrested and charged for murder.'

'So why are *you* going to let them have all the fun? You've been hunting us down for so long now, why don't you just finish the job now you have the chance?' asked Philip.

'I'm afraid you have got the wrong end of the stick. Do you really think that if I wanted you dead before this moment, you would have gotten here? I needed you to think that way, so that you would think you could actually succeed.'

'Don't make me laugh. Your men have been trying with all their hearts to kill us. We've made it this far because we have out-thought you, and that's the truth,' laughed Mark.

'Sorry to disappoint you, but if that were true, how could I possibly know that you would come out at this exact spot? Why would we have prepared this pentagram and so on? I needed you to not only find the records, but to be able to release them from the chest and bring them up here to me.

'You see, we found the Altar and the tabernacle site many years ago but it seemed some angel of GOD came along and put the orb there, so the minute we stepped onto the first step of the altar, the orb would blast us back into the darkness of the room; which meant we could only stand at a distance and look at it all.

'So we had to find four priests and give them separate tasks, which were really all this one task; and then let you get together and think that you had stumbled onto the biggest thing since sliced bread. The rest, as they say, is history,' smiled Director Forbes smugly.

'But I don't understand. Why go to all that trouble? What good are the records to you?' asked Philip.

'Oh, dear. You haven't got a clue how people in power think, have you? In the wrong hands, this is trouble with a capital T. *We* control the world and our control is always on a knife's edge. Things like this make people like me lose a lot of sleep.

'These records debunk our entire system… Anarchy would rule the streets if these got out, and we would lose our power and control. So rather than risk someone stumbling onto these records, we have tried for years to get the right bunch of priests together to find their way to them;

but the truth is most priests are more interested in little boys on the Internet.'

'But whether you have the records or don't, JAW is real and is coming. You can't win, so what's the point?' said Mark.

'Winning... ha! It's never been about winning, young man. It's about surviving for as long as you can and being on top while you're doing that. When JAW is awoken, he and his angels of war will feed for a long time on the pathetic, selfish, vain, ignorant, self-absorbed, blasphemers and ungrateful flesh and souls on this earth... who by choice, I might remind you, have chosen to reject him and the MOST HIGH for religions that make them Gods.'

'So while he's doing that... feeding, as you put it; you will run off into the wilderness with these beings or demons and find another world to corrupt.' said Philip.

'To put it bluntly, yes.'

'Do you really think these demons will keep their promise? After all, what better meal for JAW and his angels of war than the architects of this miserable world on earth? You're not going to survive; the demons will not take you once they have to leave. You're useless to them, nothing more than extra baggage,' said Mark.

'They are blinded by their own ignorance Mark, of course JAW will get them and deep down they know it. The truth is, unlike you and I, these types of people live for the power and wealth, and they don't care at what price. Believe me son, JAW will have his day with them sooner than they think or dare to acknowledge.' smiled Philip.

'Just give me what I want and then you can start trying to outrun your prison sentences,' said Director Forbes.

'It doesn't make sense. Why would you go to all this trouble? The pentagram in fire and these men standing in a circle. If you are going to let us go then why do you keep asking me to give it to you? Why don't you just reach out and take the rucksack? You can't can you? I have to give it to you, isn't that right!' said Philip.

Director Forbes pulled out a gun from under his robe and pointed it at Mark.

'Give me what I have asked for, or I will kill your son,' shouted Director Forbes at Philip.

'No. If you have the power to kill us then take it or kill us,' replied Philip.

Director Forbes smiled and pointed his gun to the ground. 'You think you've got me, don't you? But think back to when you were in the secret room. Could both of you open all of the boxes, or was it just you, Philip?' asked Director Forbes, as he raised his gun again and pointed it back at Mark. 'You may be half right in that I can't take it from you, but what about Mark? Did he pass the test of righteousness? Maybe I can kill him.'

Philip thought back to when Mark tried to pick up the orb and it blew him back onto the floor. He knew Mark had led a dark life in the army, he also knew they were dead no matter what they did; but the fact was he could not bring himself to be responsible for his own son's death, even for something as important as this.

He begged for forgiveness from the MOST HIGH for failing this last task, pleading with the MOST HIGH to do something; hoping that Mr Death would show up, or Major Stone in War Hawk. But nothing happened. He looked at Mark, the rucksack and then at Director Forbes. His stomach churned, his mouth went dry and tears of frustration ran down his cheek. It was like choosing between two of his own children, how could he possibly decide? The guilt for letting down the MOST HIGH was unbearable; so was the fact that he was considering sacrificing the life of his own son.

A lifetime seemed to pass in the mind of Philip; his hands hurt from clutching the rucksack so tightly. Once again he looked at Mark, the rucksack and then at Director Forbes. His head was spinning; all the time he hoped Mr Death would show up and save him one last time. He looked up into the heavens but only the stars looked back at him.

'Okay, here you are. Please, don't shoot him,' said Philip. He handed the rucksack to Director Forbes, who opened the rucksack greedily to check it had the records inside.

'Very good. Now I can sleep at night knowing I will only lose control of this world when JAW comes and I leave,' smirked Director Forbes.

'So now what?' asked Philip.

'Like I said, you are no threat to me Philip, so you can run along.'

'Come on Mark, let's go,' said Philip.

Director Forbes turned and began to walk towards an altar just a few feet away. Then he stopped and turned around slowly. Calmly, he shot Mark in the spine. Philip cried out and tried to catch his son as he fell to the ground.

'Why, why, why? We did what you asked. Why did you shoot my son? Oh LORD, please help me!' cried Philip.

'I'm afraid that help can only come when his son wakes up. I need a sacrifice to offer to the Beings that have brought these records to me. Now if you don't mind...' said Director Forbes, as he called over to two of his Secret Service Agents to come and pick up Mark's body and carry it to the altar. Philip tried to fight them off, but he was no match for them. He fell to the ground in a heap, sobbing and weeping, shaking uncontrollably. As the agents removed Mark's body from Philip, he could not help noticing that both of the agents had nose bleeds and were bleeding very heavily. They carried Mark's body and placed it on an altar. Mark moaned as they did, but could not move as the bullet had shattered his spine, paralysing him. Philip ran towards the altar but was stopped by the two Secret Agents, who threw him to the ground. Director Forbes walked up to him. 'Did you really think you would get to tell the world our dirty little secret?' said Director Forbes, pointing his gun at Philip.

'What are you going to do with my son?' cried Philip.

'Do you really want me to tell you? Okay then. I need him alive so that when I cut him open from his neck to his belly, I can rip his heart out while it is still beating,' answered Director Forbes, who then shot Philip in the head.

Suddenly Philip saw darkness and then he felt like he was floating upwards. As he floated, he looked downwards and saw his body lying lifeless on the ground. Director Forbes was standing over it, with smoke coming out of the end of his gun. Philip looked towards the altar and cried out to Mark, who laid lifeless on the altar. As Philip rose, he watched Director Forbes throw the gun on the ground next to his body and then walk up to the altar and pull a golden knife out from under his robe. Philip kept rising higher and higher and for the first time he could now see the shape that the fire which had surrounded him, had made. Philip continued to rise and just as Forbes was about to go out of focus, to Philips horror, he saw Forbes lift the golden knife above his head and bring it down into the upper body of his beloved son Mark. Once again Philip cried out, but he could no longer see his son, Forbes or the twenty-four men on the ground; all he could see was the outline that the fire had made of the pentagram and circle.

All this time Philip had been so consumed with the situation concerning Mark, that he had not paid any attention to the fact that he had been looking at himself lying on the ground, with blood dripping slowly down his face from a hole in the middle of his head; or the fact that he was floating into space... or, most importantly, that he was now dead in the flesh and his spirit was now free.

Suddenly a bright light shone down upon him, and for the first time Philip began to think about what was happening to him. He looked up at the light and as he did the rays pulsating from the light hit Philip with an amazing intensity of overwhelming joy and happiness. It filled Philip with a sense of well-being, such as he had never felt before. Suddenly all of his sorrows were gone and as he got closer to the light, smaller lights, like the orb in the secret room, came flying down towards him and Philip revelled in his new spiritual state. 'I'm dead!' he thought, as he filled more and more with the overwhelming feeling of happiness.

The orbs surrounded him and in a flash he was no longer in the earth's realm but was speeding along a tunnel made up of different coloured streaming lights, that whizzed by at light speed. The tunnel turned up and down, then left and right; like a cosmic roller-coaster ride.

Then out of nowhere he was standing in what looked like a golden field, that was bright like the sun for a moment and then it changed to all of the colours of the rainbow. 'It was so beautiful' he thought, as happiness filled him so much that he felt as though he might burst.

Then a large shadow filled the sky as a winged creature flew near. It was so large that when it got close enough to pick him up, it did so with just two of its five claws that wrapped completely around his spiritual body. But Philip had no fear in him whatsoever and he looked down at the beauty that was beneath him; as the creature carried him up into a place filled with humans and other beings. Philip instantly recognised this as being the place he had seen when the Ark lid had been opened, it was the side where the righteous stood; and he then realised that all that time, he had been looking at a garden like that of Eden.

The creature put him down and said, 'I have carried you here so that if you wish, you may look over the mighty gulf and say good-bye to those you love before they are tormented day and night. As from then on they will no longer be able to hear your voice, for their own screams will drown it out.'

Philip did not feel sad or fearful, even though he had just been told to say goodbye to those that he loved before they were to be tortured day and night, although on the other hand, he did wish that his family and friends could have been on his side of the gulf; but he fully accepted that the MOST HIGH, who is a fair and righteous judge, had judged them. Even if he himself did not think that way, the overwhelming feeling of happiness that he was now experiencing, meant that he was not able to feel sad or remorseful for too long. Philip realised that he was, for the first time in his entire existence, totally at peace with himself and was one step closer to the MOST HIGH and Heaven.

Back on earth..... Mark could not move. He stared up at Director Forbes as he summoned the beings from the deep, offering them a living sacrifice and plunging the golden knife into Mark's chest. Mark did not feel a thing due to his paralysis, but a single tear fell and rolled down one side of his face as he realised that what Director Forbes had just done, had ended his life on earth.

He thought of his dad and smiled in comfort, knowing he would be in Heaven now, but then sorrow filled him as he thought of the last moment when he had seen his dad on the ground and Director Forbes had pulled the trigger on his gun, sending a single bullet to his beloved dad's head.

Then Mark began to sink downwards and he could see his body as he looked up. Director Forbes was holding Mark's still-beating heart in his hand. Sadness and regret filled Mark's soul and darkness began to fill his sight, as he continued to sink deeper and deeper.

All the wrongs he had done came to his mind, all the unjust and dirty wars he had fought for his country. The lives he had taken... good and bad, soldiers and civilians, the guilty and the innocent; men, women and children. He cried out as the awful truth that he had been able to hide deep within himself up until now, came bursting in like a raging fire; it tormented him and brought him nothing but great sorrow.

Then a white cloud wrapped itself around him and filled his soul with pain and anguish. He felt a heavy depression grip his being, and he fell even quicker into the pits of Hell. He plummeted into a tunnel filled with fire and white smoke, which whizzed past him at light speed; turning left and right and up and down like a roller-coaster ride to hell. Then suddenly he stopped, and for a moment he thought he could see and hear his beloved Dad on the other side of the mighty gulf, saying goodbye to him and telling him that he would love him forever.

Then the pain became great from the millions of bodies all around him, crushing him and breaking his bones, sucking the air out of him so that he could not breathe; as he heard his neck break and his skull pop. His eyes bulged as if they were about to pop out of his head and he realised with great sorrow, that once again he was a soul within a body. He never saw, heard or thought about his beloved Dad again.

Director Forbes raised Mark's heart into the air. As he did, the Beast appeared from nowhere in its grand chair.

'We have finally got the records, as you predicted, my Lord. Mankind will not be woken to the truth until JAW is awakened. We will be able to control them for many years yet, my Lord,' said Director Forbes to the Beast.

The Beast began to speak but its mouth did not move. 'My Master wants you to be able to see all of mankind, like GOD can. You must hurry and complete the surveillance camera project; we need to know as much as possible about mankind and be able to track the begotten and chosen ones. They also want more black blood pumped out of the earth to weaken her more, so that she retaliates against the ungrateful child and ferociously destroys them all,' said the Beast.

Director Forbes did not understand the last bit, seeming confused. The Beast shook its head, saying, 'My Master wants the earth to kill as many of mankind as possible; so get control of as many of the oil-rich countries as you can, as quickly as possible, and get pumping. This will cause the earth to respond with earthquakes, hurricanes and tsunamis.'

'Yes my Lord, now I understand. Is there anything else?' asked Director Forbes.

'We need to fulfil the prophecy of the beast that has one of its heads cut off but survives; this we can use to scare mankind, as those that read the scripture will believe that the end is near. This is important, because we will be able to take away more control from the people and keep control of our enemies in a way we would not be able to without such an attack,' said the Beast.

'What do you have in mind Lord?' asked Director Forbes.

'Destroy something meaningful in this country. Say it was the work of your enemy, and use it to bring in the last phase of the new world order. But first, create one enemy, bigger than the ones you have created already. Tell mankind that they are not safe from this new and more organised enemy; remind them of the old enemy and how bad it was, and tell them this one is much worse. Then begin to hunt down this enemy in the oil-rich lands where they will come from.

'While you tell mankind you are at war, with an invisible enemy, send in your companies and pump the oil out, increasing your riches and power. At the same time you will be weakening the earth and making her angrier, which will make her attack in self-defence. This will kill more people, for which mankind will blame GOD; they will curse them and turn their backs on them, and this will make JAW extremely angry. He will be kept occupied with them the moment he awakes, giving us time to make good our escape. For mankind is an easy being to corrupt and control,' said the Beast.

'You truly are wise, my Lord. When should we destroy the buildings?'

'Spread the word that an attack from your enemies is coming, but do not destroy the buildings until JAW has been awakened. Only then will it be the right time to bring into play the last phase of the new world order; for once it begins, time on the earth will be short. Even if JAW were not coming, the earth cannot withstand much more as we have taken her to the brink of her patience.

'You have put many evil men in power all around the world, especially in the oil-rich countries; now it is time to reveal to the world just what horrible things they have been getting up to and how your peace-loving nation will blow them away for democracy and freedom.'

'Yes my Lord, you are truly wise. It will be done as you wish,' replied Director Forbes.

BIGS AND HIS SMALL CONGREGATION

'If I were to say to you... Now before you answer, I want you to clear your minds and only picture what you see when I say the words. Are you ready?' Bigs asked his small Friday evening congregation. The congregation was made up of his wife Michelle, his daughters Mart and Pas, his son Ric, his three friends Paul, Andy and Derrick and their three girlfriends.

'Yes!' they all shouted back.

'The words are *Jesus Christ*... remember, it has to be the first image that comes into your heads. Write down the description of what you see,' said Bigs.

They all began to write down a brief description of what they saw in their minds.

'Next question. What is the true religion of Jesus Christ?' asked Bigs.

'Christianity!' they all shouted.

'Wrong. Jesus never ever called himself a Christian; he had no idea of such a name. In fact, it didn't even exist when Jesus was on the earth and there was no religion anywhere called Christianity. The truth is, he was dead by the time Christianity came along. So, what is Jesus' last name?'

'Christ!' they all shouted.

'Wrong. No one who lived around and knew Jesus ever called him Christ; as his first or last name, no one. The truth is, it's a lie to talk as if his last name was Christ or to say people called him that. Okay, what is the colour of the hair of this Jesus Christ?' asked Bigs.

Some said ginger, while others said blonde or brown.

'Was it straight, curly, or Afro-type hair?'

They all answered that it was not quite straight, but slightly curly.

'So it wasn't an Afro?'

'No!' they all shouted, and then laughed because they kept speaking in unison.

'Okay, was it short hair or long?'

'Longish,' they all said together.

'Okay, so it wasn't like the typical black persons hair?'

'No.'

'Was it Chinese people's hair?'

'No.'

'Indian people?'

'No.'

'Mexican?'

'No.'

'European?'

'Yes.'

'Was the colour of his skin like a black, Chinese, Indian or a Mexican person's skin colour?'

'None of them,' they all replied.

'European?'

'Yes.'

'So the image of Jesus Christ in your minds, is of a white man with ginger, brown, or blonde hair, that's curly. Correct?'

'Yes.'

'Why do you think that is how you picture Jesus Christ? Is it, firstly, because you have seen him in real life? Is it, secondly, because you just believe he is European looking? Or is it, thirdly, because this world has planted that image into your heads?'

'The third one,' they all replied.

'So... Now think carefully and truthfully about your answer, because the truth is what will help you be a better person. Truth is your best friend, never forsake it for a lie because in the end a lie is not worth half as much as the truth. Okay, so do you think that description is correct of the real Jesus?'

'No,' they all said.

'Tell me why Michelle?' asked Bigs.

'Because Europeans weren't in that part of the world... well, not in enough numbers to make up a tribe or population like the number of Jews that lived there.'

'Derrick, what do you think?' asked Bigs.

'I agree with Michelle, those parts of the world were black. The mixing of the Europeans with the blacks and other indigenous people, then made the Arab people.'

'So if Jesus Christ looks like a man from Europe or the western world, but we know the people of that part of the world were not European or from the western world, then does that mean someone has made changes to the appearances of the characters in the Bible?'

'Yes. They must have,' said Paul.

'Or is it us that are wrong? Was it white people who first lived in that part of the world and then moved to Europe when we arrived?' asked Bigs.

'No, that part of the world has always been black and Arab,' said Andy.

'Back in the days when the changes were made in the Bible from black to white characters, they had no idea that in the future incredible advances would have been made by white people in genetic research. These advances ironically proved that their forefathers had lied and that the beginning seed of mankind had to be black.

'You see, the bloodline of the real Jesus goes all the way back to Adam and Eve and what I mean by that is Jesus' family tree is directly connected to Adam and Eve; as if they were his a million times a million great grandparents. It is a biological and genetic fact that the European genetic make-up cannot produce the African genetic make-up; but the African genetic make-up can produce the genetic make-up of all the other races.

'I won't go into the full genetic break down at this moment, but if anyone is interested in where I got this information from, it was from a leading genetics professor named Dr Leaky. It is also a fact that Abraham and David were not born in Europe and these two men and all the other people in the Bible are a part of the bloodline that Jesus came from. That genetic makeup or bloodline, is not European or from the Western world. Now why is this important? It is important because it tells us that there are people out there, some now dead, that are willing to lie just so they can say their race is the line of David and call themselves the original Jew.

'I believe the reason for this is because a long time ago, and not many people know this because it has been hidden well by such lies as the one we are talking about, the Europeans were considered animals and uncivilised. There was a time when Europeans had very little to feel good about in themselves as they had made no significant contributions in the world, compared to the many great contributions they have made in the last couple of centuries.

'In the times going back to Noah, it was Africa that was the main contributor to the advancement of civilisation. It was the Black Moors that taught the Europeans that the world was not flat and that the stars in the sky could be used to navigate the Oceans. When the Europeans finally did take to the seas, they found the world was alive and well and full of riches that they could only dream about; and we all know what happened next. They let jealousy get the better of them, and that old fiery dog the Devil told them it was not fair that the Blacks had all the riches and knowledge, and that they should take it for their own and rewrite history, and put themselves in the place of Black people.

'If only they had known they would've made up for their lack of contribution in the first part of history, by becoming great inventors of industries and producing some of the greatest inventions of the day, but they didn't know that back then so they listened to Satan and changed the face of history; and in order to do that you would have to change the bloodline of the FATHER and MOTHER OF CREATION. Which is the greatest mistake they could have ever made.

'Because the FATHER and MOTHER is merciful, they will get one last chance before the end of this worlds time to change their ways and change the lies back to the truth, especially now they know what great things they have contributed to civilisation. That's why the truth is your best friend and lies are your enemy, because once you start down the road of lies it becomes so big it's too embarrassing to admit the lie. That's what the European and Western world have inherited and unless they reject the lies of their forefathers they will become as guilty as them, but it is hard to reject that which you perceive to be done with your best interests in mind.

'To reject it must make them feel like traitors to their forefathers or make them look like they do not appreciate what has been done for them. After all, because of the changes or lies told, white people have been able to claim all of the contribution in history as theirs; making them seem like the only true candidate for such a title as the chosen people of the FATHER and MOTHER.

'That is where they keep making their biggest mistake and shortly we will all find out if it was a mistake or a worldwide conspiracy to withhold the truth, because the FATHER and MOTHER OF CREATION are real and their sons and daughters are real and they *will* one day come to reclaim the earth and all other planets and solar systems in the physical world. We must make ourselves available to serve them,' he continued...

'We must pray to the FATHER and MOTHER to use us at no cost to them. We must live our lives as if it is the only one we will get and be grateful for the gift of life, and we must not concern ourselves with Heaven and things we know nothing about; if they are ours to have, we will know when the time is right, but get it into your hearts that you are so grateful for life from the FATHER and MOTHER that you will give it back to them if they ask, but only if they ask, not any man or woman, me or a preacher.

'I have asked you to do things to prove yourselves to me, but I will not do that again. Instead I will ask you to prove yourselves to the FATHER and MOTHER.

'The men among us will train ourselves and keep ourselves in top shape, then we will offer ourselves to do the things that the FATHER and MOTHER may not wish for their saints to have to do; such as killing or going to war against the evildoers. This is what I have dedicated my life to, as I know I can't be a saint. My way is the sword, and I hope that it can be of use to the FATHER and MOTHER before I leave this earth and go to the hell that we all deserve. There is not one in this world who has not sinned. I think this world, before too long, will fall into total chaos and it is then that we will make our move and offer our services to the FATHER and MOTHER,' said Bigs. He closed the nights session with a prayer, and the men retired to the gym to smoke and discuss matters more graphically.

Bigs was still struggling with his ganja addiction, he had smoked for so long it was like second nature to him; he believed it was where his wisdom came from. Even though the voice had been talking about it as being some sort of key, he still hadn't worked out what that had meant and he wasn't even sure if he wanted to. He had begun to think that everyone was allowed one vice and this was his.

As the months passed, he noticed that the police were still keeping a close eye on him. He couldn't work out how they could get funding to pay for the twenty-four hour, seven-days-a-week surveillance they kept him under.

'They must be making out to the judge I'm some sort of terrorist or something,' he would say to Michelle.

His building firm was growing, and he had won several major contracts worth hundreds of thousands of pounds. Life was good for Bigs and his family and close friends. His children wanted for nothing, and he and Michelle were well-off materially and very happy within their family.

Bigs didn't worry much about the idea that the world was facing new terrorist threats from the Middle East, because it seemed to him as if the local terrorists had closed up shop so that the new ones could take centre stage. As far as he was concerned they all belonged to the government; as he would say, 'What type of enemy goes after the people the government doesn't care about, but never goes after the people the government does care about? Why would they blow up a shopping centre, killing innocent people who had nothing to do with their war and could do nothing to change the policy of the government; but they never touch military or government buildings?'

Bigs believed that it was all a set up and the government had constructed the perfect enemy; one that would never go after the government itself, but would only kill innocent people. When the time was right, Bigs would go after the government and its military if the FATHER and MOTHER wished, but he would not fight or kill women and children or anyone that was not part of the problem.

The months and years passed and Bigs continued in his usual routine of training, praying, smoking and talking about and to the FATHER and MOTHER OF CREATION. All he wanted was to be used by the FATHER and MOTHER someday, in whatever way they saw fit. Bigs did not know why he felt this way, he just did. It was not hard or something he tried to do, it was simply who he was: far from perfect, full of sin, yet drawn to the FATHER and MOTHER obsessively. He thought about them day and night; they were the last words he spoke before he went to bed and the first words he spoke when he woke up.

If the truth were known, Bigs did not believe for one minute that the FATHER and MOTHER OF CREATION would ever use him for anything. Yet strangely, it was because he believed they would never use him that he was free to think however he wanted to, concerning them. He could have cursed the FATHER and MOTHER like a lot of people did, who thought they were on their way to hell. He knew the FATHER and MOTHER had helped him all of his life and yet he still sinned, even after they would get him out of the trouble he had gotten himself into.

So one day he asked the FATHER and MOTHER why they keep saving him? He felt so ashamed that every time he did a devil act which would lead him into more trouble than he could handle, the FATHER and MOTHER OF CREATION would show up and save him and he would be so grateful for their help, but yet he still would go and commit another sin that would be too much for him to handle, and again the FATHER and MOTHER OF CREATION would come and save him. This went on throughout Bigs' entire life.

One night when he was sitting down with his friends, Bigs began to realise how much he went on about the FATHER and MOTHER. He was talking as usual about the FATHER and MOTHER and the voice spoke to him saying, 'They do not wish to spend all their time talking about the FATHER and MOTHER, like you do.'

Bigs thought about what was just said to him and wanted to see if it was true. So he stopped talking about the FATHER and MOTHER and listened to what they would say if he didn't speak; telling them to smoke and be merry.

'Shit, I guess some nights you guys just want to talk about football or something and here I am always going on about the FATHER and MOTHER,' Bigs said laughingly.
They all laughed. Thinking it was okay to speak truthfully in the relaxed climate, they replied, 'Yeah, sometimes it would be nice to talk about other things, or just watch a game of football or something,' they all agreed.

Bigs laughed. 'Okay, I'll try to remember that,' he smiled, trying to hide the anger that swelled within him. *'After all,'* he told himself, *'you don't have to go on all night. Not everyone is into the FATHER and MOTHER OF CREATION like you are.'* This was the first time he realised that he had something unexplainable within himself, that was totally obsessed with the FATHER and MOTHER OF CREATION. He could not understand why his friends, who were selected from his old gang of criminals, weren't into the FATHER and MOTHER like he was and it made him angry that they weren't. Yet the voice told him there were reasons that he was this way and reminded him to keep searching inside of himself for the truth.

One night as he sat with Paul, Derrick and Andrew, Bigs looked out of his window and saw a light in the sky. It changed colours as he watched it, from yellow to red and then to blue. Subconsciously, he said to Derrick, Andrew and Paul, 'That's my family... up there in the sky... can you see them?'

Andrew, Paul and Derrick looked out of the window up at the bright star.

'What, you mean that star in the sky up there?' asked Derrick.

'Look closely at it,' replied Bigs.

'Hey it's changing colours, can you see that?' said Paul to the other two men peering out of the window into the blackness of the night.

'Yes, but stars change colours, it's something to do with the atmosphere or something,' said Derrick.

'Yeah, it's changing colour from blue to red, look, ... look, it's...' Andrew stopped midsentence as he and the other men, apart from Bigs, watched in astonishment as the star began to move to the right. As it moved, it left behind it a trail in the sky that faded out after a small amount of time.

'Bigs, Bigs, are you seeing this? It's moving to the right of your house,' said Derrick, slightly nervous and scared.

'What the fuck is it Bigs?' asked Paul as he sat back down, too afraid to look out of the window anymore.

'You lot, its moving closer to the house. Oh Bigs, shit, what should we do!' shouted Andrew.

Bigs laughed. 'I told you, it's my family. Come outside with me and have a good look.'

The men followed behind Bigs as he went outside into his garden. It was a very big garden that stretched way back into the darkness.

'Boy, Bigs, do you think this is a good idea? I watched the discovery channel when it had alien abductions on it, and this is the type of thing I've always said you should never do. Man, I think we should go back inside... man I'm serious!' shouted Paul.

'Don't be a pussy Paul. I told you, it's my family; and even it wasn't, I believe in the FATHER and MOTHER OF CREATION, so I fear nothing,' said Bigs as he moved into the complete darkness of his garden; his three friends following somewhat awkwardly behind him.

They looked up into the clear black sky at the UFO as it sparkled and changed colours right above their heads, some half a mile up.

'Move for me,' said Bigs, and the UFO began to dance in the sky moving like a fly, up and down, left and right, diagonally and then vertically. Then three other UFOs joined it and they hovered in a diamond formation. Paul, Derrick and Andrew watched in disbelief as Bigs told them to move out of formation; the UFOs did, dancing around one another like an intergalactic red arrows show, before returning to their diamond formation once again. Paul ran back to the house and would not come back outside.

Bigs stared up and a tear ran down his face as he said again, 'This is my family.' After ten minutes Bigs began to get cold. 'I'm going inside,' said Bigs, but Andrew and Derrick just kept looking up at the UFOs not believing their eyes. As Bigs began to go back inside the UFOs shot off into space at such a speed, that Andrew and Derrick lost sight of them in seconds.

Back in Bigs' house all Derrick, Andrew and Paul wanted to know was, what was it that they had just been looking at and how was it they were Bigs' family? Bigs did not tell them and they had to go home wanting answers to so many questions. Bigs sat in his chair smoking a spliff and asked the FATHER and MOTHER to explain to him how he knew the UFOs were his family and how he knew they would do what he asked of them.

The next night he looked out and saw the same light in the sky and went out by himself and asked it to move for him if it was his family, and it began to dance like it did the night before. Then it was joined by six other UFOs and this time they made a shape like the letter V. Bigs looked up at them and was filled with happiness and then he noticed a dull yellow UFO, off to the right of him, moving slowly across the night sky but it did not stop, it just moved slowly and kept going until it was out of Bigs' sight. Bigs spent many hours looking into the sky and watching many different UFOs that all seemed to be moving over his house slowly, before moving on at neck breaking speeds into the depths of space.

The following day after Bigs' morning training session, he sat down with Michelle and told her about the UFOs in the sky and how for some reason, still unbeknown to him, he referred to them as his family.

'Can I come out and see them the next time they come?' asked Michelle excitedly.

'Are you sure you won't be afraid? Paul saw them and ran back in the house and wouldn't come out until they were gone and then he drove home and hasn't trained for the last two days,' said Bigs.

'I won't be afraid if you're there and you tell me it's all right,' replied Michelle.

'Okay, if they're out there tonight I'll call you.'

'Why has it taken you two days to tell me this?' she asked slightly angry.

'Because I've had to try to understand how I know what I know and see what I can see,' replied Bigs.

That night Bigs looked out of the window and saw nothing but Michelle had left some raw chicken pieces for him to give to the foxes, so Bigs went out into the pitch darkness of the night and Michelle watched him through the window for as far as she could, before he was too far gone into the darkness to be seen. She looked excitedly up into the sky but could not see much as there were clouds totally covering the nights sky. She thought 'it's not fair!' to herself, thinking she would not be able to see the UFOs.

But as Bigs walked to the back of the garden the clouds began to dissipate right before her eyes. She could not believe it, one minute there were clouds covering the whole sky, the next they had disappeared like a mighty wind had come along and blown them away in one big puff. Michelle's eyes widened and she waited to exhale for a moment before doing so, as what she looked at was so unbelievable to her it made her forget to breathe out after taking in a big gulp of air. When she saw the seven UFOs right above her house in a perfect straight line, her heart began to beat faster and she began to feel very afraid until she saw Bigs walking back down the garden path, calling to her to come out and see them; but she shook her head and watched them from the window. Bigs laughed.

'Okay I'm going back up the back. If you want me just come out and call me,' he laughed and disappeared back into the darkness.

Michelle watched from the comfort of her home but the feeling she felt wasn't that comfortable, she looked up and then sat back down and then looked up again and then sat back down. All the scary movies she had seen began to pass through her mind, especially the ones about aliens and abductions. She began to feel really scared and thought that an alien may be in the house. Her mind became more and more afraid and paranoid, as she was certain she could hear movement upstairs. She wanted to call to Bigs but that would mean going out into the garden and at that moment she could not make up her mind as to which place was the scariest, being inside the house or outside?

She looked up again at the UFOs in the sky and decided to open the window and call to Bigs, but then just thinking about calling Bigs to tell him what she had thought brought her out of the fear that had grasped her; simply because she knew what his response would have been and she played it through her mind. The first thing he would have said is 'Where is your faith in the FATHER and MOTHER? When you have fear call to them to give you faith and that will give you strength. Fear nothing but them, for all things were made by them. Did I not tell you they are my family and did you not ask me if it was okay and I said yes. Stop listening to Lucifer Michelle and be secure and positive about yourself. Now stop being stupid and come outside and meet your family.'

After she had thought about what Bigs would have said if she had called to him whilst being so afraid, she no longer felt afraid and put on her coat and walked onto the path looking up at the UFOs all the time; then she called to Bigs who came out of the darkness with a smile.

'I'm glad you remembered what I've taught you. If you didn't come out you would have been in trouble with me because you must learn to have faith and conquer your fears... I'm only joking about the trouble bit, but I am glad you did it without me having to come and get you; which I was just about to do. You must have heard me in your mind,' said Bigs smiling all the time.

'I did hear you that's why I came out. I was feeling scared but then I thought about what you'd say and it made me feel okay,' replied Michelle as she held onto Bigs tightly and stared up into the now clear black night sky, as the seven UFOs flickered brightly in colours of blue, red, yellow and white as they lined up perfectly in a straight line.

'This is our family Shell, do you want to see them move?' asked Bigs.

'Yeah,' replied Michelle.

'Move for me,' said Bigs and as he did to Michelle's amazement the UFOs began to dance once again through the night sky.

'Wow that's amazing. Gosh, you said move and they moved. So do you think they are your army? You've always talked about having to serve the FATHER and MOTHER?' she asked as they continued to dance in the sky.

'I don't know I never thought of that… You might be right Shell, that's an interesting theory,' replied Bigs as he began to contemplate what Michelle had just said.

They watched the UFOs for a couple of hours before Michelle suddenly realised that she had not brought out the baby monitor with her, so she did not know whether the children were asleep or awake and calling for her.

'Say good night then and we'll go inside now, it's getting cold,' said Bigs. He said good night to his family and so did Michelle, and with the blink of an eye the UFOs were gone.

'Wow that was totally amazing. I never thought I would see such things... and when you told them to move, the way they just started dancing around. Wow Bigs you must be someone special for them to do that just because you asked. I can't believe that,' said Michelle as she continued to analyse what had just taken place. Bigs said nothing, he just simply listened to Michelle's theories on who he might be and why they would do that for him.

'They must be something to do with the army you've being asking the FATHER and MOTHER for, don't you think?' asked Michelle, but before Bigs could say anything, she answered for him.

'You see! You thought all these years that the FATHER and MOTHER wouldn't use you, but I think you're the General or something! That's why you have always gone on about making an army for the FATHER and MOTHER OF CREATION. From the day we first met you told me that was what you wanted to do, and for some reason I never thought it was strange or weird.

'Do you remember when you told me about the part of your brain that speaks to you? I remember thinking, I wish my brain would speak to me. I'm telling you Bigs, this is why you have always thought like that. Wow, I can't believe it! Was that real just now? I wasn't dreaming, was I? Wow, I can't believe it, they must be your army!' said Michelle, not giving Bigs the chance to get a word in edgeways; the truth was, he was glad to just listen to her and her theories. If anyone knew Bigs apart from the FATHER and MOTHER, it was Michelle. He had told her everything about himself and she didn't find it strange or weird; and as Bigs had told her, it was the FATHER and MOTHER who had brought them together.

The next day Michelle told the children what had happened so when Bigs got up his kids wanted to know if it was true and when could they see the lights in the sky?

'If you won't be scared, I suppose if they're out there tonight you can have a look. But this will be the last time, my family is not a puppet show; they're not here for our entertainment and you mustn't speak of this to anyone. Do you understand?' said Bigs in a very serious tone of voice and a look which told his children he was not playing and that meant a serious smack if they broke their word; and as their Dads hands were heavy and hard, they promised and meant it.

That night one UFO appeared and Bigs showed it to his children but they didn't go outside as it was a cold night and Bigs didn't want them getting a cold, so they watched from the kitchen with the door open; to be honest the children were quite happy to view the UFO from the safety of their home.

They watched it change colours and then Bigs asked it to move for him and it did, dancing across the sky backwards at great speed and then suddenly stopping dead before changing direction and stopping dead again. It moved in a S pattern and then a circle, moving near then far and up and down; the kids loved it and when it was all over, once again Bigs just sat back and listened to what they all had to say, as they exchanged ideas and theories with great excitement. Bigs was happy to see that none of his children were afraid of what they saw and they just simply accepted the fact that what was in the sky was Daddy's family, which meant it was theirs too.

For the rest of that weekend and the first part of the week Bigs let them look up at the UFOs, but one night when he came back and found Michelle and the kids up at almost midnight looking into the sky, he decided enough was enough and banned any more sky watching. The kids protested but Bigs' word was final and as if to cement his word, the UFOs did not show up again for several months.

It was Friday night, and the small congregation gathered as usual at Bigs' house. For many weeks the buzz had been about the lights in the sky. Everyone believed they were related to the army that Bigs wanted to build for the FATHER and MOTHER OF CREATION and that it must be an answer to Bigs' prayers, for him to be used by the MOST HIGH. However, Bigs stood on the side of caution when asked what it all meant, saying, 'Your guess is as good as mine. All I want to do is serve the FATHER and MOTHER OF CREATION. How, is not up to me. You say I might be a General and if that is what the FATHER and MOTHER want, that would be great; but I would be glad to just be a soldier as well. As I've always said, to be the towel that wipes the dirt off of the bottom of the shoe of the FATHER and MOTHER is more than I deserve, and a job I would love to do. So I don't know what it means. All I know right now is that they are my family; that I do know.'

Bigs was starting to get a bit fed up with it all, for to him, all the time spent talking about UFOs was taking time away from the FATHER and MOTHER. Michelle was the first to spot that Bigs was getting fed up with the switch in focus, so she asked Bigs a question that had come to her mind some days ago.

'Do you think all those people who have become religious and have taken up the wrong religion will go to Hell?' asked Michelle.

'Those who would kill for their religion or holy book might,' replied Bigs.

'Why?'

'Because if they are willing to kill another human being because of a book or religion, then they are saying they love that book or religion as much as the FATHER and MOTHER. Nothing should be on the same level as the FATHER and MOTHER.'

'So which religion do you think is the most likely to go to heaven? Is there one? You know that Christians say they are the only way to heaven, and Muslims and Jews say the same thing. How can you know which one is right?' asked Michelle.

'Let me put it this way. A hummingbird cannot say to the woodpecker, "You cannot enter into Heaven, because you are a woodpecker and not a hummingbird." A man who thinks he knows all the things in the Universe still cannot say they know all the ways of the FATHER and MOTHER, for THEY are greater than eternity.

'There are none that are worthy of heaven, and all who believe they are worthy are fools; religion cannot change these facts. It is even more ridiculous to expect to go to heaven because you are of a specific religion, than it would be to expect that if you knocked on the Prime Minister's door, he would let you in with no questions asked because you are a citizen.

'If you were to say to any of these religions who tell you they will enter heaven because they are a Muslim, Christian, Jew or Buddhist, can you enter freely when you feel like into the palace of the King or Queen of your country, or the house of your President or Prime Minister? I can tell you no matter how important they are in religious circles and even if the King or Queen and President or Prime minister is a member of their religion, they will still not be able to just walk in because they say so.

'Yet these religious people want you and I to believe that they can make a claim that they have that right to heaven because of a book that told a story; that wasn't even about them but about specific people or persons who lived in a certain way at a certain time and who did not receive their invitations by reading a book but received their invitation direct from the FATHER and MOTHER, or maybe via an angel in some cases. These people who are talked about in the bible did not read a book and then call themselves a name of a religion and then because they called themselves a religion they entered into heaven.

'Believe me it is a million times easier to get into the palace of a person here on earth than it is to get into heaven and it is harder to get into the palace of a person here on earth than it is to get into the kingdom of the FATHER and MOTHER. Why, because you and I do not decide who gets in, nor do we do anything that gives us the right to get in. Just as we who are chosen or have favour, cannot do anything to take us away from being chosen or favoured. But one thing for certain is, that being in a religion will not give you better odds because you were chosen or favoured before you came into the world; and there is no religion outside of the physical realm, only the creator and their creations,' answered Bigs 'Yet people believe that they have this right... all because they were told so in a book!'

'So are you saying that the Bible and Qur'an are not to be trusted?' asked Paul's girlfriend.

'Like I have said before be careful of such books and of the faith you put in them. Books are always written by men or women, and although men and women have the knowledge of the FATHER and MOTHER OF CREATION and angels, they also have the knowledge of Satan and demons. Mankind has the ability to hide with whom they have allied themselves, and can hide their true beliefs behind certain types of clothing. For example, when you see a man with a vicars dog collar on, you may assume he is a man of the FATHER and MOTHER and that his intentions are good and in keeping with theirs. Yet how many times have we read about priests raping little boys whose parents believed that their children were safe with these 'holy' men?

'I'm not saying that the people who wrote the books were corrupt, but I am saying that these books have passed through a lot of hands and that not all of the people who have added things to or taken things out of these books, have done so for the right reasons. For example, the Bible has had things removed simply because they were written by women. I mean does that sound righteous to you, or does it sound as though mans negative thinking has been allowed to creep in? If so, then what you read now has been corrupted by the views of those you have trusted to tell you the truth. Also, the word 'Israel' was changed to the word 'church' and 'Jerusalem' was changed to 'Heaven.'

'The fact that the Bible makes Pontius Pilate out to be a caring, concerned Roman who has a problem with crucifying a possibly-innocent Jew, tells me this book has been tampered with. The idea that the Romans were a just and fair occupier of the land, and that Pilate was too moral to send an innocent man to death and required the Jews persuasion to do so, could only be believed by those who have little understanding of how the Roman empire operated.

'Learn to hear what is already in you, and then use these books to confirm what you have been told. Do not put the books on the same level as the FATHER and MOTHER OF CREATION, and do not automatically trust in religious figures; for all of mankind struggles with demons. Last but certainly not least, you should look for the FATHER and MOTHER OF CREATION in living things, because that's where you will find them. You will find Satan in dead things, and that includes religious books,' said Bigs.

'So you don't trust those preachers on the TV who say they can heal and all that?' asked Andrew's girlfriend.

'Again, only the FATHER and MOTHER know what's in the heart of a man. I have found that the people may believe that they are giving praise to the FATHER and MOTHER OF CREATION, when in actual fact they may be praising the preacher or themselves. A lot of the people in these churches on the TV only start saying 'hallelujah' when the preacher tells them to, or when he has told them something that glorifies themselves; such as that they will be healed or they will get a supernatural financial reward. Then a lot of these preachers also seem to need the church to give them praise for preaching well,' replied Bigs.

'So are you saying that it is wrong to join a religion?' asked Paul's girlfriend.

'If you have become religious, make sure it is for the right reason and not for what that religion may be offering or promising; or because you think it will spare you eternal damnation.'

'So why should you become religious?' asked Paul's girlfriend.

'It should be because in your heart you honestly think and believe that the religion you have chosen will be the best way to serve, praise and worship the FATHER and MOTHER OF CREATION,' answered Bigs.

'But how would you know? Like you just said, the religion you choose could be corrupted,' said Derrick's girlfriend.

'If you search for the FATHER and MOTHER OF CREATION, then you are searching for the truth. You will not stop at any one religion if you search for the whole truth, and you will search in all things, not just religion. For the FATHER and MOTHER are not just in one place; they are in the entire universe, and much more.'

'But why can't you find the truth, or what you are looking for, in just one religion?' asked Derrick's girlfriend.

'Because when one searches for the truth, there are no parameters as to where it can be found. Yet all religions have parameters; they have to in order to make themselves different from the rest. But you are right in what you said... I just don't think that you, like many people, realise what it is you say and actually do.'

'What do you mean?' asked Derrick's girlfriend.

'You said "why can't someone find the truth," but then you narrowed it down, subconsciously I think, by saying "or what they are looking for." This is the problem, the truth and what you are looking for are not necessarily the same thing. The truth has no feelings or emotions; it is merely the pure simple facts or reality. Looking for something other than the pure and simple truth is where religion comes in; that's why there are so many religions. They each take a portion of the truth, and then they remove all that does not make its followers comfortable. They only use what appeals to the religion's leaders and followers.'

'But my Mom has been a Christian all her life and I have been brought up as one too. I don't think there's anything wrong with it. We serve, praise and honour GOD. Why would GOD have a problem with that?' asked Paul's girlfriend.

'Well I don't want to get into an argument with you; if you believe in Christianity, that's your right. I tried talking to a group of Christians once and I was called a devil, amongst other things. I have learnt that people who have made their choice about what they are going to believe in, do not want to know truths that would challenge their beliefs. But I *would* say to you that the statement you just made about serving, praising and honouring the FATHER and MOTHER OF CREATION is incorrect.'

'Incorrect! Why do you say it's incorrect? I go to church every Sunday and I give thanks and praise to GOD,' interrupted Paul's girlfriend.

'It's incorrect, because Christians give praise to Christ every Sunday. The FATHER and MOTHERs name is an obscure, distant thing that you may talk about occasionally or indirectly. But as for giving them the full praise... no I'm sorry you don't. You give 99% of it to Christ. If you think I'm lying, next Sunday try counting how many times you give praise to Jesus Christ and then count how many times you give praise to GOD, as you call them.'

'Yeah, but even if you are right...'

'You see, as you think about it, you already know that what I'm saying is true.'

'Okay, maybe, but Jesus and GOD are one. To give praise to Jesus is the same as giving it to GOD,' said Paul's girlfriend.

'They are one in the sense that Jesus is their son and is therefore born from them, but Jesus is a separate being from the FATHER and MOTHER OF CREATION. Jesus and the FATHER and MOTHER are two beings, not one. When Jesus was on the cross he did not call up to himself and say "Save me, self" or "Why have you forsaken me, self," did he?' asked Bigs.

'No,' replied Paul's girlfriend.

'That's because they are two beings, although, Jesus came out of the FATHER and MOTHER and is therefore like his FATHER and MOTHER. So when you praise Jesus you do not praise the FATHER and MOTHER OF CREATION; however, when you praise the FATHER and MOTHER you praise Jesus as well. It is written in the Bible and is a well-known fact in the spiritual world and among preachers, that all prayers should be to the FATHER and MOTHER OF CREATION. If that is the case, then would it not be wise to give all glory and praise to them as well?' said Bigs.

'Sorry... you said in the spiritual world. What is that, like New Age religions?' asked Paul's girlfriend.

'I think you've asked enough questions; let someone else ask one,' said Paul. 'Sorry Bigs, mate, she's a typical Christian who's unwilling to know the truth if she thinks it's going to put her Christianity down.'

'No, don't apologise; let her ask what she wants. Go on Carroll, you were going to ask me something else. What was it?' said Bigs.

'No, I just wanted to know what you meant when you said spiritual world, that's all. I just... well like Paul said, I'm getting a bit carried away. Sorry,' she replied.

'Look, don't apologise for your beliefs. If that's what you want to believe in, then that's your right. I'm just telling you what I believe in, and that's my right. We should all be able to live with one another, even if we believe in different things. What I'm trying to say is that if you stand where I stand, you can see things that you can't see from where you stand, and vice versa.

'In answer to your question, no; the spiritual world I talk of is not New Age religion. It has been here since before mankind ever existed. We are... well, some of us are... four-part beings. Now I know in this world they say you are three parts: spirit, soul and flesh. But I've been told, I believe by the spiritual world, that we are... well, some of us are actually four parts.'

'You've completely lost me,' said Carroll.

'Well, that isn't hard to do,' laughed Paul.

'Shut up you,' replied Carroll, feeling somewhat embarrassed.

'It's like this: according to this world you have a spirit and a body, and what connects them is a soul. I also used to believe in this theory until a week ago, when I was told we are four parts: the spirit, soul, body and mind. The body or flesh, is controlled by the physical world and sometimes by the spiritual world; which can communicate with the flesh or body. All of this information is stored in the mind. The spirit is controlled by the spiritual world, which communicates with the spirit, and all of this
information is stored in the soul. The physical world is corrupt; that's why left to its own devices the body and mind would gladly eat nothing but chocolate, burgers, chips, fizzy drinks and cakes, all the time; even though these things are bad for us. The spiritual world is not corrupt and those that lean towards that side of self, eat things like fruit, vegetables, water and brown bread.

'Obviously I'm giving you a very basic example, but I hope you get the drift of what I'm trying to say. These sides of self can be at war within us and a long time ago I was taught by the spiritual side, that the first really important war on earth is called the war of self.
Furthermore, until each of us can win this war, we will bounce around like Ping-Pong balls in our own lives.'

'Have you won this war?' asked Paul's girlfriend.

'Hey, I was about to ask that,' said Andrew's girlfriend.

'Have I won that? It took me about three years to know what it meant, then another two to understand it. Now, another year on, I have the wisdom to start that process, but I know that it will take me the best part of the rest of my life to come to grips with it all. You see, when we become more spiritually aware, we begin to see how corrupt the flesh is. The problem then is that as we look at our imperfections and we begin to identify more and more problems, if the spirit connection is not strong enough we will break away and return to the flesh and mind; where we cannot see our imperfections. When we do that, we can become lost forever.'

'But what if the spirit connection *is* strong enough?' asked Derrick's girlfriend.

'Well... then the fight begins. One way to look at it is to think that we are like a computer screen. We can only deal with or look at a certain amount of information at one time, and as the war gets fiercer, our flesh will run off and do things while we are still dealing with the screen full of information before us. It really is quite hard to explain; you have to be at war with yourself to understand what I'm saying.

'People who have problems with overeating, gambling, sexual addictions, or drug or alcohol addictions, and who really want to give those things up, can understand the war of the spirit versus the flesh. A lot of addictions are caused by the flesh being out of control, and when they try to get those addictions under control, it requires the mind, soul and the spirit.'

'Oh, so don't you think the mind is a part of the problem too?' asked Derrick's girlfriend.

'I think the worse off someone is, the more likely it is that their flesh and mind are working together. I think child killers, child sex offenders, rapists and serial killers... those types are definitely flesh and mind. I mean, we all have to fight our negative selves, but you know the difference. Think about the two people who were up on charges the other day, of raping a three-month-old baby they were babysitting. That's an example of the flesh and mind being totally out of control.'

'So is there any religion out there you would say are okay?' asked Derrick.

'Look, the problem I have with religions is that they all have parameters. Another word for parameters is conditions. They all describe their GOD in a way that puts conditions over what their GOD can and can't do. I don't put any conditions over the FATHER and MOTHER OF CREATION; I dare not, nor do I want to. They are my master and I, if I'm extremely lucky, will be their servant. But I will do *their* bidding, not mine.

'Be careful when putting conditions on what type of GOD you will and won't worship and love, for true love is unconditional. I look into all religions to find the truth because I know the FATHER and MOTHER OF CREATION are real. However, if I were to be like the religious and limit my beliefs to what my religion told me, then I might end up rejecting something that is a part of the true GOD, as you say.'

'So what do you think about religions view on gay and lesbian people?' asked Paul's girlfriend.

'What do you think?' asked Bigs.

'I think it's wrong. I mean, I have nothing against gay people, but...'

Bigs interrupted, 'But your religion tells you it's wrong, so you have to take that point of view as well; even though it sounds like you may not be against them.'

'What's your opinion?' asked Paul's girlfriend.

'I think a man or a woman is more than their sexual preference, and that what they do in the bedroom should remain there. That is my only problem with gay men and lesbians; they keep wanting to make a statement with their sexual preference, rather than who they are as an entire person. Michelle and I may be lovers of a certain sexual position, but we don't have to become campaigners for that.

'I understand that gay people want the same rights as traditional couples, and I think they should get them, but I would like to know about the person, not the gay scene. On the other hand, when you make yourself out to be the cool alternative to straight sex, then it sounds a bit two-faced to ask for things like the right to getting married and the acceptance of the church.

'That to me would be like I as a black man, asking the Ku Klux Klan or the National Front to become a member of their organisation. The church and marriage were created for a set way of thinking, just like the National Front and the Ku Klux Klan.'

'So you're saying it's okay to be gay in the eyes of GOD?' asked Paul's girlfriend.

'You know, those who say they can speak for the FATHER and MOTHER are braver than I am. I can't tell you what the FATHER and MOTHER see; I'm nowhere near such a height. But I can see what the church can see, because the church is made up of people and I'm a person.

'This subject goes back to what I was saying earlier about parameters; religion sets rigid standards and ideas and then says that they are the FATHER and MOTHERs standards. The problem is, that religion cannot see what the FATHER and MOTHER OF CREATION can see and so even if the FATHER and MOTHER were set in a way, they would still know everything. Religion, on the other hand, pretends to be able to see everything, but it did not see that far more people would be gay in the future, than there were in the earlier days of the church.

'The FATHER and MOTHER knew back then how many people were gay, and they knew who was pretending to believe that being gay was wrong, to hide the fact that they were gay. Like I've said, being gay does not mean you don't love the FATHER and MOTHER OF CREATION, just as a man who is not gay does not mean that he does love the FATHER and MOTHER OF CREATION.

'In the same way, a man who kills may not be a devil, and a child who lies may not be a wicked child. We cannot see what the FATHER and MOTHER can see, so we must trust in them to judge, not you and I. So treat people how they treat you, and don't prejudge.'

'I'm sorry to say this to you, but I just think you have a problem with Christianity,' said Paul's girlfriend.

'You're right, I do. I think Paul... the so-called apostle Paul who wrote most of the New Testament... is actually the representative of the Western world and its philosophies. He, like the World at large, takes what is not his and then lies and says it belongs to him.

'Jesus never said what he taught was for the whole world, but Paul took it and called it Christianity, and now the teachings belong to Christianity. Nowhere in the Bible do you find books with the name Jesus above them, even though there were books and scriptures written by people who listened to him speak. Instead, you have people with European names like Paul, Matthew, Mark and so on... telling you about a man they never met. As a Christian, don't you find it strange that the very person your religion is supposed to be based upon, did not write any of the books or scriptures in the Bible? Why are your books titled Matthew and Luke? These men cannot claim to have sat with Jesus.

'Do you not understand that all of the men and women who really did sit with Jesus were considered, what we would call today, to be terrorists and that they would have been killed if they had been found?

'Instead you have to read books by European men who went to the land after Jesus was dead, and spoke to people who may or may not have known him, and then they wrote their own versions of his life; yet you now read them as if they were Jesus' version. The Western worlds Jesus Christ is not the real Jesus. Their names are different and I believe their images are as well. Paul is the Jesus Christ of the world, and he is a servant of Satan.'

'But how can you say that?'

'Because Satan's job... and it is a job. He is not roaming around like this world suggests, looking for a hopeless fight with the FATHER and MOTHER OF CREATION... Satan's job is to twist truth into non-truth. Paul has done that by making out that Jesus now wants the world to know what he taught.'

'And you're saying that's a lie?'

'Of course it is. Jesus was not here on his own business; he was here doing the business of the FATHER and MOTHER OF CREATION. All he would have been concerned with, would be to tell the truth to whomever the FATHER and MOTHER OF CREATION had sent him to speak to. Those who might come after and speak to the Gentiles were no business of his; that was for the FATHER and MOTHER to decide. If they had sent Jesus in a vision as Paul said, like any other angel or messenger, Jesus would have made it absolutely clear that the message was from the FATHER and MOTHER OF CREATION and that it was *their* will that the rest of the world now know.'

'I think you're wrong about Paul; he loved Jesus and only wanted to spread his word. What's wrong with that?' said Paul's girlfriend.

'Okay look. If you asked Jesus who he was in the flesh and spirit and what he believed in, he would say, "I'm a Jew by flesh and the first-begotten son by spirit, and I believe in my FATHER and MOTHER OF CREATION and the laws of Abraham." If you asked Paul who he was in the flesh he would say, "I'm a Christian, a follower of the heavenly Christ and the Virgin Mary, mother of GOD." So you need to go and work out which one you follow because by what I have just said, they both follow different people and have different religious names and laws.

'Your problem is that you think the church is the true representative of the FATHER and MOTHER OF CREATION, and they're not. You are, and all men and women are. The church is simply a place where some people go, but it is not religion or church attendance that makes them righteous... it's the desire in their hearts. Let me just say this to try and help you to understand that the church is not holy because it is the church.

'Some two hundred years ago on one of the Caribbean plantations, the owners used to brand their slaves by burning the word SOCIETY into their flesh, using white-hot metal that had been heated up in a furnace; the slaves screamed in agony, but their owners did not care. More than half of the slaves belonging to those owners had a life expectancy of just three years, before the work and brutal conditions would kill them; this three-year life expectancy covered children, women and men of all ages. The owner in question was the Church of England.

'Wow, look at the time. I think I've done enough talking for the night. Michelle must be sick of my voice by now, and it's time my little ones were getting ready for bed,' said Bigs, as he got up and began to kiss his children good night. The children moaned and said they were not tired, but Bigs insisted they go to bed. His friends also understood the hint that it was time to leave and got up to go.

Later that night, the voice said to Bigs, 'You keep saying you want to be a soldier for the FATHER and MOTHER OF CREATION. Is that what you think you are, a soldier?'

'A long time ago you told me to find the real me within and I think I've found myself. Yes, I think I could be a soldier for the FATHER and MOTHER OF CREATION,' answered Bigs.

'Go outside and look up into the night sky,' said the voice. Bigs put on his coat and went outside. Looking up into the sky, he was blown away by what he saw. Thousands of UFOs filled the sky above his house, there were so many that for the first time, Bigs felt a little nervous and scared.

'This is your family and your army, and you are their leader. They are waiting for you to find yourself and lead them. Now dig deeper within yourself, and find out who you really are. You are more than a soldier! Do you truly believe in the MOST HIGH? If you do, what do you think the eighty percent of your brain that you don't use is for?' said the voice.

'What do you mean? Are you saying I have unknown powers that I haven't yet used because I'm only using a small part of my brain, or are you saying I can find myself in there?' asked Bigs, but the voice did not answer.

Bigs stared into the sky and watched the many different types of lights in the sky. He wondered for a moment if he was going mad, if this voice inside his head that only he could hear was a sign that he was a schizophrenic or something of that nature; however, he knew he wasn't. Besides, if he was insane, then so were the people around him... they had all seen the lights and how they had danced for him. It was all so unreal.

Bigs would spend so many nights after talking with his wife and friends, trying to work out how he knew the things he spoke about. Often he would explain to Michelle that he had no idea how he knew the stuff he was talking about, and that sometimes he could find himself listening to what he was talking about and learning about it, as he spoke about it.

He had not been brought up in any religion except that of the street and his family were known as gangsters, not preachers. Bigs had spent most of his life in situations he should not have walked away from. People feared him because of all the times when he had walked into a room by himself and met ten or more people inside the room, all of whom intended to kill him, and yet when the gun shots faded and the blood had been spilled, Bigs would always be the one person who walked out alive.

So it was not as hard as it might have seemed, for Bigs to accept such a surreal truth as having a voice that spoke to him, or UFOs in the sky that moved when he asked them to; as his entire life was filled with the unexplainable.

For example, there was the last war he had fought before going straight and giving up the life of crime. It was a war with Special Branch, the Armed Forces in Britain that dealt with terrorists and serious organised crime. There was no way Bigs should have been alive, never mind free, but he was and he knew that it all had to do with the FATHER and MOTHER OF CREATION; just as he knew that what he was looking up at in the sky, was to do with them as well.

So he allowed himself a moment to be overwhelmed by it all and then he pulled himself together; asking the FATHER and MOTHER to help him find himself deep within.

A few months later, Bigs looked at Michelle one morning at the breakfast table.

'I'm going to have tattoos,' said Bigs with a smile.

'Tattoos?' replied Michelle, surprised.

'Is there an echo in here?' laughed Bigs.

'But you don't like tattoos,' said Michelle, still not sure if Bigs was joking or not.

'These tattoos are words to do with the FATHER and MOTHER OF CREATION. There are seven of them.'

'Where did this idea come from?'

'I think it was the voice, but I'm not certain. I just know I have to have these tattoos done.'

'Should I have them done too?'

'I'm not sure yet. I don't even have all of them yet, just the first two which are to go on my arms.'

'What, just like writing on a page? Are you going to write them across or down your arm?'

'No, no. They're circles, seven circles. There will be one on each arm, and then one over the belly button. I think there will be two on the chest and two on the back, but like I say, I'm not that sure yet. I just know there are seven circles and the first two are on both of my arms.'

'Wow, did you have a vision?'

'No, it was just there in my head. I can't explain it; I just know that's what I have to do next, and I have the words for the first two. Weird, isn't it?'

'So when are you going to have them done and where?'

'Well, that's where you come in, my beautiful wife. I need you to find the nearest tattoo shop for me in the Yellow Pages, then I'll go and take a look and see if it's clean enough first.'

'So do you want me to book an appointment for you, or to just find out where it is?'

'Yeah, book it and I'll go in. Then if I think it's too dirty, I won't keep the appointment. Okay, I'm going to train now. Love you.'

'Hold on, do you want me to book it for today if they have the space?'

'No, make it tomorrow. I've got to write out the words in a circle first.'

'Can you remember what it's supposed to say?'

'Yeah, it's crystal clear in my mind... it's like I've known it my whole life. I'll show it to you when I've done it.'

'Okay, I'll make some phone calls now. See you when you finish training. Love you.'

The next day, Bigs drove to the tattoo shop and sat in the waiting room, looking at all of the pictures on the walls of supposedly satisfied customers. The place looked and smelt clean and so did the equipment; which Bigs insisted on looking at, before he agreed to keep the appointment. Once Bigs was satisfied, he described the wordings and the circles to the tattoo artist, who then took them and began to copy the words and design onto tracing paper. The artist then explained to Bigs that because of his skin colour and the fact that the words would have to be enclosed in a circle which could be no wider than his arm, people would not be able to read the words. But Bigs made it clear that as long as *he* knew what it said, it did not matter.

When Bigs had the first two tattoos done, he was very proud of them; even though nobody could read what they said. They looked like two big circles of unreadable wordings on his muscular arms, however to Bigs, it seemed like that was how it was meant to be. His tattoos were not gimmicks, they had deep profound meanings that were not for the devils of this world to read. He hurried home to show them to Michelle, who was eagerly awaiting his return to see what they looked like.

A car pulled up outside of the tattoo shop and three men dressed in black got out of the car and entered the premises. As the three men walked up to the counter, one man walked behind the counter and into the back of the shop; into the room where the tattoo artist was working on a customer's tattoo. The receptionist tried to stop the man, but one of the other men told her to take a seat, pulling open his jacket slightly, to reveal his gun in its holster. The girl got the hint and sat down.

'I want the drawings and words that you just did for the last customer!' said the man dressed in black.

'We don't keep anything brought in by our customers; everything we have here is our own designs,' replied the tattoo artist.

The man in black grabbed the tattoo artist by one of his many ear piercings and threw him into a glass and wooden cabinet. The glass shattered and the wood broke, collapsing on top of the tattoo artist, who had fallen in a heap on the floor.

'Steady on old man, are you trying to kill him or what!' shouted the man sitting in the tattoo chair, whose tattoo was only half done.

'Mind your own business!' snarled the man in black.

'Well it is my business, if you hurt him he won't be able to finish my tattoo!' shouted the man in the tattoo chair.

Shooting the man in the chair a killer glare, the man in black picked up the tattoo artist. 'I will ask you one last time and if you don't answer me correctly, you will die today.'

'Okay, okay, look, it's not our policy to give out our clients' designs, but I didn't think you wanted to kill me over it. It's over there in a drawer, in the front reception area to the right... now could you phone me an ambulance, please?' said the tattoo artist, as he slumped once again to the floor.

The man in black went back into the front reception area and looked in the drawers to the right.

'Got them!' he shouted, waving the tracing paper in front of him. Then the three men walked out of the shop as if nothing had happened. They got back into the car and drove off, wheels smoking.

Bigs was proud of his new tattoos, showing them to Michelle with an attitude like that of a father showing off his new born son.

'Did it hurt?' asked Michelle, looking at them closely.

'No, not at all. It just stung a little,' remarked Bigs. 'You know, I can't bath or shower for a few days. You'll just have to wipe me down with a damp cloth.'

'What do you mean, *I* will have to? You're not an invalid!' smiled Michelle.

'Oh, I'll remember that when you need my tender loving care.'

'I'm only joking. You know I will always take care of you, my baby. Give us a kiss.'

'No, that's it... you've hurt my feelings now.'

'I was only joking. You're not serious are you darling?'

'Okay, I'll forgive you this time. Come and give me a hug.'

That night, Bigs and Michelle lay in bed discussing the voice's command that he find himself within. Bigs tossed and turned in the bed, unable to get comfortable; he was not sure he would ever find out who he was, or what it really meant to have UFOs outside of his house, that were willing to dance for him in the night sky.

'What if I'm the angel of Death?' he asked Michelle.

'Do you think that's who you are?' she asked, sitting up in the bed and nervously biting her bottom lip.

'I don't know... That's the problem, I'm not sure about that term, the angel of Death. General of war, maybe? As I've told you many times before, I have this thing inside me. I don't know what to call it... fury? Anger? All I know is that if I let it out, it will quite happily go up and down the street and kill everyone that is ignorant or vicious... and I'm not even sure... if it would just kill everybody? I've never got to know that side of me that well.'

'Why did you call yourself an angel? What makes you think that?'

'That's what I'm saying; I don't know what I think. I guess I don't think I'm an angel it's just... what else could I have said when referring to death in that sense? That I'm Death?'

'I know you'll find the answer; don't get all wound up about it.' Michelle climbed on top of Bigs and began to give him a massage.

'You know what I think sometimes? I think we are like thoughts of the FATHER and MOTHER OF CREATION. Some are good and will be kept, while others are rubbish and will be thrown away.'

'So what are we... rubbish, or good thoughts?'

'You, my dear, are definitely a good thought. You are patient, gentle and caring. I... I am a rubbish thought, always dreaming of serving the greatest being in existence. They must be fed up of me and my constant wanting to serve them, like I'm special or something.'

'Don't say that Bigs! That's not true and it means you don't believe in what has happened. I do, because I've seen it with my own eyes. Moreover, you've been teaching me amazing things that I'd never have known if you hadn't shown them to me. It's what you've taught me that has allowed me to see the UFOs and not be as afraid as I wanted to be.'

'I'm sorry; sometimes I just think this is all in my head, but you're right, you've seen my family now... Anyway, that's enough talking for tonight,' said Bigs. He rolled Michelle off him onto her back and lay on top of her as they kissed.

An hour later, Bigs stared up into space as Michelle slept. In his mind's eye he began to see a place he did not know, set in a time thousands of years ago. As he saw more and more with his mind's eye and not his natural eyes, he stared out over a valley with shrubs, small bushes and golden, dusty, sandy hills and small mountains all around it.

He looked up at the sky; it was full of fast-moving grey and black clouds, streaming across the horizon in an endless flow. Behind the fast-moving clouds, the sky looked as if it was on fire. The ground below him was full of skeletons, skulls and dead bodies with flesh that was rotting and half-eaten by crows, scavengers and wolves.

Yet his feet did not touch the floor; it was as if they were suspended in mid-air, and blood dripped from them onto the ground and bones below.

He screamed as he began to pull his arms free from the position they were in; stretched out to his sides and away from his head and body. Blood was pouring out from his wrists, but he felt no pain. He continued to pull at his wrists until his arms were finally freed...

But this presented him with a new problem; it would seem that it was not only his arms that were nailed down, but that his ankles were as well. He fell forward towards the ground, which was covered in skulls and bones, and as he fell his weight and the force of the fall freed him from his last nail. His ankles ripped free, leaving the nails in the wood they were hammered into. Bigs fell to the ground, smashing skulls and bones as he landed.

'FATHER and MOTHER it is done! Please now remove this bitter cup from me!' he shouted. He tried to stand up, but as he did he felt a thrusting sharp pain of cold metal piercing his side; a Roman soldier had plunged his spear deep into Bigs' body. He lay flat, face to the ground, resting on the dead remains of those who had suffered this fate before him. As he felt his spirit begin to break free of its mortal prison, he turned his head and eyes and looked as best and as far as he could into Heaven. With his last breath, he said, 'FATHER and MOTHER it is done.'

Bigs gasped for air as he removed himself from his mind's eye and brought himself quickly and gladly back to reality. He wiped his eyes; though he had not realized it, he was crying. He got up and went downstairs and made himself a hot drink, smoking a joint as he thought about what he had just seen in his mind.

THE SPY FORTRESS

'Home Sweet Home' said Mobile One's Operator One, as he looked up at the sign above the mountain entrance that read CHEYENNE MOUNTAIN COMPLEX. The army jeep carrying the two operators from Mobile One moved at the restricted speed of fifteen miles per hour along the long tunnel, which went two thousand feet deep within the Cheyenne mountain. The jeep pulled up just outside of a door, which was three and a half foot thick and some twenty feet high; resembling a bank vault door on steroids.

The two men got out of the jeep and walked through the massive door, where they waited for a lift to take them to the NORADs special operations room. As the doors opened, they were greeted by four armed guards, with whom they exchanged salutes. They put their faces up against two retinal eye scanners, then placed both hands on a finger and handprint recogniser before two steel doors slid apart, allowing the two men into NORADs command centre.

'Welcome back gentlemen! So the NSA has finally returned my two special ops Lieutenants. I hope those shifty bastards didn't get you to do too much covert, highly illegal shit?' said Brigadier General Vice Commander Patterson. He pulled on a cigar and billowed out the smoke with a crackled laugh.

'Umm... no sir. We have written up our reports and have them with us. This was strictly to do with Project JAW sir!' replied Mobile One Operator One, otherwise known as NORADs special operations officer, Lieutenant Coal.

'Yes sir, everything was done by the book, sir! Mobile One should have sent all activities as they happened, to NORADs special operations command centre sir!' said Mobile One Operator Two, otherwise known as NORADs special operations officer, Lieutenant Clay.

'Yes, we have all the info on that little mission. Good work gentlemen, get some rest and then get back to your desks. The skies have been busy while you've been away, we've moved up to DEFCON-4. It looks like they're getting ready to do something with Target One and we've been tracking them in and out of space, on and off for the past few months. They seem to be ready to make Target One aware of their presence and they've been coming in from all over space and out of the sea, just to park right above Target One's home.'

'Has Target One seen them sir?' asked Lieutenant Clay.

'Hell yeah! Target One has been having what looks to me like some sort of UFO gathering of close friends and family. So yeah, Target One is damn well aware of them. He's calling them family,' replied Brigadier General Vice Commander Patterson.

'So what's our new ops? That is, if you don't mind me asking ahead of time sir.'

'The same as usual. Observe them, tag 'em and bag 'em,' replied the General. This meant that they would watch the UFOs, give them radar identification numbers and then feed those numbers into the supercomputers. The computers would then automatically identify and track the UFO, anytime it entered the stratosphere.

A major walked with purpose up to the Brigadier General and saluted.

'This is Major General Thomson, Director of Commander's Special Ops Action Group. Speak your mind son, they have level one clearance.'

'We need one of these men to take up post at Peterson Air Force Base to be the spokesperson and Team Leader, as part of the special surveillance operations team.

Along with the NSA and CIA, we will be continuing the live feed and satellite link with our British counterparts, MI5, MI6 and Special Branch.'

'Well boys, you can either toss a coin or ask me to make the call. Which one is it going to be?'

'Heads or tails?' asked Lieutenant Coal, flipping a nickel into the air.

'Tails.'

'Looks like you're off to the sunny side of Colorado Springs,' smiled Lieutenant Coal, as he caught the nickel and looked at it.

'No rest for the wicked. Get your stuff; we leave immediately,' said the Major. He turned back to face the Brigadier General and saluted before heading off with Lieutenant Clay to the jeep waiting outside of the massive vault door, at the entrance to the Spy Fortress.

Once he had arrived at Peterson Air Force Base, Lieutenant Clay was only given four hours to get to know his surroundings and rest, before taking over as Team Leader.

Meanwhile, back in London..... The three men who had visited the tattoo shop to retrieve the drawings and designs of Bigs' new tattoos, stopped at a green traffic light outside of Trafalgar Square in the London's West End; to the anger of the many drivers stuck behind them in the midday traffic jam of London's busy streets. The men paid no mind to the many car horns that greeted them as they exited the car, which added insult to injury by speeding off once the men were out of the car, blowing through the now-red traffic light.

They made their way on foot to the shopping centre and headed down a flight of stairs to the loading bay of a warehouse, where one man entered a PIN code into a door lock which opened immediately. They walked along a corridor into a CCTV control room, and the man sitting in a chair directed them down some more stairs to the CCTV special operations room. When they arrived outside of the room, a camera watched their every move as the solid steel door opened.

Two armed guards asked the men for ID before allowing them into the CCTV special operations room and then they were escorted by the armed guards to a side room, where they knocked on the door and waited.

'Is that my package? You're two hours late... get your ass in here now,' shouted a thin man in a brown suit, as he stubbed out another cigarette in an already over-filled ashtray.

'Sorry we're late sir, the traffic is hell out there,' remarked one of the men as he placed his briefcase on the table in front of the thin man.

'You make me laugh... are you forgetting where we are? I've been watching you from the time you left the fucking tattoo shop all the way from South London, right up until you knocked on my door. That means I watched you stop off for fish and chips at the café in Brixton, where you spent twenty-nine minutes and four seconds eating; before driving across the river at Vauxhall bridge, which by the way, is the fucking long way to get here. Then you stopped again at a newspaper shop, where you bought three cans of fizzy drinks, and that took you another ten minutes and ten seconds to complete. Have I missed anything out?'

'Sorry sir, we were hungry and forgot to buy a drink to wash it down with,'

'Next time drink your own piss and eat your own shit,' said the thin man as he smoked another cigarette and opened the suitcase. 'You clowns are on night watch for making me wait for this. At twenty-two hundred hours you'll relieve team B... who are going to become team A if you carry on like this much longer, is that clear?'

'Yes sir.'

'Then get the fuck out of my office,' said the thin man. He left his office and went into the main CCTV special operations viewing room, where he looked up at the many monitors and plasma screens; some showed the outside of Target One's home, while others showed rooms inside Target One's home. The man looked up at one screen that showed the body heat of anyone in the house and he flicked a switch as he counted the body heat sources given off by the people in Target One's home.

'We've got a full house.'

'Yes sir, everybody is home at the moment. We heard Target One saying he was heading out in the next hour.'

The thin man smoked another cigarette, even though the sign above the door was clear to see and said smoking was prohibited.

'Okay, keep me informed when he leaves and radio team C, too; tell them they'd better not be having lunch when he leaves,' said the thin man as he went back to his office.

'Having lunch sir? I don't understand.'

'Never mind,' he replied as he entered his office. The thin man put out the cigarette in the overfilled ashtray and then put the two tracing papers into a scanner. He immediately sent a copy to the Area 51 Project JAW 67 base command centre.

Dr. Goodenberg looked at the colour photos of the words tattooed on Bigs' arms from the pictures that had been taken by CIA officers, as Bigs emptied his house bins in a vest one morning.

'Where are the damn drawings? You can't make out what the words say. Can you, Dr Jacobs? After all, this is your area of expertise.'

'No, but we're not supposed to. These are the words that only he will be able to read and understand.'

'But what about the tracing paper? Will we be able to read that?'

'Let's hope so.'

The printer began to print out the pictures they had been waiting for. Once the printer had finished printing, Dr Goodenberg and Dr Jacobs looked over the paper and smiled; the words were crystal clear. Both men sat back in their chairs studying the words carefully, then Dr Jacobs left Dr Goodenberg's office with the paper and took it back to his lab to continue his work on them and the meanings of the words; before producing a report for the President and all official Heads of organisations involved in Project JAW 67. Dr Goodenberg was also putting together a report on the progress of War Hawk, along with Major Stone who had returned from his E.B.E. abduction.

Dr Jacobs Report:
Sent to the White House, Joint Chief of Staff, NORAD, NSA, CIA, MI5, MI6 & Special Branch.

We have the first two of the seven wordings, which are to be written in circles.
The seven circles represent the seven seals, but the wordings are not representative of the seven seals.
The wordings represent the thoughts, feelings and desires of the subject wearing them. They are a personal billboard to the MOST HIGH. It is almost as if the subject is an advertisement of the MOST HIGH.
The words become seals by the subject because of their willingness to permanently mark their body with words only for the MOST HIGH. Therefore, in return, the MOST HIGH seals the subject with supernatural powers and protection.
Be advised that only the subject can mark their body in the correct wording and only the subject can withstand the power of the seven seals from the MOST HIGH. Therefore, the understanding of the wording is purely for scientific purposes and cannot be utilised for the advancement of the government or mankind.

The circle on the right arm reads as follows:
I am an Asiatic warrior, soldier of the FATHER and MOTHER, freedom fighter, defender of the Earth.
This is the description of who and what the subject is and what they are here to do.

The second circle on the left arm reads as follows:
The Way of Life, Truth, Harmony, Love, Respect, Equality and Justice.
This description is what they have come to bring to the Earth, but they have come to bring it by force and by war; because the first description is of their very nature and the second is of their intent.

Therefore, I conclude that the subject is hostile and is unapproachable, incorruptible and single-minded in their mission. At such a level, one could quite easily call them obsessed and possessed.
The seven seals on the outer skin are to show that there are seven seals within the body, meaning the supernatural powers and protection already exist.
Only by reading the remaining seals, which are yet to be written, will we be able to fully understand the makeup of the beast before us.
At this stage, it is safe to say that the subject will not fully understand or be aware of the implications of what is happening.
Only when all seven seals are written on the outside, will the subject become aware of the self within. These seals on the outside will begin to stir this realization, along with the coming awakening.
Recommended action: covert observation; no contact or reaction to any possible action taken by subject. Treat as normally as possible within the world's system, until the awakening and final seventh seal.

BIGS' LIVING ROOM

Bigs couldn't sleep; it was seven am on a Saturday morning. He hadn't had a smoke in two weeks and every day and night was agony. He couldn't take it anymore and went downstairs to get a joint. He sucked on the joint as if it was an oxygen mask filling his lungs with much-needed air, but instead it was filling his lungs with much needed nicotine and ganja. Bigs sat in his chair, trying to find out whom he was inside. He found no answers, but at least he had stopped his craving and felt a lot more relaxed.

He switched through the TV channels and stopped at a religious channel, where some black American preacher was talking about how the end times were upon mankind. Bigs was about to turn the channel when the preacher began to speak about how mankind had better not be found in these last days with anger inside them; for the foe that cometh was truly dreadful and would use the anger of mankind to fuel its fiery furnace. It would devour any of mankind found to have such anger within them.

'Great!' Bigs thought. 'I'm full of anger; there's a side to me that's so angry it scares the life out of me, and it's me. I've tried to get rid of it, FATHER and MOTHER OF CREATION, you know I have. And now this guy's saying some creature exists that uses such anger to fuel itself while it devours people like me,' thought Bigs, sighing.

'What would you call this anger inside you?' asked the voice.

'Anger,' replied Bigs.

'Would you call it extreme anger, fury, rage or wrath?'

'Wrath, that's what's inside me. Wrath... maybe. I don't know.'

'Stop lying to yourself. You know what's inside of you; you are what's inside you.'

'Yes, okay, it's Wrath... well, an essence of Wrath. Yeah, that's it. That's exactly it! It has no fear and it could consume the entire planet if I let it out or left it alone to do what it desired; but I don't, I've spent my entire life keeping it under control. I've always been afraid of it, even though it's myself. I'm the essence of Wrath. Yes, I'm Wrath; it makes perfect sense for the first time. I finally have a name for the dark side of me that I have feared all of my life. Thank you, FATHER and MOTHER OF CREATION, without you I would have never known who I am!' shouted Bigs as he ran upstairs to tell Michelle.

'I've finally worked out who I am Shell! Wake up, wake up!' shouted Bigs, as he jumped on the bed and lay on top of her.

Michelle yawned and wiped the sleep from her eyes. She smiled at Bigs as he gave her a great big wet kiss on the lips.

'Get off me,' she said jokingly, as she wrapped her arms around him and held on tight to him.

'I know who I am Shell, the FATHER and MOTHER helped me, I think... or my brain, or the voice... I really don't know but I do know who I am.'

'Well, come on then, tell me! You've woken me up now, don't keep me in suspense.'

'Wrath! That's who I am, or that's a part of me; you know, the part of me I've always feared? Well, it's Wrath; no wonder I feared it. Anyway, I just wanted you to be the first to know; you can go back to sleep now. I think I'm going to have an early morning train, if I don't feel too tired when I start. I love you,' said Bigs, as he gave Michelle another big wet kiss.

'Get off me,' she said again jokingly, as she held him tightly and squeezed him.

For the rest of the day Bigs was extremely happy, as he had finally worked out who he was; but that night Satan

Lucifer Devil came to Bigs as he slept and questioned him about what he had been saying that whole day.

'Bigs, have you done the right thing by saying you are Wrath? After all, you could be wrong, and what would the real Wrath be thinking? Who is Bigs to call himself something as important as the Wrath of the MOST HIGH? Surely Bigs, you know you could not be such an important thing. How could you believe that's who you are? Was it not you who said you were not worthy of wiping the dirt from the bottom of the MOST HIGHs feet? Now you are Wrath, the pure anger of the MOST HIGH. From the lower levels of nothing to the dizzying heights of the anger of the MOST HIGH. I would not like to be you for all the Kingdoms in Heaven if you are wrong and continue to call yourself by this name, for this is the highest level of blasphemy; and you were doing so well as seeing yourself as nothing.'

Bigs woke and looked at the clock; it was a quarter past three in the morning. He got up and went downstairs. He felt sick; terror filled his mind and body, right through to the marrow in his bones. He made a joint and pulled on it until it had filled his body; but it did not fill his mind, as he could not shake the sheer terror he felt. What had he done? He had gone around all day saying he was the Wrath of the FATHER and MOTHER OF CREATION. How could he have done such a thing without their telling him? It was just his mind and his self that had come up with the idea. He had been stressed out about trying to find himself, and he had not smoked for two weeks.

He fell on the floor where he stood and begged the FATHER and MOTHER OF CREATION for forgiveness. He had not meant to make out that he was something so important to them, or so high up in their establishment.

'Please, please, please forgive me. I am nothing. I am not even worthy to wipe the dirt from your feet. Please forgive me for my foolish thoughts and for getting carried away!' cried Bigs. He stayed on his hands and knees with his head bowed to the floor, as he continued sobbing and begging; his entire body shook.

Then out of nowhere five lights appeared; just as if Bigs had suddenly looked up at a light bulb for several seconds and then closed his eyes. Yet his eyes had been closed the entire time he had been asking forgiveness from the FATHER and MOTHER OF CREATION. To make matters more mysterious, the only light on was the kitchen light; which was not a light bulb but a fluorescent tube. Bigs looked at the lights and was disorientated momentarily, because his eyes were still closed... how could he see them? Then in that very moment the lights, which had seemed stationary, moved away from him at great speed; but it was as if it was he that was moving away from the lights. He kept moving at a great speed, until he could see the lights no more.

Bigs opened his eyes and was so shocked at what he saw that he closed his eyelids tightly again. He was even more shocked when, although his eyes were closed, he could still see the grey-faced alien with big deep black eyes looking at him.

'What is this? I wasn't thinking about aliens, why would I be seeing images of aliens?' thought Bigs. With his eyelids still closed, he waited for the grey face before him to melt back into the black space in his mind... but it didn't, so Bigs opened his eyes and to his relief, the grey face had gone.

Then suddenly his heart fell to the floor as out of the darkness, which had been Bigs' living room but no longer was, he could see a line of what looked like all types of aliens slowly coming towards him. They stretched out all around him as far as the eye could see and fear filled his mind like never before as they moved towards him slowly.

'Oh shit... I'm dinner,' thought Bigs.

THE SPY FORTRESS

CHEYENNE MOUNTAIN COMPLEX

People ran all over the place; some were carrying files and documents, while others ran to their desks or to monitors. Alarms rang and lights flashed. The main screens in the Special Operations Command Centre were filled with thousands of dots. The supercomputer could be heard all over the complex humming like it had never done before, as it worked overtime in an attempt to track and tag all of the dots on the screen. A red light above the massive vault entrance door flashed and sirens sounded to warn everyone that the massive vault door was slowly closing.

People ran towards it like rats in an overflowing sewer, trying to escape before they were trapped and drowned. There was sheer panic among all of those trying to reach the door before it closed, because they all knew that once the door was shut it would not be opened for anyone, not even the President. Anyone who did not make it in by the time the massive vault door closed, could be waiting a very long time for it to reopen. Those inside could survive for thirty days without having to reopen the door, as for many of the people on the outside, one day would be too long; most of them had no idea why the door was closing, but one possible reason was a nuclear attack by a foreign power.

NORAD COMMAND CENTRE

'Shit, it looks like a sand storm up there. What the hell is going on?' shouted Brigadier General Johnson, as he stood in the middle of the command centre looking up at the screens with his hands on his hips.

'Do you think it's an attack on the world?' asked Brigadier General Vice Commander Patterson, as he also stood in the centre and looked up at the screens.

'Get the White House on the line immediately! And get me the President!'

'Patching through Dr Goodenberg from Area 51, sir.'

'Dr Goodenberg are you seeing what we are seeing?'

'Yes, I am... isn't it amazing? There must be at least two thousand spacecrafts up there, all in the same area.'

'I don't mean to cut in and shit on your parade, but I've got the President on the other end of the phone. He's on board Air Force One, heading for a secure location. What I need to know from you Doc, is this: are they about to attack us?'

'Oh, oh of course... sorry, I get carried away sometimes, but you have to admit it is a sight. Well, no General they are not here for us. Oh no... they have come for their own Brigadier General! Gentlemen, we are entering the final stages of Project JAW, and it looks like we are going to live to see the end of it.'

The Brigadier General nodded his head, and one of the many operators switched off the link to Dr Goodenberg without as much as a goodbye.

'We can confirm sir, that this is not a hostile threat. Our information on the location of the crafts indicate that they are centralized at one location, directly above Target One's home. We have been advised that it is the final stage of Project JAW 67, sir.'

The President put down one phone, then picked up another.

'Patching the NSA Director through, sir.'

'This is Director Forbes. We're picking up an awful lot of chat throughout the East and Middle East; they're watching the show too. China and Russia also want to know what the hell is happening. You're going to have to give them something before the whole world gets wind of what's happening. We are also picking up several observatories and many amateur astrologers... they're watching too. I need authority clearance to execute Executive Order 1-9-6-7, sir.'

'You think it's time for that, so soon?'

'We need to start now so we can have everything in place within the next few weeks, just in case this situation gets out of hand and our media get wind of this. We need to distract them, and we need something big in order to do that, sir. We need to identify all of the amateur astrologers who won't cooperate and we'll have to eliminate them, sooner rather than later. Don't worry sir, this all comes under the jurisdiction of National Security. We'll deal with it, but as Executive Chief and Commander, I need your clearance now.'

'Okay, I'll give the clearance... but I hope you're right!' The President put down the phone and picked up yet another one.

'Patching the CIA Director through now, sir.'

'The shit's hit the fan sir. I need clearance to execute Executive Order Propaganda 67.'

'Okay, authorisation will be faxed through immediately. It's really happening!' The President put down the phone and was immediately joined by his advisors as Air Force One headed for the secure, secret location.

'I need you to get NASA on the line and get an update on all observatories that have the ability to spot what is going on and send that to the CIA Director at Langley.'

'Yes Mr President. Do you want me to contact Area 51 and get War Hawk up there?'

'Of course, I forgot, and it looks like everybody else has forgotten too. Yes get them up there immediately and let's see what they can do in a real situation.'

'Patching through Lieutenant General Grey at Area 51 now, sir.'

'This is the President. I need you to get as many operational War Hawks as possible up there, to show these E.B.Es that we mean business and are prepared to defend our planet.'

'Are you sure sir? Our people say they have no interest in us and are here for the subject Target One.'

'Are you questioning my orders soldier?'

'No sir, not at all. What I am questioning is our ability to do anything at this stage in the development of War Hawk. We only have four built and the tests are still ongoing. Have you not received the report from Major Stone and Dr Goodenberg yet?'

'No, I have not. What's in it that you think is significant?'

'Well, just the fact that Major Stone and War Hawk One were abducted by said craft, sir!'

'Put Dr Goodenberg on the line.'

'Yes sir, how may I be of help?'

'Do you not think this is a good scenario in which to fully test the capabilities of War Hawk?'

'Umm...yes and no sir. Yes, because it is not really a hostile situation, but we could send up one or two and see what happens. No, because we could turn a non-hostile situation into a hostile one, and then War Hawk and its pilots would be up the river without a paddle, sir.'

'Thank you Doc. Put Grey back on the line.'

'Yes sir?'

'Did you hear what the Doc said, and do you agree with his assessment?'

'Yes sir I did, and yes sir, I do agree.'

'Well, in that case send two up, just to observe. Let them see if they can keep up with any of the crafts up there.'

'Yes sir, understood. Implementing your orders now.' Lieutenant General Grey put down the phone and began to set up the operation for two War Hawks to go into outer space and observe the alien crafts as best as they could; whilst hoping that at no time the alien crafts pilots turned nasty and engaged them in a dog fight.

'Major Stone, it's time to get back into War Hawk One. Take Major Riddick with you as your wing man. Your mission is to observe a shit load of E.B.E. spacecrafts at this location.'

'Yes! This should be fun. No hostile intentions, right Kevin?'

'That's right Eric. Just get up there and see if our birds can stay within observation distance of theirs. If you think they're gonna go hostile, get your ass out of there ASAP.'

THE UNKNOWN

Bigs squinted his eyes and then rubbed them. He looked at his hands, then looked back at the aliens. It didn't make sense. How could this be real, whatever this was? He looked around him, it was as if he was in complete darkness. Blackness was all around him, yet the aliens were now some hundred feet away; he could see them clearly, without the aid of any light.

Bigs' mind was at maximum working level. He could not take much more. His heart pumped at a rapid rate, one that he had never felt before, and he tried to slow it down by telling himself that he could handle whatever happened. Then he tried to calm himself down, but panic and terror would fill his mind. He was sure these aliens were going to eat him and he began to panic even more as the reality before him sunk further into his mind.

He knew by now that if this was a dream, he would have woken up. He also knew, from his years of taking ecstasy and acid, what it was like to hallucinate. This was real. Yet his mind couldn't deal with it.

Then he felt Wrath rise inside him, as it always did when he was in danger. This made him calm down a little and gain a little focus. He remembered the FATHER and MOTHER OF CREATION and how they had always been there for him.

Suddenly, he truly realised what it meant when he had been telling everyone that the UFOs in the sky were his family. His heart rate began to slow down and he relaxed somewhat. Yet looking at the aliens before him was so surreal, it was hard for him to focus. It just didn't seem real, even though it was.

Then suddenly his body was filled with an overwhelming feeling that came from out of his stomach. It was so beautiful and amazing; it was indescribable. It was warm and full of well-being, like some wonder drug made just to make you feel the most wonderful feelings. It was as if all of the best feelings in the world had been put into a package that could be taken like a pill. Bigs knelt under the overwhelming feeling, and for a moment he could think of nothing else. Not even the aliens mattered.

Then a voice came out of the darkness, though Bigs did not know from where it came. It was like the sound of a thousand people speaking in perfect harmony, like a voice whose words went right through his body and out the other side.

'Do you bear witness? This is real! This is not a dream!'

Bigs jumped as the words vibrated through his body, passing through his bones as if it was alive. Yet the words did not hurt his eardrums, even though they had such a presence.

'Do you bear witness? This is real and not a dream!' Bigs repeated to himself, as he jumped and looked around; but could see nothing to indicate where the being was that spoke with such prominence.

'Yes I do... I bear witness that this is real and not a dream!' shouted out Bigs. Then, immediately after saying that, his mind went straight back into denial. 'This can't be real. Pathetic,' he thought to himself, as he tried to make sense of all that was going on.

Finally, Bigs' brain had overloaded. Everything he thought was now in delayed mode. His mind was one or two steps behind everything that was happening and it was still trying to come to terms with the aliens that were getting closer and closer, saying, 'We are family,' over and over again.

They slowly edged forward towards Bigs, who could now see them clearly. This did not help things, as some of them were fearsome-looking creatures that looked just like the type that would eat him. Then, for a moment, Bigs began to panic again. Yet he did not panic for long, as his mind placed his desire to panic in a queue of delayed thoughts.

Bigs tried to make sense of what was going on, such as being in a pitch black place. It was so pitch black that he could not see what it was that he was standing on; yet he could see the aliens in front of him without the aid of lights. There was so much going on. There was the wonderful, overwhelming feeling running throughout his entire body. There was a voice that spoke like a thousand people, a voice that cut through his body like a shock wave from an explosion, and that was asking him if he understood that this surreal experience was real. There were the beasts and the aliens coming towards him, telling him that he was their family. The only thing that Bigs could think to himself was 'This is not real!'

The aliens and beasts were now twenty feet away, and for the first time Bigs realised that many more were dropping down from the pitch black sky. He could not see from where or what they were coming, but he could see them coming down clearly; it didn't make any sense to his mind. Then, he looked back to the ones on the ground in front of them. He looked left to right, as far as his eyes could see. There were so many different types, and some were *so* scary. Bigs glanced at them, but his eyes always seemed to come and rest on the same one in front of him.

'It looks like a praying mantis,' Bigs thought, as he quelled another panic attack. It was green and blue in colour, and it was quite tall... around seven feet. Then Bigs' mind went back to the feeling inside him. 'It's like a continuous orgasm,' Bigs thought, 'right on the apex, that moment of complete ecstasy. It's like replaying that feeling over and over again.' Then he thought of the voice which had just asked him if he understood that what he was experiencing was real.

He looked up at the aliens and the beasts, and he began to panic for a moment. He realised, for the first time, that the aliens and beasts had wings. 'Why hadn't I noticed that before?' he thought, as he looked up and down the front line of aliens and beasts. Then again, his eyes came to rest on the alien that looked like a praying mantis with human features. It had two big black eyes, two arms and two legs, but no claws like a mantis. It was really only the shape of its head that made Bigs think of a praying mantis; the rest of it was quite human-like.

Then suddenly, he peered over his shoulder as he heard a sound coming out of his own back; it sounded like bones rubbing together. As he kept looking over his shoulders, he saw something he would not have believed was possible. The fact was, he could see what was there and he didn't believe it. 'This is not real!' shouted Bigs, as he looked over his shoulders from left to right, and saw the same thing on both sides. 'How can this be real?' he thought, once again.

Bigs looked back at the alien for answers, but there were none. He looked back over his right shoulder and then his left, and he tried to comprehend what he was seeing.

His heart rate began to soar once more, and Bigs really believed that he would have a heart attack if he did not get his heart back under control. However, his mind lost interest.

Once again he felt the overwhelming feeling, and he remembered the voice and what it had asked him. He looked at the aliens and beasts who were continually saying that they were his family, and he looked up into the blackness and saw aliens coming down with wings spread open. Then he looked back over his left and right shoulders to see his very own white coloured wings, like those of a dove, which seemed to be coming out of his back. It was all too much for his mind to take. 'How could this be real?' he thought over and over, as he continued to look at the white dove like wings coming out of his back. He looked back up and down the front line of aliens and his mind spun to a point beyond dizziness, as his eyes came to rest on the alien that resembled a praying mantis.

Then suddenly, as he looked at the alien, he and it began to rise into the blackness that surrounded him. As he and the alien rose up, he could see for the first time the rows of aliens and beasts that were behind the front line. Bigs began to panic, but only for a moment, as his mind tried to comprehend the wings sticking out of his back. His eyes gazed downwards and he looked at his feet as they dangled in the blackness; then he looked up, as he continued to ascend.

The aliens and beasts looked straight at him as they descended out of the blackness and for the first time he realised that they were all watching him. As he passed an alien that was like a humanoid, or maybe half-alien and half-human, he felt scared once again as its big black eyes watched him as it descended and he ascended. However his mind had no time for that emotion, as the feeling that flowed through him consumed his mind as it bathed in its utopia.

In his mind, he replayed the sound that came out of his back as his wings appeared. Once again, Bigs looked back over his right and left shoulders to see as much as he could of the white wings, as he effortlessly floated in the blackness that surrounded him. He looked down at the many lines of beasts and aliens and then he looked up and saw more still coming down out of the blackness. He looked at the alien in front of him and for the first time he realised that it was saying something to him, without moving its lips.

'You are...' said the alien, but Bigs did not hear anymore. His mind could not concentrate on what was being said as it wandered back to the thought that this could not be real. Again, his mind began to spin and his heart began to race. Then he forgot the thought as the feeling of wonderfulness flowed all around his body. He looked at the alien before him.

'Your name is Jesus.' The voice of the alien was then lost as Bigs' mind collapsed once again; he could not believe what he had heard. 'This has to be a dream. There is no way I'm Jesus. Now I know this is not real!' he said.

Then he made a great effort to concentrate on what the alien was saying. It was hard, but what he had just heard made him get a grip of himself for the first time.

'You are the first,' said the alien, but that was it. That was as long as Bigs could keep control of his spinning mind. It went back to the feeling flowing around his body; he went with it for a moment, but then tried again to control his mind.

'You are the MOST HIGH.'

'What?' he shouted, as he looked the alien in the face. 'No way. That's blasphemy. You can't say that! That's not true,' shouted Bigs, as his mind collapsed and he lost control of his concentration.

Bigs pulled himself together. He needed to hear what was being said; there was a serious mistake. Worse still, blasphemy was being spoken.

'You are the First-begotten son.' Bigs' mind lost concentration once again as he thought 'First-begotten son! No! There's been a mistake.' The alien did not seem to mind. It just kept saying the same words over and over; as if it knew that its words would sink subliminally into Bigs' subconscious mind.

'Your name is Jesus...'

'Jesus,' he interrupted again. 'There is no way I'm Jesus. This is madness,' he thought as the alien kept talking without moving its mouth. Bigs tried again to pay attention. Luckily for him, it seemed as if every time he tried, he regained a little bit more control over his spiralling mind.

'You are the gateway between heaven and earth and all dimensions,' the alien said telepathically. 'The MOST HIGH is...'

Once again, Bigs did not hear the rest. He broke his concentration to think about what had just been said. 'I'm the gateway,' he thought. 'There's been some sort of mistake,' explained Bigs to the alien, but the alien just smiled and continued to repeat the message.

'You are the First-begotten son of the MOST HIGH. Your name is Jesus...' but again on hearing the name Jesus, Bigs' mind nose-dived into denial and paid no more attention to what was being said.

'I'm sorry, but you have got the wrong person. My name is not Jesus! What you are saying sounds like serious stuff, and I don't want to waste your time, but believe me you have got me confused with someone else! I'm not Jesus and I'm not a gateway to anything. Sorry!' The alien just smiled and, once again, began telling Bigs who he was. For the first time, Bigs had gotten to a point in his own mind where he was intent on making the alien know that it had made a big mistake. He had regained full control of himself and he patiently listened to what the alien had to say; but only so that he could tell it one last time that it had made a mistake.

'You are the First-begotten son of the MOST HIGH, and your name is Jesus...'

'I'm not Jesus,' thought Bigs, as he began to disengage from the conversation once more. Yet the next word he heard the alien speak, stopped his thought and got his attention back straight away.

'...Wrath. You are the gateway between heaven and earth and all dimensions. The MOST HIGH is you and you are the MOST HIGH.' finished the alien.

'Say it again!' Bigs could not believe it. He had heard the word wrath... this, he was certain he had something to do with. 'Please forgive me, but this is all too much for my mind to hold.'

The alien smiled, and for the first time Bigs felt the smile from the alien. It was as if its smile had travelled from off of its lips and entered into Bigs' body or mind as a feeling, or as something solid that wrapped itself around Bigs. He could feel the smile as well as see it on the alien's face; it was beautiful, just like the utopia he had been feeling the whole time.

'Open your wings,' smiled the alien. Bigs did what he was asked, but he had no idea how he did it. As his white wings opened fully, he looked to the left and to the right. 'Wow,' he thought, as he could see them much better in their full splendour. Then, out of the darkness behind him, a blinding light that was as bright as the sun shone out. It illuminated the blackness that surrounded him, replacing its blinding blackness with blinding brightness.

Bigs looked towards the alien, as the light no longer allowed him to see his wings in their full glory. The alien smiled, and once again Bigs was filled with its smile. He looked at his arms and hands; they were glowing and were bright gold in colour. It did not make sense to Bigs' mind, but by now his mind was growing accustomed to the surreal being real; he took it in his stride as best as he could.

The alien smiled as it stared at Bigs, making Bigs feel a bit uncomfortable. It looked up into the darkness as the brilliant light shone over its body and beyond. Then it put both arms up into the air.

'He is awakening!' the alien shouted full of pride and happiness, with a really big smile that showed off its extremely sharp teeth. Then it gazed at Bigs as if it had found its long lost friend.

Bigs was confused, but this was normal. 'I don't feel like I'm awakening,' he thought, as he looked at the alien who was smiling from ear to ear.

'I don't know what you're talking about. I'm not awake. I don't even understand what is going on,' apologised Bigs.

'Don't worry. You are what you are and nothing can change that,' replied the alien. The alien then turned to its side and pointed down towards the rest of the aliens and beasts below. 'Look at your army.'

Bigs looked down and was taken aback by what he could see before him. The brilliant light emanating from behind him, lit up the blackness so that he could now see the millions of aliens and beasts stretching back as far as the eye could see. Bigs was completely overwhelmed by the sheer number of aliens and beasts that were there; and they were still coming out of the blackness, descending continuously.

'This is just too much for me to take in. You have to understand that I have never seen, felt or experienced anything like this in my life. You know... you just said I was awakening, I do not have any idea of what you mean. You keep telling me that I'm somebody and you keep telling me other things. It sounds really important, and I have to be honest... I'm really not taking it all in. I think there's been a mistake, although I did think I had something to do with Wrath.'

'Don't worry. You are what you are, and nothing can change that. Your destiny has been written and your future foretold! You are the First-begotten son of the MOST HIGH and your name is Jesus Angel Wrath (JAW). You are the gateway between heaven and earth and all dimensions. The MOST HIGH is you and you are the MOST HIGH.' grinned the alien with pride and joy.

Bigs was stunned. For the first time he heard every unbelievable word that the alien had tried to tell him a hundred odd times before, and all Bigs could say in response was 'This is not real.'

'Come, take a look at yourself.'

Before Bigs could comprehend what that meant, he found out. He immediately left his body and floated down to the front line of aliens and beasts, where he looked up at himself. Once again, Bigs was thrown into a spin. He had been doing so well up until that point and he had, for a moment at least, gotten a grip of his fluctuating heart rate and delayed mind-set. Yet now they had returned, as his mind scrambled to make sense of being able to look up at his own body.

He looked around him, and then down to where his arms, hands, body and legs should have been, but they weren't there; they were up in the air, some hundred feet away. Bigs could not get over this issue. His mind boggled at what was happening. He looked up at himself, and for the first time he could see that the light that he had thought was coming from behind him, actually wasn't; he was the light source. He was illuminating the blackness with the brilliant light that shone like the sun. Once again, his mind nose-dived into denial. The all too familiar words, 'This is not real,' came out of his mouth, which had been wide open since he had been there in the blackness. He looked at the alien who had been teaching him about himself and asked 'How can this be real?'

The alien smiled and Bigs once again felt the alien's affection for him, waft over him like a reassuring blanket.

'Come, let us go back up.' The bodiless Bigs floated with the alien back up to his body. The next thing Bigs knew, he was reunited with his flesh.

'This is all just too much; I don't know how much more I can take. I have this overwhelming feeling pumping through me and I'm always inches away from it being too much, but it never quite gets there. I have wings coming out of my back and I'm floating in the air with you, with millions and millions of beings all around me. I've just come out of my body and looked up at my body, which is glowing brighter than the sun. And you keep talking to me, telling me things that sound really important and serious. I'm not taking it all in.' The alien smiled and, as usual, it comforted Bigs.

'Do not worry. You are what you are, and nothing can change that. Your destiny has been written and your future foretold! You are the First-begotten son of the MOST HIGH and your name is Jesus Angel Wrath (JAW). You are the gateway between heaven and earth and all dimensions. The MOST HIGH is you and you are the MOST HIGH,' gleamed the alien once again.

They floated back down to where the front line of aliens and beasts were waiting. This time Bigs had his body with him, but his mind was still up there in the blackness; thinking about being out of his body and looking at his body glowing brightly like the midday sun.

Bigs was surrounded by aliens and beasts, and he felt very nervous as he looked at them and they looked at him. He noticed one alien or beast... he really didn't know what to call it. He was intrigued by the way it looked. It had four legs that were similar to those of an Elephant, but it did not stand on its legs; rather, it hovered above the ground with its legs in front of it. Its eyes were big and round, but its body was rather smaller than its legs and its wings were see-through.

Bigs marvelled over it until the alien that had been teaching him about himself, did something that caught Bigs' attention straight away. The alien put its hand into Bigs' stomach. How it did this, Bigs did not know. When he looked down towards his stomach, the aliens' hand, up to its wrist, was inside of him. He felt no pain or discomfort and Bigs, for the first time in a long time, thought, 'Oh, no! This is the part where they eat me!'

CCTV SPECIAL OPERATIONS ROOM (LONDON'S WEST END)

'What do you mean he's disappeared?' shouted the thin man at his CCTV operators.

'One minute he was on thermal imagery and the next he was gone.'

'That's impossible! How the fuck can I go to the big wigs and tell them, "Sorry sirs, one minute he was here, the next he was gone." Who is he? Fucking Houdini?'

'We're telling you the truth sir. One minute his body was giving off its usual higher than average heat source and then, just like that, he was gone.'

'Team A, come in. Over.'

'This is team A. Over.'

'Has target one left the house, back or front, to your knowledge? Over.'

'That's a negative. No one has been in or out, front or back.'

'Play back the thermal imagery of the exact time he left and play back the CCTV footage of the outside of his house at the same time.'

The operators did as they were told, and they and the thin man watched the chain of events with disbelief.

The thin man made them play it back over and over again. Each time he watched the CCTV footage, it looked more unbelievable than the last time. One minute the heat source of Bigs was clear to see on screen and within a second it disappeared into thin air.

'Un-fucking believable,' said the thin man as his cigarette fell out of his mouth onto the floor.

'The cameras must be faulty.'

'No sir, they're not.'

'How do you know?'

'Because we have a normal spy camera in that room, too.'

The thin man looked hesitant as he asked for the footage from that camera to be shown.

'It doesn't make any sense,' remarked the thin man, as he fell back into a chair and lit another cigarette. The one that fell out of his mouth lay on the floor still smouldering.

'Play back that footage again and again,' ordered the thin man, as he watched it in total disbelief.

The spy camera clearly showed Bigs on the floor in a prayer position, with only the kitchen light on; which was enough to half-light up the living room that Bigs was in. One second he was on his knees in prayer and the next second he was nowhere to be seen; without ever moving out of his prayer position.

The thin man, after exhausting every possible reason, picked up a phone and called the head of Special Branch with the unbelievable news. The head of Special Branch, who could not understand what the thin man had meant, phoned the head of MI5; who seemed to be less shocked and bewildered by the news.

The head of MI5 then phoned the head of MI6 and explained the situation to him in a more matter of fact tone of voice; he also told him that he would now be informing the Prime Minister. The head of MI6 then phoned their counter-part in the CIA, who then informed the President of the USA of the extraordinary news.

The news did not go down too well with the President, as he half choked upon hearing the news whilst eating a pretzel; causing him to fall backwards as he choked. He ended up banging the side of his face on the Presidential table in his office, leaving him with a visible bruise on one side of his face that no makeup artist would be able to cover up.

The NSA did not need to be informed as they had witnessed the entire disappearing act via the live feed, that was provided by the London base CCTV special operations room; which up-linked to the NSAs own satellites. They had also been listening in to all of the conversations by all of the involved parties, that used satellites and not secure landlines.

The CIA team was pissed off at how long they had to wait for the footage to be downloaded, from the Peterson Air Force Base's Special Surveillance Operations Team. They were especially pissed off because they knew that the NSA had watched the now infamous disappearing act as it had happened, but they were somewhat comforted by the fact that they had live pictures from War Hawks One and Two, of the spectacular display of thousands of alien spacecrafts hovering fifty miles directly above Target One's house.

NORAD. THE NORTH AMERICAN AERO SPACE DEFENCE (SPECIAL OPERATIONS) COMMAND CENTRE

'Okay, this is Brigadier General Johnson. I'll be heading these ops tonight. Major Stone, before you and your wing man make your final approach, we need to do a quick check on the DCS. I'll be handing you over to Major

Thomson, Director of Commander's Special Ops action group. Good luck gentlemen and GOD speed.'

'Okay, this is Major Thomson. Let's bring up all six DCS and see what you can see.'

'Roger that. Bringing up imagery now.'

The screens for monitoring the pictures from War Hawks One and Two, split into six individual boxes on each screen; showing space from in front, behind, left, right, above and below of War Hawks One and Two.

'Bring up front data from both crafts.'

'Yes sir.'

The two front pictures from War Hawks One and Two were magnified and shown on two other screens. As the two crafts began to get closer to the alien crafts, just the sheer number that were up there was an amazing sight for all to see. It was somewhat overwhelming, to say the least.

'War Hawk One, magnify front data to maximum and hold current position.'

'Roger that. Magnifying now and holding position. Over.'

'War Hawk Two, take up a position of 345 to rear of War Hawk One and magnify to full resolution.'

'Roger that. Taking up position 345 at rear of War Hawk One. Full resolution acquired. Over.'

'How many crafts would you say we are looking at General?' came the voice of the President over the loud speaker.

'It's hard to say sir, and with our super-computer in melt, we won't have a clear number 'til the engineers fix the damn thing. But on the last count it was 6400 and still counting and that does not include Mother One, which is still stationed a hundred and fifty miles above Target One's home, sir.'

'What the hell is going on up there?' asked the President.

'We have no idea, sir.'

'Get me Dr. Goodenberg.'

'Yes sir.'

'What a wonderful sight sir, don't you agree?' remarked Dr Goodenberg.

'No, I don't. I have no idea what is going on up there.'

'I think I do sir, if you will allow me to explain. It will be quite all right for our War Hawks to fly by and get some great shots of their crafts. I think it is now okay to do so, because I believe they are all aboard Mother One attending the awakening of JAW. Therefore, they will be too preoccupied with seeing their General, to be bothered with us; as we are no threat to them, sir.'

'General, send in your boys to take a closer look.'

'Yes sir. War Hawks One and Two, proceed and complete three fly-bys of area covered by alien crafts.'

'Roger that sir. Proceeding forward on first fly-by of area. Over.'

As Major Stone and his wingman got within touching distance of the spacecrafts, they sent back glorious data from the magnificent alien spacecrafts. There were so many, all different shapes and sizes. The biggest was Mother One, which had been around as long as Target One. It appeared in the heavens days before the birth of JAW on the earth and had followed Target One, who was JAW, ever since.

Secretly Major Stone hoped he would be abducted by Demon Destroyer, who he now saw as his friend. He looked for his spacecraft, but it was like looking for a needle in a haystack. They flew by the enormous spacecraft called Mother One. 'It has to be at least four square miles in size,' thought Major Stone.

'I wonder what the hell is going on in there?' remarked Major Riddick, the wingman to War Hawk One.

INSIDE MYSELF

'What are you doing?' asked Bigs, as he once again began to panic.

'I'm going to show you something.'

The next thing Bigs knew, it was as if he was sliding down from inside of his own head into his stomach, which was pitch black. Then, out of nowhere, he could see the alien. 'How can this be? It seems like we're in my stomach, but that doesn't make sense,' Bigs thought.

'This is your power,' remarked the alien, as it pointed to a small ball of blue, green, white and yellow light that was glowing; in what Bigs perceived to be his stomach.

'Where are we?' he asked, totally ignoring what the alien was pointing to. 'Is this my stomach?'

'Yes, this is your stomach, and this is your power.'

Bigs looked at the glowing ball of light for a moment, but it made no sense to him. How could they be in his stomach looking at a ball of light? 'I don't understand, what do you mean power? How do I use it?'

'You will know when the time is right.'

'How will I know?' Bigs was losing patience with the whole thing because as far as he was concerned, they had the wrong person anyway. It was obvious to him that they had the wrong person, as he had no idea of what was happening at anytime.

'This can't be real,' he thought for the hundredth time.

'Look, I still think there's been a big mistake. How can we be in my stomach? I don't understand anything that has happened. This ball of light... you say it is my power, but I don't have a clue what you're talking about or how I would ever know what to do with it. I mean, how do I get back here... wherever here is... and use it?'

'You will know when the time is right.'

'You keep saying that, but how will I know?'

'Do not worry. You are what you are and nothing can change that. Your destiny has been written and your future foretold! You are the First-begotten son of the MOST HIGH and your name is Jesus Angel Wrath (JAW). You are the gateway between heaven and earth and all dimensions. The MOST HIGH is you and you are the MOST HIGH,' smiled the alien.

It seemed to Bigs as if they had begun to walk along a pitch-black corridor, but that didn't make sense; as far as he knew, they were in his stomach. Bigs' mind began to lose the plot once again and span out of control. Bigs let it for a moment, but the overwhelming feeling of everything was now getting to a point that he really thought his head was going to explode. He could take no more of what was happening. The wonderful feeling of well-being was now starting to really overwhelm him.

By itself the feeling was an amazing experience and feeling, but coupled with everything else, it felt like his mind was choking and was beyond the point of overload. Everything and anything was now just too much. This last incidence of seeing the aliens' hand in his stomach and then being in his stomach looking at his power, which was a ball of light; was the beginning of the end for Bigs.

'Look, I can't take anymore, this is just too much. My mind can't cope. Can we do this again in a couple of days or something? I just need to take in what has happened and then we can continue. You are showing me and telling me things that are out of my world as I know it, and to be honest with you I don't think I'm taking it all in, and it sounds really important.'

'Okay, let's go back to the rest of them, but before we do I want to tell you something and after I tell you I'm going to have to remove it from your mind. The first thing is that I've missed you and I love you.' The alien reached forward with arms open; without thinking Bigs did the same thing, and they hugged.

'I've missed you too,' replied Bigs. He didn't know why he said it, but he felt it in his heart.

As they hugged, Bigs looked at the skin of the alien; his head reached just below the alien's armpit. He noticed how the alien's skin was remarkably similar in texture to that of a dolphin. When they parted, they walked and sat down looking out over a galaxy waterfall. It was as if they were at the end of the Universe, looking down over its edge. Bigs could not work out how they had done this because as far as he was concerned, they had just been in his stomach; but he did not waste much time trying to work it out, as he knew he couldn't. As long as he went with the flow, he could remain calm and somewhat relaxed. They spoke for some time before returning to the rest of the aliens and beasts. Once they had returned, Bigs could not remember what had been said, but in a strange way he felt as if he knew.

He stood looking at the aliens who were looking at him and once again he suddenly felt as if it was all too much.

'Please, I have to go. I'm about to lose what's left of my mind. Can we do this again? I just need some time to take in what has happened so far. Will we meet again soon?'

'Yes.'

The alien looked at the two tattoos on Bigs' arms and smiled. Bigs, on seeing this, looked at them himself. 'I have another five to do. I love the meanings of these two,' he said, as he kissed both circles of words on his arms. 'I'll see you soon, yeah?'

'Yes,' replied the alien, as he held Bigs by both arms and hugged him quickly again.

Bigs looked up and down the front line one last time and then knelt into his prayer position, bowed his head, and waited a moment before looking up. It seemed that what he had just done, had caused a bit of a commotion amongst the rank and file of aliens and beasts and it was left up to the alien that had been teaching him about himself, to calm them down.

The alien told them that Bigs was not bowing to them, but it was just the way that he felt comfortable for his journey back to earth. Bigs looked at the alien as it waved its hands to calm the rest of the aliens and beasts, and then he put his head back down and closed his eyes.

He reopened them again a moment later to see if they were ready to send him back and was shocked to see the kitchen light shining into the living room of his house. Bigs sat on the sofa and contemplated what had just happened; shaking his head several times as he did. He relit a half-smoked joint from the ashtray and sat in shock on his sofa for an hour; before getting back on his knees and saying another prayer.

He was hoping he could now go back to the place from where he had just so badly wanted to get away. Although he did not leave his house this time and he knew he was still kneeling on his living room floor; he had a vision. As he said his prayer, he saw many beings wake from their sleep as they heard his prayer cutting through the air like the sound of many trumpets. They quickly arose, saying 'we are coming, oh Lord, we are coming,' and then they began what was to be a long journey, to where Bigs was on earth.

He saw himself following an alien and they flew through the air towards a beast that was see-through. Its outline was like that of a heat wave, shimmering above the hot tarmac in the summer's sun. It had four legs and two horns and was charging like a bull; to where it was charging, Bigs did not know. Attached to the back of its body, was a shape like the bottom part of an ant or a wasp which had been cut off from the rest of the body and then attached to that part, to Bigs' surprise, was Michelle's head; her hair was like living vines and out of them flowed lights and orbs. She wailed, and as she did, living things came out of her mouth.

CCTV SPECIAL OPERATIONS ROOM (LONDON'S WEST END)

'He's back sir!' screamed the operator, as he ran down the hallway to the thin man's office.

They then both ran back to the operations room, like kids trying to be the first to the presents under the Christmas tree, tripping over one another as they scrambled through the door into the special operations room. They stopped dead as they both stared at the screens, one screen was showing the thermal body heat and the second showed Bigs still in a prayer position.

'Replay the moment he reappeared.'

'Yes sir. This is unreal. Watch.'

The thin man watched in disbelief as Bigs reappeared out of thin air and then sat up on his sofa.

'Replay it again and again.'

The doors opened and two men in suits from the Ministry Of Defence walked in and confiscated all of the data concerning the entire incident; whilst at the same time reminding the thin man and all of the operators that they were MOD employees and were bound by the official secrets act. Then they left.

Director Forbes made a personal copy for himself and told Assistant Director Collins and Special Agent Rodrigo, that the official copy was to be escorted to the NSA vaults; he then took the rest of the week off. The head of the CIA, coincidently, also took the week off.

At his next scheduled press conference, the President told the press and the media that he would be holding no official engagements over the next week.

However, he would be meeting with the different heads of religion and churches over the coming weeks, to discuss how to deal with the immorality in today's society; as he himself was a devout Christian and wanted to work with all religions to create a better America.

'It was purely by coincidence.' The British Prime Minister wanted to make that first point absolutely clear, as he too, was about to hold meetings with all the heads of religion. He told the press, 'it was nothing more than keeping good relations with the different religious leaders, in times like these.'

A week later.

Bigs, at this point, had only told Michelle what had happened to him that night. He added that, in his opinion, the government didn't want to admit that aliens were real because they knew that they were really the angels of the Bible. Like with everything in this world, the angels' commercial value was more important than their original context, so the government portrayed angels as human beings with wings rather than as aliens with wings.

He was very confused. He was sure that what had happened was real, but just like when he was there, he could not believe it. Every night since then, when he prayed, he expected to have been taken back to wherever it was, to continue the experience; but every night he was disappointed. He so desperately wanted to get back up there and he couldn't understand why it did not happen.

For many nights after that Bigs, Michelle and his friends, witnessed many different UFOs hover and fly over his home; but for Bigs this was frustrating. 'Why did they just fly by? Why didn't they stop and pick me up?' he would ask. He was no longer interested in them flying by, nor in seeing them in the sky. He wanted to be up there with them, learning more about himself and what it was he was supposed to do next. He was now ready, he just needed some time to deal with what had happened. But now all they did was fly by. 'What good was that to him?' he would complain to Michelle, night after night.

He decided to phone his Dad and tell him what had happened and then he told Andy, Derrick and Paul. Bigs began to believe he was mad, or that he had turned mad for that night.

'If it was real, where are my wings?' he moaned to Michelle.

All she could do was tell him to ask the FATHER and MOTHER OF CREATION for guidance. He then told her, and everybody else, that from now on they were to call the FATHER and MOTHER OF CREATION 'the MOST HIGH,' as that was what his family had called them.

Bigs struggled to deal with what had happened to him. Being told who he was in the way that he was told, seemed to create more questions instead of giving him answers. Every day and night he would question the reality of what had happened, telling Michelle that he didn't believe it was real because of this or that.

'I must have been in some sort of a delusional state of mind. If this was something that was real, why don't I have the ability to float like I did? Anyway, I know I'm not Jesus Angel Wrath.'

'Don't say that Bigs! Why can't you be Jesus Angel Wrath? I know you. If you say you were there, then you were there. And another thing... your mind is too strong to have had a hallucination. From the day I met you until now, you have always wanted to serve the MOST HIGH and you have never cared about how the MOST HIGH chose for you to do that. You never use the MOST HIGH'S name in vain, so I know you would not lie about this or make it up. Be patient and ask the MOST HIGH to guide you, like you've always done.'

'But why haven't they come back for me? I asked it if we would be meeting again soon and it said yes. I told the alien... I mean, that angel, that I just needed a bit of time to take it all in. So, where are they? They haven't even flown by in the last couple of nights. If I am Jesus Angel Wrath then I should be able to order them to come.'

'I order you to come and pick me up... I am the First-begotten son of the MOST HIGH and my name is Jesus Angel Wrath. I am the gateway between heaven and earth and all dimensions. The MOST HIGH is me and I am the MOST HIGH. I command you to come to me now!!!' shouted Bigs as he looked up at the sky and waited and waited, but nothing happened.

'You see! It's not real Shell but I know it happened. I was there. I don't understand. Do you know that when I was there and it was all happening, I just wanted to get away so badly. I was so afraid at one stage, as I've now told you what... a hundred times? But anyway, I knew then that if I got back home I would start talking like this... as if it didn't happen. That's why I know it was real, because I think like I do. I mean, when you have a dream you accept things without the questioning and when it all gets too much, you wake up. Well, I questioned every second I was there, and I kept trying to wake up every second I was there; only to find out what I already knew... that I was already awake. You're right Shell, I've got to ask the MOST HIGH to help me understand. I have to work on this inside of myself, otherwise it will turn me mad.'

As the weeks and months passed, Bigs waited. He expected that at any minute he would be picked up by his family, but it didn't happen. He became consumed with finding out whether or not he was mad, but all of the people around him knew that he wasn't; they knew that he had a gift, but they could not convince him. Bigs spent less and less time on his business, but luckily for him it ran itself as long as someone answered the phone and made the appointments. Michelle took on those tasks, and Andy made sure that the appointments were kept.

Bigs cried a lot at night. All he had ever wanted to do was to serve the MOST HIGH. He kept trying to work out how he had gotten to this point. He wished he could just walk away and forget it had ever happened; after all he had a wonderful family, a successful business, was extremely fit and healthy and he was enjoying the trappings of life, but he couldn't walk away. He would give all of that up, if the MOST HIGH told him to. What was he meant to do?

Bigs stared into space and began to see with his mind's eye. He saw himself in a mirror, first from behind. He was once again in a pitch-black environment, but he could see himself clearly in the mirror; there was something about the self-image he could see in the mirror. It was as if, although he was looking at himself from behind, it was not himself that he could see. As he circled around to the front, he began to feel afraid, very afraid.

Staring at himself, face to face, he realised why he was so afraid, and he knew where he was. He was deep within himself; it was a forbidden place, he never came down here. This was the place he had buried his darker self... the side he was so afraid of, the madman within. But Bigs now knew that this side of himself was called Wrath; it wasn't bad, it was good, but that did not make him feel any better looking at himself. This side of his self still frightened the life out of Bigs. He stared at himself, face to face, but the eyes of this side of him were like fire and emitted a vibe that sent shivers down his spine. It wasn't long before Bigs could look at himself no more. He ran for the upper parts of himself; a long way away from the deep depths of the prison, in which he held the side of himself that he feared the most.

Bigs removed himself from his mind's eye and fell on his hands and knees, asking the MOST HIGH to teach him how to free himself from within.

'It is you that must teach yourself, for it is you that has imprisoned yourself and it is you that has taught yourself to fear who you are. Lucifer helped, of course, but that is no excuse. It is Lucifer's job to make you doubt yourself, and it is your choice whether you take his advice or not,' said the voice.

Bigs knew, from that moment on, that the hardest thing he now had to do was to stop fearing his own self. He had to undo a lifetime's work as quickly as possible. 'Bingo!' shouted Bigs as he laughed, praising the MOST HIGH. 'I understand. For the first time, I understand that the smoke is the key!' thought Bigs. He realised that he had become so in love with the smoke because, in his mind, it helped him keep Wrath deep down inside him, imprisoned. Any time he felt Wrath coming up, he would smoke and the effected would be that he couldn't be bothered to get angry. He laughed, as he could see where Lucifer had helped him to think that way. He could see how that type of thinking and the years of smoking, had made him so addicted to it.

'When you stop smoking, the countdown to the end of this world begins,' said the voice.

However, what Bigs didn't know was that knowing this didn't make things any easier; like he had thought that it might. It actually made things much harder; for the real war of self was now about to begin.

INSIDE THE WHITE HOUSE AND NUMBER 10 DOWNING STREET.

The meeting of all government religious heads.

The six o'clock news reported on the ongoing discussions, that the British Prime Minister and the

President of the USA were having with religious leaders. The discussions were centred on how to bring the world out of the moral cesspit, into which it had fallen; and how to bring all religions together to work as one, in order to solve the moral decline in today's society. The program showed the heads of fifteen different religious leaders being driven into the White House and into no.10 Downing Street.

The heads of the different religions were shown into the meeting rooms and took their seats, on both sides of the Atlantic. Unbeknownst to the outside world and the news reporters, the exact same questions were being asked and the exact same answers were given, on both sides of the ocean.

'Well, let me first say hello to everyone and I hope you had a pleasant journey here? I hope you all know why you are here; you know about the grave times we are now entering. Before we begin, would anyone like refreshments of any kind other than those that are on the table?' The Prime Minister looked around the table to see if there were any requests, but there were none. He and his team of advisors sat down on one side of the table, while the religious leaders sat down on the other side.

'So, if everyone is comfortable, we will now get on with the business you are here for. If you could all take out of your bags and briefcases, the one letter that has been entrusted to you for the past two thousand years or so, then we can begin,' said the Prime Minister.

The fifteen rabbis, imams, archbishops and high priests opened their satchels and briefcases, pulling out scrolls that looked extremely rare, old and valuable; which they handled as if they were newborn babies or the most delicate butterflies with wings still wet and not yet hardened. They unrolled the scrolls to reveal one letter on each of them, written in Aramaic.

One of the advisors to the Prime Minister walked around the dark brown oval oak table with a pen and notebook in hand, writing down the letters on each scroll; each letter was written on an individual piece of paper in the notebook. A second advisor then went around the table and did the exact same thing and lastly a third advisor.

When all three men had taken their seats the rabbis, imams, archbishops and high priests rolled up their individual scrolls, with the same care and attention with which they had opened them, and placed them back into their satchels and briefcases. At that time, they were politely asked to go and have lunch before being taken on a grand tour of number 10.

The three advisors then had each page with a letter on it, torn out of their notebooks and the matching, corresponding letters were put together into two piles. The three advisors who had written down the letters were then asked to leave.

Two translators entered the room and were given one pile each to translate into English letters. Once they had completed their task, they were also asked to leave the room. The letters, now in their English form, were then copied out several times so that the different people still remaining in the room, could each look at the letters without having to share.

A secure up-link between the two countries was then enabled. The 'for-your-eyes-only' information was looked at and discussed at great length, with only the members of their secret organisation. The fifteen letters could now be made into three words that would be the final and absolute proof, that Target One was the Antichrist. One at a time, each letter was put on to the table in the correct order. One member counted each letter that was put down, while another member read out the letter as it was put down.

'One.'

'J.'

'Two.'
'E.'
'Three.'
'S.'
'Four.'
'U.'
'Five.'
'S.'
'Six.'
'A.'
'Seven.'
'N.'
'Eight.'
'G.'
'Nine.'
'E.'
'Ten.'
'L.'
'Eleven.'
'W.'
'Twelve.'
'R.'
'Thirteen.'
'A.'
'Fourteen.'
'T.'
'Fifteen.'
'H.'

As the last letter was read out, the two men sat down. Director Forbes then read out the letters, stopping when the first word was made and stating it before reading out the next set of letters. He stopped to read out the second word, and then he did the same with the last word.

'So to confirm with our brothers in Great Britain, I shall read out the words one last time. Each word is made up of five letters. The first is J, e, s, u, s which spells the word Jesus. A, n, g, e, l spells Angel and W, r, a, t, h spells Wrath. Together they read Jesus Angel Wrath. Everybody concur?' asked Forbes.

'Aye,' they all replied.

'These words have been kept in secret for thousands of years. Only the real Jesus would know this name and he has now revealed himself to us. We must take our findings to our Master, but before we do we must implement the last phase of the New World Order. Our time of control and on the earth, is almost at an end. Gentlemen, you know what to do,' said Director Forbes, as he and his counterpart in England burnt the papers, destroying their information.

One month later.

The six o'clock news reports:
USA to free oppressed people from insane, murderous, religious dictator in Afghanistan.
USA and Europe Security Services say attack on their countries imminent.
Governments say new laws needed to tackle the threat.
Backlash, on new laws introduced by USA and Europe. Civil rights campaigners say new laws stink of Big Brother state and that citizens' rights are being eroded.
Congress defeat government's new laws in USA.
MPs defeat government's new laws in Europe.

Director Forbes discussed the defeat that the secret organisation had just suffered, whilst trying to implement the last phase of the New World Order with his Master the Beast, at the Skull and Bone Mansion.

'We have been successful with starting the war in Afghanistan. We can build on this like we have planned and say that we are now going to deal with the evil dictators of the world. We can go into Iraq and control the oil, once and for all.'

The Beast breathed out fire as it spoke, but its mouth did not move. 'And the attack on your country?'

'Everything is being put in place as we speak, and will be ready shortly.'

'When this is done, you will have no problem with implementing the final stage. No politician will want to look as if they are weak or not ready to defend their country from such an attack.'

'Yes, Master, but what about the UN and civil rights groups? We cannot control them as effectively as we used to.'

'Even they will be less effective once the attack takes place. The people of the western world have been programmed to see such an attack as war, and we have taught them that war is okay as long as we are doing the killing. So as long as they think that the new laws will enable their country to win the war, they will not care how moral that war is.

'We must be able to arrest all of those that do not subscribe to our programming in this final hour, as it will take JAW many years to come to terms with who he is. When he does, we will have left a third of the world in such a state that he will be pre-occupied for some time with his poor little starving and dying children; whose cries reach all the way up to heaven.

'So we must take out the threat, which is all of those that subscribe to Islam. They will try to make their move once the world sees the First-begotten son heading for Africa and the rest of the third world.'

'Yes, Master, we will have everything in place and ready to complete our final phase.'

Eight months later.

The six o'clock news reports that the USA is attacked like never before.

Thousands are killed by a new extremist terrorist group called Al-Qaeda.
USA and Europe Security Services say: more attacks on their countries are imminent.
Government says: new laws needed to tackle the threat.
New laws bypass Congress. President says: 'We are at war with a new enemy and that means new tactics. We cannot wait for Congress to make up its mind. We must act now, not later.'
New laws bypass European Parliament. President of Europe says: 'We are at war with a new enemy and that means new tactics. We cannot wait for Parliament to make up its mind. We must act now, not later.'
New laws bypass Australian Parliament. Prime Minister of Australia says: 'We are at war with a new enemy and that means new tactics. We cannot wait for Parliament to make up its mind. We must act now, not later.'
Civil rights campaigners say: citizens rights do not exist anymore, not even government officials have any say.
USA and Britain say: they must stop Iraqi dictator from launching an attack on US and British soil.
Security Services say: Iraqi dictator is involved in supplying arms to terrorist groups, and that if he is not stopped soon, nuclear terrorism will be next.
UN says: no more bloodshed, war is not the answer in Iraq.
USA and Britain insist that war with Iraq is imminent.
Civil rights campaigners say: first citizens rights were removed with the new laws and powers, then the government officials who did not sign up for the new ways lost their power, and now not even the UN can stop America and the UK from carrying out their own personal agendas around the world.
USA and Britain say: they don't need the UN and will go it alone in Iraq. When told that such a war would be illegal, the USA and Britain respond that they don't care.

A poll shows that even though most Americans and British citizens know that such a war would be illegal, they still back their governments. They state that their countries are at war with extremist Islamic terrorist groups who are prepared to kill innocent men, women and children; and that under such circumstances their governments have to do whatever is necessary, in order to stop or kill the enemy within and without.

Director Forbes turned off his TV, leant back in his chair and smiled as he drank his malt whiskey.

THE REAL UNDERWORLD

Deep down, some hundred miles beneath the earth's surface, a deep river flowed through the rocky caverns. Eventually it became shallower, coming to a gradual stop as it reached the rocky and muddy shoreline. The waters of the deep were normally pure and without cargo, but on this day the waters washed a single body up onto the shore. The inhabitants of the deep were not accustomed to having life from the surface of the earth, washing up on their shores.

There were very few places where the two worlds could connect, and those that did exist had been deliberately kept separate by powerful orbs and their force fields; which repelled both those on the surface and those underneath. The naked man's clothes must have washed off, as the sometimes violent river currents carried him from the surface, to the deep depths of the underworld.

Slowly, the naked man began to open his eyes. He coughed and spat out the water that filled his stomach. He was so weak, that he could hardly turn his head around to see where he was; as he lay with his back to the ground. As the water reached the end of its journey it kept nudging at his body, as if it was trying to make him get up.

He gingerly wiped the cold muddy water from his eyes and found enough strength to turn onto his stomach. He clawed his way out of the water completely, while he tried to focus his eyes; as he stared into the dimly lit cave where he now found himself. He could see slightly better, but his eyesight was still blurred. It was not clear enough for him to see his surroundings, but he could make out red, yellow and white lights in the distance, that seemed to move backwards and forwards.

'They must be some sort of fireflies, they seem to be flying in tandem,' he thought, as he squinted his eyes to try and clear the blurriness. Slowly, as he watched the lights, his eyes regained more and more focus. The more he watched the fireflies moving in pairs in the shadows of the cave, the more he tried to focus.

He looked up and could see the fireflies way up in the roof, of what he assumed was a cave. Water dropped down from the ceiling of the cave and fell into his eyes and his mouth; but this was not normal water. As it entered his eyes it cleared his blurry eyesight instantly, and the drops that fell into his mouth filled him as if he had eaten a full course meal. Filled with sudden strength and energy and with cleared vision, the naked man stood, wiped his eyelids clear and looked around him.

'Oh, shit!' he shouted, as he stared at the fireflies that had seemed to be in pairs. The naked man first wished that his eyes were not so clear, then wished that he was not where he was. He looked at the yellow, red and white lights, which were not fireflies at all but the individual eyes of beings staring at him from the shadows. The naked man spun around and looked up and down then left and right, but no matter where he looked, he saw eyes looking at him.

The beings moved out of the darkness and as they did, their full features could be seen. They looked like ghouls and goblins, with pointed fingers and long, straight nails. Their skins were grey, green and slimly and their teeth were like daggers.

He tried to remember how he had got there, but his mind was blank. 'Where the hell am I?' he shouted, as the ghouls and goblins crept ever nearer and closer. It became clear that they were not coming to welcome him but they were coming to eat him, and as they got closer the naked man knelt and prayed as if it were his last prayer.

Then suddenly, out of the heights of the cave, he heard a swooping sound. He looked up to see what looked like a man, with wings like that of a bat, swooping down towards him and then grasping him with feet like those of a golden eagle. He was lifted just in the nick of time, up out of the reach of the ghouls and goblins.

They flew through the cave and out of the cave's mouth, into what looked like fields and forests. He looked up and at first it looked like the sky was on fire, but then as he kept on looking, he realized that it *was* on fire.

Suddenly they came to rest in the large branches at the top of a massive tree, some three hundred feet high. The naked man looked closely at the thing carrying him. 'It's like a vampire, but that could not be possible,' thought the man, as he stared at the creature who stared back at him. Then it laughed and to the astonishment of the naked man, it seemed to be able to read his mind. 'Well, well, well. You seem to be a long way from home, Agent Smith.'

THE FINAL COUNTDOWN

Every year, Bigs would hope that this anniversary would be the one to reunite him with his family; and every year he was disappointed. He had passed the stage of expecting every week or month to be the one when they would be reunited; and slowly and reluctantly, he began to accept the fact that there was something he had to do in order for the reunion to take place. The worst thing was that he knew, as he had always known without a question of a doubt, what he had to do next; and it frightened the life out of him.

Bigs knew that he had to take on the governments and their authorities, the army and the police forces. But it was not that part that he was so afraid of, it was how he would have to do it. He would have to reunite with the whole of himself in order to complete his mission, and that meant releasing his Wrath side. There was also the next phase that had to be completed in order to reach the point of most fear. To release his Wrath, he had to stop smoking. Lucifer's game plan became more and more clearer to Bigs, the more he attempted to stop smoking. The two things he needed to complete in order to be truly free, were going to be the two hardest things he had ever tried to do.

All Bigs could do was ask the MOST HIGH to help him and to forgive him for his foolish transgressions; and then be patient as his prayers might not be answered for a long time. 'What a fool I have been,' thought Bigs, as he saw the error of his ways.

Over the next three years, Bigs tried numerous times to stop smoking, but failed miserably. He could manage a week or two, at best, and then he would find some feeble excuse to start again. The most common excuse was that if he could smoke only one and then not smoke again, it would mean that he had given it up for real and wasn't just hiding from it. Of course, the one always turned into two, and that would be the end of his attempt to stop smoking.

Some nights Bigs would cry to the MOST HIGH, begging them to remove what he now saw as a curse over his life. He would laugh at how he would have never had seen his smoking as a curse before; for all those years it had seemed like his best friend, something that he never ever wanted to be without. He had been willing and had wanted to die smoking. Now, it was not his best friend; it was his enemy. It had its claws deep in him and it would not leave him alone.

He had given up his business as he could not concentrate on anything, other than the night he was taken up. Although his business was earning hundreds of thousands of pounds a year, to Bigs it meant nothing. He was consumed with the need to understand and to find out if what had happened to him was real. To do that, he had to go back to the one place he hated the most... religion... as it held the answers; though to Bigs, religion was only using the MOST HIGH'S word to make itself look legitimate, but nevertheless, religion had the word of the MOST HIGH.

As Bigs listened to the scriptures being read on the Christian networks, he began to hear a code that was left there for him; things that the voice had told him and asked him about were there. Answers he had given in reply to a question from the voice, answers that he was not sure were really correct, were there; they were there in the words that were written more than two thousand years ago. Also, the way in which Bigs thought and the way in which the voice had told him to think, were there; the way he thought, had been written in the Bible more than two thousand years ago. Situations that Bigs had found himself in, situations which should have cost him his life, even a description of how he would look to the MOST HIGH to save him and the fact that the MOST HIGH would; they were there, written in the Bible more than two thousand years ago.

Bigs did not expect to find such personal answers awaiting him in the Bible. He was amazed to find out that he had lived a life that was similar in so many ways to the lives of the men in the book. He had not expected to find answers to his present situation. It was desperation that had driven him back to religion and to the Bible; a book that he had never read, but had only glanced at whilst pretending to sing hymns at weddings and funerals.

For the life of him, Bigs couldn't work out why if what he thought had happened was real (and he was certain that it was), but he had nothing to show for it. At first, when smoking was brought into it by the voice that told him 'the smoke is the key,' that had reinforced his disbelief in the whole thing. He had no idea what smoking had to do with anything, though, that was something that he now understood.

He still could not understand why he had no abilities on earth and then one night, as he was listening and searching for the answers to his questions and verifying the answers given to him by the voice, one by one it was all being proven to him as real; and on this night in question he found the answers to the biggest problems he had with the whole thing.

Why didn't he have the powers right now, why didn't he have the powers to open his wings like he had done that night? If he was who he had been told he was, why couldn't he command the angels to come to him, why couldn't he float in mid air, and so on?

The voice would ask, 'And what would you do if you could use these powers right now? Use them to play video games better? What good are they to you if you have no real faith in the message given to you? For you are of little faith.'

Bigs, as usual, did not understand at first what he had been told. As far as he was concerned, he had faith; he believed in the MOST HIGH and was willing to serve them. How could the voice say he was of little faith, and what did that have to do with what had happened? Bigs had passed such a point, hadn't he?

So he was pleasantly surprised that night, when he watched a preacher talking about certain scriptures that dealt with the issue of faith. The preacher quoted scriptures that spoke of the fact that the only way to please the MOST HIGH was through faith. Once again, Bigs was able to verify something that the voice had told him; something that he did not have any understanding about or that he had not ever read or learnt.

Once again, it was a wonderful feeling. Also, in that instance, Bigs realised that he had spoke of such things before but had never before experienced what he had said. He had said several times that things should come first from within, and then one should seek to qualify them through the Bible and the Qur'an.

This puzzled him as he began to see just how much he talked about stuff that he did not know; although he knew it was true without knowing it, as it was not an assumption, he just knew deep within himself that it was fact. At that point, he came to understand how the voice had been speaking through him on so many occasions; it was quite mind-blowing to try and understand how one could say something, without knowing what you were saying.

One night Bigs found meaning in this puzzle, as a preacher quoted scriptures that described the mystery of talking about what one does not know; the scriptures told how the Holy Spirit often did that to the men of the MOST HIGH. Bigs sat up, had he really heard the true name of the voice? Was its real name the Holy Spirit? 'Are you the Holy Spirit?' asked Bigs, but the voice did not answer. This was not unusual, as there had been too many times to count when Bigs would ask the voice or the MOST HIGH something and would not get an answer for minutes, hours, days, months or even, in some cases, years. However, when it came to the MOST HIGH or the voice, Bigs was always patient; he always knew that when the time was right he would get the answer he was seeking.

He told Michelle of his discoveries, and she reminded him of the time when it had all just happened. She reminded him about when he had been taken up and told who he was and she reminded him of how, for months and years, he nearly tore himself apart with the longing for them to take him back. She reminded him of how he had so many unanswered questions and how over the years, all of them had been answered, one by one. They were answered because he had kept his faith in the MOST HIGH and had not given up; even though he could not see how his questions could ever receive meaningful answers.

The one thing Bigs knew from the beginning was what he had to do next (assuming that he was who he had been told he was). He had to be one hundred percent certain that this message was from the MOST HIGH, before he would begin what was already written and programmed inside of him.

Bigs now understood why he did not have his powers or wings. Finally, he had been given the answer and it made one hundred percent sense to him. For the first time in years, he was glad that he did not come back to earth with his powers because if he did have his powers he would not have been able to walk by faith into what was his birthright. If he could not walk by faith into it, then he could not please the MOST HIGH; for it is only through acts of faith in the MOST HIGH, that anyone can please them.

With this understanding, a very heavy weight was lifted off of his shoulders. It was confirmation that all that had happened was true. What else could explain how all of the answers he was looking for, were waiting for him in a book full of the words of the MOST HIGH? Coincidence? Bigs thought not.

This was all of the proof that he had needed to truly believe, that what he had been told that night was true. That did not mean that it was now easy for him to be JAW, as that in itself was now part of the next challenge. If the truth be known, it was probably the one thing that he would not complete before actually reaching the full glory of being JAW. However, even with most of his fears and doubts put to rest, he would continue to look for answers as to why it was so hard for him to believe in who he was.

Bigs now found himself in a strange and surreal place. He was now in between worlds, reaching and striding towards being JAW, but at the same time while he moved towards his true self, he was still Bigs and he still had a family to support. He was now seriously lacking in his effort to support them, and he had to make one of the biggest decisions of his entire life.

One option was to stop concentrating on pleasing the MOST HIGH through faith, which to many people seemed like nothing more than madness or some sort of mental breakdown. The other option was to do what those very people would suggest to do... forget it all and take back control of his business before it was too late; before he had nothing left and could not feed or support his family like he should. After all they were more important and to do that was not madness, it was the proper and right thing to do. Such was the opinion of most people.

Bigs wanted to do both, but it became painfully clear that it was not possible. He had to make a choice. The MOST HIGH over this world or this world over the MOST HIGH. Lucifer, on hearing his cue, tried to infiltrate Bigs' mind.

'It would be irresponsible of you to leave this world's system, in order to take up a system that will not prove itself to you, until you pass a point of no return. If you are wrong, it will be too late. You will have lost your home and maybe even your family and don't forget all of those people out there that are wishing you will fail and fall on your face, so they can say behind your back, "I told you so. He's lost his mind." It's too risky, and it's not worth the price if you are wrong. You have a successful business and money, and all of those people who have been wishing you would fail are having to eat their words right now. Don't spoil it all. If that message was true, then it is up to them to come to you. If you are wrong Bigs, not only will you leave your children homeless and in the hands of the people who have wished for your downfall, but you will also leave them unprotected. At the very best you will be in prison, and at the worst you will be dead. And for what? An idea? A dream? A delusion? Who really knows what it was.

'Ask yourself, "Do you really think you are JAW?" Of course you don't. That, above all things, is something that you cannot bring yourself to believe. Why should such a burden be put on your shoulders? All you have ever asked for, is to serve.'

Bigs awoke in the middle of the night and fear came over him for a moment, then he laughed. 'You're wrong Satan Lucifer Devil, I *will* give everything I have to the MOST HIGH, for it is them that have given me everything that I have; not you, nor those people who have no idea why I'm willing to risk it all just to die. Even knowing I died trying to serve the MOST HIGH is the greatest honour that I could wish for. Without the MOST HIGH, I am nothing, but with the MOST HIGH, nothing is impossible.

'I couldn't care less if the whole world thinks I'm mad to do what I will eventually do. It is not any of them who have helped me, or saved me, or guided me, or looked after me. Like you said, they have all wished for my downfall. Why would I care about any of them? They mean nothing to me; they are blasphemers and idol worshippers, lovers of this world and its dead materials. Why would they know what I do? I am not they, and they are not I. I live and die for the MOST HIGH. They live and die for this world.

'My only concern is that my wife and children understand me, and I'm glad to be able to say that they do. They back me and bless me, while you and your world curse me and backstab me. Know this, Satan Lucifer Devil, I will not stop until I have reached my destiny for the MOST HIGH. I'm not afraid for my family for they are blessed like me, with the love and protection of the MOST HIGH. I have pity for the fools that come against the house of the MOST HIGH, which is my family and I.'

This little spat with Satan Lucifer Devil strengthened Bigs. He took comfort in the fact that, instead of waiting for days and weeks, he had instantly responded to the fiery darts of the Devil. For the first time, Bigs could now distinguish between his own thoughts and the unclean, unseen spirits that were speaking to him. Like most people in the world, Bigs had always thought that if a thought was in his mind, it was because he had thought it.

These thoughts were unlike those from the Holy Spirit, which seemed to make itself clear by the way that it spoke. These were not just thoughts; the job description of an unclean, unseen spirit or demon was to try to make a person think that the negative thought or idea it injected into their mind, was their own idea or thought. They were supposed to slip in unclean thoughts, at a time that would not make them stand out as being alien to one's own thoughts. Satan Lucifer Devil was the absolute master of such tactics, however, Bigs was now able to quickly identify such tactics; and as a result, he was able to move more easily towards his destiny.

Bigs was so grateful for the backing and support of his family. His family was the MOST HIGH – his wife Michelle, his now four children, plus his army of aliens and beasts. Then one night as he smoked his joint, he calmly turned to Michelle and said, 'This is my last smoke, Shell.'

'Really? Why do you say that?'

'The MOST HIGH has told me that it's time.'

'Wow.'

'I can tell you that if the MOST HIGH doesn't do something, then I will be smoking again by tomorrow evening. However, they have told me, so I don't have to worry. You know I can't do this without them. I hope this is true and not just some devil trick.'

'Does it feel like it's a trick?'

'No, not at all. To be honest with you, I'm ninety-nine percent certain; yet I've tried so many times in the past and failed.'

'But like you say, this is not you. This is the MOST HIGH.'

'The day I stop smoking is a day I have never been able to see until now. That's why I know it's the start... because only the MOST HIGH could make me see this day. In a lot of ways, this day is more unbelievable to me than being JAW. Anyway, we'll see tomorrow.'

One year later.

What a year it had been for Bigs and his family. Bigs rejoiced in the fact that it had been a full year since he had last smoked a joint or anything else. He was also proud that he had been able to show the MOST HIGH how much they had meant to him, by walking away from his business and from the world's point of view. He had done so, even though he did not know how long his money would last or how he would pay back his investors. What he believed, more than anything, was that the MOST HIGH would provide the way when they saw fit to do so.

With every day that passed, Bigs grew stronger in his beliefs. He knew that Satan Lucifer Devil would use everything in his worldly power to try and make him think that he was mad, foolish and living a lie; but Bigs had already learnt this trick of the Devil's. He had learnt it when he was told by the MOST HIGH to change his lifestyle from that of a gangster, to that of a businessman. Satan Lucifer Devil would use people around Bigs to try to put doubt in his mind and Satan Lucifer Devil would also use his world system to put a strain on Bigs; in an attempt to make him go back to his old lifestyle. Yet back then, as now, Bigs was single-minded and forged ahead; while all of those that were not his family tried to make him doubt himself and the MOST HIGH.

The one thing that Bigs still couldn't do was believe that he was JAW. It was just too hard for him to believe. He had spent his entire life seeing himself as last, and now he was first. Through his research he had come across the scriptures that said, that those that think they are last will be first and that those that think they are first will be last. Once again, the scriptures confirmed that the way in which the Holy Spirit had taught him how to think, was in line with the written word. Bigs took great comfort in that.

However, it did not change the fact that he had lived all of his life thinking that he was last. He had grown very comfortable with that thinking. So to now try and see himself as first, as high up as anyone could be, was something he still struggled with. He did not try to hide it from the MOST HIGH, from Michelle, or from his children. Nevertheless, he was determined to make it to where the MOST HIGH had told him he would be.

He began to get less concerned with who he was and more concerned with the fact that it was the MOST HIGH's message to him. He now believed this because over the years he had asked the MOST HIGH to let him know if it was all a mistake, or a lie by some mischievous demons. He told the MOST HIGH that he did not care about a title unless they did, and that he could not find it in himself to believe or comprehend such a title.

If he had been called a soldier of the MOST HIGH that would have been the greatest honour to him... more than he could have dreamed of. However, at no stage did he ever imagine being any of what was told to him that night.

He would say to the MOST HIGH, and to Michelle, and to his children, 'How can I lift my mind up to such a height? I have tried but I cannot do it.

'If I were just the First-begotten son of the MOST HIGH, I could not believe it.

'If I were just JAW, it would be impossible for me to imagine.

'If I were just the gateway between heaven and earth and all dimensions, my mind could not be able to grasp such status.

'And last but certainly not least, if I were just the MOST HIGH and the MOST HIGH were me; I would say that I must have fallen down and hit my head.

'Each of these names is beyond my wildest dreams. In fact, these are dreams I would never dare to have; in case the real being who was these things heard my thoughts and came after me for having the nerve to have delusions of such grandeur. Yet I am all of these things. So how can I ever possibly comprehend such importance, given where I am right now? Even when I am in my full glory, it will be years before it really sinks in. That night, I knew what it felt like to be a lottery winner of millions of pounds.

'So, I have decided that to try and think in the way that I have thought, is the wrong thing to do. What I will do, if it pleases you the MOST HIGH, is believe in you. I will believe that you know my situation and that you know that I did not wish for this, or even think of such things. I will believe that you know that in my heart, my purest desire and dream is to serve you.

'I cannot make the leap to such a height. I do not know how to do so, even though I have seen it with my own eyes. I will make you my foundation and my rock, like I used to do, until that night. I now realise that I had began to think differently, and that because of my status and my name, I tried to make them my foundation and my rock. You are and always will be my everything. No matter what my name is, I exist to serve you.'

Bigs was ready, but something was still not quite right. He knew that he had to confront the authorities of the world and he had planned to do so as soon as his money had completely run out; which was just about to happen.

So, he wrote letters to the authorities telling them that he was JAW and that he would not be paying any more taxes. He told them that, if they wished to, they could attempt to arrest him or take away his home.

As time passed and Bigs' bills began to mount, the day finally came for his home to be repossessed. Bigs could not bring himself to begin, something was holding him back. He reluctantly left his house and had to move into his in-laws' home. This was not how Bigs had envisioned his final path to glory. He was taken aback by the whole situation. What had gone wrong?

He retraced his steps and tried to find out what was missing. How could his plan, go so drastically wrong? The tax collector came to his home looking for money and Bigs refused to pay him, and there was nothing the tax collector could do. However, when it came to the repossession of his home, he had no desire to battle over it. From the Holy Spirit came the thought that this was not the time, the place, or the correct thing over which to go to war.

The idea of moving in with his in-laws, who Bigs knew didn't really like him, seemed impossible. What was the point? How had he miscalculated so badly?

He had concentrated on the MOST HIGH being his rock and his foundation and he had discovered that from the night when he was taken and told who he was, he had entered into a covenant with the MOST HIGH. Part of that covenant was to place himself in a situation where the odds were extremely stacked against him. For example, a situation with ten police officers, all armed with semi-automatic submachine guns pointed at Bigs, while he stood armed with only a sword. Such a situation may sound like suicide, but it would not be. It was what was required in the covenant between the MOST HIGH and Bigs.

He was JAW, and he must have the greatest of faith in the MOST HIGH, who is his FATHER and MOTHER. He would stand before the armed officers, but not armed with a sword; as that would just be a worldly symbol of his intent. He would stand before the officers armed with the power and the authority of the MOST HIGH, knowing that the MOST HIGH would not let the armed police officers kill him or have authority over him.

Bigs knew and believed this with all of his heart, and yet he still could not begin; something was not yet complete. Bigs scratched his head, trying to find the missing piece. He knew that he had doubts about who he was, but he also knew that he believed in the MOST HIGH and that they would not let any harm come to him. He had a lifetime of experience to prove that. So what was it? Why couldn't he begin?

He asked the MOST HIGH to show him what he needed to do. He thought back all those years to the time of his awakening, and to how his alien brother had told him so confidently, that he would know what do to when the time was right. Well, he knew for sure what to do, now. So why couldn't he start?

His thoughts were constantly interrupted by Michelle's family, who called him lazy and ambitionless. To make matters worse, Michelle's mom had invested money in his thriving construction company, before Bigs made up his mind to leave it. Now she was on the warpath to recoup her money.

Bigs promised her that when he had completed what he was doing she would get back every penny, but that did not stop her from being her usual negative self towards him and everything that he did. Bigs had lost the peace and quiet of his home. He had now been tossed into a house that was at war with itself and with him. He longed for peace so that he could work out what had gone wrong and what he needed to do to rectify it.

Satan Lucifer Devil was about to have his field day with Bigs, and he made sure that Bigs had as little time as possible, to work out what was to come next. Bigs' in-laws constantly told Michelle that she was like a slave, because she looked after Bigs and his family so well. Michelle's dad turned on her and his grandchildren, and he began to tell them that after living in his house for six months, they just had to leave. He wanted them to leave for no other reason than that the children played too much and made too much noise. When he was growing up, he could not play and make noise, so he wanted them out of his house; even though he knew that they had nowhere to go. Worse still, Michelle had given birth to their fifth child a year earlier, who was now a one-year-old boy; still, her dad did not care. Satan Lucifer Devil laughed, and he knew that this distraction would slow Bigs down and prevent him from getting closer to what he should be doing next.

Michelle's mom, dad and sister were Satan Lucifer Devil's perfect tools. He had Bigs right where he wanted him. His in-laws squabbled amongst themselves and there was little love between them on the surface. They hardly agreed on anything except when it came to their dislike for Bigs... that would always unite them. For the moment, Bigs was powerless to act; yet he knew that his day would come. The MOST HIGH had always given him his day against those foolish enough to come against him.

For almost a year and a half, Bigs spun in a circle. He could not concentrate enough to work out what it was he should be doing now. Because of his situation, he fell back into thinking that he should go back to work. Then he would say 'No. He had to follow the path towards the MOST HIGH, no matter what.'

He went back and forth, not really doing anything, while his in-laws constantly made it clear to him he was not their family and that he should be glad that they had let him stay in their home. Bigs tried to concentrate, but he would always get distracted by Michelle's dad.

This made Wrath boil over inside him, and Bigs began to spend most of his days just trying to keep Wrath down and under control. Unbeknownst to Bigs, this was exactly what Satan Lucifer Devil wanted. Bigs did not realise that the very thing that he was doing, was one of the things that he would have to stop doing if he was ever to become his true self.

He told Michelle's dad that he should be ashamed of what he was doing. How could a man tell his daughter and his grandchildren to go, when they had done nothing to him? How could he tell them to get out of his house, knowing that they had nowhere to go, knowing that they had a one-year-old baby and a three-year-old little girl. Bigs told him that he needed to stop drinking, because it was quite clear to Bigs that the drinking was affecting him; and that the way he acted towards his own grandchildren was, in Bigs' eyes, because he was an alcoholic.

Michelle's mom, dad and sister began to argue with Bigs, telling him that he was out of order in calling Michelle's dad an alcoholic. They began to shout at Bigs, but Bigs paid them no mind as he was at war within himself; trying to keep Wrath from getting out and doing unthinkable things to those that had dared to come against him.

After it had all died down and Bigs was by himself, the Holy Spirit spoke to him. 'If you were truly ready you would not fear your Wrath, for it is of the MOST HIGH and it will not rise against the just and the righteous. Only the ignorant, vain and proud will cause Wrath to rise in you, and that side of you will deal with them justly. This alliance amongst your so-called in-laws will not last long. This man is restless and has no peace here. Soon he will move on and when he does, you must begin to write,' said the Holy Spirit.

'Write what?' asked Bigs, but the Holy Spirit did not answer. So, Bigs told Michelle of his dilemma. He told her that even though he knew that the Holy Spirit was right, he would not let his Wrath be unleashed on her family. He told her that he hoped her dad would leave soon, but he felt bad for saying that, as this was his home and not Bigs'.

Bigs tried to keep away as much as he could. So they both watched and waited and just as the Holy Spirit had told him, Michelle's dad decided to go back to his homeland. He said that there was nothing left for him here but argument and unrest. He complained that he had no one to talk to, and he took his belongings and left.

This was a relief for Bigs, as he did not know how long he could have put up with Michelle's dad's abusive attitude towards his children. Bigs was extremely angry with himself for allowing this situation to get the better of him; for allowing Michelle's dad to be abusive towards their children, just because it was his house. From that moment on, Bigs did not like any of Michelle's family. He felt awkward and bad for feeling like that, because he was living in their home. 'But how could they stand by and let Michelle's dad talk to his grandchildren like that?' thought Bigs.

His in-laws continued to use the time that Bigs and his family were staying there, to try and drive a wedge between Bigs and Michelle. They told Michelle that she shouldn't be running around after Bigs and cooking for him all the time, they told her that she was a slave to do such things; and they asked her if she was afraid of Bigs because that's what it looked like to them. They asked her, 'What does he do for you?'

When they finally realised that they could not break what the MOST HIGH had put together, they turned on Michelle. They told her, hoping it would really hurt her, that she had been cut out of the family will because she was married to Bigs. Satan Lucifer Devil laughed, because he knew that Bigs was having to spend most of his time dealing with their poison.

However, what Michelle's family didn't know was that Bigs had told Michelle, before they moved into her

mom's house, what her family would do and what they would say. Michelle hoped that Bigs would be wrong but she knew by now, after being with him for almost twenty years, that he could read the future and that he was able to show her things that she could not see. The night before they told her that she had been written out of the will, Bigs had warned Michelle; because of his warning, Michelle's family had not succeeded in causing unrest in their
relationship. They would now try something else, and she had best be ready for whatever it was.

Michelle was broken-hearted by what her family had said and done to her. They had made her feel like a stranger, because she was loyal to her husband Bigs and their five children. Yet, Bigs knew that these things had to happen; as they had said so many times before, he and they were not family.

Bigs tried to make Michelle understand this, that not everyone had to get along. They were who they were, and he and his family were who they were, and it was quite obvious that the two families were heading in different directions. However, because it was their house, they
should try to adopt the lower standard; which meant there was a double standard and Bigs, Michelle and the kids were on the lower of the two standards.

Michelle's family were always making clear, that if Michelle's children left a plate unwashed, there would be hell to pay; yet if the plate was left by one of the in–laws, it didn't matter. This double standard drove Bigs mad, especially as it was his family that did all of the cleaning in the house anyway. He complained that his in-laws were quick to criticize and moan at his children for leaving their dirty plates in the sink, even though they would wash them later. The fact was, they never said thank you to him, to Michelle or to his children, for vacuuming and dusting the whole house every other day. They said that he was out of order to bring that up; after all, they were letting him stay in their home.

In the winter, Michelle was concerned with the cold, as she had two young babies to keep warm. When she asked if the heating could be turned up in the night, she was told that she should tell the babies to learn to cover up. Yet when her thirty-five-year old sister complained that she was cold, the heating was turned up to maximum.

Michelle could see how her family were making an enemy of Bigs; this worried her, since she knew who he really was. She asked Bigs, 'Would you still hold it against them once you have completed your transformation to JAW? After all, they did not know who you were.'

Bigs laughed, saying, 'Then you had better tell them; though I can tell you now that it won't make any difference. Your family do not know me because the MOST HIGH obviously does not want them to. Or maybe you're right, maybe you just need to tell them who I am. But be warned that if you do, and if they still come against me; the consequences will be far greater than they are now.'

'Please tell me what you think I should do. I can see that they are making you dislike them, and I know that if I don't warn them, I will feel like it is my fault when they pay for it at their judgement day. Yet now you are saying that if I say something and they continue, it will be worse than now. I don't want them to go to hell, Bigs.'

'First of all it's up to my FATHER and MOTHER, the MOST HIGH, to decide; not me. But if I have any say, then I would put in a good word for your mom. I'm not too fond of her, but she has helped us. To be honest with you though Shell, I don't think they have a chance. They blaspheme too much and they are into idol worship, with all of their superstitions. If I was their only hope, then they are fast making that a non-reality.'

'So what should I do? Nothing?'

'The question really is, can you do anything? I believe that if you tell them who I am, they will reject me and say that it is not possible, or worse. But even if you don't tell them who I am, at their judgement day they will have still rejected me because I am who I am; whether they know my name or not. So what you have to consider is this: Do you think they will accept who I am, if you tell them? Do you think they will change their ways towards me, or will they condemn themselves further?'

'Tell me what do, Bigs. I don't want them to be condemned.'

'The truth is, Shell, they are already condemned by their own actions. I know this, because we don't get along. I can tell you in advance about the things people will do, but it is not because I can read the future; it's because I can see the unclean, unseen spirits that are either trying to control them, that are controlling them, or that are a part of them. The differences between the three situations that I have just mentioned are, that in the first two instances there's a battle going on between the person and the spirit; a battle for the body that could go either way. Though, with the third there is no battle; the person has, for whatever reason, given over control to the unclean spirit. I believe this has happened with your family, like it has with most of the world.'

'So, are you saying that I shouldn't tell them?'

'I believe that if you tell them, the unclean, unseen spirits will tell them to come against me, as long as I'm in their house and I look like I'm down and out; though, the only way to know is to tell one of them and see what happens. However, I have to say that I think they already have an idea.'

'Really? Why do you think that? I haven't told them anything, I swear.'

'I didn't say that you did. It's just that people with... and I'm not trying to be nasty when I say this... but people with such sad lives will often sneak a look or listen to the lives of people who seem to be happy. So I would be surprised if they haven't been listening in on our conversations while we've been here. Anyway, if it makes you feel like you have done all you can do, then tell your sister first; but I promise you though, she is going to run me down with negative comments.'

'No, I don't think she will. She's been saying lately that she goes to Bible studies and is getting more spiritual.'

'Oh, my, Michelle. You really are blind to the ways of this world. She probably says that because she's been listening in to our conversations; she's trying to act like she knows about the Bible and who I can or can't be. Anyway, if you believe that, then go and tell her; but say it like it's in confidence and I bet you she will betray you.'

'Okay, I will, because I believe in you and I believe you are JAW. I don't want my sister to be condemned if I can help it in any way.'

Michelle told her sister, in confidence, that Bigs was the First-begotten son of the MOST HIGH; she also told her sister his whole name. Her sister immediately began to ridicule the whole idea saying 'It sounds like he is psychotic,' she then asked Michelle. 'Was he smoking at the time? I bet it's the smoke that has turned him mad, he has all the signs of that; he's so OCD, he keeps going on about cleaning, always wanting everything to be so clean. I study the Bible, and I can tell you that such a name is to do with revenge; that means that he's a Devil worshipper.' she barked.

'No, Wrath means anger.' shouted Michelle.

'No. I do Bible studies once a week, I know what it means,' she snapped and walked out before Michelle could reply.

Then, when Bigs was sitting downstairs, she shouted out, 'I have to get out of here, because there are too many Devil worshippers in this house for my liking.'

Bigs laughed and looked at Michelle with a smile. 'What did I tell you? Do you see, now? As far as she knows, I don't know that you have told her. Now in her mind she's just tried to put you in an awkward situation. She thinks I will ask you, what is she talking about, and that you will either have to tell me the truth or lie to me.'

After that day Michelle did not try to save any other members of her family, as she could now see that they would not believe in Bigs.

One month later, Bigs decided that it was time to tell Michelle's mom who he was. That was if Michelle's sister hadn't already told her, but even if she had, Bigs wanted to tell her personally; so there could be no excuses. If they wanted to make fun of him then so be it; he did not wish to protect them anymore.

Michelle's mom was worried about the bills, as she was getting old and no one was helping her to pay the mortgage. Bigs had always told her that he would pay her what he owed her, once he had finished his project; but because no one else in the house was helping her, she began to put pressure on him to go and get a job.

Bigs would ask her what her daughter was doing... why wasn't she helping her out? She worked and would be the beneficiary of the home once her mother died; but Michelle's mom would tell him that it was none of his business, that Michelle's sister was her daughter and did not have to help her pay the bills. She said, 'Once in a while she buys me nice things, and that's good enough.'

Bigs would say that he had told her that he was going to pay her when he had finished what he was doing; nothing had changed, and that was still his plan. He had no money right now and she would know when he did have money, as he would be leaving her house the minute he could; but if she was not happy, then she could tell him to leave. He told her that he knew that she worried, but that she needed to have a little faith in the MOST HIGH and in him. Then he told her who he was and what his name was, and told her that was why she didn't need to worry.

The next day, still feeling upset about her bills, she began to curse Bigs. She said that she was tired of his crap and tired of hearing him talk about the MOST HIGH. She began to mock him and his relationship with the MOST HIGH, saying that he was still a lazy good for nothing. But then the next night she brought home a box of chocolates for Bigs, Michelle and the children.

Michelle said, 'I think she's sorry for what she was saying. I think it's the pressure from worrying about the bills and about how she won't be able to work next year.'

'I understand Michelle, but it makes me so angry when someone talks negative about my relationship with the MOST HIGH. However, because your mom has done some good things for us over the years, I'm going to forget about it; at least until the next time she starts about something.'

'Thank you.'

'Don't thank me, thank the MOST HIGH. They remind me that I owe your mom and until I pay her back, I will tolerate her up and down ways. I don't mean to be funny, but if she could just stop drinking she would be able to get a clearer perspective on things.'

Satan Lucifer Devil knew these things would get under Bigs' skin and would slow down his progress greatly ... and they did. Bigs spent fifty percent of his time dealing with Michelle's family issues, instead of working out what it was, he was supposed to write. The double standard in his in-laws' house drove him mad, and he would waste entire days being pissed off at the situation, instead of concentrating on what came next.

His children became an escape goat for his in-laws own failures, and Bigs felt they were sometimes being picked on; though this was not to say that the in-laws did not buy things for the children, or spoil them. But the good things always take care of themselves, and it was always material things that she gave them. Bigs, on the other hand, sometimes felt that what was needed was moral guidance or loving emotional reassurance; as they would buy the children clothes, but treat them like second-class citizens.

Bigs felt that it would have been better if his in-laws had never bought them one present in their entire lives, but instead, had treated his children as if their home was his children's home; unfortunately it was the other way around. For Bigs' own part, they had treated him the way that he would have treated them, if the shoe had been on the other foot. He understood how hard it must have been for them to put up with him, and Bigs honestly didn't care less if they liked him or not. However, his children were another matter, and this was the reason that he did not like his in-laws.

A great deal of time had passed and Bigs had lost a lot of time thinking about the problems with his in-laws, instead of writing whatever it was he was meant to write. Then one day he finally realised that the Devil had done one over on him, and had tricked him into wasting so much time. So Bigs decided to sit at the computer and see what would happen.

He had been diagnosed as dyslexic, so he wasn't too convinced that he would be able to write anything of any meaning; yet he looked at the screen and before he knew it, he had written ten pages. He could not believe his eyes... it was as if it was not him writing at all, and before long he had a title in mind: 'The Last Message for Mankind Before the End of the World.'

Now, once again, he had found the answer to a question that was important. He now knew why he could not begin the war against the world and its authorities, as he had to warn the world first with this book; even though it did not mean that anyone would read it or that any publisher would publish it. In his mind he had doubts; he could not see this world wanting something like this to be out there, and even if it were, how many people would really want to know *his* truth?

This world would not believe him without proof, and when he proved it, it would be too late. He had nothing to prove to the world, but he had everything to prove to the MOST HIGH. He was also starting to learn that just because he could not see the point, that did not mean there was no point; this was especially true when dealing with the MOST HIGH. Bigs had come to realise that faith is so important when dealing with the MOST HIGH, because as human beings our ability to see beyond the tips of our own noses, is hard at times. Yet it is impossible to see what the MOST HIGH can see or to know what they know; so if we are to be in fellowship with them, then we must learn to see with faith. Otherwise, we will not be able to walk with them at all.

What mattered to Bigs was that he was writing the book for anyone willing to know the truth about the real GOD, the MOST HIGH, and his First-begotten son Jesus. Bigs knew that once it was written and if it was the will of the MOST HIGH for the world to know about it, it would be so. He knew this because as each day passed he became better at seeing by faith and not by sight.

He finished the book and let the MOST HIGH's will be done with it.

He was now ready to begin the end of the world. So he planned to let the book circulate for a year, as long as he could live on its proceeds; but if he couldn't, it would mean that no one wanted to know, or that Satan Lucifer Devil and his wicked men had stopped its progress. Either way, it would mean that mankind's time was already up, and the book would not be of use to anyone.

THE BEGINNING OF THE END AND THE END OF THE BEGINNING

One Year Later

The book had become a number one best seller and millions of people had read it. Some read it because they wanted to know as much as possible about how the world might end, while others read it because they thought it would be a good read. Then later, some read it because they wanted to read the book that had stirred up so much controversy, and others became believers. There were those, as well, who called the book blasphemy.

Bigs did not care why they bought the book; it was enough that they had bought it and read the message. But after he had made millions of pounds from worldwide sales and had paid his mother-in-law what he owed her; he donated all the proceeds to charities and then set up a website for those who could not afford to buy the book.

The time had come. Bigs had done what was asked of him, and he could do no more. It was now up to the world and to those organisations that called themselves followers, believers and the appointed of the MOST HIGH (whom they called GOD and ALLAH); to either spread the word or disclaim the word that he had brought to the world.

The truth was, Bigs did not care who believed him. He was not here for this world but for the world that was to come, and he had the honour of bringing it in for the MOST HIGH. As far as Bigs was concerned, this world had gained an extra year, and it had no idea of how lucky it was in having this extra time.

He closed the door quietly behind him, as it was the early hours of the morning and he did not wish to wake his wife and children. This was ironic, as he was about to wake the whole world to his presence as the First-begotten son of the MOST HIGH.

He placed his specially made sword and nine millimetre Beretta, onto the leather front seat of his brand new car and drove slowly down his long gravelled drive. Moving through his electric gates he looked back at his million-pound home with a smile, before putting his foot to the floor and speeding off along the quiet roads of the suburbs; heading for the inner part of south London.

Bigs searched the streets looking for his target and the CCTV cameras followed his every move. Where was his prey, the final step to immortality? His heart raced, this was it. He had finally solved the entire puzzle and had climbed over all of the hurdles that the wicked men and their masters had put before him. He had weathered the storm of Satan Lucifer Devil and its continual onslaught of fiery darts from hell. The legions of unseen, unclean, spirits and demons that had besieged him day and night, all of his life, were nothing more than piles of dead meat, rotting in their cells in eternal hell.

All who knew of the deadly game that was to unfold on this night, trembled like never before. The twenty-four wicked men, their master the Beast and its army of E.B.Es, watched in fear via the NSA satellite in London's West end. Lieutenant Clay at Peterson Air Force base was also watching Bigs' movements, along with his special surveillance operations team. Watching from Area 51 via Peterson Air Force base were Lieutenant Colonel Grey, Major Stone, his wingman Major Riddick and Dr Goodenberg. MI5, MI6 & Special Branch also watched from their HQs. Every one held their breaths; this could be the end of the world as they knew it.

NORAD COMMAND CENTRE.

Brigadier General Vice Commander Patterson looked up at the big screens, which showed thousands of dots that indicated the UFOs were filling the night sky in the earth's atmosphere.

The alarm bells rang and warning lights flashed as once again, the massive vault door began to close; but this time it was for real. Once the vault door closed, it would not open again for thirty days. Vehicles raced along the tunnels of the CHEYENNE MOUNTAIN COMPLEX, as the drivers did not want to be left outside once the massive vault door closed.

Lieutenant Coal looked at his monitors in disbelief as the supercomputer hummed, as it had on the night of Bigs' awakening. Now, as then, it tried to track and identify all of the UFOs in the sky.

Bigs was starting to get frustrated. 'Where are the police when you need them!' he shouted. After an hour of searching, he gave up and moved to plan B. He pulled up in a cloud of white tyre smoke, as his car skidded to a halt outside of a phone booth. He had picked this phone booth just in case plan A did not work.

The phone booth was twenty feet away from a CCTV camera and Bigs was sure they would not be able to miss him as he stepped out of his car, with his three foot sword in one hand and his nine millimetre Beretta in his waist belt. Bigs picked up the phone and dialled 999.

'This is the emergency services, how may I help you?' asked the male operator. Bigs looked up at the CCTV cameras.

'I need you to listen very carefully! You may already know why I'm calling.'

'No sir, I have no idea who you are or what your emergency situation is. My name is Gary, and I'm listening to whatever it is you want to tell me.'

'Okay... in that case you may know of me as Ronnie Bigs, of 73 Bury Road, South London. Or perhaps I should say that the police will have records of me under that name and address.'

'Okay, but I don't understand what the problem is. Are you hurt in any way? Is someone at this address hurt?'

'No, I'm not hurt and no one else is, just listen! The name I have just given you is not my real name. My real name is JAW, and you need to inform your CCTV camera operators to look at the phone booth at King's Point, South London on the corner of Crowns Road. You need to inform the police that there is a man standing there with a samurai sword and nine millimetre gun.'

'Is this a joke or a prank call?.... Shit!' shouted the operator, as he heard a bang come over the phone.

'Does that sound like I'm joking?'

'No sir, it doesn't, but what do you hope to get out of this? I will have to inform Trojan, the armed response unit.'

'Good, now we're getting somewhere. You tell them that I'm the First-begotten son of the MOST HIGH, and that my name is JAW. I have come to bring the authority of the MOST HIGH to earth, and all those who wish to come against me shall feel the Fury of the MOST HIGH descend upon them; for I am that Fury manifested in the flesh.'

'Okay, sir, try to remain calm. Can I try to talk to you, to try and find out why you are feeling like this and if there is any other way of defusing this very serious situation?'

'Just send your authorities to try and stop me; that's all I need. Oh, and tell them I'm not in the mood for talking. If they dare come to challenge me, they'd best be ready to go to hell or to bow to the authority of the MOST HIGH, which I represent.'

'Okay, sir, I have notified our armed response units, and they are en route as we speak. I just want to suggest to you that whatever the problem is, talking is a better way out than suicide.'

'Ha, ha, ha, ha! Believe me, it is you and your world that is about to complete the suicide it started a long time ago! Now, after all this time that you have been given by the MOST HIGH to repent your wicked and vain ways; your time is finally up. I hope you kissed the ones you love the most before you started work tonight, as you may not get another chance. If you haven't, I suggest you leave your post and rush home and do so.' Bigs put down the phone and looked up at the CCTV camera. He pulled out his sword, showing its razor-sharp blade to the CCTV camera. He then fired off two rounds into the sky as a testament of his intent, will and attitude of no surrender. Bigs looked up at the camera, shouting 'Come on!' before taking up his position and waiting for the armed response unit to arrive.

THE SECRET LOCATION

Several voices shouted at once in total panic, until the beast shouted at them to be quiet.

'What do we do now Master? Surely it is time we left the planet?'

'Yes, I agree, we should leave now before it's too late!'

'What if it's already too late?'

The beast rose out of its chair, and fire filled the whole room. As it did, the twenty-four men fell to the floor, begging not to be consumed by the fire. The beast withdrew the fire and opened its mouth to speak; as it did fire poured out of its mouth.

'You are the leaders of this world and the most powerful men on the planet, and yet you cower like chickens.'

'But Master, surely you're not suggesting that we could possibly take on the Antichrist?'

'If you interrupt me again, I will kill you. My point is that you did not become the most powerful men in the world by chance. I told each of you back then when you were nothing, that because of me you would become the most powerful men on this planet. And I am telling you now that the Antichrist will spend little time in the Western world. His attentions will be on the third world and the suffering children of that part of the world. That is, if he is truly ready to begin. We must not show any signs of weakness now. Send your armed police force to where he is and have them carry out their normal duties.'

'Master, I do not mean to question you, but please help me to understand... if we send the armed police, won't they be killed by the Antichrist? Would it not be better to ignore him, as we have done up until now?'

'Yes Master; if we call his bluff and he does not bow, won't we have helped him complete his final phase to full glory?'

'You fools, do you think that it is you or I that has kept him from his full glory? No matter what we do, when it is time, it is time. Nothing will be able to stop him from reaching his full glory. All we have been doing is checking how close that time may be from beginning. That is why we must send in the armed forces, to see if it is that time.'

'You mean as bait?'

'What else have we ever used the security forces for when dealing with the Antichrist? Now, I must go and prepare for the final phase, if that is what this is. Do not deviate from my plan,' said the Beast, as it and its E.B.Es vanished into thin air.

The Prime Minister of the United Kingdom made the call to Special Branch, who had intercepted Bigs' call from the phone booth and had placed one of their men on the line to act as an emergency service operator.

'This is the PM. Send in the SAS.'

'Yes sir, they are en route as we speak and are in normal Trojan armed forces uniform. We have had the area cordoned off for the last hour, and special ops have been driving by, acting as normal people. We have two undercover units stationed one hundred meters away from Target One. ETA of SAS two minutes, sir.'

'Good, this must run by the book. The target is not to have any idea that he is not dealing with the normal armed response unit. And believe me, the target has had a lot of experience going up against our armed response units.'

'Yes sir, they have been fully briefed and have studied the armed response tactics and operations manual.'

'Good. Well, we will be watching, and let's hope he backs down before anyone gets killed.'

The CCTV camera pointed at Bigs, watching his every move. In response, he gave it the finger. Bigs watched the couple in the car that was parked on the roadside some hundred feet away and laughed before looking back up at the camera. 'Do you think I'm that stupid? What we have here is the classic double surveillance: boy and girlfriend parked a hundred meters on one side, and the lonely cab driver who has just stopped for a bit of a midnight snack, parked exactly one hundred meters on the other side of the road.'

Bigs debated whether he should shoot them for being so dumb, or whether he should play along with the charade. 'After all, what could they do to me?' he thought. He looked at his watch; time was getting on, and Bigs was starting to get bored with the waiting, so he began to walk towards the couple in the parked car. As he did, he began to hear the sound of sirens in the distance, quickly getting closer.

'Finally,' Bigs thought, as he repositioned himself and waited for the sirens that he could hear, to become blue and white flashing lights.

'This is it, FATHER and MOTHER. I don't know what is going to happen next, but I do know I trust in you and will go wherever you tell me to. I will not bow to their authority and I know you will do whatever pleases you. That will please me, as I have only ever had one desire, one obsession and that is to serve you. It is an honour to be used by you, the MOST HIGH, as your tool. Guide me now as you have always done and whether there are a thousand against me or just one, I will not be moved. I know you are with me, as you have always been, and I am with you, as I have always been.' Bigs raised his sword in the air as he saw the armed police van coming towards him, with sirens blazing and lights flashing. He pulled his nine-millimetre pistol out of his waist and fired off two well-aimed shots at the van's tyres.

The police van skidded to a halt some hundred meters away. The doors flew open and ten armed police officers jumped out one by one, pointing their guns towards Bigs. For Bigs, this was just like in the olden days, when he would be in gang shootouts and the odd one or two shootouts with the police. He was right at home, only this time he had no intention of holding back his rage.

As everything went into slow motion, Bigs wore a huge smile on his face. He was finally home, back on the battlefield, only this time it was for the MOST HIGH. He began to run towards the armed police, who were shouting 'Armed police, put down your weapons. Armed police, put your weapons down now!'

In response, Bigs shouted, 'First-begotten son of the MOST HIGH, put down your weapons or feel the fury of the MOST HIGH! Do it now!' Both sides continued to shout and run towards one another.

Bigs could feel and hear his heart pounding as adrenalin pumped through his veins; his muscles bulged and the veins in his neck pulsed. Then his stomach felt just like it had on the night of his awakening. For a single moment Bigs became distracted, lost in the overwhelming feeling of happiness running over his body. 'It's so beautiful,' he thought, as the feeling of utopia once again filled his body and mind. Bigs began to think he was hyperventilating as the wonderful feeling almost choked him. 'It must be this situation,' he thought, as he could hardly focus.

'This is your last chance,' shouted the police, who had stopped running towards Bigs and had taken up aiming positions on the street. Each officer aimed their infrared lights at points all over Bigs' body.

Bigs tried to refocus on the armed officers in front of him, instead of the wonderful feeling inside of him. He was a bit confused; why was this feeling that he had not felt for almost seven years, now suddenly back with him? 'Is it a good thing?' he thought.

'This is your last chance! if you don't lay down your weapon we will open fire! Do you understand?'

Bigs' body was so pumped up on adrenalin that he could feel every beat of his heart all over his body. His heart rate was going through the roof; it was beating so hard that he could hear it, like a bass drum, in his ears. His knees felt weak and began to buckle, and then he fell to his knees.

'FATHER and MOTHER, please tell me what is happening to me? Why do I feel like I did that night when I was awakened? I feel dizzy... have I overestimated my ability to handle the situation? Is this fear that grips me and chokes me? What am I to do?' thought Bigs.

'Have faith and trust,' came the reply from the Holy Spirit.

'Okay, now slowly put your weapons down on the floor and lie down face first on the floor!' shouted one of the armed officers.

Bigs looked back at the CCTV camera as he put his gun down onto the ground.

'That's it, now slowly put the sword down and lie on your stomach!'

Bigs looked back towards the armed officers and smiled. 'You guys are what, SAS? Only the best could have the slightest of chances against me. Your formation is not the normal armed police forces formation; they aren't that brave... they never aim without cover, never!' Bigs began to pull himself up; his head was pumping and his eyes could hardly see straight but it did not matter. He knew the MOST HIGH had everything under control; all he had to do was not surrender and the victory would be his.

'Do not stand up! Lie back down now or we'll....'

'Or you'll what? Shoot? I'm betting on it. You cannot beat me, for I am backed by the power and authority of the MOST HIGH and this is just my beginning.'

Bigs stood and raised his sword. Taking a deep breath and holding it, he ran towards the armed officers; only releasing his breath as he yelled, 'For the MOST HIGH!'

Everything then went in to slow motion. Bigs could see the armed officers yelling words, as their breath was made white by the coldness of the air; but he could not hear them. His body was filled with utopia and his mind was filled with the MOST HIGH. He saw the recoil of the armed officers guns as they fired, and for a second he could see the bullets as they moved rapidly towards him. Then there was blackness.

Bigs opened his eyes, but he was not sure if they were open; he could only see blackness, as if his eyes were still shut. He tried to get his bearings but felt disorientated, almost as if he had been asleep and had awoken in an unfamiliar position. Then it occurred to him that his thighs were up against his stomach and his head was slumped over his knees; as if he had collapsed into a neat heap, like the crease in a paper fan.

Still bewildered, he raised his head slightly and saw his hands. Now he was certain that he was in a prayer-like position. But this did not make any sense to him. He had just been running towards the police and now he was in total silence and complete darkness. Had he been shot and was he now dying or dead? Where was he and what had happened to the police? Then he realised, that all the time he was still experiencing the feeling of overwhelming utopia.

Something was very familiar about how he was postured and how he was feeling. It was as if he had been in that same position and had that same feeling somewhere before... Then his eyes widened as he realised the familiarity of his situation. This was exactly how he felt when... Bigs looked up slowly and almost passed out as his mind registered what his eyes could see.

It was his family, the aliens and beasts, and it was as if he had never left; they were exactly where they were when he thought he was getting ready to come back to earth. That time when he knelt and took one last look at them, and he saw the alien that had told him who he was, calming down the other aliens and beasts who did not understand why he had knelt as if to pray. But that was seven long years ago, it didn't make sense; how could the alien still be calming them down after seven years?

Bigs stood and looked at the alien that he had been talking to all those years ago. 'I've been waiting for seven years for you to come back; every day that passed was like a nightmare. If it weren't for the MOST HIGH, the Holy Spirit, my wife and children; I would have gone mad waiting for you to come back for me! You said it would not be a long time before we met again. Although I have to admit now, looking back, that the seven years have gone quite quickly and I have learnt an awful lot in that time. But nevertheless, you lied when you answered my question: do you remember my question?'

'Of course I do. You asked me if we would meet again soon, and I answered yes. I believe you asked me that same question four times,' replied the alien.

'So what happened? It's been seven long years... and why are you still calming everyone down? I didn't know the prayer position was such a big deal. You should have just told them it was because that's the way I came; that you took me from earth after I had finished saying my prayers.'

'The reason it was a big thing was, first of all, because you are who you are and secondly, the rest of your army did not understand what you were doing; as in their minds you weren't going anywhere.'

'What do you mean I wasn't going anywhere? Why didn't you tell them I had to go back to earth and that we agreed to continue this soon?'

'I couldn't tell them you were going anywhere, because you weren't.'

Bigs looked lost and confused. He really felt like he had been hit in the head by one of the bullets, because what the alien was saying to him didn't make any sense.

'Let's start again. First, do you agree that I have been back on earth for the last seven years?'

'No!'

'What?'

'I said, no, I do not agree with that. You have not been on earth for the last seven years.'

'Well, where have I been?'

'You have been on your knees.'

'For seven years?'

'No, more like seven seconds. That's about how long it has taken me to calm everyone down and try to make them understand that you just needed a few seconds to get your bearings and get used to the idea of who you are. Now I think you are ready to lead your army into glory for the MOST HIGH, don't you?'

Bigs did not know what to say, but the one thing he knew he wasn't ever going to say again was, that this could not be real. He took a second to comprehend the fact that the seven years of life on earth, that he had believed he had just experienced, had actually been no more than seven seconds of readjustment to his true self in this amazing place. The overwhelming feeling of utopia was wonderful, and Bigs never wanted to be without it again, not even for seven seconds.

He opened his wings, which once again shone like the light from the midday sun, and rose above his army into the air. Then he looked at his friend, the alien, that he had been talking to all of the time and said, 'You know what? In all that has happened, I didn't ask you your name.'

'I am your humble soldier and brother, whom you like to call DD.'

Bigs smiled and took in a deep breath. Then he raised his double-edged sword.

Shouting 'For the MOST HIGH!' he opened the gateway between heaven and earth and all dimensions.

To be continued…

www.ingramcontent.com/pod-product-compliance
Lightning Source LLC
Chambersburg PA
CBHW020631300426
44112CB00007B/78